Word Formation as a Naming Device

Word Formation as a Naming Device

PIUS TEN HACKEN AND RENÁTA PANOCOVÁ

EDINBURGH
University Press

Edinburgh University Press is one of the leading university presses in the UK. We publish academic books and journals in our selected subject areas across the humanities and social sciences, combining cutting-edge scholarship with high editorial and production values to produce academic works of lasting importance. For more information visit our website: edinburghuniversitypress.com

© Pius ten Hacken and Renáta Panocová, 2024, 2025

Edinburgh University Press Ltd
13 Infirmary Street
Edinburgh, EH1 1LT

First published in hardback by Edinburgh University Press 2024

Typeset in 9 on 12pt Noto Serif
by Cheshire Typesetting Ltd, Cuddington, Cheshire

A CIP record for this book is available from the British Library

ISBN 978 1 4744 8701 6 (hardback)
ISBN 978 1 4744 8702 3 (paperback)
ISBN 978 1 4744 8703 0 (webready PDF)
ISBN 978 1 4744 8704 7 (epub)

The right of Pius ten Hacken and Renáta Panocová to be identified as the authors of this work has been asserted in accordance with the Copyright, Designs and Patents Act 1988, and the Copyright and Related Rights Regulations 2003 (SI No. 2498).

Contents

List of Figures and Tables		ix
Preface		xi

1	Naming Concepts	1
	1.1 The nature of concepts	1
	1.2 The nature of names	3
	1.3 The nature of naming	9
2	Naming in the History of Morphology	15
	2.1 Traditional grammar	16
	2.2 Historical-comparative linguistics	19
	2.3 Saussure's general linguistics	21
	2.4 Bloomfield and the Post-Bloomfieldians	25
3	Historical Relationships between Current Theories of Morphology	29
	3.1 Word formation in generative linguistics	29
	3.1.1 The early stages of generative grammar	30
	3.1.2 The lexicon in generative grammar	33
	3.1.3 Elaborations of the Lexicalist Hypothesis	35
	3.1.4 Generative Semantics	38
	3.1.5 Generative morphology as a basis for the study of word formation	41
	3.2 Word formation in functionalist frameworks	43
	3.2.1 The position of word formation in the language system	43
	3.2.2 The object of word formation	45
	3.2.3 Foundation and motivation	47
	3.3 Selection of current theories and frameworks	49
4	An Approach to the Analysis of Naming	54
	4.1 Words and phrases	55

	4.2	Lexemes and word forms	58
	4.3	Paradigms	61
	4.4	Naming and transposition	62
	4.5	Onomasiological coercion	65
5	Distributed Morphology	68
	5.1	Distributed Morphology as a framework	68
	5.2	The treatment of relevant contrasts in DM	71
		5.2.1 Words and phrases	72
		5.2.2 The borderline between inflection and derivation	75
		5.2.3 Paradigms	79
		5.2.4 Transposition and the formation of names	82
		5.2.5 Onomasiological coercion	85
	5.3	Word Formation and Naming in DM	85
6	Lexical Morphology	89
	6.1	Lexical Morphology as a framework	89
	6.2	The treatment of relevant contrasts in LMP	94
		6.2.1 Words and phrases	94
		6.2.2 Lexemes and word forms	97
		6.2.3 Paradigms	100
		6.2.4 Naming and transposition	103
		6.2.5 Onomasiological coercion	104
	6.3	Word formation and naming in LMP	105
7	The Lexical Semantic Framework	107
	7.1	LSF as a framework	107
	7.2	The treatment of relevant contrasts in LSF	112
		7.2.1 Words and phrases	112
		7.2.2 The borderline between inflection and derivation	114
		7.2.3 Paradigms	116
		7.2.4 Transposition and the formation of names	118
		7.2.5 Onomasiological coercion	122
	7.3	Word formation and naming in LSF	124
8	Construction Morphology	127
	8.1	Construction Morphology as a theory	127
	8.2	The treatment of relevant contrasts in CxM	133
		8.2.1 Words and phrases	133
		8.2.2 The borderline between inflection and derivation	137
		8.2.3 Inflectional and derivational paradigms	139
		8.2.4 The distinction between transposition and the formation of names	141
		8.2.5 Onomasiological coercion	144
	8.3	Word formation and naming in CxM	145

Contents

9	Relational Morphology	149
	9.1 Relational Morphology as a framework	149
	9.2 The treatment of relevant contrasts in RM	154
	9.2.1 Words and phrases	154
	9.2.2 Lexemes and word forms	158
	9.2.3 Paradigms	161
	9.2.4 Naming and transposition	164
	9.2.5 Onomasiological coercion	166
	9.3 Word formation and naming in RM	168
10	Cognitive Grammar	172
	10.1 Cognitive Grammar as a framework	172
	10.2 The treatment of relevant contrasts in CG	177
	10.2.1 Words and phrases	177
	10.2.2 Lexemes and word forms	183
	10.2.3 Paradigms	185
	10.2.4 Naming and transposition	187
	10.2.5 Onomasiological coercion	189
	10.3 Word formation and naming in CG	190
11	Štekauer's Onomasiological Theory	193
	11.1 Štekauer's onomasiological theory as a framework	193
	11.2 The treatment of relevant contrasts in Štekauer's onomasiological theory	200
	11.2.1 Words and phrases	200
	11.2.2 Lexemes and word forms	204
	11.2.3 Paradigms	206
	11.2.4 Naming and transposition	208
	11.2.5 Onomasiological coercion	210
	11.3 Word formation and naming in Štekauer's onomasiological theory	212
12	Natural Morphology	216
	12.1 Natural Morphology as a framework	216
	12.2 The treatment of relevant contrasts in NM	220
	12.2.1 Words and phrases	221
	12.2.2 Lexemes and word forms	224
	12.2.3 Paradigms	225
	12.2.4 Naming and transposition	227
	12.2.5 Onomasiological coercion	229
	12.3 Word formation and naming in NM	230
13	An Assessment of Similarities and Differences between Theoretical Frameworks	233
	13.1 The set of naming expressions	233
	13.1.1 A framework for the use and extension of the mental lexicon	234

		13.1.2	Naming vs description	237

        13.1.2 Naming vs description   237
        13.1.3 New names vs adaptation of existing names   240
  13.2 The meaning of new names   245
  13.3 Properties of a good theory of word formation
        as a naming device   251
        13.3.1 Traditional distinctions relating to morphology   251
        13.3.2 Morphology and functions of language   252
        13.3.3 Two roads into the lexicon   254
        13.3.4 Selection criteria for word formation as a naming
                device   255

Bibliography   258
Author index   274
Example index   280
Subject index   285

Figures and tables

Figures

1.1	Three manifestations of a word	7
1.2	Processes in naming and use of names	12
3.1	Halle's (1973: 8) model	36
3.2	Representation of Jackendoff's (1975) model of the lexicon	38
3.3	Partial word formation nest for *učiť* ('teach')	49
5.1	Model of grammar assumed in DM	70
5.2	The structure of *Hartkäse* in DM	73
5.3	A possible structure of *explore* and *exploration* in DM	83
5.4	The structure of *exploration* in DM	84
5.5	Representation of the non-transpositional reading of *installation*	85
6.1	The model of Lexical Morphology and Phonology by Kiparsky (1982)	92
10.1	Diagrammatic representation of a symbolic structure in CG	174
10.2	Diagrammatic representation of a higher-level symbolic structure	174
10.3	Diagrammatic representation of a combination of symbolic structures	175
10.4	Structure of *Hartkäse* in CG	180
10.5	The structure of *harter* in CG	180
10.6	Three levels of schematic construction of the Slovak accusative form *gitaru*	186
10.7	Semantic contrast between a verb and its nominalization in CG	188
11.1	Štekauer's model of naming	194
11.2	Internal structure of the Word-Formation Component in Štekauer's model	197
12.1	A model of NM	217
13.1	Processes in the extension and use of the mental lexicon	234

Tables

1.1	German and Slovak words for *computer*	11
2.1	Examples of Grimm's Law	20
3.1	Two criteria for classifying models of word formation	43
4.1	Examples of Dutch plurals and diminutives	59
4.2	Paradigm of the Slovak noun *gitara* ('guitar')	61
6.1	Selected differences between lexical rules and post-lexical rules	95
6.2	Examples of Slovak diminutives	99
6.3	The analysis of *innocuous* in SOT	101
6.4	The analysis of *unknown* in SOT	102
6.5	Paradigm of the Turkish noun *el* ('hand'), from Lewis (1967: 29)	103
8.1	Partial conjugation of French *recevoir* ('receive')	140
10.1	Degrees of composition according to Langacker (1987a: 450)	179
10.2	Examples of gender markings in Spanish nouns	183
10.3	Selected case forms of some feminine nouns in Slovak	185
11.1	Naming process resulting in *comfort eater* in Štekauer's model	197
11.2	Paradigm of the borrowed noun *bloger* ('blogger') in Slovak	206
11.3	Dokulil's types of transpositional onomasiological category	209
13.1	Positions on the distinction between lexicon and syntax	238
13.2	Mechanisms for distinguishing naming units from inflection and transposition	242

Preface

Word formation is a mechanism for producing new words. There is an extensive literature on word formation. Most of this literature focuses on the question of how the form of a particular word is produced on the basis of existing linguistic elements. Here we take a different starting point. Our question is rather why a new word is formed and how this influences the formation of the resulting word. We assume that both questions are legitimate and interesting, but the second question has been studied much less. As a new word connects a form and a meaning, it can be seen as a bridge. In the first question the observer is at the form-side of the word and assumes the existence of the meaning-side without paying much attention to its details. In the second question, the observer takes a bird's-eye perspective of the bridge, overlooking both sides and their connection.

In order to study how word formation is used in naming, we have chosen a number of current theories of morphology and discuss how they deal with questions of naming. As a starting point, we explain in Chapter 1 what we mean by naming and introduce some concepts and ideas we use in discussing it. In Chapters 2 and 3, we give a concise historical outline of the study of naming. Chapter 2 presents the earlier background, up to the mid-twentieth century. Chapter 3 describes the later developments. At the end of Chapter 3, we motivate our selection of eight current linguistic theories that cover word formation. Some of them present themselves as a theory of morphology, others as a theory of the lexicon, or even as a general theory of language. However, when a theory covers word formation, it is legitimate and interesting to inquire how naming is accounted for.

Our methodology in this study is to select data that we consider typical as illustrations of various aspects of the naming function of word formation and find out what our selected theories have to say about them. We present these data in Chapter 4. Our selection starts with a number of contrasts that illustrate the difference between naming expressions and expressions that describe something. Then we turn to the contrast between new naming expressions and adaptations of naming expressions to the syntactic context.

Finally we have examples where naming determines to some extent the meaning of the resulting word. By selecting our data in this way, we wanted to ensure that we have a good mixture of general and specific questions, so that theories are likely to cover at least some of the contrasts we illustrated in our data. Our data are from English, German, Dutch and Slovak.

In Chapters 5–12, we discuss eight different theories. These chapters all have the same overall structure. Section 1 gives an outline of the theory, introducing the main mechanisms that are used in word formation. Section 2 goes over the data from Chapter 4 and explains how the theory under scrutiny can account for them. Section 3 summarizes how and to what extent the theory considered in this chapter is successful in its coverage of the naming aspect of word formation. In this summary, we also compare the theory with theories we discussed in earlier chapters.

Finally, Chapter 13 gives a general evaluation of the theories we discussed. On the basis of the analyses in Chapters 5–12 we consider how particular properties of the theories contribute to the successful account of word formation as a naming device and propose a view of the mental lexicon in which naming finds a natural place. Without coming down in favour of any single theory, we explain why and how some theories fare better than others. In doing so, we also bridge the opposition between formal and functionalist theories.

In writing this monograph, we considered a readership consisting of researchers and PhD students in word formation, morphology, lexicon and adjacent fields. We explain theoretical concepts and data with this readership in mind. This means that we take for granted that readers know basic concepts of word formation and morphology, but we explain naming in more detail. We also assume that they can interpret English data, but explain the German, Dutch and Slovak data in sufficient detail for them to understand what is at issue.

Although we hope that readers will be motivated to read the entire book, we understand that not all readers will be interested in all chapters to the same extent. The core chapters are the discussions of the eight selected theories in Chapters 5–12. We made an effort to make each of them readable independently of the other theory chapters. Comparisons are limited to the final section of each chapter and are accompanied by cross-references to the relevant discussion. In order to understand our methodology, we recommend, however, that readers first go over Chapter 1 and Chapter 4. As a conclusion, Chapter 13 is relevant to all readers, but the points we make will be understood better when more theory chapters have been read.

In writing this book, we relied on each other as well as on a number of other people. Coming from different theoretical backgrounds, we managed to work with most theories by combining our skills and experience. For Distributed Morphology, we received valuable comments from Maria Bloch-Trojnar, who added a perspective we did not cover. Needless to say, any deficiencies in the resulting chapter are the exclusive responsibility of the authors. Before we started writing, we benefited from the generous help of Laura Quinn of Edinburgh University Press, who guided us through the book proposal reviewing process. We also thank Sam Johnson, who took over her role as contact during her maternity leave. We thank Katharina Stolz and Klara Volaucnik for their help with the compilation of the bibliography and the index. This work was supported by the Scientific Grant Agency of the Ministry of Education, Science, Research and Sport of the Slovak Republic and Slovak Academy of Sciences VEGA under the project No VEGA 1/0130/21.

CHAPTER 1

Naming concepts

In the same way that communication is the reason why language exists, naming is the reason why we have word formation. The relationship between communication and language has been discussed in some detail.[1] The relationship between naming and word formation has received much less systematic attention. Without any doubt, naming is a relevant factor in the application of word formation. However, to what extent naming determines the organization and nature of word formation can be debated. The purpose of this book is to give an overview of how naming is covered in a range of current theories of morphology.

Naming is the creation of a new association of a name and a concept. In this chapter, we elaborate each of these terms in order to set the background for the remainder of the book. Section 1.1 discusses the nature of concepts, section 1.2 the nature of names, and section 1.3 shows how naming can be understood as the process of creating an association between a name and a concept.

As this book is about word formation, we will not give a full overview of the discussion about the nature of concepts and names. Instead, we will outline and motivate our own position that underlies the analysis in subsequent chapters.

1.1 The nature of concepts

A concept is a unit of meaning. Although we will not present a precise delimitation of its size, we can say that it is a fairly small unit. It is smaller than a proposition or a text. At the same time, many concepts can be decomposed into smaller units.

---

[1] The discussion has mainly focused on how and to what extent the communicative function of language determines the way it is organized as a system. Newmeyer (1998) gives an overview of this discussion.

The difficulty of delimiting the size of the unit of *concept* is similar to the difficulty in delimiting that of *word*. For many speakers, a word is what is written together. Linguistically, this is problematic, because we find contrasts such as (1).

(1) a. teapot
    b. tea pot
    c. tea-pot

All three expressions in (1) refer to the same concept. (1a) is more frequent, but corpora such as BNC (2007) and COCA (2008–2020) give occurrences of (1b) and (1c) as well. According to the orthographic criterion, (1a) is a word, but (1b) is two words and for (1c) the number of words depends on one's analysis of the hyphen. Other criteria that have been invoked involve phonological, morphological, syntactic and semantic properties. Di Sciullo and Williams (1987: 1–2) argue that there are four different concepts of word, each with its own delimiting properties.[2]

In the case of *concept*, there is an obvious link to the understanding of *word*. In many cases, a concept is the meaning of a word. However, not all words have a conceptual meaning. We can illustrate this by means of (2), from BNC (2007).

(2) When she entered the house, it was silent and empty.

In (2) we have a sentence of ten words. Four of these words refer to concepts. The other six are function words. Whereas *house* has a lexical meaning that corresponds to a concept, *she* only has a grammatical meaning, which can be encoded entirely in terms of features. For word formation and naming, function words are less relevant. It is rare that new function words are adopted and if this happens, there is no rule system for producing them. If we want to have a third person singular pronoun that is unspecified for gender, we have to resort to some creative means, not to a regular word formation rule. The distinction between lexical words such as *house* and function words such as *she* is well established. We take a concept to be the meaning of a lexical word.

We can think of a lexical word as a word whose meaning can be described by relating it to the outside world. *House* in (2) refers to a kind of object, *silent* and *empty* to properties and *enter* to an event. The concepts behind these words are understood as units. This does not mean that they cannot be decomposed. Both *silent* and *empty* have a negative component that can

---

[2] Although Di Sciullo and Williams (1987: 1) start with the claim that '[t]here are three different ideas of what a word is', which they call *morphological objects, syntactic atoms* and *listemes*, they mention a fourth, phonological word, later (1987: 2). Orthographic words play no role in their study.

be distinguished. One could describe *silent* as 'without noise' and *empty* as 'without objects'. Despite this possibility of decomposition, they still each reflect a single concept.

It is more difficult to establish the upper boundary of concepts. It is intuitively fairly clear that the entire sentence in (2) does not refer to a concept. What about *silent and empty*? BNC (2007) has 26 occurrences of the three-word sequence. However, it has 33,993 occurrences of *silent* and 52,962 of *empty*. Even the order is not fixed, as there are 30 occurrences of *empty and silent*. This suggests that *silent and empty* is not an established expression in British English. It is likely that in (2) they are intended as two separate properties. It is possible to conceive of *empty and silent* as a single concept, but if we want to do this, we can come up with a single word for it.

We assume that whether something is a concept or not depends on the way it is encoded in a speaker's mind. In line with Rosch's (1973) research on the representation of colours and shapes and Labov's (1973) experiment on artefacts, we assume that a natural concept has a prototype structure. Such a structure is determined by a number of focal examples that serve as prototypes and graded properties that determine how close a possible instance is to these prototypes. Jackendoff (1983: 135–157) gives a detailed and well-argued exposition of such a theory.

In the literature on naming, proper names take a prominent position. On one hand, we find the entire research field of onomastics, cf. Hough (2016), on the other, studies rooted in the philosophy of language, e.g. Bochner (2021). In onomastics, the central question is how names for places, persons, etc. are chosen. In philosophical studies of proper names, it is not so much the choice as the status of these names that is the focus. Proper names do not have prototypes in the same way as lexical words. *Groningen* is a city in the Netherlands. There is also a town *Groningen* in Suriname. Unsurprisingly, given the historical connection between the Netherlands and Suriname, the town in Suriname was named after the Dutch city. The two are not instances of a single concept *Groningen* with one more central than the other. Even when many objects have the same name, each object is named separately. Many Italian cities and towns have a *Piazza Garibaldi*, but there is no concept of *Piazza Garibaldi* of which they are instances.

In this book, we will assume that a concept is a unit of meaning in a speaker's mind. It corresponds to a lexical word or a multi-word unit with an equivalent type of meaning. We consider lexical words to be opposed to function words and to proper names. Concepts have a prototype structure.

1.2 The nature of names

As argued in section 1.1, names are typically words. In order to investigate their nature, we can consider whether a particular word exists and how we verify this. The examples in (3) highlight some different aspects of these questions.

(3)   a.   collapser
      b.   kritharaki
      c.   polycystid

When asking someone how to determine whether something is a word of English, the most common answer, especially from non-linguists, is to look it up in the dictionary. For English, OED (2000–2023) is probably the most prestigious authority. Craigie and Onions (1933: viii) give (4) as the most important guiding principle of the OED.[3]

(4)   The first requirement of every lexicon is that it should contain every word occurring in the literature of the language it professes to illustrate.

When we look up (3a) in OED (2023), we find that it is not included.[4] Does that mean that *collapser* is not a word of English? One of the considerations is how a word gets into the OED. Especially for this dictionary, there is a long tradition of basing decisions about the inclusion of words on their occurrence in texts. As Gilliver (2016) describes, this principle was pursued long before electronic corpora could be used to support such decisions. It is also reflected in (4) by its formulation of 'occurring in the literature'.

At the time of the first edition of the OED, users were entirely dependent on the dictionary editors to look for occurrences of new words, but nowadays, we can use large corpora ourselves. In fact, iWeb (2018), a corpus of about 14 billion words collected from websites, gives 24 occurrences of *collapser*, including the one in (5).

(5)   A collapser is a clickable switch for hiding a section of the Status Line.Collapsers can be used to hide or display sections of the status line and adjust the number of available functions at an instance.

The way (5) is formulated, especially its explanatory character, suggests that *collapser* is perceived as a new word. However, because it is based on word formation, it is not a word that is difficult to understand. The base *collapse*

---

[3] (4) is the first of the principles presented in the *Proposal for the Publication of a New English Dictionary* in 1858. As described by Gilliver (2016: 28–32), this document was an important milestone in the process that eventually led to the compilation of what we now know as the OED. In the preface to the third edition, Simpson (2000: 10) calls it a 'myth' that the OED 'includes every word [...] of the English language. Such an objective could never be achieved.' For more discussion, see ten Hacken (2012).
[4] Correct as of 19 September 2022.

is a common word of English and the nominalization with *-er* is a very productive word formation process. If the use of the word catches on, we can expect that in a future update of OED (2023), *collapser* will be included.

A somewhat different situation occurs for (3b). The word *kritharaki* is a Greek word (κριθαράκι) for a typical dish in Greek cuisine. OED (2023) does not include it. A search in iWeb (2018) yields 11 occurrences, mostly in recipes. The question whether (3b) is a word of English is different from the same question for (3a), because in the case of (3a) the emphasis is on *word* and in the case of (3b) it is on *English*. For *collapser*, the real question is whether it is a word. When we reply in the affirmative, we know immediately that it is a word of English, because it is based on an English word formation rule applied to an English base. For *kritharaki*, there is no question whether it is a word of Greek. The question is whether it is also a word of English. If we take OED (2023) as an authority, we should say it is not. If we want to go by iWeb (2018), we can say it is.

Let us now turn to (3c). Here we have the reverse situation compared with (3a–b). OED (2023 [2006]) gives an entry for *polycystid*, classifying it as either a noun or an adjective and assigning the meaning in (6).

(6) A parasitic protozoan of the former gregarine group Polycystidea (also called Cephalina), characterized by having the cell divided into protomerite, deutomerite, and usually also epimerite.

In (6) we have the meaning of the noun. Both examples of the adjective give *polycystid gregarine* as the context, which suggests that the putative adjective is in fact the noun occurring as the modifier of a compound. For the noun, OED also gives two examples. All examples are from 1888–1926. No occurrences are found in iWeb (2018). Here the question is rather whether *polycystid* is still a word of English.

Cases such as (3) may suggest that it is wrong to give OED (2023) the authority to decide whether an expression is a word of English. The OED, like any dictionary, is made by lexicographers who take decisions about the inclusion of words. If we take these decisions as authoritative, the question whether something is a word of English is not an empirical one.

In fact, lexicographers tend to refer to the corpus as an authority (cf. ten Hacken 2012). Instead of to a dictionary, we may therefore assign the authority to a corpus. We may say, for instance, that occurrence in iWeb (2018) determines whether something is a word of English. There are three problems with such an assumption. First, any particular corpus has its limitations. Even if iWeb (2018) is huge, it is only a selection of the use of English. As it is based on websites, it is biased and may not contain expressions that are only used in other contexts. We can cater for this by removing the limitation to a particular corpus. This is the classical position adopted in lexicography.

The other two problems of relying on a corpus are more persistent. In (7), we give two examples from iWeb (2018).

(7) a. For example, knowing another langauge will give you an edge in most multinational corporations.
b. The TEFL program gave me a whole new appreciation of English langauge and taught me a lot about how languages work and how we learn.

Both examples in (7) contain the word *langauge*. Obviously, this is a misspelling for *language*. In (7b), we even have the correct spelling in the same sentence. With 974 occurrences, the frequency of *langauge* is in fact much higher than that of *collapser* and *kritharaki*. Nevertheless, there is no question that *langauge* is not a word of English. It is an error. Errors occur in language use and therefore also in corpora. Whereas for the non-occurrence of expected words, we can enlarge the corpus to increase the chance of finding them, for errors the only solution is to exclude them on the basis of a decision. For some corpora, such decisions are taken in the compilation. For all corpora, the user is ultimately responsible for the conclusions they draw. The reason why OED (2023) has an authority that iWeb (2018) does not have is that the lexicographers at OED are trained to take such decisions.

The final problem with corpora is that they only give the form of a word. The interpretation is added by the reader. This can be seen in an example like (8).

(8) a. The poet tells us how the King saw his men speared and shot down.
b. If I was the boss here I would. I'd spear him without warnin'.

In (8), we have two occurrences of the verb *spear*, taken from historical sources and quoted by OED (2023: *spear*, v. 3). The question is what *spear* means. In (8a), we might think of 'challenge with a spear' or 'pierce with a spear' or 'kill with a spear'. These senses are related, but the outcome of the events is different. The context of 'and shot down' suggests that the men were at least wounded. If we take this interpretation in (8b), however, we are on the wrong track. According to OED (2023), it means 'dismiss' here. This information is not directly encoded in the corpus, but must be inferred by contextual knowledge. This knowledge interacts with our knowledge of language in a way similar to that used in (7) to determine that *langauge* is an error and not a word of English.

What we have seen in this discussion of the examples in (3) is that words manifest themselves in three different ways. We can label them lexicographic, usage-based and cognitive. The lexicographic manifestation is found in dictionaries and based on decisions by lexicographers. More generally, it is found in sources that claim or are assigned an authority over the language. In this manifestation, a word is not an empirical entity as it is based on a conscious decision by an authority. The usage-based manifestation is found in corpora. More generally, it is found as a physical signal.

Naming concepts

This physical signal can take the form of sound waves, letters, or signs of sign language. In its physical representation, language is empirical, but it does not contain the meaning of a word. The cognitive manifestation is vested in the knowledge of an individual speaker. Here, a word is a combination of form and meaning stored in the speaker's brain. As this storage exists physically, the word is an empirical entity in this sense. As different speakers have separate brains, no two speakers share a word. However, language use in communication leads to pressure on speakers to harmonize their knowledge. This means that speakers who are in contact with each other tend to have similar mental representations of the words they use. The relations between these manifestations of the word are represented in Figure 1.1.

In Figure 1.1, the three manifestations are represented with the following properties:

- Word as signal: the usage-based perspective, sound waves or letters. Here the word is only a form. It is an empirical entity. It is produced and interpreted by the corresponding knowledge in the speaker and in the hearer.
- Word as knowledge: the cognitive perspective, realized in the brain. Here the word is a combination of a form and a concept, both represented as prototypes. This knowledge is different for each speaker. It is an empirical entity. It is used to produce and interpret the signal.
- Word as entry: the lexicographic perspective, realized in a dictionary. Here the word is represented by a dictionary entry. The word itself is not an empirical entity, but based on its manifestation as a signal, interpreted

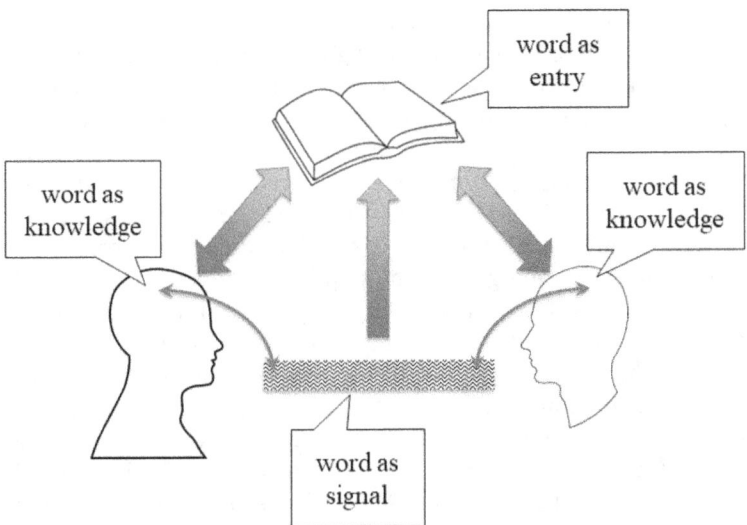

Figure 1.1 *Three manifestations of a word*

by the cognitive representation in the lexicographer's brain. Speakers can consult the entry and adapt their use and knowledge of the word.

The three manifestations are of course not our own inventions. It is easy to recognize Chomsky's (1965: 4) distinction between competence and performance as the basis for the word as knowledge and the word as signal, respectively. Chomsky (1986: 19–20) introduces the distinction between I-language and E-language, which roughly correspond to the word as knowledge and the word as entry, respectively. Ten Hacken (2007: 41–53) gives a more detailed analysis of the Chomskyan concepts of *competence, performance, I-language* and *E-language*.

Although the notions of *competence* and *performance* are often perceived as evolving from generative linguistics, there is no particular need to restrict them to this approach. Here, we are interested in words, whereas generative linguistics has a focus on syntax. The distinction between competence and performance has often been criticized, but the arguments do not generally affect the way we use *word as knowledge* and *word as signal* in Figure 1.1. One type of criticism, exemplified by Hymes (1971), is that competence in Chomsky's (1965) sense is not sufficient to explain language as it is used. Instead of grammatical competence, Hymes proposes communicative competence. Whether or not we agree with this view, it does not challenge the basic opposition between words as knowledge and words as signal. Another type of criticism, often raised by second-language teachers, is that it is impossible to determine whether a particular error is an error of competence or performance. However, this is not an argument against the existence of the opposition between the two, but at most an argument against the classification of errors into these categories.

Another element of the representation in Figure 1.1 that is sometimes criticized as reflecting (only) generative linguistics is the idea that languages are not empirical entities. The word as a lexicographic entry does not occur naturally. The idea that named languages such as English or German do not exist as empirical objects was recognized as a consequence of the distinction between competence and performance by Chomsky (1980). It has sometimes been formulated in a provocative way, e.g. Uriagereka's (1998: 27) statement that 'English doesn't really exist'. A more nuanced exposition of the idea, focused on the emergence of new words, is ten Hacken (2020a). Ten Hacken and Panocová (2022) illustrate how the study of a word formation process can be related to the notion of English as a language.

As explained by ten Hacken (2020d), a language label such as *German* is used in two fundamentally different ways. In one sense, *German* is used in the classification of speakers. In this sense, it is part of a list of languages and the statement *X is a speaker of German* means that the language of *X* is assigned to the class with the label *German*. The second sense of *German* is used in evaluating texts and utterances. It sets up a standard against which speakers and their performance can be judged. It is used in second-language

Naming concepts

acquisition and in translation. When translating a text into German, a native speaker of German should not use their native language, but the German standard. Of course the distance between the native language and the standard may vary for different speakers, but it is essentially the standard that is used for the evaluation of a translation.

In both senses, *German* is not an empirical entity. In the list of languages used for classification, we have to decide which languages will be on the list. Especially in a dialect continuum, the question of how many and which languages there are cannot be fully linguistically determined. The break-up of Serbo-Croatian, described by Greenberg (2005), is a recent example of how such decisions can be essentially political. For the standard, the question is who has the authority to determine it. For various languages, language academies have been set up. They deliberate and decide on cases where speakers disagree. This is not an entirely empirical process. There is no place where one can find the standard before it has been created consciously.

On the basis of such considerations, we take it that the distinctions in Figure 1.1 are not specific to generative linguistics. In fact, one finds the insight of the non-empirical status of named languages also in non-generative sources such as Piller (2016) and Coulmas (2018). Here we will adopt the analysis of the nature of words as names in Figure 1.1 as a basis for our study.

1.3 The nature of naming

In order to illustrate the process of naming, let us consider the following scenario. Two people, Arnold and Betty, go to a pizzeria and while sitting at their table, they observe the traditional way pizzas are produced. One of the things they observe is the wooden instrument that is used to put the pizzas in the oven and take them out. As they are talking about what they see, they may refer to this instrument in different ways. Some possibilities are listed in (9).

(9) a. instrument for putting pizzas in the oven
    b. pizza shovel
    c. peel
    d. pala

In (9a), we have a description. This is not a name and it may vary in details of its form without changing its reference. In (9b–d), we have three different names for the instrument described in (9a). If Arnold and Betty do not know the word for the instrument, they may settle for (9b). This is a compound consisting of two words they know. If one of them knows the trade, they may end up using (9c). The word *peel* is more common in the sense of the skin of a piece of fruit (e.g. *lemon peel*), but there is a homonym of French origin, which COED (2011: *peel*²) qualifies as archaic and describes as 'a baker's shovel for carrying loaves into or out of an oven'. In Italian, (9d) is used. As pizzas are originally Italian, Arnold and Betty may also use it in English in order to emphasize their knowledge of or respect for the Italian terminology. The three names in (9b–d) illustrate different naming mechanisms. In (9b), we see the result of word formation, in (9c) of sense extension and in (9d) of borrowing.

With the three names in (9b–d) as candidates, an obvious question to ask is which of these is the correct one. This question asks for a norm. In the light of Figure 1.1, we might derive the norm from three sources. One takes the word as knowledge as the basis. In this case, we consider Arnold's and Betty's mental lexicons and try to find out which word is stored there. We can say that Arnold and Betty each decide for themselves what is the right word. The second approach is to take the signal as a basis. We can look up the expressions in (9b–d) in a corpus. In iWeb (2018), (9b) has only 2 occurrences. For (9c) and (9d), we find many occurrences, but most of them do not have *peel* and *pala* in the relevant sense. We can of course go over the occurrences and sort them semantically, but in that case we do not keep to the signal in a strict sense, because we use our knowledge of language (or someone else's) to interpret the examples. Finally, we can use an authoritative source such as a dictionary. In our view, it is possible to study word formation without settling questions pertaining to the correctness of the resulting words in the language. It is also appropriate to do so, because correctness is not a property that can be established on a neutral basis.

If it is not possible to establish the correct word for a concept without resorting to an authority, we expect to find cases where several words for the same concept are in competition. A well-known, but still interesting example of the competition between different names is the word for *computer* in German and in Slovak. In both languages, there are three variants. Table 1.1 gives their frequency in DeReKo (2021) and SNK (2022).[5]

In Table 1.1, the three words for *computer* are listed in the same order. The first is an unadapted loanword from English. As ⟨c⟩ is orthographically marked in both languages,[6] the second form is an orthographic adaptation with the more regular ⟨k⟩. The third form is a different type of adaptation. It is based on the translation of *compute*, *rechnen* in German and *počítať* in Slovak, and an agentive suffix corresponding to -*er* in English. For each of these forms, the columns marked 'Frequency' give the frequency per million words and 'Per cent' the share of the form in the total of the three variants. As is obvious from Table 1.1, the adapted forms with ⟨k⟩ are not popular. In German, *Computer* is much more frequent, but *Rechner* is still frequent enough for most speakers of German to know it as well. In Slovak,

---

[5] Search date 25 September 2022. DeReKo: W Archiv öffentlich. SNK: version 10.0.
[6] In German, ⟨c⟩ occurs only in loanwords and in the digraph ⟨ch⟩. In Slovak, ⟨c⟩ is pronounced /ts/, except in the digraph ⟨ch⟩.

Table 1.1 *German and Slovak words for* computer

German	Frequency	Per cent	Slovak	Frequency	Per cent
Computer	35.254	83.738	computer	1.711	2.366
Komputer	0.006	0.014	komputer	0.118	0.163
Rechner	6.841	16.249	počítač	70.476	97.47

it is rather *počítač* which has become the standard and KSSJ (2003), a standard one-volume dictionary of Slovak, does not give *computer* as an entry.

Words such as German *Rechner* and Slovak *počítač* are often described as loan translations. We should keep in mind, however, that this is not a category that stands in opposition to word formation. Rather *loan translation* and *word formation* describe different aspects of the same word. Word formation is a rule-based mechanism for naming concepts. The decision which rules to use and how to use them belongs to the domain of motivation. In the case of (9b), the motivation stems from selected aspects of the concept to be named. In the case of *Rechner* and *počítač*, the motivation is likely to stem from the English word *computer*. It is not always possible to verify whether it is the structure of a foreign word or properties of the concept that serve as motivation. The two factors may also reinforce each other. Ultimately, motivation is something that is valid for an individual speaker.[7]

On the basis of these considerations, we can represent the formation and use of words as names for concepts as in Figure 1.2. In Figure 1.2, we see a sequence of four processes. Naming is the creation of a new association between a concept and a name. As indicated by the arrow, the starting point is the concept. Lexicalization is the storage of the pair of a name and a concept in the mental lexicon. Naming and lexicalization take place in an individual speaker. By the use of the mental lexicon, the speaker can form sentences and other complex expressions that are associated with a meaning. This is represented in Figure 1.2 as *intended performance*. Intended performance is a representation of an expression which includes both form and meaning. It is still within the speaker's cognition and serves as the basis for an utterance or a written text. The actual production leads to the signal, which only has a form and can be observed directly.

The process of naming in Figure 1.2 has been the main focus of our discussion in this section. The three procedures of word formation, sense extension and borrowing as illustrated in (9b–d) are the main processes that are used in naming. The competition between different processes, as illustrated

---

[7] Motivation is especially important in language acquisition. It is by no means necessary for a motivation to be linguistically valid for it to work for an individual speaker. This is particularly true in second-language acquisition, where mnemonic aids can be based on hints from the first language that have no historical or linguistic role in the second language. Thus, the consonants in Dutch *duur* and Slovak *drahý*, both 'expensive', may be used as a mnemonic aid, although they are not historically connected.

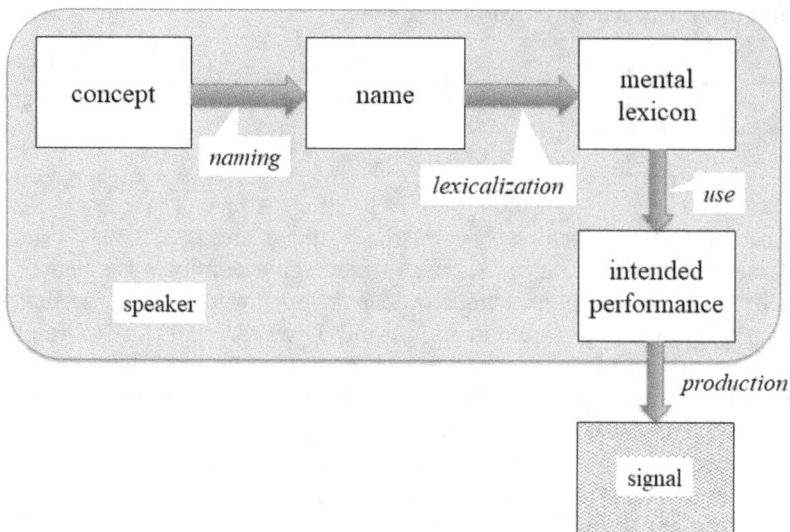

Figure 1.2 *Processes in naming and use of names*

in Table 1.1, shows that the concept does not determine which procedure is taken. At the same time, we observe that in a particular speech community, one of the expressions emerges as the standard.

In the literature, we find different meanings of *lexicalization*. Thomas (2013b) gives a systematic overview. A common interpretation of *lexicalization* is focused on the specialization of meaning. The idea is that after a complex word has been stored in the lexicon, it acquires an additional or more specific meaning. This is a diachronic interpretation that is gradual in nature. It depends on a sequence of events, because the specialization only starts after the initial formation. The gradual nature is visible in that the specialized meaning may be more or less removed from the compositional one and the relative prominence of the specialized meaning with respect to the compositional one may vary along a continuous scale. This is the interpretation advocated by Brinton and Traugott (2005: 91–92). It is not the one we use in Figure 1.2. To us, it seems highly improbable that a word is formed first, then lexicalized and only after that used for a specific concept.

Another interpretation discussed by Thomas (2013b) is the one used by Jackendoff (1990) in the context of what in his later work would be called the Parallel Architecture. Jackendoff uses *lexicalization* to refer to the selection of a portion of a semantic representation as a unit to assign a name to. In Figure 1.2, this portion of a semantic representation corresponds to 'concept'. The formation of concepts is presupposed in Figure 1.2. It is without any doubt an interesting topic, but it is not the focus of our study here.

As mentioned in the description of Figure 1.2, we use *lexicalization* to refer to the process of storing a name in the mental lexicon. This implies

Naming concepts

that lexicalization follows naming. Specialization is a feature of the process of naming. We assume that in naming, the starting point is a concept and the result is a name that fits the concept. This is what we call *onomasiological coercion*, an idea we will discuss and illustrate in more detail in section 4.5. Onomasiological coercion explains why, for instance, Dutch *woordenboek* (lit. 'word-EN-book') refers to a dictionary. It never referred to, for instance, 'book containing words' before coming to mean 'dictionary'. Onomasiological coercion also applies to borrowing. Thus, Slovak *interview* can only refer to a setting of a conversation with a journalist, not to, for instance, a job interview. This is because only for the concept designated by Slovak *interview*, a new name was necessary.

Naming and lexicalization are often not necessary. The contrast between (9a) and (9b–d) illustrates the distinction between naming and description. Description, as in (9a), depends only on the use of lexical entries. In Figure 1.2, it corresponds to the situation where the speaker skips naming and lexicalization and starts with their existing mental lexicon. In fact, in ordinary communication, this is the most common procedure.

Bauer (1983: 48–49) uses *lexicalization* for the final stage of a process that starts with *institutionalization*. Compared with institutionalization, lexicalization requires an aspect of the word that is not retrievable from a productive rule. As Figure 1.2 takes the perspective of a single speaker, it does not represent this social aspect. Institutionalization depends on the general use in a speech community. In Figure 1.1, it corresponds to the formation of a 'word as entry'.

As elaborated in ten Hacken and Panocová (2011), naming is sometimes perceived as the action of a speech community, but it is only individual speakers that can actually take any action in this process. Ten Hacken (2019a: 58–65) makes the point that the most common use of a word formation rule is not for the creation of a new name, but for the interpretation of a name that occurs in a discourse or text. In terms of Figure 1.2, this interpretation process can take two forms. If the hearer knows the concept, the occurrence of the unknown word in the discourse or text serves as a motivation for naming it. If not only the name, but also the concept are new to the hearer, the naming process is applied in reverse, i.e. the hearer tries to reconstruct the concept on the basis of the name. As argued by ten Hacken (2013b: 38–41), there are three types of information a hearer can use to infer (properties of) the concept, listed in (10).

(10)   a. The recognition that X is not in the mental lexicon.
        b. The form of X.
        c. The context in which X is used.

In (10), the new word is indicated by X. The reversed naming process is triggered by (10a). For word formation, (10b) refers to the component parts and the word formation rule, e.g. *woord* ('word') and *boek* ('book') in Dutch *woordenboek* ('dictionary'). For borrowings, it is a word in the donor language, e.g. English *interview* for Slovak *interview*.

To sum up, we assume that a concept is a unit of meaning to which a name is applied. Names can be perceived as words in a signal, words in the mental lexicon and words in a dictionary. New names are generally motivated, either by a word formation rule or by other words in the same language or in another language. Naming takes place in a particular speaker. We use *lexicalization* for the storage of the resulting name in the mental lexicon.

CHAPTER 2

Naming in the history of morphology

In this chapter we consider the place of word formation in the study of morphology in a number of linguistic theories of the nineteenth and twentieth centuries, as well as its consequences for their treatment of naming. This will serve as a background for the discussion of theories of morphology in subsequent chapters.

Taking the nineteenth century as a starting point is not arbitrary, because it marks what is usually considered the starting point of systematic, theory-oriented linguistic research (cf. Robins 1979: 164). However, we start in section 2.1 with what has been called *traditional grammar*. Many later theories are presented by their proponents in opposition to traditional grammar. In traditional grammar, the focus is on a single language and the purpose is to formulate rules of correct usage. For Latin, this type of grammar has a long tradition. For many other languages, the eighteenth and nineteenth centuries constituted an important transition period, because vernacular languages were increasingly used in a variety of domains previously dominated by Latin. This tradition continues in the compilation of descriptive grammars for individual languages, which often present normative judgements on the basis of their descriptions.

In section 2.2, we turn to the historical-comparative approach, which dominated the field of linguistics in the nineteenth century. Central aims were demonstrating the relationship between languages and reconstructing their common ancestor. Current research in historical linguistics continues this tradition, although it is no longer dominant in the field of linguistics and supplements the older methods with ideas originating from various later approaches.

Section 2.3 is devoted to Saussure's theory of language. Published posthumously, Saussure (1916) has been a work with enormous influence on the subsequent development of linguistic theory. With his distinction between synchronic and diachronic linguistics, Saussure sets off his theory from the historical-comparative approach. Central elements of this theory are the distinction between *langue* and *parole* and the sign consisting of an arbitrary connection of a *signifiant* and a *signifié*. Various strands of European structuralism have developed these ideas, but the Prague School of linguistics proved to be particularly influential in further developments.

Section 2.4 takes up the theory of language developed by Bloomfield (1933) and his successors in the Post-Bloomfieldian tradition. As opposed to the European traditions, American structuralist linguistics did not start from the assumption that the object language was understood by the linguist when its study would begin. This led to a focus on utterances rather than meaning. Generative linguistics emerged in contrast to Post-Bloomfieldian linguistics, but continued using many of its insights and techniques. Corpus linguistics constitutes a more direct continuation of the Post-Bloomfieldian tradition.

2.1 Traditional grammar

The term *traditional grammar* is a kind of exonym in the sense that it is in general not used by linguists working in it, but by their opponents proposing alternative frameworks. Here, we will take it to refer to the type of study that results in grammatical descriptions of individual languages. For Latin, grammars of this type have a long tradition, because there were no native speakers of the language that served as a standard in a variety of domains in Medieval and Early-Modern Europe. An eighteenth-century example of such a grammar is Hoffmann (1777).

With the increasing use of vernacular languages, the need for their grammatical description arose. As described by Tieken-Boon van Ostade (2011), the English grammar of Robert Lowth, published in 1762, was written primarily in order to help speakers of English whose native language diverged from the standard as adopted by elite speakers. This is typical of one type of motivation behind such grammars. Grammars written for second-language learners have a similar motivation.

A different type of motivation for writing a grammar of a language occurs in a context when the language in question has not been established. Sussex and Cubberley (2006: 101–105) describe this for Slovak. In the eighteenth century, there was no standard Slovak language, but only a range of dialects. Grammars of Slovak compiled in the nineteenth century emphasized either the similarity to Czech or its difference and independence. There is also an extensive literature in Slovak on this issue. A similar motivation can be found in dialect grammars. In his grammar of Basel German, Suter (1992: 17) states the purpose as both describing the language as it is spoken and guiding the speakers to its proper use.

A common feature of traditional grammars of both types is the tension between descriptive and normative purposes. In grammars of the first type of motivation, the standard is taken to exist and is the subject of the description, which is then interpreted as a norm. In the second type of motivation, the grammar sets a norm on the basis of the selective description of linguistic features. It should be noted that the two types are idealizations. In fact, the role of a grammar in setting the standard can be seen as located on a continuum between these two poles, where the point depends not only on the grammar, but also on the user.

The role of morphology and the place of word formation in traditional grammars depend of course both on the object language and on the views of individual grammarians. For this purpose, we can distinguish three types. The first type describes languages without native speakers, the second type describes languages for native speakers and the third type describes modern languages for learners.

A typical example of the first type is Bornemann and Risch's (1978) standard grammar of Ancient Greek, written in German. The main text consists of three parts, *Lautlehre* ('phonology'), *Formenlehre* ('morphology') and *Syntax*. It is followed by three appendices, *Abriß der Wortbildungslehre* ('outline of word formation'), *Die homerische Sprache* ('the language of Homer') and *Zur griechischen Metrik* ('on Greek metrics'). It should be noted that a bilingual dictionary such as Collins (1999) translates both *Formenlehre* and *Wortbildung* as 'morphology'. The former is inflectional morphology. As anyone who has learned Latin or Greek will know, much of the learning process concerns the declension and conjugation. Accordingly, the part on *Formenlehre* takes up over 40 per cent of the text of Bornemann and Risch's grammar (including appendices), with another 28 per cent, included in the part on *Syntax*, devoted to the use of the different inflected forms. Word formation has been assigned to an appendix, which takes up 4.4 per cent of the text. This appendix consists mainly of a list of suffixes, sorted by syntactic and semantic criteria and illustrated with examples.

A slightly different example of this type of grammar is Whitney's (1879) classical grammar of Sanskrit, written in English. It starts with chapters on orthography and phonology. These are followed by chapters on syntactic categories and their inflection, which make up 63 per cent of the text. They treat both the formation and the use of inflected forms. Two final chapters are devoted to derivation and compounding. They comprise almost 20 per cent of the text. Most of the chapter on derivation consists of a list of suffixes like in Bornemann and Risch (1978). The chapter on compounding offers a typology of compounds, based on the Sanskrit grammatical tradition.

Grammars of classical languages are an important domain of traditional grammar. They focus largely on inflection. Word formation appears as an afterthought in grammars of Ancient Greek and Latin, but because of its strong place among traditional Sanskrit grammarians, it is more prominent in grammars of Sanskrit.

As an example of the second type of grammar, directed at native speakers, we will consider Haeseryn et al.'s (1997) grammar of Dutch. This is a two-volume standard work of almost 1,700 pages. Volume 1 is mainly devoted to the word, volume 2 to syntactic constituents, sentences and general (syntactic) phenomena. Dutch is not a highly inflected language, but the formation and use of inflected forms takes up most of volume 1. The last chapter of this volume, and with 165 pages by far the longest, is devoted to word formation. The primary organizing principle is the syntactic category of the output word. The secondary principle is the type of formation (e.g. conversion, suffixation). After that the text is organized by semantic category.

Another example of this type is Romieu and Bianchi's (2005) grammar of Occitan. With 470 pages, it is more modest in size. Whereas Haeseryn et al. (1997: 14–24) briefly address the question *Welk Nederlands wordt in de ANS beschreven?* ('Which Dutch is described in [this grammar]?'), Romieu and Bianchi (2005: 25–64) discuss the dialects and history of Occitan extensively in order to determine the scope of their grammar. Also, the phonetics and orthography take up a much larger share of the text. This reflects the lack of a generally accepted standard in Occitan. Inflection and phrasal syntax are combined in the longest part of the book. This is followed by a section on complex sentences and one on *Morfologia e semantica lexicaus* ('morphology and lexical semantics'). Here *morfologia* refers only to word formation. The chapter on word formation (2005: 453–485) consists of lists of affixes and compound types with examples, ordered by form-based criteria and alphabetically.

In grammars of modern languages written for native speakers, word formation is generally treated in some detail. The organization of the chapters on word formation is generally based on formal principles, especially at the higher levels of the structure, which makes sense because it facilitates finding the relevant information.

The third type of grammar is the one for learners of modern languages, i.e. languages one learns in order to communicate with its native speakers. Here, word formation often has a very subordinate position. Thus, Zubiri's (2000) grammar of Basque, written in Spanish, does not address word formation at all. The same applies to Timberlake's (2004) grammar of Russian, written in English, and ten Cate-Silfwerbrand's (1973) grammar of Swedish, written in Dutch. Butt and Benjamin's (2004) grammar of Spanish, written in English, has no chapter on word formation as such, but there is a brief chapter on diminutives and augmentatives (2004: 549–555). Holton et al.'s (2004) grammar of Modern Greek, also written in English, has a brief chapter with some examples of affixation and compounding (2004: 241–248). Kotyczka's (1976) grammar of Polish, written in German, has some examples of suffixation and prefixation on the final pages (1976: 150–152). Wiedenhof's (2004) grammar of Mandarin, written in Dutch, does have a full chapter, *Morfologie* (2004: 251–277), but this chapter treats the use of bound morphemes without distinguishing inflection and derivation.

In grammars of modern languages for learners, word formation is not generally treated in any systematic way. The degree and type of treatment is determined by the question of what a learner is likely to encounter. Thus, Kotyczka (1976) focuses on highly productive affixation processes, which he exemplifies without giving any constraints on their application. Such a description is useful for decoding words encountered by the learner which are formed according to these rules.

The presentation of traditional grammar at the start of this chapter is motivated by its role as a reference point for many other approaches and theories. Traditional grammar does not constitute a theoretical approach. It is defined by its purpose of describing the grammar of a language. Although the tradition of writing grammars is older than any of the theories treated in the rest of this book, individual grammars are often newer and may use the insights of some of these theories. Individual grammars are written for the purpose of supporting learners or native speakers. In grammars for learners, word formation is not usually treated systematically. As far as it is treated, it is geared towards the recognition of new words. In grammars for native speakers, more attention is paid to it, because the users may consult them for guidance on the formation of a new word.

2.2 Historical-comparative linguistics

Historical-comparative linguistics is an approach to the study of language that dominated the field in the nineteenth century. Although it lost this dominance in the course of the twentieth century, it is still represented in current research. The approach is comparative in the sense that it compares different languages with the aim of showing their relationships and historical in the sense that it studies older stages of the languages and aims to reconstruct common ancestors of related ones.

The starting point of historical-comparative linguistics is traditionally taken to be Sir William Jones's 1786 statement to the Royal Asiatic Society in Calcutta (Robins 1979: 134). Although his statement has often been read as foreshadowing the discovery of the Indo-European language family, Robins (1987) shows that this interpretation is too anachronistic. However, Jones did highlight the relationship of Sanskrit to Greek and Latin and the significance of his statement consists in the fact that it triggered a systematic study of this relationship. The main linguistic domains used for the comparison were morphology, the focus of work by Franz Bopp (1791–1867), and phonology, for which the work of Rasmus Rask (1787–1832) was an early example. In the case of morphology, the idea is that grammatical morphemes are less subject to borrowing and as such reflect an older, indigenous layer of the language. In the case of phonology, the idea is that general, regular changes can be observed.

Perhaps the most famous generalization of the early period of historical-comparative linguistics is what is known as *Grimm's Law*. It is a generalization named after Jacob Grimm (1785–1863), but based to a large extent on insights from Rask (cf. Robins 1979: 171). Some examples reflecting this law are given in Table 2.1.

Table 2.1 *Examples of Grimm's Law*

Latin	pater	trēs	cordis
English	father	three	heart
Dutch	vader	drie	hart

In Table 2.1 Grimm's Law is illustrated only for voiceless stops. The three languages serve as representatives of different stages in the development. In all words, the focus is on the first consonant. The Latin examples represent the common starting point for a large group of Indo-European languages. The English examples represent the first sound change, which is common to Germanic languages. Here the voiceless stops become fricatives. The Dutch examples illustrate the second sound change, where the fricatives become voiced. Similar changes can be traced for voiced and aspirated stops. Grimm (1893 [1822]: 496–507) gives examples from Ancient Greek, Gothic and Old High German to support the statement of the regularities.

In Table 2.1, the words in the same column are translations of each other. In *cordis*, the genitive is given to show the final -d- of the stem. The focus is on the form of the words, but the meaning is important as a way of demonstrating that the words in the different languages correspond. This is an attitude that is very common in historical-comparative linguistics. It is directly connected to the type of question that is the focus of linguistic research. The purpose of this type of research is to identify systematic correspondences in order to reconstruct elements of the common parent language.

A modern overview of the results achieved in comparative Indo-European linguistics, Beekes (1995), divides the presentation between methodology, phonology and morphology. While the part on morphology is about two and a half times as long as that on phonology, it is mostly on inflection. Only 5 of the 288 pages of text are devoted to word formation (1995: 168–172). An example of the perspective is the list of nominal suffixes (1995: 169), which is grouped according to the last phoneme. The description of individual suffixes addresses their distribution and makes generalizations about the suffixed words, but does not attempt to circumscribe the meaning of the suffix. One has to keep in mind here that these suffixed words are forms reconstructed on the basis of the comparison of various languages. Therefore, word formation is only used in the reverse direction. Although naming is implied, it does not play a role in the analysis.

A quite different type of research within historical-comparative linguistics is represented by Paul (1886). Here, the historical component is prominent. Indeed, Paul (1886: 19–20) argues explicitly that there is no scientific approach to the study of language other than the historical one.[1]

---

[1] Paul (1886: 19) speaks about the 'wissenschaftliche betrachtung der sprache'. There is of course a well-known mismatch between DE *wissenschaftlich* and EN

Paul also uses examples from various languages. However, more than the reconstruction of a common ancestor, the use of examples from different historical stages and different languages serves the purpose of drawing cross-linguistic generalizations.

The difference in outlook is visible in the chapter 'Entstehung der wortbildung und flexion' ('Origin of word formation and inflection', 1886: 274–298). Examples in this chapter are drawn mainly from German, French and Latin, of course in different historical stages. Reconstructed forms are rare. A central topic of the chapter is the difference between compounding and syntactic constructions, which is captured in what Paul (1886: 278) calls the *isolation* of the entire expression with respect to the components. Isolation is a psychological phenomenon and implies that the component parts of the expression are not fully present in the entire expression. This can be reflected in a non-compositional meaning, phonological changes, the absence of inflectional endings, etc. In Paul's analysis, the comparison of the underlying syntactic expression and the compound involves two historical stages. Derivational affixes are the result of a further reduction of a component of a compound.

It is interesting to consider the place of naming in Paul's (1886) theory. Whereas compounds name concepts, syntactic constructions describe them. Paul (1886: 282–284) discusses compounds of the type *bienenkönigin* ('bees queen', i.e. queen bee) and a number of similar types, linking them to various syntactic constructions, including older preposed genitives, e.g. OHG *then hîuuiskes fater* ('the family$_{GEN}$ father'), where the ending of *then* marks it as modifying the second noun. When Paul (1886: 277) claims that there is no clear boundary between compounding and syntax, this implies that he does not recognize a clear distinction between naming and description.

Historical-comparative linguistics is often considered as the branch of linguistics concerned with the reconstruction of common ancestor languages and family trees. However, there is also a tradition centred around the question of how to explain linguistic changes. Here we find an interest in the origin of word formation and its distinction from syntax.

2.3 Saussure's general linguistics

Ferdinand de Saussure (1857–1913) started his career as a representative of historical-comparative linguistics, but his influence derives mainly from his course on general linguistics. This posthumous work was compiled by his colleagues Charles Bally (1865–1947) and André Sechehaye (1870–1946) on the basis of his students' lecture notes. The history of its compilation means

---

scientific. Throughout his work, Paul does not observe the German tradition, now orthographic rule, of capitalizing nouns.

that the relation between the published text and Saussure's actual ideas has been the subject of extensive research, of which Depecker (2012) gives a brief overview. We will take Saussure (1916) as a basis here, because it is the version that has influenced later research.

Three ideas that are central for our study here are the distinction between synchronic and diachronic perspectives, the distinction between *langue* and *parole*, and the binary nature of the sign. The first of these is a direct reaction to the assumptions made in historical-comparative linguistics. Saussure (1916: 114–140) discusses the distinction in some detail and clearly prioritizes the synchronic perspective. In stark opposition to Paul (1886), he claims that traditional grammar ('la grammaire classique') is more scientific than historical-comparative linguistics ('la linguistique inaugurée par Bopp', 1916: 118).

For the study of word formation and naming, both synchronic and diachronic perspectives are relevant. A purely synchronic perspective cannot directly account for the choice of a name. The formation process is inherently diachronic, because it links a state before the name emerged to a state after. Synchronically, we can study word formation only in terms of the structure of complex words and the word formation rules underlying them. Naming is not in either of these.

A second basic idea of Saussure (1916) is the opposition between *langue* and *parole*. One can think of *langue* as the system of language and *parole* as the use of this system by individual speakers, but for Saussure the system of language is realized not in individual speakers, but only in a group of speakers, the speech community (1916: 30). By making *langue* at the same time a social rather than individual phenomenon and placing it in the brain, Saussure created a tension he did not manage to resolve in his lifetime. The lexicon must be considered part of the language system for the language to work at all, but no two speakers have exactly the same lexicon. A word such as *quillet* 'small plot of land' is rare enough that most speakers of English will not know it, but OED (2000–2023) has a record of quotations from the sixteenth to the late twentieth century. Is *quillet* then part of the English *langue*?

An important observation by Saussure is that individual speakers cannot change the *langue* (1916: 104). If interpreted strictly, this would make word formation impossible. However, in a slightly looser sense, it can account for the barrier to the use of new words. Whereas it is common to use a phrase not stored in the language system, new words are much rarer. The acceptance of a new word in a speech community is not automatic and depends on a variety of factors that may differ between speech communities. These factors typically include the recognition in the speech community that a new word is needed, the status of the speakers using it and the perceived appropriateness in relation to other words. Speech communities differ in their tolerance of new words. Thus, Aufinger (2022) gives evidence for the hypothesis that in German, new words are accepted more easily than in French.

The third main idea from Saussure which is important for the discussion of word formation is the analysis of the word as a *signe*, consisting of a *signifiant* and a *signifié* (1916: 98–100). It is not sufficient to equate *signifiant* with form and *signifié* with meaning, because both of them must be representations that are sufficiently abstract to be shared by the members of a speech community and applied to a variety of realizations. The relation between the two components is arbitrary in the sense that it is not possible to derive one from the other (1916: 101).

Saussure's model of the *signe* gives us a basis for representing word formation. Word formation is one way of creating a new *signe*. When word formation is used for naming, the starting point is a *signifié*. The arbitrariness of the *signe* is reflected in the fact that different *signifiants* can in principle be chosen. The social nature of the *langue* implies that the choice of a name depends on the speech community. At the same time, as observed by ten Hacken and Panocová (2011), any action in the naming process can only be carried out by individual speakers.

Saussure's ideas were developed in various places throughout Europe. In Geneva, Bally and Sechehaye and their students continued working within Saussure's tradition, and Amacker (1995: 240) mentions that Bally used the designation *Geneva School* for this group. The most influential current of thoughts inspired by Saussure's ideas, however, was no doubt that of the *Cercle linguistique de Prague*, in English known as the *Prague School*.

The *Cercle linguistique de Prague* (CLP) was founded in 1926 by an international group of linguists under the direction of Vilém Mathesius (1882–1945). Sergej Karcevskij (1884–1955) provided a direct link to the Geneva School, as he was a student of Bally and Sechehaye in Geneva as well as an early member of the CLP. One of the internationally most famous members was Roman Jakobson (1896–1982). A central document outlining the group's views of linguistics is *Thèses* (1929), a set of hypotheses proposed for discussion at the First Congress of Slavic Philologists in Prague in 1929.

The central idea of the CLP was that language is determined by its function. They considered language a 'system of purposeful means of expression' (Vachek and Dušková 1983: 77).[2] The functional view means that the study of linguistic units is oriented towards their task or role in delimiting an expression, in selecting a form from a paradigm and in determining the flow of discourse. From the perspective of a speaker's communicative needs, Mathesius (1936: 97–98) makes a distinction between functional onomatology, i.e. using names for selected elements of reality, and functional syntax, i.e. organizing these names into sentences reflecting a specific situation.

---

[2] Quoted from the translation of *Thèses* (1929) in Vachek and Dušková (1983). The original reads 'la langue est un système de moyens d'expression appropriés à un but' (*Thèses* 1929: 7).

The language system is, according to the CLP, organized in a number of strata, levels or planes, ordered linearly. Although there was some discussion on details, the following levels are more or less generally assumed:

- Text: As language occurs in the form of texts, this must be the starting point of the analysis.
- Syntax: Here the units are sentences, clauses and phrases. They are identified as parts of a text. In the system, sentence patterns are the focus.
- Lexicon: Here the units are words or lexemes. They are considered as meaningful and described in the vocabulary.
- Morphology: Here the units are morphemes. The focus is on the structure of words.
- Phonology: Here the units are phonemes. This concept was proposed by Trubetzkoy (1939) to distinguish phonology from phonetics.

At the levels of both the Lexicon and Morphology, the units are Saussurean signs. At these levels, naming takes place. The higher levels are used for description.

The connection between adjacent levels was discussed among the members of the CLP, but no uniform theory about it was published. There was wide agreement on the assumption of morphophonology as an interlevel between morphology and phonology. Word formation can be considered an interlevel between morphology and the lexicon. Collocations can be located at an interlevel between the lexicon and syntax. Mathesius (1940: 80) proposed the concept of a naming unit or denomination. He distinguished two types, descriptive and simple. He illustrates it by the contrast between *airman* and *pilot*, where the former has an internal structure linking it to other words and the latter does not. In this contrast, *airman* is motivated by its relation to *air* and *man*, whereas *pilot* does not have a similar type of motivation.

Whereas Trubetzkoy focused on the opposition between phonemes and their relation to phonetic realizations, Jakobson (1932) studied the distinction between phonological and morphological oppositions. For phonology, it is possible to analyse phonemes into bundles of features. Instead, in the domain of morphology, Jakobson proposed the concept of markedness. A good example is the contrast between singular and plural, as in *box* and *boxes*. The plural implies the existence of the singular, but the reverse does not hold. The plural is therefore marked, which is also reflected in the form.

Based on its focus on the function of language, the work of the CLP introduced a number of important new notions compared with Saussure's theory. A central innovation is the set of levels of representation, which provides a more articulated view of language as a system. Against this background we can also locate word formation. Mathesius's distinction between description and naming is essential for the study of word formation in its role as a naming device. Jakobson's concept of markedness can be used to characterize morphological relationships of the type that arise in word formation.

Apart from the Prague School, there were a number of other linguists who developed Saussure's ideas in different directions. In Denmark, Louis Hjelmslev (1899–1965) proposed the framework of Glossematics. In 1931, he co-founded the *Cercle linguistique de Copenhague*. A central component of Saussure's theory he expanded on was the idea that a *signe* and its components, *signifiant* and *signifié*, are first of all different from others. Under the influence of logical positivism, Glossematics was strongly form-oriented. Its main theoretical exposition, Hjelmslev (1943), appeared in Danish and, although an authorized English translation appeared in 1953, its influence beyond Denmark was limited (Fudge 1995: 263). In Britain, J. R. Firth (1890–1960) was inspired by a different aspect of Saussure's theory of the *signe*. His emphasis was on the syntagmatic and paradigmatic relations among *signes*. This led to the study of collocations which was further elaborated on in corpus linguistics. As Palmer (1995) describes, Firth inspired many linguistic researchers in Britain.

This overview of some key elements of Saussure's theory and some theories based on it is necessarily selective and concise. However, it introduced the main concepts we need from these theories for our discussion of word formation as a naming device in subsequent chapters.

2.4 Bloomfield and the Post-Bloomfieldians

There is a traditional distinction between European and American linguistics. As argued by Joseph (2002: 1–17), there is a genuine difference in outlook underlying this distinction, but they should rather be thought of as prototypes than as theoretical frameworks with clear boundaries. Moreover, the geographic basis of the labels is sometimes misleading, because not all linguistics in Europe belongs to the former nor does all linguistics in America qualify as the latter. The work of Leonard Bloomfield (1887–1949) can be considered the foundation of the American tradition. The Post-Bloomfieldians, in particular Zellig Harris (1909–1992) and Charles Hockett (1916–2000), developed and modified his ideas to make them more radical in some respects.

Bloomfield's (1933) overview of linguistics has been hugely influential. As an overview, it does not present a single narrow approach. Thus, it also presents results from the historical-comparative tradition and it includes a substantial chapter on the comparative method (1933: 297–320). However, at the outset, Bloomfield (1933: 22–24) presents the stimulus-response model as the proper foundation for linguistic research, which sets his work and that of his successors apart from the European traditions, both the historical-comparative and the Saussurean ones.

A central assumption in the stimulus-response model is that language should be studied only as behaviour. On one hand, this is opposed to a focus on writing, literature or 'correct' speech (1933: 21-22). Instead, Bloomfield considers language as first of all realized in actual unmarked speech. On the other hand, the focus on behaviour excludes the use of mentalist data (1933: 31-34). Bloomfield argues that there is no objective access to mentalist observations, so that they cannot be the basis for any scientific inquiry. This attitude accounts for a strong bias towards form rather than meaning. Bloomfield claims that '[i]n order to give a scientifically accurate definition of meaning for every form of a language, we should have to have a scientifically accurate knowledge of everything in the speakers' world' (1933: 139). This view was also inspired by the tradition of field linguistics, which in the American context often starts without access to anything else than the form.

Bloomfield's (1933: 207-246) overview of morphology has been a basis for most morphological research afterwards. The overview is systematic and includes many examples from a variety of languages, which explains its influence. At the same time, it is written from a particular theoretical perspective, which is then given an additional authority by the systematic and authoritative nature of Bloomfield's text. Thus, when introducing the opposition between inflection and word formation, he presents it as pertaining to 'many languages' (1933: 222) and states immediately that '[t]his distinction cannot always be carried out' (1933: 223). Similarly, he mentions the distinction between morphology and syntax as a 'traditional division [that] is justified', but cannot always be maintained (1933: 184).

Bloomfield's central notion in the domains both of morphology and of syntax is what he calls the *construction*. Bloomfield describes it as one of the 'three great classes' of grammatical forms, the others being sentence types and substitutions. He characterizes the construction as 'the grammatical features by which they [i.e. the constituents of a complex form] are combined' (1933: 169). By focusing on constructions, Bloomfield reconciles grammatical traditions distinguishing morphology and syntax and dividing the former into inflection and word formation with observations of languages in which such distinctions raise problems.

Bloomfield (1933) proposes a general theory of language. As such, naming also falls within the domain of his theory. However, the focus of attention is clearly a different one. The study of word formation as a naming device presupposes a distinction between word and phrase as well as a distinction between word formation and inflection. Bloomfield does not assume that such distinctions can be maintained for all languages. Moreover, an account of naming is not possible without reference to the study of meaning, for which the behaviourist framework offers very little footing.

The Post-Bloomfieldians were a group of linguists who developed Bloomfield's theory and approach. The most important theorists among them were Zellig Harris and Charles Hockett. Whereas Bloomfield (1933) gives a general overview of the field of linguistics, Harris and Hockett developed a system of linguistic analysis that focused on some selected aspects from Bloomfield's overview and made a number of constraints much more explicit and absolute than Bloomfield had done. Ten Hacken (2007: 130-155) proposes a systematic analysis of their research programme.

The Post-Bloomfieldian approach to linguistics is strongly corpus-based. Harris (1951: 12) identifies linguistic work as consisting of collecting a corpus of data and analysing it. He immediately adds that the corpus is not closed before analysis starts and should be representative of the language (or dialect) in the sense that another sufficiently large corpus would lead to the same results. Hockett (1947: 322) describes data collection in similar terms. Whereas linguistic analysis in the system of the Prague School starts from the text and gradually moves to smaller units, Harris and Hockett use the corpus as a basis for a bottom-up analysis, starting with the identification of the smallest units. This means that the order of the levels of analysis we saw in section 2.3 is reversed.

Theoretical discussions among Post-Bloomfieldians often turned on the conditions that must be fulfilled by the procedure of analysing the data. Harris's (1951) book can be read as a catalogue of such procedures. Hockett (1942: 20-21) proposes 'six requirements which seem essential for a correct system'. Two of these are of special relevance here. One is a general prohibition of mentalism. This is a tightening of Bloomfield's (1933) point of view, but it is clearly in his spirit. It implies that hypotheses about speakers' thoughts or intentions play no role in the analysis of corpus data. The other one is a prohibition of what is called *circularity*. The idea is that the analysis starts from the primary data in the corpus and first produces a phonological analysis. The phonological analysis of a corpus leads to an inventory of phonemes and a set of rules for their context-dependent realization in the language represented by the corpus. Morphological analysis takes the result of phonological analysis as a basis. The morphological analysis of a corpus leads to an inventory of morphemes and a set of rules for the realization of allomorphs for the language represented by the corpus. Circularity occurs when morphological considerations play a role in phonological analysis. As shown in ten Hacken (2007: 151-152), there was some discussion about circularity among Post-Bloomfieldians, but not about mentalism.

When we consider the place of word formation and naming in this context, Post-Bloomfieldian linguistics offers even less of a foundation for the study of naming than Bloomfield (1933). A first problem is that naming depends on meaning. Meaning is not recorded directly in the corpus. It appears only in the interpretation of the text. However, interpretation is speaker-specific and inseparable from a speaker's mental processes. The strong emphasis on barring mentalism thus makes it impossible to study the semantic component of naming. This reduces the data that can be gathered from a corpus to the appearance of a new form in a particular linguistic context.

The impact of the constraint against circularity is less clear. Obviously, as word formation involves morphemes, it requires phonological analysis to be completed. Morphological analysis should be described in a way which indicates the licit sequences of morphemes in a language. It is less obvious, however, how word formation as a process should be placed with respect to morphological analysis. The corpus-based approach assumed by Harris and Hockett is strictly synchronic. In its naming aspect, however, word formation has an inherently diachronic component to it. By adding a new word for a new concept, the system is changed. The change can only be observed in a corpus by comparing two stages of the language, before and after the act of naming. This corresponds to a common type of corpus use in lexicography, where first attestation dates of words are searched for, but there is no parallel in the systems proposed by Harris (1951) and Hockett (1942, 1954).

On this basis, we can conclude that Bloomfield (1933) leaves the door to the study of naming open, but does not offer much support when this direction of research is chosen. By contrast, the Post-Bloomfieldians introduce a number of constraints that make the study of naming all but impossible. The most important among them are the exclusion of the use of meaning in the analysis of the data and of the comparison of stages before and after the naming in order to identify the application of a word formation rule.

CHAPTER 3

Historical relationships between current theories of morphology

In the history of twentieth-century linguistics, the emergence of generative grammar is without any doubt a crucial development. In the domain of morphology, the contrast between the period before and after this emergence is less marked than in other areas of linguistics, but for most of the eight theories discussed in Chapters 5–12, generative grammar constitutes an essential reference point, either as a basis they work with or as a counterpoint they reject. Section 3.1 will therefore describe some of the major developments in generative grammar and their influence on the treatment of word formation as a background for the discussion of the theories in Chapters 5–12. Section 3.2 outlines some of the main developments in non-generative, functionalist linguistics that serve as a source of inspiration for some of the theories. Section 3.3 will then motivate the selection of theories for Chapters 5–12 and place them into the theoretical discussion covered in Chapter 2 and in sections 3.1 and 3.2.

3.1 Word formation in generative linguistics

The start of generative grammar is often taken to be the publication of Chomsky (1957). Although it is not a general overview of Chomsky's early theory, this brief monograph was influential in spreading his new approach to doing linguistics, presented as being in opposition to the mainstream at the time. As early as the early 1960s, the term *Chomskyan revolution* was used to refer to the development that saw this new approach becoming mainstream.[1] Here we will focus on the elements of the theory that are relevant for word formation.

---

[1] Voegelin's (1958) review of Chomsky (1957) already refers to it as triggering a revolution. The term *Chomskyan revolution* seems to have been used in print for the first time by Thorne (1965). Newmeyer (1986b) argues for the idea of a Chomskyan revolution on the basis of a mix of theoretical and social features. Ten Hacken (2007: 156–182) analyses the transition as one between different research programmes. Both

After a description of the framework presented by Chomsky (1957) and applied to compounding by Lees (1960) in section 3.1.1, section 3.1.2 outlines the motivation and the consequences of the introduction of the lexicon by Chomsky (1965), which led to Chomsky's (1970) Lexicalist Hypothesis. Section 3.1.3 presents two early elaborations of the Lexicalist Hypothesis, by Halle (1973) and Jackendoff (1975). An alternative development of Chomsky's (1965) model is represented by Generative Semantics. For word formation, Levi's (1978) theory of complex nominals is the most elaborated proposal in this direction. Section 3.1.4 describes her foundational assumptions and the aspects of her analysis that we find most relevant as a background for the theories we discuss in Chapters 5–12. Finally, section 3.1.5 formulates some generalizations about generative theories of word formation and proposes a classification along two parameters.

3.1.1 The early stages of generative grammar

The first widely noticed publication of generative grammar is Chomsky (1957). It evaluates the mainstream linguistic theory of the time and proposes an alternative. The mainstream against which Chomsky (1957) reacted was the Post-Bloomfieldian approach of Zellig Harris and Charles Hockett described in section 2.4. The new approach was marked by a shift in emphasis to syntax, a new conception of the nature of language as an object of study and a new set of questions to be answered. We will discuss these innovations in their relation to word formation. For a more general discussion of morphology in early generative grammar, see ten Hacken (2019c, 2020c).

The shift in emphasis in the new approach is reflected in the title of Chomsky (1957), *Syntactic Structures*, as well as in the central position of syntax in the architecture of grammar. In Post-Bloomfieldian linguistics, Hockett's (1942: 20–21) requirements on a proper analysis method prohibited circularity. The idea was that phonological analysis had to be completed before morphological analysis started. Syntax would be the next step. As a result, most research was focused on methods for the identification of phonemes in order to establish the phoneme inventory of a language and the distributional rules for phonemes. Only for languages for which this step was completed could the identification of morphemes and of their distribution be studied. Syntax is, in this view, the distribution of morphemes at a larger scale. The circularity constraint determined a view of the morpheme from below, i.e. as a unit composed of phonemes.

Chomsky (1957) proposes the opposition between Deep Structure, generated by phrase structure rules, and Surface Structure, derived from Deep Structure by the application of transformation rules. Chomsky's (1957: 26)

---

also discuss and reject various arguments against the analysis of the emergence of Chomskyan linguistics as a revolution.

first example of a grammar starts with *Sentence*. Even though the sentence is ultimately composed of morphemes in a way that Post-Bloomfieldian linguists would recognize, the idea that these morphemes are approached from above, i.e. the sentence they appear in, rather than from below, i.e. the phonemes they are composed of, reverses the perspective.

A more revolutionary innovation is the proposed set of legitimate questions to be asked in linguistics. Chomsky (1957: 49–60) discusses the goal of linguistic theory and considers three options of how to relate grammar and corpus (1957: 51). The strongest option assigns the linguistic theory the role of a discovery procedure. This means that the theory offers a method for extracting a grammar from the corpus. While certainly compatible with Harris (1951) and Hockett (1954), the only place where such a goal of linguistic theory is formulated explicitly seems to be Chomsky's (1953) own presentation of Post-Bloomfieldian linguistics. The other options Chomsky (1957: 51) considers are the theory as a decision procedure or as an evaluation procedure. In the former, the compatibility of a grammar with a corpus is established, in the latter the theory compares the merits of different grammars in the light of a corpus. Chomsky argues that 'it is unreasonable to demand of linguistic theory that it provide anything more than a practical evaluation procedure for grammars' (1957: 52).

Apart from this view of the nature of linguistic theory, also the view of the nature of language as an object of study in Chomskyan linguistics marked a revolutionary innovation compared with the Post-Bloomfieldian framework. Although references to the opposition between competence and performance are missing in Chomsky (1957), ten Hacken (2007: 104–105) argues that there is no reason to assume that this signals a different view of the nature of language on the part of Chomsky at this stage of generative linguistics. At most, it shows a less elaborated view than the one found in Chomsky (1965: 4).

The earliest stage of generative grammar was marked by the absence of a lexicon. Chomsky (1957: 26) includes rewrite rules such as (1) in his grammar.

(1) a. T → *the*
    b. N → *man, ball*, etc.
    c. Verb → *hit, took*, etc.

The grammar Chomsky presents at this point is only meant for expository purposes, which explains the use of *etc.* in (1b–c). Chomsky (1957: 32) proposes to derive *took* from *take* and *past* by means of a morphophonemic rule.

The only well-known systematic study of a word formation phenomenon in this early stage is Lees (1960). At the time, it was the most extensive application of the new framework proposed by Chomsky. Lees proposes an account of English compounding using only phrase structure rules and transformations. Ten Hacken (2009b: 55–60) gives a brief summary of the account from the perspective of the study of compounding. Two examples of deep structures used by Lees (1960) are given in (2).

(2) a. The mill produces textiles.
 b. (i) The plant is for N_a.
 (ii) The plant assembles autos.

In (2a), Lees (1960: 147) gives the deep structure of *textile mill*, in (2b) the one for *assembly plant* (1960: 142). Despite its appearance, the deep structure should not be read as a sentence. In (2a), we have the leaves of a tree structure generated by phrase structure rules, including some of the type illustrated in (1). They are represented as a sentence that can be generated from the same deep structure. In (2b), two separate tree structures are used, with N_a marking a position that is underspecified. A series of transformations results in the stepwise derivation of the compound. In the case of (2b), the first transformation combines the two separate structures into a single tree.

One of the most striking aspects of Lees's (1960) account is its apparent complexity. Lees (1960: 142) gives a sequence of eight transformations taking (2b) as its starting point and yielding *assembly plant* as its output. The motivation for this approach is that each of the intermediate stages can also serve as a basis for other surface structures with shared aspects of form and meaning. In the case of (2a), the sentence is the one that results from the deep structure if only minimal transformations are applied. This is compatible with the idea that semantic interpretation is derived from Deep Structure and phonological realization is based on Surface Structure.

One of the most criticized properties of Lees's (1960) account is its systematic and extensive overgeneration. In (2), some elements are present that do not appear in the compounds at Surface Structure. In (2a), the verb is deleted in the course of the derivation, leaving only the two nouns. In (2b), the verb is retained in a nominalized form, but its object *autos* is deleted. The reason for including *produces* in (2a) and *autos* in (2b) is that they are part of the meaning of the compound. In (2a), the verb is the most plausible one for the connection of these two nouns, but it cannot be deduced from one or the other separately. In the case of *textile market* or *water mill*, a different verb should be inserted. The plausibility of the verb depends on world knowledge. In the case of (2b), the choice of *autos* is more specific. An assembly plant is a factory where cars are built by assembling components produced elsewhere. The idea that it is cars and not other products that are produced in this way is not just a matter of world knowledge. More obviously than in the case of the verb (2a), it depends on naming. The specification of the deep structures in (2) is then the reflection of the way the relevant compounds are used for naming.

As the most elaborate study of word formation in early generative grammar, Lees (1960) offers an account of compounds in English based on the assumption that the deep structure encodes the meaning of the expression realized in the surface structure. The naming aspect of the compound is reflected in the specification of a descriptive equivalent in the deep structure. This means that the meaning is made explicit. However, because the rules have to be of a general nature, it also leads to an extensive overgeneration. In principle, all verbs are generated in the position of *produces* in (2a) and all nouns in the position of *autos* in (2b). Any restrictions have to be based on explicit features, e.g. that the verb is transitive in (2a) and the noun inanimate in (2b). Such restrictions are not sufficient for a significant limitation of the number of possible deep structures for one compound.

3.1.2 The lexicon in generative grammar

From the perspective of our topic in this monograph, a crucial innovation in generative grammar in the early 1960s was the introduction of the lexicon. Chomsky (1965: 84–90) proposes a modified system in which the deep structure of a sentence is no longer generated entirely by phrase structure rules. Instead of being introduced by rules such as (1), individual words are in the lexicon. Phrase structure rules generate a structure which ends with markers (or dummy symbols), written as Δ, that incorporate all the features of the node. An operation called *lexical insertion* then selects an element from the lexicon for each Δ that matches its feature specification.

As a result of this change in the grammatical architecture, there were now three components that could contribute to the account of a particular phenomenon. Whereas Lees (1960) assumed that compounding should be covered entirely by phrase structure rules and transformations, the lexicon offers a third possibility. Chomsky (1970) discusses the distribution of tasks between these three components.

We can identify as a crucial component of Chomsky's (1970) reasoning the desire to separate the generative component of the grammar from the naming function. However, Chomsky does not formulate it in this way. His reasoning is illustrated by the examples in (3) and (4).

(3) a. John is easy to please.
    b. *John's easiness to please

(4) a. John is eager to please.
    b. John's eagerness to please

Chomsky (1970: 188–189) discusses the idiosyncratic contrast between *easiness* in (3) and *eagerness* in (4) in syntactic terms. It can also be analysed in terms of the relation between the adjective and the derived noun. The meaning of *easiness* is illustrated in (5), taken from BNC (2007).

(5) 'The upper classes', he remarked, 'are too "bottled up" to be of any use as colourful screen material, too stiffened with breeding to relax into the natural easiness and normality required by the screen.'

In (5), *he* refers to Alfred Hitchcock (1899–1980), the famous film director. The use of *easiness* in (5) shows that its semantic relation to *easy* is different to the one *eagerness* in (4b) has to *eager*. This results in the difference in syntactic behaviour illustrated in the contrast between (3b) and (4b). Chomsky formulates this as a 'matter of productivity' (1970: 188). He contrasts the nominalization of adjectives by means of *-ness* with the nominalization of verbs with *-ing*. Another aspect in which this contrast can be found is in the choice of the suffix. Whereas *-ing* applies to all verbs, adjectives can be nominalized with a range of alternative suffixes.

On the basis of such arguments, Chomsky argues for what he calls the 'lexicalist hypothesis', which implies that 'derived nominals should have the form of base sentences' (1970: 212). This means that (4b) does not arise by inserting *eager* into the deep structure and applying a transformation to derive *eagerness* in the surface structure, but by inserting *eagerness* directly into the deep structure. The relationship between *eagerness* and *eager* is not expressed in syntax, but only in the lexicon.

At this point, the precise distribution of tasks between the lexicon and the phrase structure rules remains an empirical issue to be settled for each morphological process. However, an important observation can be made on the basis of the examples in (6).

(6) a. The book is readable.
b. the book's readability

In (6b), the use of *-ity* rather than *-ness* is an idiosyncratic aspect that must be covered by including it in the lexicon. However, if *-ity* is attached in the lexicon, its base *readable* must also be in the lexicon. Therefore, Chomsky (1970: 212) deduces that the formation of adjectives with *-able* must also take place in the lexicon, even though it is more regular. In his conclusion, Chomsky suggests that 'the transformationalist hypothesis is correct for the gerundive nominals and the lexicalist hypothesis for the derived nominals' (1970: 215).

By introducing the lexicon, Chomsky (1965) makes it possible to separate the naming function of word formation from the descriptive function of regular syntactic processes. The discussion of the Lexicalist Hypothesis by Chomsky (1970) shows a very pragmatic approach, in which the classification of specific processes as covered by syntactic rules or in the lexicon should be decided on an individual basis.

3.1.3 Elaborations of the Lexicalist Hypothesis

The 1970s saw a revival of the study of morphology in generative linguistics, based on different elaborations of the ideas outlined by Chomsky (1970). Two early proposals that developed these ideas in different directions are Halle (1973) and Jackendoff (1975). Halle (1973: 8) proposes the model in Figure 3.1.

The four components in the top line of Figure 3.1 constitute the lexicon. What is called the *dictionary of words* is the input to lexical insertion. In order to account for the selection of correctly inflected forms in the syntactic context, Halle (1973: 9) proposes that the lexical insertion operation inserts entire paradigms, so that the correct form can be selected from the paradigm.[2] These paradigms are the units of the dictionary of words. This dictionary of words is the result of rules of word formation operating on the list of morphemes. Halle (1973: 10) gives the example in (7) to illustrate the form of a word formation rule.

(7)   [VERB + al]$_N$

The dotted line from the dictionary to the word formation rules indicates that the application of the rules depends on information available only in the dictionary. Halle (1973: 10) gives the example of *arrival*, which uses (7), but depends on the information that *arrive* is a verb, which is only found in the dictionary. Halle (1973: 13–15) argues that the phonological output should also be available as information guiding the application of word formation rules.

The filter between the word formation rules and the dictionary is the mechanism invoked to explain that (7) does not apply to *confuse*, so that *confusal is not in the dictionary. In general it handles 'exceptions and idiosyncrasies of all sorts' (Halle 1973: 11). As Scalise (1984: 34) notes, a major objection to Halle's model is that the filter is not a finite device. If its decisions are not based on rules generalizing over classes of individual cases, the number of potential forms that need to be recorded is infinite. Given that the human brain is finite in size, an infinite device cannot be a proper account of how language is implemented in the brain.

It is immediately clear from Figure 3.1 that Halle's view of word formation is strongly biased towards the formal aspect. In fact, whereas the phonological interpretation of syntactic structures is represented, their semantic interpretation is not. Whereas Halle (1973: 13) discusses how it should be explained that the /t/ in *soften* is not pronounced by the interaction of word

---

[2] The problem of selecting the correct form is complicated by the assumption that lexical insertion takes place at Deep Structure, but the correct inflected form depends on properties that are only visible at Surface Structure. Thus, the passive transformation determines which noun phrase has to agree with the verb. In Figure 3.1, syntax is not divided into Deep and Surface Structure.

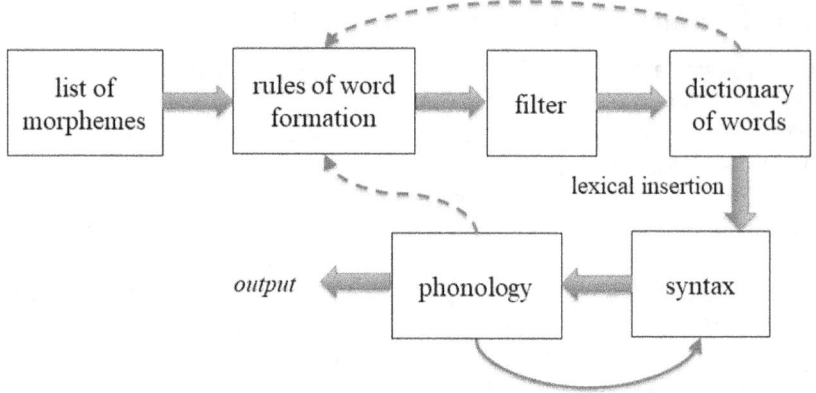

Figure 3.1 *Halle's (1973: 8) model*

formation rules with the phonology, semantic idiosyncrasies are simply assigned to the filter. The information that *blackbird* refers to a bird of the species *Turdus merula*, even though other birds, e.g. crows, are also black and female blackbirds are brown, is not explained, but only listed in the filter.

Jackendoff (1975) offers an alternative elaboration of the Lexicalist Hypothesis. The differences between Halle (1973) and Jackendoff (1975) start with the scope of their papers. Whereas Halle designates his as *prolegomena to a theory* in the title, Jackendoff's abstract starts 'This paper proposes a theory of the lexicon' (1975: 639). Also, the nature of the theory is different. Jackendoff argues for what he calls a *full-entry theory* and conceptualizes word formation rules as redundancy rules. The former means that a complex word such as *decision* has a fully specified entry. This entry does not contain references to *decide* and to the nominalization rule with *-ion* so as to minimize its contents, but specifies the phonological, syntactic and semantic information about *decision*. The word formation rule connects the entries of *decide* and *decision* in such a way that redundant information does not count fully to the effort of storing it. By conceptualizing word formation rules as redundancy rules, Jackendoff does not have to use a filter of the type Halle (1973) has in his model.

Jackendoff (1975) does not give a model of the type represented in Figure 3.1. However, he gives many examples of dictionary entries. These entries contain a phonological representation, the syntactic category, subcategorization information and a semantic specification. As an example of such an entry, (8) gives Jackendoff's (1975: 643) entry for *decision*.

(8) a. /decīd + ion/
    b. + N
    c. + [NP_1's ___ on NP_2]
    d. ABSTRACT RESULT OF ACT OF NP_1'S DECIDING NP_2

The idea of word formation rules as redundancy rules can be illustrated by determining which parts of (8) count towards the storage burden in the mental lexicon. In (8a), the phonological representation of the base depends on the entry for *decide* and that of the suffix on the rule for *-ion*. In fact, Jackendoff (1975: 648) refers to 'the *-ion* ending, which appears as part of the redundancy rule 3'. This suggests that *-ion* is part of a redundancy rule that models the word formation process, rather than an entry of its own. The syntactic category in (8b) is the output of this redundancy rule and the subcategorization in (8c) is taken over from *decide*. In (8d), the semantic effect of the rule for *-ion* is applied to the meaning of *decide*. Therefore, the only cost of storing (8) is to record which parts are from the entry for *decide* and which parts from the redundancy rule for *-ion*.

On this basis, we may tentatively represent Jackendoff's (1975) model as in Figure 3.2. A first striking difference to Figure 3.1 is that Figure 3.2 only represents the lexicon. This reflects the idea that Jackendoff focuses only on the internal organization of this component. The words in the lexicon include complex words as well as simplex words. The redundancy rules relate them to each other. It would be incorrect to formulate this as a statement that complex words are related to simplex words, because the interaction is more complex. On one hand, we find cases such as *transformational*, which is related to *transformation*. Here a complex word is related to another complex word. On the other hand, we find cases such as *aggression*. This is a simplex word, because there is no corresponding verb *aggress*, but it can still refer to the redundancy rule for *-ion*, which connects it to regular formations such as *decision*.[3]

Compared with Halle (1973), Jackendoff (1975) pays more attention to the meaning of words. In the case of *blackbird*, the complex word with its meaning of *Turdus merula* is specified in a lexical entry. This means that alternative meanings, such as 'crow', though plausible from a morphological perspective, do not play a role in determining the actual meaning. There is no point at which the 'crow' meaning of *blackbird* needs to be excluded. The most that can be said is that the restriction to one species counts more heavily in determining the cost of storing the entry.

From the mid-1970s, an increasing number of PhD dissertations were devoted to morphology in generative grammar. In 1974, there were the dissertations by Mark Aronoff, published in 1976, and Dorothy Siegel. In 1978,

---

[3] Jackendoff (1975: 647) refers to the 'hypothetical roots **aggress*, . . .', but OED (2000–2023: *aggress* v.) gives examples starting from the late sixteenth century and places it in frequency band 4 ('most words remain recognizable to English-speakers, and are likely be used unproblematically in fiction or journalism'). If we interpret Jackendoff's statement as a statement on what we called *words as knowledge* in Figure 1.1, the two observations are not incompatible. Moreover, the general point that there are entries of this type does not depend on the validity of an individual example.

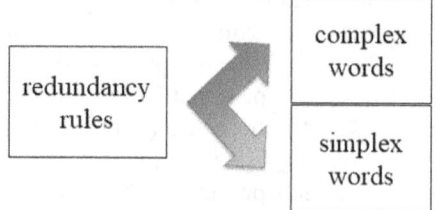

Figure 3.2 *Representation of Jackendoff's (1975) model of the lexicon*

Margaret Reece Allen's was defended and in 1980 Rochelle Lieber's. Rather than discussing each of these, we will address selected ideas they introduced when we present modern theories in Chapters 5–12.

3.1.4 Generative Semantics

In describing the models of Halle (1973) and Jackendoff (1975) as elaborations of the architecture that resulted from the introduction of the lexicon by Chomsky (1965) taking it in opposite directions, we run the risk of presenting an overly teleological view of the history of generative grammar. In fact, the view of Chomsky (1970), which served as the basis for Halle's (1973) and Jackendoff's (1975) theories, represented a minority position at the time (cf. Newmeyer 1986a: 82). The majority of generative linguists in the late 1960s and early 1970s embraced the views of Generative Semantics. Because of their vehemence and acrimonious nature, the discussions between proponents of Generative Semantics and supporters of Chomsky's views have been described as the *linguistic wars*, a term Newmeyer (1986a: 117) attributes to Paul Postal. Most of the discussion focused on syntax, but here we will highlight and contextualize some ideas that relate to morphology and have played a role in subsequent theorizing.

A central difference between Chomsky's (1965) model and the model of Generative Semantics is the relation between syntax and semantics. For Chomsky (1957), the division between Deep Structure and Surface Structure in syntax is motivated by the fact that Deep Structure is interpreted semantically and Surface Structure is interpreted phonologically. Although in subsequent work, Chomsky changed the relation between Deep Structure and Surface Structure, in all of his frameworks up to and including the latest versions of the Minimalist Program, semantics is conceived of as an interpretive module, derived from a syntactic representation. In fact, with the introduction of traces as empty categories indicating the position a constituent occupied before a transformation, the role of Deep Structure diminished and semantic interpretation could be based on what used to be Surface Structure.

In Generative Semantics, a development in the opposite direction can be observed. An increasing amount of semantic information was represented syntactically at Deep Structure, until there was no distinction between

Current theories of morphology

Deep Structure and semantic interpretation. One can also represent this development as an inversion of the relationship between syntax and semantic representation. Whereas Chomsky derived semantic representation from syntax, Generative Semantics derives syntax from semantics. Newmeyer (1986a: 92) considers the point when Deep Structure lost its role as the basis for semantic interpretation as the birth of Generative Semantics as a new model.

As an illustration of the result of the decision to take a semantic as the source of a syntactic derivation, we can consider the analysis of *kill* by McCawley (1968: 73), given in (9).

(9) a. [CAUSE X [BECOME [NOT [ALIVE y]]]]
    b. [CAUSE X [BECOME [[NOT ALIVE] y]]]
    c. [CAUSE X [[BECOME [NOT ALIVE]] y]]
    d. [[CAUSE [BECOME [NOT ALIVE]]] x y]
    e. [kill x y]

In (9a), we have the starting point of the derivation, i.e. the deep semantic representation. (9b–d) are subsequently derived by means of a predicate raising transformation. The structure in (9d) serves as the point for lexical insertion, resulting in (9e). In (9b), [NOT ALIVE] could have been lexicalized as *dead* and in (9c) [BECOME [NOT ALIVE]] as *die*. As an example of lexical insertion in a morphologically complex word, McCawley (1968: 75) gives *redden* in (10).

(10) a. [CAUSE [BECOME [RED]]]
     b. [Ø [en [red]]]

Whereas in (9d–e), the entire predicate is replaced by a lexical item, in (10), each of the semantic components is represented by a separate lexical item. Subsequent transformations will ensure that (10b) surfaces as *redden*. The verb *redden* can appear in two types of frame, illustrated in (11) on the basis of examples from COCA (2008–2020).

(11) a. She felt her face redden with a certain pleasure as well as embarrassment
     b. They were picked while still green ... and gassed with an excess of ethylene gas fumes to redden their skins

Obviously, (10) only models the causative meaning in (11b). The intransitive use in (11a) can arise because in (10b), the meaning component CAUSE is lexicalized as Ø.

A typical omission in the reasoning behind derivations such as (9) is that the alternative outcomes in the derivation are not used as equivalents. The contrasts in (12) illustrate this.

(12) a. My boyfriend killed someone.
b. My boyfriend caused someone to die.
c. They tried to kill us during the night.
d. They tried to cause us to die during the night.

The examples in (12a) and (12c) are from COCA (2008–2020). While (12a) and (12b) have an overlapping meaning, the focus is different. In (12a), the way the death of the referent of *someone* came about is typically caused more directly by the referent of *my boyfriend* than in (12b). If the death was caused by an error in the dosage of a drug, (12b) is more appropriate than if it is caused by stabbing. This explains why (12d) sounds somewhat odd.

The most well-known example of an extended analysis of word formation in Generative Semantics is Levi's (1978) theory of English nominal compounding. In this theory, Levi aims to save the basic insight of Lees's (1960) account while avoiding the problem of the excessive power of transformation rules. She divides nominal compounds into two types, one with a predicate as a part of the head and one without. In the former case, the predicate is available as a way to connect the two components of the compound, as in (13).

(13) a. cell division
b. constitutional amendment
c. blood donor

It should be noted first of all that in the deep structure assumed in Generative Semantics, the relational adjective in (13b) is indistinguishable from the corresponding noun and *donor* in (13c) contains a verb that is not phonologically realized as such. The resulting compound designates an act in (13a), the result of an act in (13b) and an agent in (13c). Levi distinguishes four nominalization types. For the cases without a predicate as part of the head, Levi proposes nine Recoverably Deletable Predicates (RDPs), three of which are reversible. Some examples are given in (14).

(14) a. song bird
b. sugar cube
c. industrial equipment
d. love song

In (14a–b), the RDP MAKE is used. This RDP is reversible. In (14a), the head is the subject of MAKE and in (14b) it is the object. In (14c), the RDP is FOR and in (14d) ABOUT. The examples in (13) and (14) are taken from Levi's (1978: 280–284) appendix. It should be noted that the selection of a single RDP or nominalization type is not part of the derivation. The compounds in (14) have twelve interpretations, one for each RDP and direction. The ones in (13) have sixteen, adding to the twelve based on RDPs the four for nominalization. The selection of one of these options and the further specification of the meaning is the result of what Levi (1978: 10–12) calls *lexicalization*. She excludes this component of the meaning of compounds from the scope of her theory.

From a naming perspective, the discussion of lexicalization is of particular interest. By separating the rule-based meaning components of compounds from those that cannot be covered by rules, Levi (1978) distinguishes the effects of the compounding mechanism from the effects of naming. However, the mechanism of lexicalization is not further discussed, which raises the suspicion that Levi only uses the appeal to lexicalization as a way of excluding phenomena she cannot account for from the scope of her theory. Levi's use of lexicalization was criticized, for instance, by van Santen (1979: 250), because it is not correctly characterized as a strategy for disambiguation. Rather it is a completely separate route for the interpretation of compounds. Moreover, van Santen observes that lexicalization is much more widespread than Levi assumes. The fact that *song bird* in (14a) refers to a class of birds is also an effect of lexicalization.

3.1.5 Generative morphology as a basis for the study of word formation

Sections 3.1.1 to 3.1.4 outlined the main developments in the modelling of morphology in generative grammar. A crucial change in the model was the introduction of the lexicon as a component by Chomsky (1965). The lexicon makes it possible to distinguish between syntax and morphology. Syntactic rules use entries of the lexicon to build up larger structures. Morphology is concerned with the internal structure of lexical entries. However, the precise implementation of such a distinction was a matter of debate. Thus, the question of the autonomy of morphology is at the centre of the discussions in Everaert et al. (1988).

A traditional distinction in generative morphology is the one between transformational and lexicalist models. Among the models discussed above, Lees (1960) and Levi (1978) are transformational, whereas Halle (1973) and Jackendoff (1975) are lexicalist. The basis for the distinction is that transformational models use movement and deletion operations in the derivation of a complex word, whereas lexicalist models only use concatenative rules and readjustment rules. In these considerations, the emphasis is on the mechanisms for generating the correct form.

When we focus on the naming function of word formation, a different distinction is more prominent. It has been widely noted that the result of word formation rules often has a much more restricted meaning than can be predicted on the basis of the rule. There are two main approaches to this problem, which can be labelled *overgeneration* and *initial specialization*. In a model with overgeneration, more results are generated than are necessary and the unwanted ones are deleted. Halle (1973) proposes an overgeneration model with a filter. He does not apply the overgeneration and the filter to meaning, because he does not address meaning directly, but we can assume that the filter which eliminates unwanted forms will have a similar function with respect to the meaning. Levi (1978) also has a system with overgeneration. Each compound has twelve interpretations based on different RDPs and four additional readings if the head is deverbal. In order to account for the more specific meanings of actual compounds, she proposes lexicalization. For Levi, lexicalization is the specification of a particular meaning of a compound by its storage in the lexicon. The specification that takes place in lexicalization is not determined by a rule and the process is not limited to the selection of one of the possible forms generated in her theory. It can involve a further restriction or a more radical change of the meaning. Levi (1978: 239) gives examples such as *nose job* as cases that are basically covered by her theory, but have a more specific meaning because of lexicalization. In cases such as *honeymoon*, lexicalization replaces the entire regular process.

In opposition to these overgeneration models, we find models that assume initial specialization. Here the meaning of a complex word is determined at the start of the operation. One such model is the one by Lees (1960) for nominalizations. In his model, the meaning is determined in the deep structure. This is illustrated for *assembly plant* with its deep structure in (2b). The fact that an assembly plant is used for assembling cars rather than photocopiers or other objects is encoded in the deep structure at the start of the derivation. That this information is not retrievable from the form of the complex word has been criticized on formal grounds. However, it can also be seen as the actual predicament a hearer faces whose lexicon does not contain *assembly plant*. They have to work out what is assembled from the context of use or their world knowledge, or use external sources (e.g. another speaker or a dictionary). Another way to encode initial specialization is Jackendoff's (1975) Full Entry Theory. Here, the lexical entry is fully specified. This means that *assembly plant* has the specification of 'for cars' in the entry to start with. As this information cannot be derived from the redundancy rules modelling word formation, it counts fully to the cost of the entry.

The classification of theories on the basis of the two criteria discussed here is summarized in Table 3.1. The distinction between transformational and lexicalist theories is a standard one. The distinction between the two types of model in the columns of Table 3.1 can be summarized for the example of *assembly plant* as follows. Whereas in initial specialization, the semantic component 'for cars' is specified at the start, in overgeneralization models it can only be specified after the application of word formation rules. As far as Halle (1973) covers it, it must be in the filter which applies between the word formation rules and the dictionary of words. Levi (1978) assigns twelve interpretations to the compound. The choice between them and the addition of any further meaning components can only occur in

Current theories of morphology 43

Table 3.1 *Two criteria for classifying models of word formation*

	Initial specialization	Overgeneration
Transformational	Lees (1960)	Levi (1978)
Lexicalist	Jackendoff (1975)	Halle (1973)

lexicalization. As illustrated in Table 3.1, the distinction between overgeneration and initial specialization is independent of the one between transformational and lexicalist approaches.

3.2 Word formation in functionalist frameworks

In the *Thèses* (1929), the basic properties of lexicology and word formation as understood by the *Cercle linguistique de Prague* had already been formulated. These properties were tightly linked to the functionalist view of language. Traditional grammars of Czech in the 1930s generally included separate sections on word formation which would, however, only give a detailed description of lexical means and word formation patterns (Dokulil 1994: 123). Only after World War II were more theoretical and methodological issues discussed, leading to two contrasting positions as to the place of word formation in the system of language. In section 3.2.1, we outline these positions, defended by Miloš Dokulil and Ján Horecký. Section 3.2.2 presents the notion of onomasiological category and its role in the study of word formation. Finally, section 3.2.3 explains the difference between foundation and motivation and the concepts of word formation paradigms and nests.

3.2.1 The position of word formation in the language system

Central in the theorizing about word formation in the Prague School tradition were the questions of the position of word formation within the language system and its relationship to other components of this system. Here we focus on the two probably most influential views in the Praguian tradition, represented by Miloš Dokulil (1928–2002) and Ján Horecký (1920–2006).

Dokulil (1962: 221) argues for a special position of word formation, which he also calls *derivology*, among the components of the language system, separate from morphology, lexicology and syntax. On one hand, word formation is part of lexicology. At the same time, word formation is also part of morphology, 'being distinguished from syntactic morphology by the term *lexical morphology*' (Dokulil 1994: 127).[4] While it is obvious that word

---

[4] Dokulil (1994) is a summary in English of his earlier theory with some updates prepared for a volume about Prague School linguistics. Dokulil (1962) also contains summaries in Russian and in English.

formation is connected with both the lexical and the morphological level, Dokulil (1964) claims that word formation can also be understood as having a specific position with respect to syntax. However, he does not make this distinction from syntax explicit, as his main focus is on positioning word formation in relation to morphology and lexicology.

In contrast to Dokulil, Horecký (1959) places word formation in lexicology. This view is based on Mathesius's distinction between two fundamental functions of language, which Horecký (1959: 29) calls *pomenúvacia funkcia jazyka* and *usúvzťažňovacia funkcia jazyka* in Slovak.[5] The former covers all means used for naming elements of extralinguistic reality. It is implemented in lexicology. The latter encompasses the linguistic tools that are used to express relations among individual naming units in a statement, i.e. morphology and syntax.[6] Dokulil (1962: 15) disagrees with Horecký in this interpretation. The central question is whether word formation is a part of grammar. The answer depends on the definition of the term *grammar*. Whereas Horecký links the distinction between grammar and lexicon to the two functions from Mathesius, Dokulil denies this dichotomy and formulates as the central question whether what he calls *lexical morphology*, i.e. morphology of naming, is part of grammar or not.

Dokulil's theory is based on Czech, which, in his opinion, is a language without clear-cut distinct boundaries between word formation and inflectional morphology. He gives two main reasons for this. First, 'the means primarily proper to morphology (grammatical word-formative suffixes and inflexional endings) may secondarily serve as means of word-formation' (Dokulil 1962: 222). Second, there are some morphological categories that 'are not unequivocally classed with either lexical or inflexional morphology' (Dokulil 1962: 222). These may be exemplified, for instance, by number on nouns, aspect and tense forms of verbs, or comparison of adjectives. Despite the absence of a clear distinction between word formation and inflection, Dokulil claims it is possible 'to distinguish in principle between the two indicated levels' (1962: 222). He considers the degree and quality of abstraction to be the main difference between word formation and inflectional categories. This means that word formation categories are always connected with classes of lexical semantics, whereas inflectional categories 'are only built up on lexical meanings, and abstract from them' (1962: 222).

The discussion between Dokulil and Horecký was carried out over a long period and attracted contributions from various other linguists. It did not

---

[5] The former is related to *meno* ('name$_N$') and *pomenovať* ('name$_V$'), the latter to *vzťah* ('relation') and *súvzťažný* ('mutually related, correlative'). *Jazyka* is the genitive of *jazyk* ('language').

[6] The distinction between inflection and word formation is presupposed in Prague School linguistics. For Horecký (1959), *morphology* does not include word formation, although the two are not strictly separated from each other. Dokulil (1994) uses *syntactic morphology* to refer to inflection.

3.2.2 The object of word formation

In the functionalist approach of the Prague School, the object of word formation is considered from two perspectives, which Dokulil (1962: 9; 1994: 127) calls *genetic* and *functional-structural*. While the genetic aspect concentrates on 'formation in the proper, processual meaning of the word, on the processes of word formation', the functional-structural aspect concentrates on 'the result of these processes on the patterning of words and on its impact on the system of language' (Dokulil 1994: 127). For instance, when we consider *acceptable*, the genetic aspect focuses on its formation from the verb *accept* and the suffix *-able*, whereas the functional-structural aspect highlights its position in the lexicon and its composition of two morphemes.

Dokulil argues that, in a synchronic perspective, word formation should cover the mechanisms by means of which new words can be formed, the rules that govern these mechanisms, the input and output categories and classes, and the relations between words on the basis of their word formation structure. This is in opposition to the diachronic perspective, in which word formation should cover the developments of these four aspects. Dokulil (1968: 206) admits that for individual words, it is often difficult to determine whether for a speaker they are formed when speaking or retrieved from the lexicon. This distinction is primarily a question of lexicology. In word formation its impact is limited to whether an open series is extended by one item or not.

The word formation structure of a complex word reflects the language-specific thought processes that were active in the naming act. This does not only apply to new words, but also to words that are stored and retrieved. In the Prague School approach, naming starts from 'the psychological contents which are to be named, and it handles the question how these psychological items should be patterned to be expressed by correlative structures existing in the language' (Dokulil 1994: 133). This brings us to the concept of *onomasiological category* (OC) which is central in Dokulil's theory. Onomasiological categories are understood as 'basic conceptual structures establishing the foundations of naming activity in the given language' (Dokulil 1994: 133). This means that the process of conceptualizing takes place in the human mind. Conceptualization includes registering the object and classifying it. It serves as the preparation for the step of forming an expression in line with the word formation means of the language. Dokulil (1962: 47) distinguishes three onomasiological categories: mutational (relational), transpositional and modificational. The mutational category is the most basic type. It is illustrated in the Slovak examples in (15).

(15) a. zamestnávateľ ('employer')
     b. jazykoveda ('linguistics')

In (15a), we have a noun derived from the verb *zamestnávať* ('employ'). The suffix *-teľ* is used to form a noun designating a person who performs the action denoted by the verb. In (15b), we have a compound consisting of *jazyk* ('language') and *veda* ('science') with the linking element *-o-*. The onomasiological structure is always binary. It consists of an onomasiological basis and an onomasiological mark. In (15a), the onomasiological basis is the suffix *-teľ* and in (15b), it is *veda*. The onomasiological mark determines this basis. It is the verb stem *zamestnáva-* in (15a), the noun with the linking element, *jazyk-o-*, in (15b).

The onomasiological basis is always simple, which means 'there can only be a difference in the level of abstraction, e.g. substance, animate being, man' (Dokulil 1994: 133). The onomasiological mark can be simple, as in both examples in (15), or complex, as in (16), also from Slovak.

(16) drevorubač ('woodcutter')

In (16), the onomasiological basis is the suffix *-ač*, which expresses an agent. The onomasiological mark in (16) consists of the noun *drevo* ('wood') and the stem of the verb *rúbať* ('cut down').

The examples in (15) and (16) are all of the mutational category. The concepts of one category constitute the onomasiological basis and they are specified by the concepts of either the same or a different category representing the onomasiological mark. In (15) and (16), the basis is in all instances a SUBSTANCE. This substance is specified by an ACTION in (15a) and (16), and by another SUBSTANCE in (15b). The other categories are QUALITY and CONCOMITANT CIRCUMSTANCE. They are illustrated in (17).

(17) a. rýchly   ('fast$_{ADJ}$')
     b. rýchlosť   ('speed')
     c. rýchlo   ('fast$_{ADV}$')

In (17a), we have an adjective whose meaning is a QUALITY. In (17b), we have a noun whose meaning is the same QUALITY. The derivation of (17b) from (17a) is a transposition. In (17c), we have the corresponding adverb, which expresses a CONCOMITANT CIRCUMSTANCE. The category of modification is illustrated in (18).

(18) zamestnávateľka ('employer$_{FEM}$')

In (18), we have a derivation based on (15a), where the suffix *-ka* expresses feminine. As opposed to mutation, a modification only adds information. The added category in this modification produces a marked member of an contrastive pair.

As opposed to the word formation structure we discussed in relation to examples (15) to (18), Horecký (1959, 1964), Bosák and Buzássyová (1985)

Current theories of morphology

and Furdík (2004) also consider the morphematic structure of complex words. The contrast can be illustrated by the two structures assigned to *učiteľka* ('teacher$_{FEM}$') in (19).

(19) a. uč-   i-   teľ-   ka
        teach   theme   agent   feminine
    b. učiteľ- ka
        teacher feminine

In the morphematic structure (19a), *učiteľka* is decomposed into four morphemes. The thematic vowel *-i-* also occurs in the verb *učiť* ('teach'). The agent suffix is the one we saw in (15a) and the feminine suffix the one in (18). In the word formation structure (19b), only the last operation in the formation of *učiteľka* is recorded. The word formation structure is always binary. In this functionalist approach, no tree structures are used. A recent discussion of the relationship between morphematic and word formation structure in Slovak is Ološtiak (2019). Dokulil (1968: 205) introduces the German term *Wortgebildetheit* for the morphematic structure and contrasts this with *Wortbildung* for the word formation structure. This contrast is sometimes used in the German literature, e.g. Fleischer and Barz (2012: 5).

3.2.3 Foundation and motivation

A basic property of a derived word is that its form and meaning can be linked to the ones of another word, the deriving word. In (19b), *učitelka* is the derived word and *učiteľ* the deriving word. Dokulil (1962: 11; 1994: 131–133) uses two concepts to express this relation, which he calls *foundation* and *motivation*. They represent different aspects of what is basically the same relationship.

When we consider the relation between *učiteľka* and *učiteľ* from the perspective of foundation, we can say that *učiteľka* was formed from *učiteľ*. This is the genetic (diachronic) use of the term. Synchronically, *učiteľ* is the prius and *učiteľka* the posterius. In this example, Dokulil (1994: 131) would call *učiteľ* the 'foundating naming unit' and *učiteľka* the 'foundated unit'. Foundation is a formal relationship between the two words and it represents the word formation structure of the foundated unit. It is prominent especially from the speaker's perspective.

When we consider the relation of the same two words from the perspective of motivation, we can say that the existence of *učiteľka* can be explained by the existence of *učiteľ* and vice versa (Dokulil 1962: 11). Motivation takes into account the meaning of the two words and represents first of all the hearer's perspective. In understanding *učiteľka*, the hearer relates it to *učiteľ*.

As mentioned in section 2.3, motivation was a central concern of Prague School research. Mathesius used it to distinguish descriptive naming units such as *airman* from simple naming units such as *pilot*. Whereas descriptive naming units are motivated, simple naming units are not. Several researchers in this tradition used motivation as a basis for theoretical statements about the structure of the vocabulary of languages. Thus, Sambor (1975) and Furdík (1978) found that motivating words are generally more frequent than their motivated counterparts. Furdík (2004: 24) uses the ratio between motivated and non-motivated words as a way of characterizing the vocabulary of languages. Thus, for Slovak the ratio is 65:35, for Russian 66:34, for French 57:43, for Hungarian 80:20 and for Finnish 88:12. This shows that in related languages, the ratio is similar. It also shows that in Finno-Ugric languages, which have a lot of agglutinating morphology, there are relatively fewer simple naming units than in Slavic languages. In French, which has less elaborate word formation morphology, there are more simple naming units. Ološtiak and Ivanová (2015) use a larger set of words as a basis for their research and arrive at a higher level of motivated words. For Slovak, they give a ratio of 86.2 per cent of motivated and 13.8 per cent of non-motivated words (2015: 128). Whereas Sambor (1975) and Furdík (1978) focus on token frequency, Furdík's (2004) and Ološtiak and Ivanová's (2015) research uses type frequency as a basis.

A different elaboration of the research into motivation concentrates on the way several words are related to each other. We can distinguish word formation chains, paradigms and nests. An example of a word formation chain is (20).

(20) a. učiť ('teach')
b. učiteľ ('teacher')
c. učiteľka ('teacher$_{FEM}$')

In (20), we see a sequence of motivated words. The chain links (20a) to (20b) and then to (20c), which means that (20b) is motivated by (20a) and motivates (20c). An example of a word formation paradigm is (21).

(21) a. učiť ('teach')
b. učiteľ ('teacher')
c. učivo ('teaching material')
d. učilište ('vocational school')
e. učenie ('teaching')
f. zaučiť ('train (on a new job)')

In a word formation paradigm, we have a motivating word, here (21a), and a series of motivated words. Each of (21b–f) is motivated by (21a). In a word formation nest, we find the combination of word formation chains and word formation paradigms, as in Figure 3.3.[7]

---

[7] Several of the words in Figure 3.3 are translated in (20) and (21). This is not the case for *učiteľstvo* ('teacherhood'), *učiteľský* ('pertaining to teachers'), *zaučenie* ('training$_N$'), *zaučený* ('trained$_{ADJ}$'), *zaúčať* ('train$_{IMPF}$').

Current theories of morphology

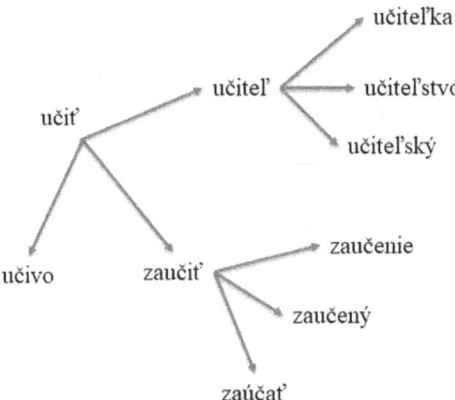

Figure 3.3 *Partial word formation nest for* učiť *('teach')*

In the word formation nest in Figure 3.3, we see the word formation chain of (20) represented with arrows at the top and a selection of the paradigmatic relations in (21). Some new words have been added to illustrate how the nest represents the recursiveness of motivation. Word formation chains, paradigms and nests are also sometimes called derivational chains, paradigms and nests. There was a certain degree of terminological development in this respect from Dokulil (1962: 13) to Horecký et al. (1989: 33–39) and to Furdík (2004: 73–77).

3.3 Selection of current theories and frameworks

For the discussion of individual theories in Chapters 5–12, we used the criteria in (22).

(22) a. The scope of the theory includes word formation.
b. The theory is being developed by its originator and/or a substantial research community.

Examples of theories we exclude on the basis of (22a) are Network Morphology and Paradigm Function Morphology. Network Morphology was presented by Corbett and Fraser (1993) as a formalism for the organization of Russian inflectional morphology. A more recent presentation is Brown (2019). Network Morphology is inheritance-based. The inheritance is between generalizations about inflection classes. This means that word formation is not covered. Paradigm Function Morphology was first proposed by Stump (1991). Stump (2019: 285) describes it as 'a precise but flexible way of defining complex inflectional systems'. Hippisley (2020: 1094–1096) considers the possibility of covering lexical relatedness, exemplified by regular agent nouns in Russian, in Network Morphology and Stump (2019: 299–301) devotes some thoughts to an account of regular derivational mechanisms in English in Paradigm Function Morphology, but the guiding principles of both frameworks remain determined by the coverage of inflection paradigms. To the extent that such theories have anything to say about word formation, it is about the form of a word as filling a slot in a paradigm. Therefore, we do not include these theories in our discussion.

Examples of theories we exclude because of (22b) are Anderson's (1992) A-Morphous Morphology and Beard's (1995) Lexeme-Morpheme Base Morphology (LMBM). Both represent theories that develop a few specific theoretical assumptions into a full model of morphology. In both cases, the models generated a lot of controversy.

Anderson (1992) takes a process-based view of morphological rules. For him, a morphological rule changes the form and meaning of its input, but does not leave any traces in the structure of its output. There is a morphological rule turning $print_V$ into *printer*, but there is no morpheme corresponding to *-er* and *printer* does not have any internal structure. Although this can be seen as a legitimate elaboration of Hockett's (1954) Item-and-Process model, the abolition of the morpheme as a structural unit was rejected by most other morphologists. Anderson (1992) presents a good amount of data and analyses, but he did not develop his theory further and there was no group of researchers who did.

Beard (1995) elaborates the idea that the form and the meaning of complex words is determined by independent sets of rules. This is the so-called Separation Hypothesis. As Carstairs-McCarthy (1992: 182) notes, his theory has suffered from an infelicitous choice of terms. Some interesting analyses in LMBM have been published by Bloch-Trojnar (2006, 2013), but even this researcher now no longer works in this framework. Beard has meanwhile left academia.

Although A-Morphous Morphology and LMBM were much discussed in the 1990s, not much further research within these frameworks was published and their initiators did not continue to work with them. As a result, modern overviews of morphological theory, e.g. Audring and Masini (2019) and Lieber (2020), mention them in their historical overviews, but do not include them in their overviews of contemporary theories. The discussion they generated did influence other theories, but because of the distance from mainstream assumptions, this influence consists rather in the strengthening of arguments motivating these mainstream assumptions than in the adoption of ideas from A-Morphous Morphology or LMBM. Therefore, it seems appropriate to exclude these theories from the scope of our monograph.

Among the theories we discuss in Chapters 5–12, we can distinguish three groups. The first consists of theoretical frameworks that are adopted and developed by larger groups of researchers in generative morphology, the second includes theories developed by individual researchers inspired by generative morphology in combination with other theoretical insights and in the third group we find theories with a functionalist foundation.

In generative morphology, Distributed Morphology (DM) can be considered the current mainstream. It was first formulated by Halle and Marantz (1993) and went through a series of adaptations, triggered at least in part by developments in generative syntax. In Chapter 5, we will present and discuss the current version as it is presented in McGinnis-Archibald (2016), Siddiqi (2019) and Bobaljik (2020).

Before the emergence of DM, the dominant approach to morphology adopted Chomsky's (1970) Lexicalist Hypothesis as a basis for devising the lexicon as a component of the model of grammar. The general tendency was to put more emphasis on the study of individual phenomena than on the specification of the global model. As a consequence, it is difficult to identify a single model accepted by the researchers in this current, which continued after the emergence of DM. We take Lexical Morphology and Phonology (LMP) as developed originally by Kiparsky (1982) as representative of this theoretical orientation and discuss it in Chapter 6. It is interesting to contrast LMP and A-Morphous Morphology in relation to criterion (22b). Both theories are considered 'old', but whereas A-Morphous Morphology is a framework that is at most acknowledged as one that should be argued against, many ideas stemming from LMP continue to be used by morphologists even if they do not consider themselves adherents to LMP.

In the second group, we find four researchers with different types of relationship to generative grammar who developed their own theories. Interestingly, their relative age correlates with the closeness of their relationship to generative grammar. We treat them from younger to older and from closer to more distant from generative grammar.

The first is Rochelle Lieber. She completed her PhD at MIT, directed by Morris Halle, in 1980 and has worked at the University of New Hampshire ever after. She is prominent in morphology not only because of her research, but also because of various handbooks she edited and a textbook that is now in its third edition. In her early work, she focused on the structure of words in a way that reflected the contemporary generative mainstream in morphology. Thus, Lieber (1983) proposes unlabelled trees. Lieber (1992) even advances the idea of abolishing morphology as a special component. Lieber (2004) reorients her research towards lexical semantics as reflected in morphology. In Lieber (2016a) she introduces *Lexical Semantic Framework* (LSF) as the name for her theory. This is the theory we will discuss in Chapter 7.

Then we turn to Geert Booij. He is Dutch, studied in Groningen and completed his PhD at the Universiteit van Amsterdam in 1977. He was a professor at the Vrije Universiteit Amsterdam from 1981 to 2005, then moved to Leiden until his retirement in 2012. The Netherlands is an important country for generative morphology, because it was one of the first countries where generative grammar became the mainstream in linguistics and it has a strong tradition of morphological research. Booij played a pivotal role because of both his publications and his organizational activity. Under the influence of Goldberg (1995), he gradually moved away from the generative mainstream. This culminated in his proposal of Construction Morphology (CxM) in Booij (2010), an approach that originally shocked many morphologists in his environment, but has gained increasing acceptance. We will discuss CxM in Chapter 8.

Ray Jackendoff started out more closely to the generative core and further removed from morphology. He completed his PhD at MIT, directed by Noam Chomsky, in 1969. He worked at Brandeis from 1971 and moved to Tufts in 2005. Highly active in the 'linguistic wars',[8] he was a fierce proponent of Chomsky's views against Generative Semantics. We came across his work on the structure of the lexicon in section 3.1.3, but his main field of research is semantics. Starting with Jackendoff (1983), he developed a formalism of Conceptual Semantics. Here the focus is on the semantic structure of words and sentences and its correspondence to syntactic structure. In Jackendoff (2002), this is expanded into a full model of language, which he calls *Parallel Architecture*. It is from this perspective that Jackendoff approaches morphology, starting with Jackendoff (2009). Originally closely aligned with Booij's Construction Morphology, he gradually moved towards his own morphological theory, called *Relational Morphology* by Jackendoff and Audring (2020), which we will discuss in Chapter 9.

As a final member of this group, Ronald Langacker completed his PhD at the University of Illinois Urbana-Champaign in 1966. He then moved to UC San Diego, where he was a professor from 1975 until his retirement in 2003. Like Jackendoff, he contributed above all to the study of semantics, but in the linguistic wars, he was closer to the Generative Semantic side. Although he denies that his theory of Cognitive Grammar, for which Langacker (1987a, 1991) provides the foundation, is a development of Generative Semantics, this background is visible in some assumptions. In the same way as for Jackendoff, his interest in morphology was triggered by the analysis of the semantics of words. We will discuss his theory in Chapter 10.

In the final group, we find two theoretical approaches inspired by the functionalist-structuralist tradition. The first is more linked to a particular researcher, the second to a group of researchers.

We start with the work of Pavol Štekauer. He is Slovak and completed his PhD at Comenius University in Bratislava in 1991. He worked at Prešov University until 2005, when he went to the Pavol Jozef Šafárik University in Košice as Professor of English Linguistics. Central in his research has been the development of an onomasiological theory of word formation and the interpretation of complex words, based on the work that had been carried out in the Prague School tradition. Štekauer (1998) introduces this approach

---

[8] Newmeyer (1986a: 117–138) gives a brief overview of this period in the history of generative linguistics and explains the origin of the term.

and describes the individual steps leading from a concept to a name for the concept. Updates of the system were proposed by Štekauer (2005, 2016). Štekauer et al. (2012), applied the approach in more typologically oriented research. He also co-edited some handbooks with Rochelle Lieber. Štekauer's onomasiological theory will be discussed in Chapter 11.

Then we turn to Natural Morphology (NM). NM was founded in 1977 by Willi Mayerthaler, Wolfgang Dressler and Wolfgang Wurzel. It takes as its starting point a development of the concept of markedness that originated in the Prague School tradition and was elaborated further by Stampe (1973). The three initiators developed this theory in different directions. Mayerthaler (1981) formulates criteria for universal naturalness, Wurzel (1984) focuses on language-specific aspects of naturalness in inflectional systems and Dressler (1985) elaborates NM for word formation processes. As most works by Mayerthaler, Wurzel and Dressler were published in German, their impact outside the German-speaking area was rather limited, but within this area, a lot of research was carried out in NM. This research will be discussed in Chapter 12.

By selecting these eight frameworks and theories, we consider that we have taken a fair general overview of work that has been done in word formation research in recent decades. In a single monograph, it would be unrealistic to give a full presentation of each theory in its own terms, highlight their research results and compare them with each other. Instead, we will consider each theory in relation to a set of data we consider indicative for the way they approach naming.

CHAPTER 4

An approach to the analysis of naming

In this monograph, we aim to compare the approach to the naming function of word formation in a range of current theories of morphology. An immediate problem this raises is that naming is not recognized as a topic in many of these theories. The linguistic phenomena do not seem to correspond between the different theories. By *linguistic phenomenon*, we mean here a grouping of observations about the data into classes for which generalizations can be made. On the basis of these generalizations, a theory is formulated.

As naming is not recognized as a linguistic phenomenon in many theories, they will not address it as a problem to be accounted for. One may be tempted to take such theories at their word, i.e. to assume that if they do not treat naming as a phenomenon, they have nothing to say about naming. In our view, however, this would be unfair towards these theories and unhelpful in recognizing their explanatory potential.

The alternative we propose here is to put more emphasis on the data. Instead of focusing only on high-level concepts such as naming, we break down these concepts into component parts and link them to individual examples. As the theories we selected are all intended to cover the area of word formation, it can be expected that they have something to say about the examples we choose. By using the same examples, with some minor variation, for all theories, we highlight the comparative analysis of the theories. In order to set out the basis for the discussion of the individual theoretical frameworks, this chapter will introduce and elaborate a number of concepts that we find essential for the discussion of naming and outline a number of examples that we will use in the presentation and discussion of the theories in subsequent chapters.

As a starting point, in section 4.1 we will discuss the distinction between morphology and syntax. This addresses the contrast between words and phrases. The data illustrating this distinction will be taken from compounding. Compounds and phrases both consist of more than one word, but only compounds are words that function as a name. It would be possible also to

An approach to the analysis of naming

discuss clitics in this context, because they are grammatical elements with a syntactically determined distribution. However, cliticization has fewer connections with word formation, as clitics are functional elements.

As a further conceptual distinction, section 4.2 turns to the contrast between inflection and derivation. The data to illustrate this distinction focus on the criteria by which lexemes and word forms can be recognized. A related issue is the question of paradigms, to which we turn in section 4.3. Although traditionally paradigms have mainly been associated with inflection, there have been various proposals to extend the notion to word formation.

On the basis of these concepts, it is then possible to discuss two issues that are central to our understanding of naming. The first is the contrast between naming and transposition (section 4.4), the second what we call *onomasiological coercion* (section 4.5). In explaining the latter, it will also become clear why the productivity of a rule is less crucial for our purposes and will not play a separate role in our discussion.

4.1 Words and phrases

It is a controversial question whether the word constitutes a relevant domain and, if so, in which respects. Some theories of language make a distinction between the rules governing the structure of words and those accounting for the structure of sentences. Other theories assume that the basic units of both are morphemes and there is no principled way to distinguish morphological and syntactic rules. In line with our programme as outlined above, we will not take a firm position on this before discussing individual theories, but present a number of examples of contrasts that every theory will have to account for.

The word can be seen as the interface between morphology and syntax. For morphology, the word is the highest level of structure, whereas for syntax, words are the basic units which are combined into phrases. In this context, compounds are of particular interest, because they are words but they consist of components that can be analysed as words themselves. Ten Hacken (2020b) gives a general overview of the main questions raised by the study of compounds. Here we will only focus on a number of pairs of compounds and phrases that can be considered minimal contrasts.

The first contrast is from German. It is illustrated in (1)

(1) a. Hartkäse ('granular cheese')
    b. harter Käse ('hard cheese')

Both (1a) and (1b) consist of *hart* ('hard') and *Käse* ('cheese'). Formally, they differ in the sense that (1b) has an inflectional ending on the adjective, marking a combination of gender, number, case and definiteness, whereas (1a) has none. The stress pattern also differs, with the main stress on the first syllable in (1a) and on the noun in (1b). These formal distinctions correspond to a semantic contrast. Whereas (1a) refers to a type of cheese, (1b) refers to cheese with a particular property. A typical example of (1a) is parmigiano. The precise scope of *Hartkäse* can be a matter of debate. Thus, Germany and Switzerland have different rules on how to determine whether a cheese variety is a *Hartkäse* or not. As a consequence, Appenzeller is a *Hartkäse* in Germany, but not in Switzerland. In any case, however, (1a) refers to a position in the taxonomy of cheeses, whereas (1b) refers to a relative property of a particular instance.

As described by Fleischer and Barz (2012: 152–159), the formation of compounds of the type in (1a) is a productive word formation mechanism in German. For theories that do not distinguish morphology and syntax, the challenge is to account for the contrast between (1a) and (1b). For us, the correlation between the formal and the semantic contrasts is especially relevant.

For our second example, we turn to Slovak and consider the contrast in (2).

(2) a. čajová lyžička ('teaspoon')
    b. čistá lyžička ('clean spoon')

Both examples in (2) include the noun *lyžička* ('spoon'), which is actually a diminutive of *lyžica* ('spoon'). We will return to diminutives in section 4.2 below. Morphosyntactically, (2a) and (2b) are highly similar, because the noun is modified by an adjective that agrees with it in number, gender and case. The difference is that *čajový* ('tea$_{ADJ}$') is a relational adjective, whereas *čistý* ('clean') is a qualitative adjective. Relational adjectives are syntactically adjectives, but have a meaning that is identical to that of a noun in non-head position of a compound. This explains the English translation as a compound in (2a). In the case of *čajový*, the corresponding noun is *čaj* ('tea$_N$').

Both (1) and (2) give A+N examples. Compared with (1), the pair of examples in (2) also contrasts an expression that designates a type with one that predicates a property over the object referred to by the noun. Syntactically, however, they are different. Whereas in (1), the contrast correlates with the absence or presence of an inflectional ending, in (2) the adjectives both agree with the noun. As discussed by ten Hacken (2019b), this has led to classifications of the type illustrated in (2a) as phrase or compound depending on whether the syntactic or semantic properties are privileged. In the Slovak grammatical tradition, examples such as (2a) are called *združené pomenovania*. This expression is difficult to translate into English. The first word is a passive participle of the verb *združiť* ('join'), the second the nominalization of the verb *pomenovať* ('name$_V$'). The closest equivalent may be 'multi-word unit', but this expression has a broader meaning than *združené pomenovanie*, which only applies to cases such as (2a).

An approach to the analysis of naming

For the next example, we turn to English. The contrast in (3) requires sentential context.[1]

(3) a. She points to a bird's nest in a low branch.
    b. The mother cuckoo lays its egg in another bird's nest.

In English, the so-called Saxon genitive, illustrated in (3) by *bird's nest*, can be used in different ways. In (3a), *bird* is generic and *bird's nest* indicates a concept. In (3b), *bird* is modified by *another* and the sequence *bird's nest* does not designate a separate concept. One consequence of this contrast can be illustrated by (4).

(4) a. It was watching us from another tree.
    b. In most cases, it does not notice this and breeds the egg.

If (4a) is used as a continuation of (3a), it is not possible to interpret *it* as referring to *bird* in *bird's nest*. It can only be saved by a context that provides an antecedent in another way. If (4b) is used as a continuation of (3b), *it* can be interpreted as referring to *another bird*. We can express this difference in the constituent structures in (5).

(5) a. [a [bird's nest]]
    b. [[another bird]'s nest]

Whereas *bird's nest* in (3a) is a constituent, as represented in (5a), in (3b) it is not, as seen in (5b).

As a final example, we will present a more complex case. It is usually assumed that in languages like English, N+N combinations are compounds. Within this class, however, we find two different phenomena, as illustrated in (6).[2]

(6) a. Mount Pleasant is a charming historic seafood village that, thanks to the bridge, is now a commuter suburb of Charleston.
    b. She writes of her pilgrimage to the Eastern Orthodox Church of St. George in the Chicago suburb of Cicero.

In (6a), *commuter suburb* is intended as a type of town. A suburb is a town attached to an adjacent larger town or city. A qualification as *commuter suburb* indicates that people living here generally commute and that this circumstance characterizes the nature of the town. In (6b), the expression *Chicago suburb* does not imply the existence of a concept with this name. It

---

[1] Examples from COCA, retrieved 17 August 2021.
[2] Examples (6) and (7) from COCA, retrieved 19 August 2021, *she* in (6b) replacing 'Frederica Mathewes-Green'.

is simply an indication of the location. The construction in (6b) is also frequent in referring to people, especially in news stories, as illustrated in (7).

> (7) His father was a Chicago postman, and his mother also worked at the post office.

The use of *Chicago postman* does not imply that there is a concept designated by this expression. This construction is similar to the deictic compounds discussed by Downing (1977). Schlücker (2013) discusses examples of this kind in German.

In this section, we presented four contrasts. The crucial examples are (1), (2), (3) and (6). In each case, we gave an example of an expression that is used as the name of a concept and one of a formally similar expression that does not name, but only describes a concept. In the discussion of the theories in Chapters 5–12, we will be interested in how they account for these contrasts.

4.2 Lexemes and word forms

The distinction between lexemes and word forms depends on the delimitation of inflection. A lexeme unites the word forms that are inflectionally related to each other. Ten Hacken (2014) gives an overview of the questions that arise in this context and concludes that the contrast between inflection and derivation should be considered from a terminological perspective. Therefore, the need for a systematic distinction and the strength of a particular definition of inflection depend on the theory selected. As a consequence, we cannot make any fair evaluation or comparison of theories if we impose a particular definition to start with.

As with the distinction between words and phrases, it is better to start with data. In the case of lexemes and word forms, the formation of plural and diminutive nouns in languages such as Dutch and Slovak constitutes a good starting point. Both in Dutch and in Slovak, nouns generally have a plural and a diminutive form, except when their meaning is incompatible with these categories. Some regular Dutch examples are given in Table 4.1.

Dutch has two main endings for the plural of nouns, *-s* and *-en*, as illustrated in Table 4.1. The choice between them is in part determined by prosodic and other phonological considerations, but it is not entirely predictable. The diminutive is marked by the suffix *-tje*.[3] In the case of *huisje*, the *-t-* is elided. The rules governing elision and modification of the ending are rather complex and not always univocal.

---

[3] The suffix is sometimes given as *-je*, e.g. by Haeseryn et al. (1997: 654), but we follow Booij's (1995: 69–73) argument that *-tje* constitutes a better starting point for an account of the allomorphs.

An approach to the analysis of naming

Table 4.1 Examples of Dutch plurals and diminutives

	Form	Article	Form	Article
Base form	vogel ('bird')	de	huis ('house')	het
Plural	vogels	de	huizen	de
Diminutive	vogeltje	het	huisje	het

Dutch has two genders, common and neuter, indicated by the definite articles *de* and *het*, respectively. Plural nouns always have *de* and diminutives always *het*. However, this is traditionally conceptualized differently. For the plural, it is said that *de* is the plural form of the article (Haeseryn et al. 1997: 189), whereas for the diminutive, it is said that the noun is of neuter gender (Haeseryn et al. 1997: 153). One reason for this is illustrated in (8).

(8) a. De vogel vloog naar de boom.
    'The bird flew to the tree'
 b. De vogels vlogen naar de boom.
 c. Het vogeltje vloog naar de boom.
 d. De vogeltjes vlogen naar de boom.

As illustrated by the verb forms in (8), the verb agrees with the number of the subject, but not with diminutive. The verb is plural in (8b) and (8d). One could of course argue that the form of the article in (8c) shows agreement with the diminutive, but the plural diminutive in (8d) has the plural form of the article. Thus, it is more economical to assume that *het* in (8c) marks the neuter gender of the diminutive noun.[4]

Another reason for the different treatment of plural and diminutive can be derived from the semantics of the different words. A plural such as *vogels* does not evoke a new concept, but a number of instantiations of the same concept. In the case of the diminutive, this is different. It is odd to speak of a small instantiation of a concept. A more natural way of perceiving this is that there are two concepts, one for *vogel* and one for *vogeltje*. These concepts are related, but they are not structured in the same way. Although a small bird, e.g. a sparrow, may be a prototypical example of both, the prototypicality decreases much more rapidly with increasing size in the case of *vogeltje*. An *adelaar* ('eagle') is a good example of *vogel*, but hardly acceptable as an instance of *vogeltje*. Therefore, we can say that *vogeltje* has a meaning that is related to, but does not include the meaning of *vogel*. By contrast, the meaning of *vogels* is nothing more or less than the combination of the meanings of *vogel* and the plural.

---

[4] Ten Hacken (2013a) discusses the case of Fula, which has an inflectional system with agreement based on diminutive and augmentative as well as singular and plural.

There are also words that are formed as a diminutive, but have a meaning that is further removed from the base. Examples are *kaartje* and *stokje*. Dutch *kaart* can have a range of meanings, e.g. geographical map or playing card. The diminutive *kaartje* can be related to these meanings, but it can also have meanings for which *kaart* is rarely or never used, e.g. ticket (for a theatre, train, etc.) or business card. The basic meaning of *stok* is 'stick'. The diminutive *stokje* can refer to a small instance of a stick, but it also has specialized meanings, especially in the plural, e.g. chopsticks, salty sticks, for which the non-diminutive form can hardly be used.

In Slovak, the plural is part of the inflectional paradigm that we will discuss in section 4.3. The diminutive is a frequent and rather regular process that applies to most nouns whose semantics allow for it. Gregová (2015) gives a detailed account of the formation of diminutives, also covering diminutive verbs, adjectives and adverbs.

Some examples of diminutives with their corresponding base are given in (9).

(9) a. vankúš – vankúšik ('pillow')
    b. lavica – lavička ('bench')
    c. strom – stromček ('tree')

The three examples in (9) illustrate different formation processes. They also exemplify different levels of lexical specialization of the diminutive. All of them can have the sense of 'small instance of X'. In (9a), this exhausts the meaning of *vankúšik*. In the case of (9b), there is a sense that for benches that are meant for outside, *lavička* is more common, whereas for inside use, *lavica* is more usual. Some typical collocations, as found in SNK (2022), are given in (10).

(10) a. školská lavica ('school bench')
     b. parková lavička ('bench in a park')

The relational adjectives in (10) indicate whether the bench is intended for indoor or outdoor use and reversing the combinations sounds less common. In (9c), *stromček* is often used in the sense of Christmas tree. Although the full form is *vianočný stromček* ('Christmas$_{ADJ}$ tree'), the adjective can easily be left out when the reference can be reconstructed from the context.

In this section, we explained the difference between the plural and the diminutive in languages such as Dutch and Slovak. The crucial contrast in Dutch is the one between *vogels* and *vogeltje*. It will also be interesting to consider how cases such as *kaartje* and *stokje*, which (also) have a more specialized meaning, are dealt with. In Slovak, diminutives are less predictably formed, because there are different suffixes involved, but their semantic behaviour is similar to their Dutch counterparts.

4.3 Paradigms

When we consider the realization of the plural in Slovak nouns, we have to take into account its place in the inflectional paradigm. An example of a Slovak nominal paradigm is given in Table 4.2.

The idea of a paradigm of the type illustrated in Table 4.2 is twofold. On one hand, it is expected that any noun has a realization for the combination of features determining the paradigm. These features depend on the language system. On the other hand, large groups of nouns follow the same patterns. For feminine nouns, there are four such patterns, depending on the presence or absence of the final -*a* in the nominative singular and the character of the preceding phoneme. The pattern in Table 4.2 is the most frequent one.

From the naming perspective, it is important that once we have the base form and the gender, we can infer the entire pattern. Of course, it may be the case that certain forms are not used, because they are not necessary. Thus, language names such as *slovenčina* ('Slovak') have the pattern in Table 4.2, but they do not normally have a plural. However, the plural is available, so that if we want to speak of *Englishes*, the Slovak equivalent *angličtina* can readily be pluralized.

As a consequence of the existence of such patterns, we have to distinguish between the choice of *gitara* as the name for a musical instrument and the choice of, for instance, *gitaru* in a sentence. The former is an act of naming, the latter a matter of adaptation to the syntactic context.

Inflectional paradigms occur in many languages. Of course they only occur for inflected word classes and the pattern is only obvious if the paradigm consists of a certain number of forms. For Dutch nouns, it is a matter of theory whether we want to account for the singular–plural alternation by means of a paradigm. For Slovak nouns, the case–number combinations require a pattern-based account.

As we saw in section 3.2.3, the notion of paradigm is sometimes also extended to word formation. Horecký et al. (1989: 44) call a word formation paradigm the ordered set of complex words which take the same basic word as their motivator. Štekauer (2014) calls them *derivational paradigms*. Examples in Slovak are (11) and (12).

Table 4.2 *Paradigm of the Slovak noun* gitara *('guitar')*

	Singular	Plural
Nominative	gitara	gitary
Genitive	gitary	gitár
Dative	gitare	gitarám
Accusative	gitaru	gitary
Locative	gitare	gitarách
Instrumental	gitarou	gitarami

(11) a. blog
     b. blogovať
     c. blogový

(12) a. bloger
     b. blogerka
     c. blogerský

In (11), discussed in more detail by Ološtiak (2021), we see a loanword from English in (11a) and two derived words in (11b–c). The agent noun (12a) is a borrowing from English as well, with only minimal orthographic adaptation. The verb in (11b) and the adjective in (11c) as well as the feminine noun (12b) and the relational adjective (12c) have been formed in Slovak. The idea of derivational paradigms is that, as soon as a noun such as (11a) or (12a) is borrowed in Slovak, derivations such as (11b–c) and (12b–c) can be used almost automatically. The three words in (11) together constitute the result of one naming act. In (12), we also have three words that are the result of a single naming act. The relationship between (11) and (12) is less automatic in the sense that the loanword *bloger* was selected as a name rather than, for instance, the Slovak derivation **blogovateľ*, formed in the same way as *učiteľ* ('teacher') from *učiť* ('teach') as discussed in section 3.2.2.

Štekauer (2014: 362) distinguishes two aspects of derivational paradigms. In their static aspect, (11) and (12) are used to encode the relationships between the words. In the dynamic aspect, the same paradigms are used to form new complex words. The non-actual words of a paradigm are potential words in the static aspect and new words when they are formed in the dynamic aspect. Based on derivational paradigms, Körtvélyessy et al. (2020) introduce the related notion of *derivational network*, understood as 'a network of derivatives derived from the same word-formation base (simple underived word) with the aim of formally representing specific semantic categories' (2020: 11). Ivanová (2020) discusses derivational networks in Slovak, and Hoeksema (2020) derivational networks in Dutch.

It is interesting to compare the different perspectives that give rise to derivational paradigms and to productivity. In the case of productivity, the starting point is a rule. The question is whether the rule can be used and to what extent it is actually used to produce new forms. In the case of derivational paradigms, the starting point is rather the choice of a form to designate a particular meaning. The question is how a particular form with the intended meaning would relate to other words in the lexicon. In this study, we focus on naming. As such, the productivity of rules takes a rather subordinate position in our discussion.

4.4 Naming and transposition

A conventional definition of *derivation* is the one given by Lieber (2020: 427) in (13).

(13) Derivational morphology is defined as morphology that creates new lexemes, either by changing the syntactic category (part of speech) of a base or by adding substantial, non-grammatical meaning or both.

In (13), Lieber gives two conditions for a formation to be classified as derivation, both of which are, in the technical sense, sufficient. Although the view in (13) is widespread, there is also another tradition, as outlined by ten Hacken (2015: 192–196), which distinguishes between cases only authorized by the first condition and cases where the second condition applies. This tradition can be traced back to the Geneva School (Bally 1922; Sechehaye 1926), but it is also well represented in the Prague School (Dokulil 1962, 1968). Based on insights from this tradition, ten Hacken (2015: 196) proposes the definition of *transposition* in (14).

(14) Transposition is a process that
    a. changes the syntactic category of a word,
    b. does not change its semantic category, and
    c. does not modify, add or delete any semantic features.

The idea of transposition and its relevance for naming can be illustrated on the basis of the contrast in (15).

(15) a. I would argue that this remains an issue open to empirical exploration even under contemporary conditions.
    b. I would argue that this remains an issue open to being explored empirically even under contemporary conditions.

In (15a) and (15b), the same idea is expressed. (15a) is from BNC (2007), (15b) is a reformulation. The basic difference is that in (15a), the noun *exploration* is used and in (15b), the verb *explore*. Other differences follow from the choice of syntactic category. One might reformulate (15b) more elegantly by using a different construction, but we deliberately minimized the difference in formulation. The point is that *explore* and *exploration* do not have a different meaning, but only a different syntactic category. This makes *exploration* a transposition according to (14). What is crucial for our purposes is that the formation of *exploration* cannot be used for naming a new concept, because of this absence of a new meaning. Therefore, not all formations that belong to derivational morphology as defined in (13) are within the scope of naming.

The analysis of transposition is complicated by the fact that many such derivations also have different meanings. This is illustrated for *installation* in (16), both examples from BNC (2007).

(16) a. At the first summit of the non-aligned nations in 1961 the Cuban President had declared that 'the peoples reject the installation in

their territory of foreign military bases implying an imminent danger of war' not only for reasons of principle 'but by mere instinct of self-preservation'.
b. The soldiers, carrying pistols and M-16 rifles, got into a pickup truck outside the hotel and were taken to a Salvadorean military installation.

In (16a), the construction with *installation* can be paraphrased as *that foreign military bases are installed in their territory*. The noun refers to the process of installing. In (16b), *installation* refers to the base or complex that has been installed, i.e. the result of the process.

In other languages, there are two words corresponding to *installation*. In German, there is *Installierung* and *Installation*, in Slovak *inštalovanie* and *inštalácia*. In German, *Installation* is much more frequent than *Installierung*. DeReKo (2021) gives a frequency of 7.503 per million for *Installation* and of 0.739 per million for *Installierung*.[5] There is also a difference in meanings, as illustrated by the examples in (17).

(17) a. die Installation der Heizungsanlage
'the installation of_the heating_system'
b. veraltete Installationen erneuern
'outdated installations renew', i.e. replace outdated installations
c. die Installierung der Heizungsanlage
d. *veraltete Installierungen erneuern

Examples (17a–b) are from Duden (2021: *Installation*). They illustrate a contrast in readings similar to the one in (16). In (17c–d), *Installierung* replaces *Installation*. As the problematic nature of (17d) shows, this only works for the process reading.

In Slovak, the frequency of both words is higher, but the difference is of the same scale. SNK gives 13.41 per million for *inštalácia* and 0.92 per million for *inštalovanie*.[6] The meaning difference is similar to the one for the German word pair, as illustrated by (18).

(18) a. inštalácia tlačiarne
'installation printer$_{GEN}$', i.e. the installation of a/the printer
b. pokazená inštalácia
'out-of-order installation', i.e. an installation that is out of order
c. inštalovanie tlačiarne
d. *pokazené inštalovanie

---

[5] DeReKo-2021-1, W-ohneWikipedia-öffentlich, size 11,760.1 million words, *Installation* 88,237 occurrences, *Installierung* 8,685 occurrences.
[6] Retrieved 25 August 2021. Relative frequency is given directly. Absolute frequencies: *inštalácia* 21,735, *inštalovanie* 1,487.

An approach to the analysis of naming

Examples (18a–b) are from KSSJ (2003: *inštalácia*). As the ungrammaticality of (18d) shows, *inštalovanie* does not have a result reading.

The difference between German and Slovak on one hand and English on the other is that in German and Slovak there is a second noun that can be derived from the verb and that can only have the transpositional interpretation. In English, this can be achieved with the nominalized participle, e.g. *installing*, although this corresponds more closely to the German nominalized infinitive, e.g. *Installieren*.

In this section we presented the contrast between word formation as a naming device and transposition. Transposition can be a classification for a lexical item, e.g. *exploration*, or for a reading of a lexical item, as illustrated for *installation* in (16). As illustrated in (17–18), we can also find cases where two morphological formations from the same base correspond to the scope of *exploration* and *installation*. In the discussion of individual theories, we will be interested in how this contrast is accounted for.

4.5 Onomasiological coercion

A final aspect of naming we want to discuss here is the relationship between the aspects of the meaning that can be predicted and the full meaning of a complex word. It can be illustrated on the basis of *doorman*. COBUILD (2023) gives the definition in (19).

(19) a. A doorman is
 b. a man who stands at the door
 c. of a club,
 d. prevents unwanted people from coming in, and makes people leave if they cause trouble.

In (19), we have divided the definition into components to facilitate its discussion. It consists of four parts. The repetition of the headword in (19a) is a consequence of COBUILD's policy of providing full-sentence definitions (cf. Hanks 1987). The fact that *doorman* is a compound explains the meaning components in (19b). The components *door* and *man* have to be linked and although *stands at* is not included in the compound, it is a plausible relation. By contrast, (19c–d) are entirely undocumented in the form of the word. The question is, then, where the specification of the location of the door in (19c) and of the role or task of a doorman as described in (19d) come from.

It is sometimes claimed that meaning components such as (19c–d) arise as a result of lexicalization. As Hilpert (2020: 1722) puts it, 'linguistic elements undergo a number of types of formal and semantic changes once they have become lexicalized'. This view implies that *doorman* is first lexicalized in a sense described by (19a–b) and then semantic changes apply to add (19c–d). There are two problems with this view. First, it does not explain why the semantic changes take place. Second, it does not explain why lexicalization in the sense of (19a–b) took place. It is somewhat implausible to assume that a new word is first formed and only then speakers start thinking about what it might mean. This would be like inventing a machine and then trying to discover what it might be used for.

In this context, it is interesting to look at the words for the concept explained in (19) in some other languages. In German, it is *Türsteher*. This is a synthetic compound consisting of three parts, *Tür* ('door'), *steh-* ('stand$_V$') and *-er*, an affix with much the same function as agentive *-er* in English. Here we see that the relation 'who stands at' in (19b) is lexically expressed, but 'man' is not. In Dutch, we find *uitsmijter*. This also consists of three components, *uit* ('out'), *smijt-* ('throw$_V$') and the same affix *-er*. Here, it is not (19b), but a central element of (19d) that is expressed in the word. In Slovak, the translation is *vyhadzovač*. This is the regular agent noun corresponding to the verb *vyhadzovať* ('throw_out'). Thus, in Slovak the same naming strategy is used as in Dutch, but there is a difference in the realization. Although particles or prepositions often combine with verbs in Dutch, there is no verb **uitsmijten*. The combination of *uit* and *smijt-* in *uitsmijter* is more similar to a synthetic compound than to the agent noun formation in Slovak.[7]

What we find then is that in different languages, the words for the concept described as (19b–d) start from different aspects of its meaning. In English and German, (19b) is the starting point for the choice of a name, but they make a different selection of two of the three elements to be expressed. In Dutch and Slovak, it is (19d) that serves to provide the material, where in Slovak a readily formed verb is available, whereas in Dutch the corresponding meaning is a combination of a verb and a preposition.

We can interpret these data from two opposite angles. When we are interested in how the form is chosen for the concept, we have here an illustration of a certain degree of what Saussure (1916: 100–103) called *l'arbitraire du signe*. The meaning of the words in the four languages are not arbitrary, but their motivation is partial in the sense that the concept does not determine which meaning elements are selected to motivate the choice of form elements. From the opposite perspective, the question is how the forms in the four languages get their meaning. None of the elements of (19b–d) is such that it must be expressed directly in the form. However, ultimately all of them will be part of the meaning of the word that is formed. Therefore, the only plausible source of this full meaning is the concept that serves as the point of departure. That is to say, when a form is chosen to name a particular concept, the meaning of whichever form is

---

[7] It is not possible to use *uit* without an object as in **Hij smijt mensen uit* ('he throws people out'). The object can be realized as a noun phrase, e.g. *Hij smijt mensen uit de club* ('he throws people out [from] the club'), or as a so-called R-pronoun, e.g. *Hij smijt mensen eruit* ('he throws people R-out'). The R-pronoun replaces a personal pronoun as the object of a preposition (cf. Bennis 1986: 176).

selected will correspond to the concept we are naming. This is what we call *onomasiological coercion*.[8]

The study of word formation as a naming device evokes a discussion of which meaning elements of the concept to be named are used as a motivation for the choice of a form. The question of productivity has a less central position in such a discussion. Productivity is a property of rules. This property may influence the prominence of a particular rule in the naming process, but the choice of one rule rather than another is mostly motivated by the perceived fit with the concept. Therefore, productivity will not be an issue that we study systematically when we discuss the different morphological theories and frameworks in Chapters 5–12.

In our discussion of the different morphological theories, one of our questions will be how onomasiological coercion is covered. We will take the example of *doorman* with its equivalents in German, Dutch and Slovak as a starting point.

---

[8] This name was introduced by ten Hacken (2013a: 69). Ten Hacken (2019a: 58–66) gives a more detailed theoretical elaboration of the concept.

CHAPTER 5

Distributed Morphology

Distributed Morphology (DM) is a framework presented originally by Halle and Marantz (1993). It was quickly adopted by a significant section of generativist linguists working on morphology and has become the mainstream in generative morphology. As can be expected, in a period of almost three decades and with many researchers elaborating it, DM is not a diachronically unified theory and even its synchronic consensus does not concern all aspects of the framework. Here we will focus on the version as laid out in the recent overviews by McGinnis-Archibald (2016), Siddiqi (2019) and Bobaljik (2020), but take into account the historical origin of certain ideas and some elaborations in selected sources. Section 5.1 gives an overview of the aims and the organization of the grammar of DM. Section 5.2 addresses the data presented in Chapter 4, showing how they can be accounted for in DM and which problems they raise. On the basis of these analyses, section 5.3 gives a general characterization of the treatment of word formation as a naming device in DM.

5.1 Distributed Morphology as a framework

The first presentation of DM to a wider audience is Halle and Marantz (1993). Bobaljik (2020: 976) mentions as important precursors a paper presented by Halle at the 1990 NELS conference and Bonet's (1991) PhD thesis, supervised by Halle and Marantz. Its central ideas build on a larger current of morphological thought that at the time of its origin was rather a minority position.

Halle and Marantz (1993) present their approach as an alternative to Anderson (1992) and Lieber (1992), but their main criticism is directed at the former. Given that Anderson's A-Morphous Morphology was not significantly developed after 1992 and Lieber developed a new theory with a strong lexical-semantic orientation after 1992, it is remarkable that McGinnis-Archibald (2016) still takes the same sources as representatives of the opponents of DM.

A central assumption in DM is the rejection of the Lexicalist Hypothesis. Originally proposed by Chomsky (1970), the Lexicalist Hypothesis was directed against Generative Semantics and became the dominant approach in the course of the 1970s (cf. section 3.1). Anderson (1992) and Lieber (1992) represent two different elaborations of it. However, Siddiqi (2019: 146) refers to Lieber (1992) as a major source of data arguing against the Lexicalist Hypothesis.

Halle and Marantz (1993) appears in the same volume as Chomsky's (1993) exposition of the Minimalist Program (MP). In a postscript, Halle and Marantz (1993: 166–170) address the relation between the two. Meanwhile, DM has become the most commonly adopted theory of morphology within MP. As MP went through a series of modifications in its history, DM adapted to them. The most important change in MP was Chomsky's (2000) introduction of Phases. Whereas Halle and Marantz (1993) introduced a level of Morphological Structure (MS) in between S-Structure and PF, MS was abolished with the introduction of Phase Theory (Siddiqi 2019: 148–149).

Bobaljik (2020: 976–977) presents (1) as the leading ideas characterizing DM.

(1) *Basic assumptions of DM*
    a. Syntax all-the-way-down
    b. Late Insertion

For (1a), it is important to understand the direction of *down*. It is based on the general representation of the model of grammar with connections between the levels of representation, which has deeper structures higher up and structures closer to the surface lower down. For word formation, Harley (2009a: 129) formulates the aim of DM as 'to present a fully explicit, completely syntactic theory of word formation'. This means that the components that make up the output of word formation are manipulated by syntactic rules, not by any specific rules of word formation.

For (1b), it is important to understand the temporal sequence implied by *late*. Here the same representation of the model of grammar is viewed as a sequence of steps, with deeper structures being earlier than structures closer to the surface. The idea of (1b) is that syntax does not see the phonological realization of its basic units. The entire path from the starting point of the derivation to LF has phonologically unspecified nodes in the tree.[1] If syntax does not treat *cat* and *dog* differently, it does not have to

---

[1] With the introduction of traces of movement by Chomsky (1973), the level of Deep Structure as introduced by Chomsky (1957) lost most of its functions, as the information it contains can also be retrieved later. Chomsky (1981: 5) refers to D-Structure as opposed to S-Structure. From S-Structure, PF and LF are derived. PF is the phonetic representation and LF stands for Logical Form. Chomsky (1977: 166) presents LF as including 'whatever features of sentence structure [that] (1) enter directly into semantic interpretation of sentences and (2) are strictly determined by properties of (sentence-) grammar'. In MP, there is no longer a coherent structure corresponding to

Figure 5.1 *Model of grammar assumed in DM*

see which of the two it handles in a particular tree. In the original framework, this means that lexical insertion, which specifies the exact identity of a node, takes place on the path between S-Structure and PF. In Phase Theory, it is between Spell-Out and PF.

The model of grammar evolving from Phase Theory can be represented as in Figure 5.1. *Numeration* designates the set of nodes to be included in a structure. The arrow to LF represents the sequence of steps for building up a structure that includes all these nodes and is grammatical. *Spell-Out* marks the point where for a part of the structure it is decided to make it pronounceable. This is the path to PF.

There is no specific place for the lexicon in Figure 5.1. In DM, the function of the lexicon, as it was assumed in generative linguistics of the 1970s and the 1980s, is distributed (hence the name) over three lists, as in (2).

(2) Lists in DM
 a. Lexicon: The set of terminal nodes in syntax, identified by features
 b. Vocabulary: The set of nodes identified by features and phonological content
 c. Encyclopedia: The set of nodes identified by listed meaning

The Lexicon, which is not the same entity as the one we refer to as *lexicon* in the paragraph before (2), is a list that contains items that are not phonologically specified. The items contained in (2a) constitute the units that are used in the path from Numeration to LF in Figure 5.1. They are feature bundles that only contain the information that is necessary to build up a syntactic structure.

D-Structure. The input is only a set of entries selected from the lexicon and added one by one by means of Merge operations.

The Vocabulary is a different set of items. It contains phonologically specified units with the syntactic features that make a proper matching possible. For *cat* and *dog*, there is one entry in the Lexicon, but two in the Vocabulary. The Vocabulary is used to assign phonological content to a syntactic structure on the path from Spell-Out to PF.

The Encyclopedia is the place where idiosyncratic aspects of meaning are listed. Entries of the Encyclopedia can be basic lexical entries, in which case they correspond to Vocabulary Items, or combinations of basic lexical entries that do not have an entirely compositional meaning. Harley and Noyer (2003: 470) use *idiom* as a term for the items that have to be listed here, a use of the term that is reminiscent of Hockett (1958: 171–173). The Encyclopedia is not mentioned by Halle and Marantz (1993). Harley and Noyer (2003: 471) note that the relationship between the Encyclopedia and the Vocabulary is a matter of debate. However, Siddiqi (2019: 165) describes the Encyclopedia and its interface with the grammar as an 'area that remains effectively untouched'. It is difficult to relate it to the components in Figure 5.1. Harley and Noyer (2003: 465) introduce a node labelled 'Conceptual Interface ("Meaning")' with incoming arrows from PF, LF and Encyclopedia. Siddiqi (2019: 150) has a similar representation, with several arrows from the Encyclopedia suggesting a stronger contribution.

Another important element of the formalism that was introduced after Halle and Marantz (1993) is the distinction between *f-morpheme* and *l-morpheme*. Harley and Noyer (2003: 468) attribute it to Harley and Noyer (1998). Here *f* can be thought of as standing for *functional* and *l* for *lexical*. The idea is that *f-morphemes* are all in competition for the insertion into nodes that match their features. For *l-morphemes*, the situation is different. They have a meaning that is specified in the Encyclopedia and do not compete in the same way as *f-morphemes*. Siddiqi (2019: 163) mentions that there have been several proposals on how to understand the precise nature of *l-morphemes*, but no general agreement has been reached.

Characteristic of work within the DM framework is that syntax takes priority over the lexicon, phonology and semantics. The functions of the lexicon are distributed among three lists. The Lexicon (not identical to the lexicon) is connected to syntax, which is the only generative engine. The Vocabulary is connected to phonology, which receives a fair bit of attention because Vocabulary Insertion identifies individual morphemes. The Encyclopedia encodes lexical meaning, but is hardly elaborated in practice.

5.2 The treatment of relevant contrasts in DM

In this section, we will go over the data we presented in Chapter 4 and indicate how they can be treated in DM. The structure of the section follows the structure of Chapter 4.

5.2.1 Words and phrases

The examples marking the borderline between words and phrases we used in section 4.1 all concern compounding. As such, it is in particular Harley (2009a) which gives useful information. The first contrast is the German one repeated here as (3).

(3) a. Hartkäse ('granular cheese')
    b. harter Käse ('hard cheese')

Whereas (3a) is a compound and designates a type of cheese, (3b) is a phrase and predicates a property over a quantity or instance of cheese. Both contain the components *hart* ('hard') and *Käse* ('cheese').

A first observation is that these components only appear after Spell-Out. They are in the Vocabulary, not in the Lexicon. In the syntactic derivation going from Numeration to LF in Figure 5.1, *hart* is not distinguished from *weich* ('soft') and *Käse* is not distinguished from *Schinken* ('ham'). What is specified is only that the nodes refer to an adjective in the positive degree and to a masculine noun.

In the Vocabulary, *hart* and *Käse* each have an entry, but it is not specified for syntactic category. That the former is an adjective and the latter a noun is the result of functional categories they combine with. In a phrase such as (3b), *hart* is combined with a range of functional categories. One of them assigns the syntactic category of adjective, others are responsible for the features that are together realized as *-er*. *Käse* is also combined with functional categories, although they are not phonologically realized. Harley (2009a: 139–140) proposes that compounds are the result of incorporation, i.e. the components combine before they are assigned a syntactic category. For (3a), this results in a structure such as Figure 5.2.[2]

In Figure 5.2, $\sqrt{}$ stands for Root. Roots are underspecified for syntactic category. Of the functional categories, only the ones assigning a syntactic category to a root are represented in Figure 5.2. The Root *hart*, $\sqrt{HART}$, combines with the functional category a^0 to produce an adjective, but it might in principle also combine with a v^0 or n^0 to yield a verb or noun, respectively. In the derivation of (3b), $\sqrt{HART}$ combines with a^0 and $\sqrt{KÄSE}$ with n^0. However, in the case of a compound as in (3a), $\sqrt{KÄSE}$ forms a complex Root, $\sqrt{}$ in Figure 5.2, before combining with n^0 to form a noun. Following the representation of Harley (2009a: 140), we represent the complex Root as $\sqrt{}$ rather than as $\sqrt{HARTKÄSE}$.

---

[2] Figure 5.2 is a simplified version of the tree Harley (2009a: 140) gives for *nurse shoe*. She embeds the tree in Figure 5.2 in an nP that also includes a $\sqrt{P}$. This $\sqrt{P}$ contains the original sites of the roots that are moved to the n^0 we represent as the top node in Figure 5.2.

Distributed Morphology

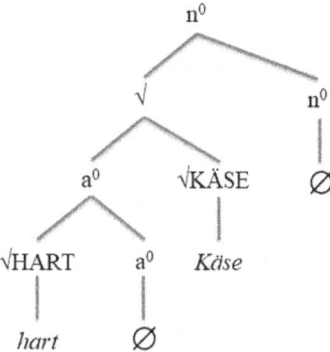

Figure 5.2 *The structure of* Hartkäse *in DM*

In DM, it is formally impossible to have two Roots as sisters, which is why there must be a functional category a^0 dominating √HART. This is somewhat counterintuitive, because it is not the adjective *hart* but rather the Root √HART which is the non-head of the compound. For a compound such as *Normalform* ('normal form'), it is not possible to decide whether *normal* is a noun or an adjective.[3] It can be either in different contexts, and within the compound, there is no way to determine the correct syntactic category, because *normal* in this position is not syntactically active.

The meaning of (3a) as a special type of cheese can only be recorded in the Encyclopedia. Entries in the Encyclopedia are mappings. The entry for *Hartkäse* connects the structure in Figure 5.2 with the aspects of the meaning that cannot be predicted by its compositional analysis.

It is interesting to compare the contrast in (3) with the Slovak examples repeated here as (4).

(4) a. čajová lyžička ('teaspoon')
    b. čistá lyžička ('clean spoon')

In (4a) we have a relational adjective (RA). Whereas in (3a), the adjective is incorporated in the compound, which is visible in the absence of inflection,

---

[3] Although the noun *Normal* is not very frequent, it is used (also) in a sense that is highly relevant in the context of the compound *Normalform*. DeReKo (13 October 2022) gives (i).

(i) Man hat ein Normal und vergleicht mittels eines Messgerätes das Normal mit dem unbekannten Wert.
('One has a *Normal* and compares by_means_of a measuring_tool the *Normal* with the unknown value')

Here *Normal* designates a kind of standard, which is close to its meaning in the term *Normalform* as used in mathematical linguistics.

the RA in (4a) is inflected in exactly the same way as the qualitative adjective in (4b). Whereas *hart* in (3) is a Root, *čajová* in (4a) is a combination of three basic elements. Although *čaj* ('tea') is a noun, the Root √ČAJ does not have a syntactic category. The element *-ov-* is a marker of adjectival status. This means that the category-neutral √ČAJ corresponds to *čaj* when combined with n^0 and to *čajov-* when combined with a^0. The final *-á* in (4a) and (4b) is a realization of feature projections in the same way as *-er* in (3b). The structure of (4a) is parallel to that of (4b) and does not display any incorporation of the type illustrated in Figure 5.2. The difference between (4a) and (4b) is only reflected in the Encyclopedia. The fact that (4b) refers to a property of a spoon whereas (4a) refers to a type of spoon is expressed in an Encyclopedia entry for (4a). In this respect, (4) is parallel to (3).

The next contrast concerns *bird's nest*. The ambiguity of this expression is illustrated by the examples repeated here as (5).

(5) a. She points to a bird's nest in a low branch.
    b. The mother cuckoo lays its egg in another bird's nest.

In (5a), *bird's nest* is a constituent and no particular bird is introduced as the nest's owner. In (5b), *another bird* is a constituent and it refers to an actual bird. This structural difference is of course visible in the syntactic derivation from Numeration to LF in Figure 5.2. In the Vocabulary, the same items are inserted, but into a different structure. Only for *bird's nest* in (5a) will there then be a matching entry in the Encyclopedia. This is equally necessary for the literal sense of a type of nest as for transferred senses such as a particular haircut.

The last contrast to be discussed in this section concerns the N+N combinations in (6).

(6) a. a commuter suburb of Charleston
    b. the Chicago suburb of Cicero

The modifiers of *suburb* have a different role. In (6a), *commuter* specifies the function of the suburb, in (6b) *Chicago* the location. In fact, *Chicago* in (6b) has the same role with respect to *suburb* as *Charleston* in (6a). Crucially, a *commuter suburb* refers to a type of suburb, but *Chicago suburb* does not imply the existence of such a type. DM offers two mechanisms to account for this contrast, the Encyclopedia and noun incorporation. In the Encyclopedia, *commuter suburb* should have an entry giving the specific properties of the concept. For *Chicago suburb*, it is sufficient that the components are listed in the Encyclopedia. As for incorporation, it is plausible that *commuter suburb* but not *Chicago suburb* has a structure like the one in Figure 5.2.

Summarizing this section, we can conclude that the Encyclopedia is crucial in recording meanings of expressions that serve as semantic units. A stronger structural connection can be encoded with the incorporation structure for compounds as proposed by Harley (2009a). The precise conditions for incorporation and the diagnostic criteria to recognize that such an incorporation has taken place will need to be specified for a proper use of incorporation in delimiting the domain of compounding.

5.2.2 The borderline between inflection and derivation

The question whether inflection and derivation are distinguished or not has historically been approached in different ways. The explicit assumption in DM is that they are not distinguished. Here, it is not our purpose to investigate whether this decision is justified, but rather how certain data that illustrate the distinction are covered in DM. As outlined in section 4.2, we use the contrast between plural and diminutive as our example, especially in a language like Dutch where both are productive but do not form part of a larger paradigm. For *vogel* ('bird') we only have the forms in (7).

(7) a. vogel   sg
    b. vogels   pl
    c. vogeltje   dim-sg
    d. vogeltjes dim-pl

Harley and Noyer (2003: 474) suggest that some of the pertinent differences between inflection and derivation are caught in DM by the contrast between f-morphemes and l-morphemes. They immediately note, however, that 'certainly not all f-morphemes would normally be considered "inflectional"' (2003: 474). This formulation suggests that f-morphemes encompass a larger class than inflection. Obviously, function words such as determiners and complementizers are also f-morphemes. In fact, it is mostly assumed, following Marantz (1997), that only lexical roots are l-morphemes. Lowenstamm (2014) proposes that some derivational affixes should also be treated as l-morphemes, but his main purpose with this proposal is to explain the order of stress-shifting affixes with respect to stress-neutral affixes.

The question at this point is whether or to what extent the difference between plural and diminutive as in (7) can be expressed in terms of the distinction between f-morphemes and l-morphemes. The crucial difference between f-morphemes and l-morphemes concerns the way lexical insertion takes place. For f-morphemes, all Vocabulary Items compete and the best match gets inserted. The competition is decided by the number of matching features. For l-morphemes, the features specified in the node constitute constraints on the class of Vocabulary Items. The choice between alternatives in the same class, e.g. *merel* ('blackbird') and *vogel*, cannot be determined by features.

Bobaljik (2020: 979–981) discusses the competition between different suffixes for past tense and nominalization. He gives the example of English *-ness, -ity, -th*, etc. He assumes that they are different f-morphemes to the extent that they have systematically different syntactic or semantic properties. Otherwise they should rather be analysed as allomorphs, i.e. different realizations of the same morpheme.

Dutch has two regular plural endings, -s and -en. In section 4.2, we saw the contrast in (8).

(8) a. vogel   vogels   ('bird')
    b. huis   huizen   ('house')

Phonological properties of the stem determine that -s is the only correct ending in (8a) and -en the only correct ending in (8b). The prosodic structure of *vogel*, with its unstressed final syllable ending in -l, conditions the use of the -s ending and after the final sibilant of *huis*, only -en is possible. The plural and noun features exclude all other f-morphemes. These other f-morphemes are in principle also competing, but they do not play a role in the decision, because there are better matches. Following Bobaljik's idea for English nominalization, we can say that -s and -en are allomorphs. However, the idea that -s and -en are competing f-morphemes is supported by the observation that the conditions for their selection are not mutually exclusive, as in (9).

(9) a. methode   methodes
    b. methode   methoden

For *methode* ('method'), both plurals in (9) are possible. The unstressed final syllable allows for -s, but the absence of a final stem consonant also makes -en possible. There is no syntactic or semantic difference between the two plurals. They are in free variation. In other cases, illustrated in (10), there is no free variation, but the selection of the affix does not follow from the rule.

(10) a. winkelier   winkeliers   *winkelieren   ('shopkeeper')
     b. scholier   *scholiers   scholieren   ('pupil')
     c. broer   broers   *broeren   ('brother')

In (10a–b), we see two derivations with the same suffix -ier, each of them selecting only one plural suffix, but not the same one. The prosodic structure would favour -en, because -ier is stressed, but most of the examples with this suffix given by de Haas and Trommelen (1993: 180) follow the pattern in (10a). Booij (2002: 32) lists a number of suffixes that interfere with the prosodic generalization, including -ier. In (10c), we have an idiosyncratic exception. As a monosyllabic noun, *broer* should have a plural in -en. Perhaps the plural in -s can be explained because historically *broer* is a shortened form of *broeder*, which has the correct prosodic structure for a plural in -s. Van Dale (2022: [1]*broeder*) gives the long form only as archaic or in a religious sense ('friar'). The examples in (10) show that there is no simple complementary distribution, but only a prosodically motivated tendency with lexical exceptions.

Modern standard Dutch only has a single ending for the diminutive, -*tje*. However, there are many allomorphs of this suffix, as illustrated in (11).

(11) a. vogel   vogeltje   ('bird')
     b. huis   huisje   ('house')
     c. boom   boompje   ('tree')
     d. kom   kommetje   ('bowl')
     e. haring   harinkje   ('herring')

As opposed to the plural endings, which are phonologically independent realizations of two different suffixes, the variants of -*tje* can all be derived from a single basic form by means of general phonological rules. In DM, they are more appropriately realized as the result of readjustment rules applied to -*tje* than as the outcome of competition between -*tje*, -*je*, -*pje*, -*etje* and -*kje*. The question is whether -*tje* is an f-morpheme.

The main difference between f-morphemes and l-morphemes is that only the latter have a reference, i.e. a link to the outside world. L-morphemes have an entry in the Encyclopedia. The plural and the diminutive both have a clear meaning that can also be expressed by a separate lexical entry. For the plural we can use *meerdere* ('several') and for the diminutive *klein* ('small'). However, we observe the contrast in (12) and (13).

(12) a. meerdere vogels
     b. *meerdere vogel

(13) a. klein vogeltje
     b. kleine vogel

Both in (12a) and in (13a), the adjective can be thought of as redundant or emphatic. However, whereas the adjective can stand instead of the diminutive affix in (13b), the ungrammaticality of (12b) shows that this is not possible for the plural. If we accept that this agreement distinction is a relevant condition for the identification of f-morphemes, the plural is an f-morpheme (or two f-morphemes, -*s* and -*en*), but the diminutive is not.

Another aspect of the difference is semantic. Whereas the diminutive triggers the formation of a different prototype, the plural does not. Although all instances of *vogeltje* are also instances of *vogel*, their evaluation on a scale of prototypicality is not the same. A *meeuw* ('seagull') is a good example of *vogel*, but a marginal example of *vogeltje*. Such a prototype marked by the diminutive suffix is not necessarily determined as small. Thus, *weekendje* ('weekend$_{DIM}$') does not refer to a shorter period than *weekend*. The difference in meaning is rather subtle, but there are two aspects that stand out. They are illustrated in (14) and (15).

(14) a. een weekend in Parijs ('a weekend in Paris')
　　 b. een weekendje in Parijs

(15) a. Volgend weekend ben ik jarig.
　　　　 'Next weekend am I year$_A$', i.e. Next weekend is my birthday.
　　 b. *Volgend weekendje ben ik jarig.

In the case of nouns referring to a time, e.g. *weekend*, the diminutive focuses on the events taking place in this time. In (14), the diminutive adds a positive evaluation, but both examples can be translated the same way. In (15), the diminutive is ungrammatical, because *weekend* is used as a pure time indication, whereas the diminutive would imply an event. A similar change of focus occurs when the diminutive is applied to mass nouns, as illustrated in (16) and (17).

(16) a. een fles wijn ('a bottle [of] wine')
　　 b. een goede wijn ('a good wine')

(17) a. *een fles wijntje
　　 b. een goed wijntje

As illustrated in (16), mass nouns have a systematic ambiguity referring either to a quantity or to a type. As shown in (17), the diminutive eliminates this ambiguity, because the quantity reading is no longer available, so that (17a) is ungrammatical. In (17b), a vaguely positive evaluation is implied, comparable to (14b), as well as a lack of ambition for it to be a great wine.

The crucial point of examples (14) to (17) is that the suffix *-tje* has a regular referential meaning at least to some extent. The referential component of the meaning is less specific than for most adjectives, but can trigger ungrammaticality if the context is incompatible. The type of meaning that is added depends on the semantic class of the base. As such, it is largely comparable to the behaviour of adjectives such as *goed* ('good'). This adjective also has a rather vague meaning that is specified further by the semantic class of the noun it modifies. Therefore, we may consider the idea to analyse *-tje* as an l-morpheme.

Creemers et al. (2018) take up Lowenstamm's (2014) idea of a distinction between some derivational affixes being f-morphemes and others l-morphemes in their discussion of Dutch derivational morphology and propose a division into three classes. Between the conventional Level I affixes (which they call Level Ia) that may have allomorphs, may change the stress of the base they attach to and may attach to bound stems, and the conventional Level II affixes that have no allomorphs, do not change the stress of the base and do not attach to bound stems, they propose a Level Ib, which includes affixes that behave like Level Ia, except that they cannot have allomorphs. Like Lowenstamm (2014), Creemers et al. (2018) set as their primary goal the explanation of the order of affixes. They claim that affixes at Level Ib and Level II are f-affixes, whereas those at Level Ia are l-affixes (2018: 66). Interestingly, although they mention -*tje* and suggest it is an f-affix (2018: 78), they do not include the suffix in the appendix with the classification of suffixes (2018: 82). As an inflectional category, the plural is not in the scope of their investigation, but it can be assumed that it is realized by f-suffixes.

A different question concerns the cases where the diminutive noun has a meaning that is not covered by the base noun. In section 4.2, we gave the examples of *stokje* ('stick$_{DIM}$'), which can have the meaning of chopstick, whereas *stok* ('stick') does not have this meaning, and *kaartje*, which can mean 'ticket for an event or for public transport', whereas *kaart* means 'card' or 'map'. Here it is obvious that the complex word must have an entry in the Encyclopedia to encode the non-predictable meaning. We would argue, however, that the more subtle changes in meaning such as the one for *vogeltje* and *weekendje* also deserve separate entries.

When we evaluate the success of the distinction between f-morphemes and l-morphemes in accounting for the difference in behaviour of the diminutive and the plural, we have to consider that the proposals by Lowenstamm (2014) and Creemers et al. (2018) focus on the order of affixes. Our interest here is mainly their difference in naming behaviour. The discussion of examples (12) to (17) showed that the diminutive creates a new concept with its own prototype, whereas the plural only adds a functional meaning component to an existing concept. Obviously, the plural is realized by an f-morpheme. For the diminutive, neither option is particularly attractive. If it is an f-morpheme, as suggested by Creemers et al. (2018: 78) on the basis of phonological properties, we cannot account for the difference from the plural in its influence on naming, as it is in the same class. If it is an l-morpheme, it would be predicted that it has a meaning of its own. However, as (14) to (17) illustrate, it is very difficult to pin down this meaning. Ultimately, this means that diminutive nouns get their meaning in the Encyclopedia in a way that is not (yet) theoretically explained.

5.2.3 Paradigms

The syntactic approach to morphology adopted in DM is hardly compatible with paradigms. Thus McGinnis-Archibald (2016: 392) states that 'the paradigm space is a virtual one' and 'paradigms themselves play no role in morphology'. The idea of a virtual paradigm space means that the grid expressing the combinations of features for the case and number forms of Slovak *gitara* in section 4.3 remains implicit. The individual forms can be generated because each attribute corresponds to a functional category and the functional head occupying the position encodes the value. In a different way of putting this, Siddiqi (2019: 160) states that 'lexemes do not exist in any meaningful way in DM'. He calls the idea of lexemes incorporated in our example of *gitara* 'epiphenomenal' (2019: 161).

A claim that there are paradigms such as the one for *gitara* can be interpreted in at least two ways, paraphrased in (18).

(18) a. If something is a noun in Slovak, it has forms for six cases in two numbers.
b. There is a class of feminine nouns with the endings illustrated in Table 4.2.

The claim in (18a) is what is intended by the virtual space of McGinnis-Archibald (2016) and the epiphenomenal status of Siddiqi (2019). What exists is the possibility of forming each of the individual word forms when they are needed. Organizing them into a grid is artificial, but not impossible.

The claim in (18b) is of a different kind. Traditional grammar has generally tried to organize the correlations that exist between word forms into neat paradigm classes. In Latin, there are five declensions. However, as any learner of Latin will know, it is not sufficient to learn five grids of the type exemplified in Table 4.2. Thus, the second declension contains masculine nouns in -*us* such as *dominus* ('lord'), neuter nouns in -*um* such as *bellum* ('war') and masculine nouns in -*er* such as *liber* ('book'). The third declension is even more heterogeneous.

Organizing case and number forms for nouns in languages such as Latin into a system of paradigms is a theoretical challenge. Carstairs (1981) and Carstairs-McCarthy (1994) discuss the principles by which forms as they are found can be organized into a system of paradigms, but McGinnis-Archibald (2016: 392) notes that the principles he proposed have been argued to be empirically unsuccessful. Corbett and Fraser (1993) propose a default mechanism as a more flexible solution in their Network Morphology.

Anderson (1992) uses the properties referred to in (18) as part of his argumentation to make a strong distinction between inflection and derivation. Whereas derivation is the formation of lexemes in the lexicon and takes place before lexical insertion, i.e. before syntax, inflection concerns the choice of a form from the paradigm to fit the syntactic context, i.e. after syntax. As we saw in section 5.1, DM rejects this so-called *split morphology*. This explains part of the resistance to claims such as (18).

When we consider paradigms from the perspective of naming, (18a) is a good basic assumption and the availability of any generalizations such as (18b) is extremely helpful. Presumably, *gitara* in Slovak is a borrowing. When it was borrowed, it was useful to assign it to a major inflection class of nouns on the basis of its phonological shape. There are also borrowings that are invariable, e.g. *atašé* ('attaché') or *zoo*, but usually, when the form of a borrowed noun in Slovak matches the nominative singular form of one of the major inflectional classes, it is assigned to this class and inflected regularly.

In the case of word formation, the assignment of an inflection class is generally unproblematic. The inflection class is either determined by the word formation process or it follows from the base. In Slovak, the former is common in suffixation, the latter in prefixation. An example of suffixation is *učiteľka* ('teacher$_{FEM}$') from *učiteľ* ('teacher'). The suffix *-ka* determines the inflection class of the result, which is the same as the one for *gitara*. An example of the latter is *nadstavba* ('superstructure') from *stavba* ('structure, construction'), where both nouns are in the same inflection class as *gitara*.

Bobaljik (2020: 984–985) mentions a related view on the nature of paradigms. He proposes a universal that the superlative of adjectives is based on the comparative. In a language like Slovak, this is illustrated by paradigms such as (19).

(19) a. starý ('old')
     b. starší ('older')
     c. najstarší ('oldest')

We can formulate this as an implicational relationship. The superlative is formed not from the positive form, but from the comparative. In English, adjectives can have a comparative with *-er* or with *more*, but whenever an adjective has the comparative with *-er*, it has the superlative with *-est*, and whenever it has the comparative with *more*, it has the superlative with *most*.

At first sight, Bobaljik's account may seem to weaken the point against paradigms. However, his view of paradigms is independent of claims such as (18). Instead of a grid determined by independent features, Bobaljik has a set of implicational relations.

It is interesting to compare Bobaljik's account of paradigms with the Slovak derivational paradigms in (20) and (21), which we discussed in section 4.3.

(20) a. blog ('blog$_N$')
     b. blogovať ('blog$_V$')
     c. blogový ('blog$_A$')

(21) a. bloger ('blogger$_N$')
     b. blogerka ('blogger$_{FEM}$')
     c. blogerský ('blogger$_A$')

Although the different items in (20) and (21) do not belong to the same lexeme, their contrast can largely be expressed in features. In (20), we can assume a Root √BLOG which both in English and in Slovak can be turned into a N, V or A by merging with a functional category. In English all three are phonologically Ø, whereas in Slovak two of them have phonological effects. In (20b), the suffix triggers a specific meaning. For Slovak, SSJ (2006–2022) gives the meaning in (22).

(22) uverejňovať články s rôznou témou na vlastnej al. inej nekomerčnej internetovej stránke
'publish articles with various themes on (one's) own or (an)other non-commercial internet page'

The specialized aspects of the meaning in (22) have to be recorded in the Encyclopedia. Ološtiak (2021: 782) suggests two possibilities for how *bloger* in (21a) can be related to *blog* in (20a), one based on borrowing, the other on word formation. The point about the latter is that *-er* is not a Slovak affix. If *bloger* is not reanalysed, we can assume a Slovak Root √BLOGER in (21), which merges with a functional category expressing N in (21a–b) or A in (21c). In (21b), a further functional category, correlating with the meaning component 'female', is realized as *-k(a)*. In the other case, i.e. if *bloger* is a word formation result, the root in (21) is the same as in (20) and *-er* is the reflection of a functional category. However, this functional category cannot be an agent-forming suffix in the same way as in English. There are only few borrowings from English with this suffix and the English stem does not correspond to a Slovak verb directly.

When we compare the examples in (20) and (21) with Bobaljik's example with the superlative, a similarity is that we can identify a chain of relationships in both examples. For (19a), (19b) and (19c), we have a parallel in (20a), (21a) and (21b), as *blogerka* is derived from *bloger*, not directly from *blog*. A difference is that in (20) and (21) we have more than one form that is derived. Both of (20b–c) are derived from (20a) and both of (21b–c) from (21a). By contrast, only (19c) is derived from (19b). A further difference is that the examples in (20) and (21) do not give rise to a plausible universal corresponding to Bobaljik's claim that the superlative is always based on the comparative.

In sum, DM treats paradigms as an epiphenomenon. As far as generalizations about the existence and the phonological shape of related inflectional or derivational forms can be made, they do not play a role in the organization of the grammar. Bobaljik's (2020) proposal to derive the superlative from the comparative may give an interesting lead as to the treatment of paradigms, but it remains unclear how and to what extent it can be generalized.

5.2.4 Transposition and the formation of names

The phenomenon of transposition was illustrated in section 4.4 by the contrast in (23).

(23) a. an issue open to empirical exploration
b. an issue open to being explored empirically

The two expressions in (23) are semantically equivalent. Syntactically they have the same external value, i.e. they can be inserted in the same contexts,

Distributed Morphology

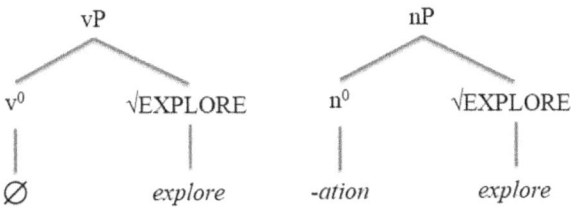

Figure 5.3 *A possible structure of* explore *and* exploration *in DM*

but different internal structures. This difference in structure is entirely conditioned by the fact that *exploration* in (23a) is a noun and *explore* in (23b) a verb. Given the approach to syntactic categories in DM, one might assume that the contrast between *explore* and *exploration* can be represented as in Figure 5.3.

The order of nodes and the phonological value are only determined in Spell-Out, but in a tree structure, it is not possible to represent unordered branches. In Figure 5.3 and other trees in this section, we follow DM custom in placing the root at the end and insert the phonological realization to identify the nodes. As represented in Figure 5.3, it might be intuitively appealing to take the DM assumption that Roots do not have a syntactic category until they are combined with a functional head with the relevant category as a basis to represent transposition as reflected only in the contrast between these functional heads. In the case of *explore* and *exploration*, the Root would be the same, but whereas the v^0 node is phonologically empty, the n^0 has a value of *-ation*. In pairs like *range*$_N$ and *range*$_V$, both category-bearing nodes would be phonologically realized as Ø.

In fact, it is assumed that √EXPLORE does not have an argument structure until it is combined with v^0. This means that we need to have the functional projection with v^0 in order to account for the interpretation of *an issue* in (23). Although we can use the left-hand structure of Figure 5.3 for *explore* in (23b), we need the structure in Figure 5.4 for *exploration* in (23a). Borer (2014) and Harley (2014) adopt such a structure and use it to have *-ize* as the realization of v^0 in cases such as *categorization*. The interpretation of *an issue* as the object of *explore* is represented by inserting a full VP between nP and vP.

Let us now turn to the cases of ambiguity discussed in section 4.4. As an example of an ambiguity between transposition and word formation as a naming process, we gave the contrast in (24).

(24) a. the installation in their territory of foreign military bases
     b. [they] were taken to a Salvadorean military installation

In (24a), *installation* has a structure as in Figure 5.4, so that *foreign military bases* can be interpreted as an argument. In (24b), the meaning of

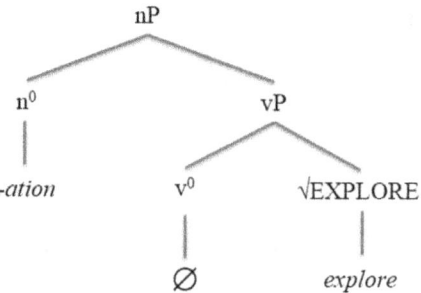

Figure 5.4 *The structure of* exploration *in DM*

installation as '[military] facility, base or complex' has to be specified in the Encyclopedia. Harley (2009b: 339) proposes that countability plays a crucial role in such cases. Whereas the transposition in (24a) cannot be pluralized, *installation* in the sense used in (24b) can.

Alexiadou et al. (2010: 560) propose the structure in Figure 5.5 for what they call the 'telic reading' of German nouns in *-ung*, which display the same type of ambiguity as the one illustrated in (24). Following an idea first developed by Picallo (2005), they assume that the Num-projection only exists for countable nouns and that countability is expressed in the Class-projection. The Class-projection also encodes gender. Picallo (2005: 108) states that gender is a precondition for number. Whereas in (24a), *installation* has [–count], so that it has no Num-projection, in (24b), it has the structure in Figure 5.5. As shown in Figure 5.5, there is no separation of morphology and syntax, with a VP projection internal to nP.

The idea of distinguishing the two readings of *installation* in (24) by assigning them structures such as Figure 5.4 and Figure 5.5 is appealing for two reasons. First, it accounts for the result reading by means of a syntactic property that constitutes a significant difference from the transpositional reading. Second, it makes the result reading in (24b) an elaboration of the process reading in (24a). This is in line with the empirical findings of Thomas (2013a) as summarized by ten Hacken (2019a: 80–82). In her analysis of the representation of nouns in *-ation* in OED (2000–2012), Thomas (2013a) found that the process reading is in most cases attested earlier.

In the case of the German and Slovak equivalents of *installation*, these aspects of the account can be used as well. The fact that German *Installation* and Slovak *inštalácia* have both readings, whereas German *Installierung* and Slovak *inštalovanie* only have the one corresponding to (24a) can be explained by the absence or presence of Num. In the German case, it must be assumed that *Installation* but not *Installierung* may have Num. The reading of *Installation* with a Num-projection has an entry in the Encyclopedia.

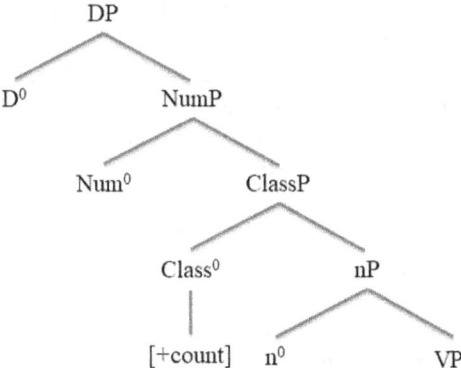

Figure 5.5 *Representation of the non-transpositional reading of* installation

5.2.5 Onomasiological coercion

As an example of onomasiological coercion, we discussed *doorman* in section 4.5 as well as its equivalents in German, Dutch and Slovak, listed and literally translated in (25).

(25) a. Türsteher ('door_stander') DE
b. uitsmijter ('out_thrower') NL
c. vyhadzovač ('throw_out-er') SK

Taking as a basis the dictionary definition in COBUILD (2023), we noted in section 4.5 that the four languages selected different elements for the lexicalization. Whereas English and German use the location, Dutch and Slovak take the function of the person as a starting point.

In DM, the specialized meaning of these words can be accounted for by assigning them an entry in the Encyclopedia. The Encyclopedia encodes the meanings of what Di Sciullo and Williams (1987: 1) call *listemes*. As noted in section 5.1, the Encyclopedia remains underdeveloped from a theoretical perspective. Therefore, assigning the task to the Encyclopedia means in fact that nothing more is said than that there is an unpredictable meaning. How much and which aspects of the meaning are predictable remains unaccounted for.

5.3 Word formation and naming in DM

Given its general orientation, DM does not assign naming a prominent position in the account of morphology. The basic assumptions listed in (1) make syntax the core of language. In DM, syntactic mechanisms determine the entire derivation of an expression and late insertion ensures that only the minimally necessary information about lexical items is available at any point in the derivation.

DM distributes the function of the lexicon over three different lists, as in (2). The Lexicon, the Vocabulary and the Encyclopedia encode different aspects of lexical information. Naming, which we characterized in Chapter 1 as the creation of a new association of a name and a concept, appeals to the interaction of the Vocabulary and the Encyclopedia. The name is a pronounceable form listed in the Vocabulary and the concept, reduced to the non-compositional aspects of the meaning of a form, is listed in the Encyclopedia.

In section 5.2, we considered how different aspects of what we consider naming can be covered in DM. Many of our examples take the form of a contrasting pair, in which one member displays naming and the other does not. An example of a contrast that can be treated well in DM is the two uses of *bird's nest* in (5). Here we have two structures as in (26).

(26) a. [a [[bird]'s nest]]
     b. [[another bird]'s nest]

In (26a), *bird's nest* is a compound noun. In the DP-analysis, first proposed by Abney (1987), the determiner *a* is the head and has the NP *bird's nest* as its complement. In (26b), *bird's nest* is not a constituent. An example where such an approach is more difficult to implement is the contrast between relational and qualitative adjectives. In (4), we illustrated this with the Slovak contrast between *čajová* ('tea$_A$') and *čistá* ('clean') as modifiers of *lyžička* ('spoon'). It is possible to express in DM the distinction between denominal and simple adjectives. Thus, the Root √ČAJ is combined with a functional category a^0 to give *čajov-*. However, we also have contrasts such as (27).

(27) a. dopravná informácia   ('traffic$_{ADJ}$ information')
     b. dôležitá informácia   ('important information')
     c. potrebná informácia   ('necessary information')

The contrast in (27a–b) is similar to the one in (4). In (27a), *dopravná* is an inflected form of the relational adjective *dopravný* ('traffic$_A$') corresponding to the noun *doprava* ('traffic$_N$'). It contrasts with the qualitative adjective *dôležitý* ('important') in (27b). In (27c), however, *potrebný* ('necessary') is at the same time a denominal adjective derived from *potreba* ('need') and a qualitative adjective. Structurally, it is in the same class as *čajový* and *dopravný*, but it is not a relational adjective, so that (27c) is not a name, but a regular A+N phrase. Therefore, it is not possible to identify relational adjectives in structural terms.

In section 5.2, we came across a number of cases in which the syntactic approach to the characterization of the contrast involves specific

Distributed Morphology 87

mechanisms that are typical of DM. For the contrast between German A+N compounds and phrases in (3), we can use incorporation. As illustrated in Figure 5.2, A+N compounds such as *Hartkäse* ('granular cheese') have a complex root, resulting from the incorporation of the adjective, whereas corresponding phrases such as *harter Käse* ('hard cheese') do not.

In the case of Dutch plurals and diminutives, we considered the possibility of using the contrast between f-morphemes and l-morphemes. However, whereas it is clear that the plural should be an f-morpheme, it is not at all obvious that the diminutive should be an l-morpheme. The problem is that for complex words with an l-morpheme we expect a compositionally derived meaning. This is not given in the case of the diminutive. Even for regular cases such as *vogeltje* ('bird$_{DIM}$') in (13), we find that it has a separate prototype from its non-diminutive counterpart *vogel* ('bird'). It is also difficult to assign a specific meaning to -*tje*. The evaluative aspect in *weekendje* ('weekend$_{DIM}$') is equally regular, but distinct from the aspect of size in *vogeltje*.

We encountered an interesting solution in the case of transposition. We can see the effects most clearly for German cases such as *Installation* in (28).

(28) a. die Installation der Heizungsanlage
 ('the installation of_the heating_system')
 b. die Heizungsanlage installieren
 ('the heating_system install' i.e. install the heating system)
 c. eine veraltete Installation
 ('an obsolete installation')

In (28a), we have a transposition of (28b). For *Installation* in (28a), the structure is as in Figure 5.4, with a v^0-projection inside an n^0-projection. The v^0-head is phonologically empty but it determines the argument structure. In (28b), the same v^0-projection is phonologically realized as -*ier*-. In (28c), a Num-projection is added on top of the n^0-projection. This corresponds to the possibility of pluralizing (28c), which is not possible for (28a), but at the same time removes the possibility of realizing the verbal argument.

In sum, DM sets as its purpose to account for the structure of expressions and its relation to the phonological realization. Naming is not considered a separate topic. For compounds such as *doorman* in section 5.2.5, DM representatives are generally satisfied with the idea that the special aspects of their meaning, which we attribute to onomasiological coercion, are simply specified in the Encyclopedia. Also, in cases in which syntactic generalizations can be made, these generalizations are form-oriented. For *Hartkäse* ('granular cheese'), the incorporation analysis accounts for the absence of inflection on *hart* ('hard'). The fact that any speaker of German knows that an A+N compound of this type must be the name of a concept, not just a description of an object, is treated as something accidental. The same can be observed for paradigms. Several authors state that paradigms are epiphenomena in DM. This is unproblematic for the production of the forms, but it misses a generalization when it comes to naming.

An interesting approach is suggested by Borer (2014). In the context of transposition examples such as (28), she not only proposes the contrast between structures such as Figure 5.4 and Figure 5.5, but also tries to formulate rules for determining domains in the tree that trigger a search in the Encyclopedia. If such an approach could be generalized, we might also be able to account for the fact that A+N compounds in German are names for concepts. Even in this case, however, it is not naming as a process, but names as the result that constitute the basis for the explanation.

CHAPTER 6

Lexical Morphology

The theory of Lexical Morphology and Phonology was developed by Kiparsky (1982, 1983). Lexical Morphology is based on the central idea that morphology is organized in a set of levels as originally proposed by Siegel (1974). Each level represents an interaction between morphological rules and phonological rules. The output of a word formation process at each level is followed by the application of appropriate phonological rules before it moves to another level or to syntax. In later work, Kiparsky (2000, 2005) combined this approach with Prince and Smolensky's (1993) Optimality Theory in Stratal Optimality Theory. Although less unified than Distributed Morphology, its ideas underlie many other morphological studies in generative grammar. In this chapter we will concentrate on the version of the theory presented by Kiparsky (1982, 1983), as well as more recent overviews by Carstairs-McCarthy (1992: 70–79), Štekauer (2000: 311–329) and Katamba and Stonham (2006: 89–151). Section 6.1 gives an overview of the main tenets of the theory of Lexical Morphology and Phonology. In section 6.2, we discuss the distinctions between words and phrases and between inflection and derivation, as well as the treatment of paradigms, transposition and onomasiological coercion. Finally, section 6.3 evaluates the place of naming in this theoretical framework.

6.1 Lexical Morphology as a framework

The theory of Lexical Morphology and Phonology (LMP) was first presented in Kiparsky (1982). Kiparsky himself views his theory as 'a convergence of several originally independent strands of research' (1982: 3). A first source is Aronoff's (1976) word-based theory of morphology and the lexicon. The second source is the idea of level-ordering, first proposed by Siegel (1974) and elaborated by Allen (1978) and others. The third source is Mohanan's (1982) PhD dissertation on Lexical Phonology. The central assumption of lexicalist morphology is that morphology is in the lexicon.

This corresponds to Chomsky's (1970) Lexicalist Hypothesis as explained in section 3.1.3.

Born in Helsinki, Paul Kiparsky completed his PhD supervised by Morris Halle at MIT in 1965. He taught at MIT until moving to Stanford in 1984 (Garrett 2008). His explorations of the relationship between phonology and morphology were at the centre of generative linguistic theory in the 1970s and 1980s. Kiparsky (1982: 3) formulates the three central assumptions of his theory in (1).

(1) a. The derivational and inflectional processes of a language can be organized in a series of levels.
b. Each level is associated with a set of phonological rules for which it defines the domain of application.
c. The ordering of levels [. . .] defines the possible ordering of morphological processes in word formation.

The idea of a hierarchical organization of morphology in levels, as formulated in (1a), is already present in an early form in Pāṇini's ancient work on Sanskrit. It was taken over by Whitney (1879: 371) in his grammar of Sanskrit and by Bloomfield (1933: 237–244), who distinguishes primary and secondary affixation in English. Chomsky and Halle (1968: 364–370) formulate the distinction in terms of + and # boundaries. Siegel (1974) then introduced the term *level-ordering morphology*. She organizes the lexicon in such a way that there are different levels of entries and rules that are connected to each other. This means that each level in the lexicon is linked with a set of morphological rules that form a lexeme or a word form.

In (1b) the set of morphological rules at each level is paired with a corresponding set of phonological rules, which determine how the output is pronounced. The rules of lexical phonology are cyclic. Level 1 rules are available as long as the derivation is at level 1, but as soon as a morphological rule applies that belongs to level 2, a new set of phonological rules can apply instead of level 1 rules.

In (1c), the organizing principle for the division into levels is formulated. The possible ordering of morphological processes determines the order of affixes. At the same time, earlier processes tend to be less formally regular, semantically uniform and general in application than later ones. Kiparsky (1982: 8) illustrates this by the semantic differentiation between *brethren* formed at level 1 and *brothers* formed at level 3.

Kiparsky's model can be seen as word-based, rather than morpheme-based. Katamba and Stonham (2006: 89) link Lexical Morphology and Phonology with the Word-and-Paradigm model and other more traditional approaches.[1] For Kiparsky (1982: 6), affixes do not have lexical entries in the

---

[1] The Word-and-Paradigm model was elaborated for Latin by Matthews (1972). Blevins (2016) gives a historical overview and an updated, more general version.

lexicon and have no lexical features either inherently or by percolation, as opposed to what Lieber (1980) assumes. This means that each affix in LMP is introduced by a general rule following the template (2).

(2) Insert A in env. $[Y\_Z]_X$

In (2), Y and Z together represent the subcategorization frame of A and X is associated with the inherent categorial specification in line with Lieber (1980). For instance, for the Agent noun *influencer* the rule in (3) is presented.

(3) a. Insert *er* in env. $[V\_]_{NOUN,+Agent}$
    b. Insert *er* in env. $[influence\_]_{NOUN,+Agent}$

The morphological rule in (3a) operates at level 2 and derives the noun *influencer* from the verb *influence* in the instantiation (3b). The suffix *-er* is inserted in the context of the corresponding morphological category. The resulting lexical item is put into the categorial frame $[\ ]_X$ where X represents a set of features, namely that it is an Agent noun in (3).

According to Kiparsky, it is sufficient to formulate appropriate verb-particular meaning conditions. Then the meaning of the suffix can be left unrestricted in principle. In this way, it is possible to account for the meaning distinction between cases such as *cook* and *cooker* in (4).

(4) a. Insert ø in env. $[cook\_]_{NOUN,+Agent}$
    b. Insert *er* in env. $[cook\_]_{NOUN,+Instrument/Device}$

In (4a) we derive the Agent noun from the verb *cook* by a rule competing with (3a), which does not insert *-er*. This contrasts with (4b), which derives the Instrument noun by a rule like (3a), but with a different feature in the result. The formation of (4a) takes place at level 1, whereas the derivation of (4b) is at level 2. The frames with the features linked to the stem *cook*, i.e. the properties of the resulting word, differ in (4a) and (4b). The morphological rule at level 1 then obligatorily inserts ø at level 1 and the suffix *-er* at level 2.

The model of LMP by Kiparsky (1982) can be represented as in Figure 6.1. It is divided into two main parts, lexical and post-lexical. The lexical part concerns word formation whereas the post-lexical part is activated when the outputs of the lexical part are used in syntax. Kiparsky presented the model only with reference to English, but there is no principled reason to exclude its use with other languages.

The lexical part in Figure 6.1 lists simplex items labelled as underived lexical entries. Kiparsky (1982) proposes a stratification of English morphology in three levels. Level 1 includes affixation of the type Chomsky and Halle (1968) associate with + boundaries (primary affixes), e.g. *-ity, -ive, -th*, as well as irregular inflection, e.g. irregular plurals such as *feet, women*, or irregular past tense forms such as *kept, drove*. Level 2 covers affixation linked with a

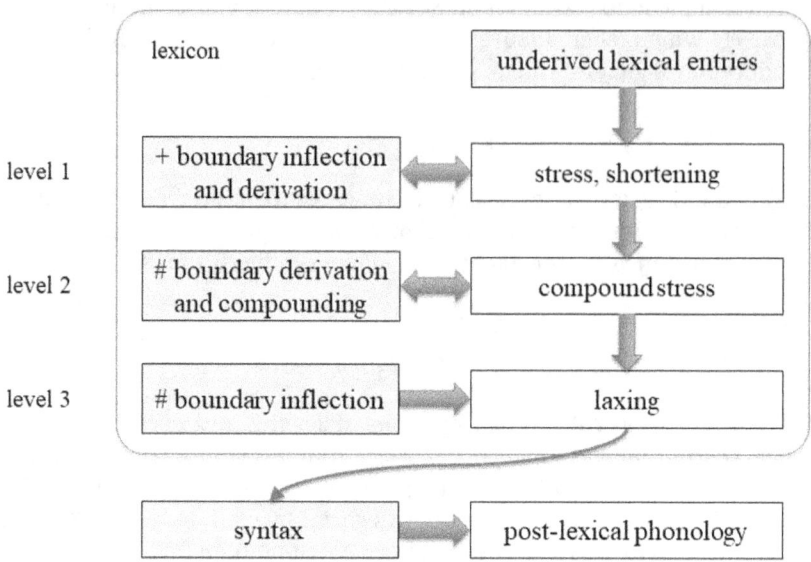

Figure 6.1 *The model of Lexical Morphology and Phonology by Kiparsky (1982)*

boundary (secondary affixes), e.g. -*ness*, -*less*, *un*-, and compounding. Level 3 deals with regular inflection. Whereas Allen (1978) proposes to have compounding at a separate level after level 2, Kiparsky follows Lieber (1980) and takes compounding and affixation to be both at level 2.

In different models of level ordering theories that have been proposed, the number of levels assumed for English ranges from two to four. In Figure 6.1 we see that Kiparsky (1982) recognizes three levels. However, Kiparsky (1983) claims that two levels, level 1 for primary (irregular) morphology and level 2 for secondary (regular) morphology including compounding, are sufficient. Halle and Mohanan (1985) distinguish four levels, placing compounding on level 3 and regular inflection on level 4. This corresponds to Allen's (1978) Extended Ordering Hypothesis. Katamba and Stonham (2006: 139) explain that the difference in the number of levels is a matter of the methodological solution applied. There are two ways to ensure that one rule precedes another. One is to place one rule at an earlier level than the other one, which results in more levels in a model. The other way is to place the two rules at the same level and introduce ordering principles. This leads to fewer levels. Kiparsky (1983: 3–4) proposes the generalizations in (5) for the ordering of levels.

(5) a. [I]n the morpheme order of English words, all primary suffixes must precede all secondary suffixes, and all primary prefixes must follow all secondary prefixes.
b. Internal brackets are erased at the end of every level.

Kiparsky (1983: 3) illustrates (5a) with the examples *Mendelianism, Mongolianism* where the primary suffix *-(i)an* attaches first and triggers a stress shift. The suffix *-ism* is only added afterwards and phonologically it is stress-neutral. Words such as **Mendelismian, *Mongolismian* are then excluded by (5a). The differences between *-(i)an* and *-ism* can be accounted for by placing *-(i)an* at level 1 and *-ism* at level 2 in the model of Figure 6.1. This also means that the boundary symbols + and # are deleted from the phonological representations and the combinatorial restrictions of the affixes are simplified. In (5b), we have the Bracketing Erasure Convention (Pesetsky 1979; Mohanan 1982). Its application ensures that the internal structure of *Mendelian, Mongolian* formed at level 1 is not accessible at level 2 where *-ism* is added.

The Elsewhere Condition is another principle that plays an important role in Kiparsky's model. It was first introduced by Kiparsky (1973) and Kiparsky (1982: 8) gives the slightly modified version in (6).

(6) Rules A, B in the same component apply disjunctively to a form Φ if and only if
   (i) The structural description of A (the special rule) properly includes the structural description of B (the general rule).
   (ii) The result of applying A to Φ is distinct from the result of applying B to Φ.
   In that case, A is applied first, and if it takes effect, then B is not applied.

The formulation of the Elsewhere Condition in (6) is a blocking principle in which a more specific rule, applied at an earlier level, blocks the application of a more general rule at a later level. This is exemplified in (7).

(7) a. feet   *foots
    b. applicant *applier

In (7) we see the outcomes of two competing rules, one of which is ungrammatical in English. In (7a), *feet* is an irregular plural, produced by a more specific rule, which applies at level 1. The alternative regular form, **foots*, cannot be generated, because the Elsewhere Condition in (6) blocks the application of the regular rule at level 3 in Figure 6.1. The suffixation of *-s* is a more general rule than the ablaut. In (7b), we have two competing agent formation rules for the verb *apply*. The suffix *-ant* triggers a stem modification and has to be applied at level 1. It is a more specific rule than the one in (3a), which adds *-er* and applies at level 2. As mentioned by Kiparsky (1982: 6), the more regular and semantically more coherent nature of the processes at later levels coincides with a greater productivity. This is in line with Aronoff's (1976) conclusions.

The organization of morphology into levels was adopted in several other theories of morphology. One of these theories, in which Paul Kiparsky was involved as well, is Stratal Optimality Theory (SOT). In SOT, Kiparsky combines some insights from LMP with Prince and Smolensky's (1993) Optimality Theory. The main source for SOT is a forthcoming book to which we do not have access at the time of writing.[2] Where it is useful in the discussion of the data in section 6.2, we will explain the relevant parts of the theory on the basis of available sources.

6.2 The treatment of relevant contrasts in LMP

In this section, we will go over the data we presented in Chapter 4 and indicate how they can be treated in LMP. The structure of the section follows the structure of Chapter 4.

6.2.1 Words and phrases

The relationship between words and phrases in LMP is determined by the distinction between lexical rules and post-lexical rules as can be seen in Figure 6.1. Kiparsky (1983: 5–6) observes that the rules of lexical phonology apply at a certain level in the lexicon whereas the rules of post-lexical phonology 'apply to sentences after they have been put together from words by the syntax'. Kiparsky (1983: 5–6) lists nine differences between lexical and post-lexical rules. Table 6.1 summarizes selected properties of lexical rules and post-lexical rules.

The properties selected in Table 6.1 are directly linked to the structure of the lexicon. First of all, lexical rules form words in the lexicon whereas post-lexical rules apply only after the words have been formed and are used in the syntax. This means that lexical rules can only apply to words, not to phrases. Phrases are then the domain of application of post-lexical rules. The second property, governing access to the structure, follows from the Bracketing Erasure Convention. Lexical rules are cyclic in the sense that at each level the output of a word formation process undergoes the phonological rules that operate at this level. Post-lexical rules are not cyclic because they apply to the phonological phrase as a whole and only once. There is no similar pairing between syntactic rules and phonological rules as there is between levels of morphological and phonological rules. Lexical rules are structure-preserving, which means that the output of every level must be a well-formed word in line with phonotactic and other constraints in a given language. Post-lexical rules do not have this

---

[2] The book is announced as *Paradigms and Opacity: Volume 1*, by Paul Kiparsky on the website of the University of Chicago Press, https://press.uchicago.edu/ucp/books/book/distributed/P/bo3535536.html (22 November 2022).

Lexical Morphology

Table 6.1 *Selected differences between lexical rules and post-lexical rules*

Lexical rules	Post-lexical rules
Word-bounded	Not word-bounded
Access to word-internal structure assigned at same level	Access to phrase structure only
Precede all post-lexical rules	Follow all lexical rules
Cyclic	Apply once
Structure-preserving	Not structure-preserving
May have exceptions	Automatic

constraint. Finally, a post-lexical rule applies automatically in the sense that whenever the conditions are met, the rule takes effect. This also means that there are no specific contexts in which the application may be blocked. This contrasts with lexical rules, which may have lexically specified exceptions; for instance, the formation of *length, depth* is allowed, but not *narrowth.

Although LMP was designed mainly with reference to English, in principle it can apply to any language. The German examples in (8), presented in section 4.1, illustrate the contrast between words and phrases.

(8) a. Hartkäse ('granular cheese')
    b. harter Käse ('hard cheese')

In (8) we have two expressions with the same basic components, but (8a) is a compound and (8b) a phrase. In German, this contrast is directly expressed in the form, because the adjective bears the main stress in (8a) and is inflected in (8b). Semantically, (8a) designates a type of cheese and (8b) describes a cheese. In LMP, (8a) is formed at level 2 where the word formation process of compounding is placed. The descriptive construction in (8b) can only be produced by rules of syntax, which in LMP constitute a component distinct from the lexicon.

Kiparsky (1982: 30) treats A+N compounds such as *whitefish, blackbird* and *greenhouse* as conventional designations of a hyponym of the noun, without a direct compositional relationship to the adjective. This means that *whitefish* refers to a kind of fish but not to 'a fish that is white'. Similarly, the meaning of the German A+N compound in (8a) is not assigned a compositional interpretation as it is not a 'cheese that is hard' but rather 'granular cheese'. Kiparsky proposes to continue using *A+N compound* as a purely terminological label. The A+N compound in (8a) is like an idiom, which can be accounted for by listing. The contrast between (8a) and (8b) reflects the distinction between lexical rules and post-lexical rules.

It is interesting to compare the contrast in (8) with the Slovak A+N examples repeated here as (9).

(9) a. čajová lyžička ('teaspoon')
    b. čistá lyžička ('clean spoon')

In both examples in (9), the noun *lyžička* ('spoon') is modified by an adjective that agrees with it in number, gender and case. In (9a), the noun is modified by the relational adjective *čajový* ('tea$_{ADJ}$'). Semantically, the relational adjective has a meaning corresponding to the meaning of a modifying noun in a compound. In LMP, (9a) results from the application of lexical rules at level 2. In (9b), the noun *lyžička* ('spoon') is modified by the qualitative adjective *čistý* ('clean$_{ADJ}$'). The meaning of (9b) assigns a property to the noun. Therefore, in LMP, the formation of (9b) is the output of post-lexical rules. Thus, although *čajová* in (9a) is inflected, it can be treated in the same way as *Hart* in (8a), because semantically the two adjectives are used in a similar way.

As a third example of a contrast between words and phrases, we discuss the Saxon genitive in English. In section 4.1, we presented the examples repeated here as (10).

(10) a. She points to a bird's nest in a low branch.
     b. The mother cuckoo lays its egg in another bird's nest.

In (10a) *bird's nest* designates a concept whereas in (10b) it is not a constituent. In LMP, we might assume an analysis similar to (8) and (9), with a distinction between lexical and post-lexical rules correlating with the meaning. However, the position of the Saxon genitive in English is somewhat problematic in LMP. In Figure 6.1 we saw that + boundary inflection is placed at level 1 whereas # boundary inflection is at level 3. The question is which category *'s* belongs to. In principle, Kiparsky separates irregular inflection with + from regular inflection with #. The former applies before and the latter after all derivation and compounding. This makes it difficult to account for other compounds like (10a), e.g. *driver's licence, women's shoes*, as described by Rosenbach (2002: 9–10). In such cases, attaching *'s* must take place before the formation of the compound, but with compounding at level 2 and *'s* as regular inflection at level 3, this is not allowed by the model in Figure 6.1.

Kiparsky (1982) does not give an explicit treatment of the Saxon genitive. However, his separation of regular and irregular inflection between two different levels solves some problems shown in (11).

(11) a. lice-infested   *rats-infested
     b. almsgiving   *almgiving
     c. excess profits tax *excess profit tax

In (11a) an irregular plural can occur inside a compound because it is formed at level 1 whereas compounding is at level 2. At the same time, this level-ordering rule excludes the formation of unattested forms with a regular plural.[3] A different contrast is in (11b). Here, Kiparsky (1982: 9) claims that *pluralia tantum* nouns are inherently marked [+PLURAL] in the lexicon. The Elsewhere Condition then blocks the application of a general plural rule to inherently plural nouns. The example in (11c) is treated as a systematic occurrence of plural inside compounding. Kiparsky (1982: 10) analyses (11c) as a phrase involved in compounds and he assumes 'some limited recursion from phrase-level syntax back to morphology'.

For the Saxon genitive as exemplified in (10), Carstairs (1987) proposes that it is a phrasally attached clitic. This follows an idea originally formulated by Jespersen (1934). In fact, in (10b), *another bird* is a noun phrase. However, in (10a), we have a different use of the same element, because it is not *a bird*, but only *bird* that serves as the anchor for *'s*. This means that in (10a), *bird's* should be formed at level 1, whereas in (10b), *another bird's* is syntactic. It should be mentioned, however, that there is no phonological reason why *bird's* in (10a) should be formed at level 1.

The last contrast to be discussed in this section involves the N+N combinations in (12).

(12) a. a commuter suburb of Charleston
     b. the Chicago suburb of Cicero

Commuter suburb in (12a) indicates a concept of a suburb where people live who typically commute to their work. This contrasts with (12b) where *Chicago suburb* merely specifies the location. Kiparsky (1982) refers to Downing (1977) who actually discusses this contrast. She uses the term *deictic compounds* for concepts that are used in conversation to refer to a temporary circumstance. As an example, *apple-juice seat* can refer to the seat in front of which there is a glass of apple juice. Lexicalization of such compounds is less probable because their formation is based on temporary needs. Therefore, it is reasonable to assume that *commuter suburb* in (12a) is formed at level 2, but *Chicago suburb* in (12b) in syntax.

6.2.2 Lexemes and word forms

In Kiparsky's (1982) LMP model, as represented in Figure 6.1, both inflection and derivation are covered. Derivation is divided between levels 1 and 2 and inflection between levels 1 and 3. At level 1, + boundary processes take place and at levels 2 and 3, # boundary processes. This means that only regular inflection is found at level 3.

In section 4.2, we introduced the formation of the nominal plural in Dutch, illustrated by the two examples repeated in (13) for convenience.

---

[3] However, Selkirk (1982: 52–53) discusses examples such as *parks commissioner*, where the plural is not only included but also semantically active in the sense that a *parks commissioner* is responsible for several parks.

(13) a. vogel ('bird') → vogels ('birds')
b. huis ('house') → huizen ('houses')

The examples in (13) display the two main plural markers of Dutch nouns. In (13a), the plural is formed by the ending -s and in (13b), the noun is pluralized by the alternative ending -en. The selection of the suffix is governed largely phonologically, on the basis of the prosodic contour of the stem. Based on Kiparsky's (1982: 6) discussion of the English plural, we can assume that the rules for the plural forms *vogels* ('birds') and *huizen* ('houses') are as given in (14).

(14) a. Insert *s* in env. [N__]$_{\text{NOUN.+Plural}}$
b. Insert *en* in env. [N__]$_{\text{NOUN.+Plural}}$

The rules in (14) operate at level 3 and form the plural of the noun *vogel* with (14a) and *huis* with (14b). In the case of *huizen*, the voiced final consonant in the stem is the underlying form, which is devoiced in the singular. For the correct assignment of the plural ending, it is necessary that *vogel* undergoes the rule (14a) but it is not subject to (14b), which is in turn the only rule governing the plural formation of *huis*. To the extent that this can be formulated in terms of phonological properties of the base, this can be stated as additional constraints on the application of the rule.

The distinction between level 1 on one hand and levels 2 and 3 on the other is determined by the nature of the boundary separating the morphemes. Level 1 works with + boundaries and levels 2 and 3 with # boundaries. Both inflection and derivation can involve + boundaries. This is primarily a phonological property. For # boundaries, derivation is at level 2 and inflection at level 3. The distinction between these two levels is presupposed. This point is prominent when we consider the diminutive in Dutch and in Slovak.

For the Dutch diminutive, two examples we presented in section 4.2 are *vogeltje* ('bird$_{\text{DIM}}$') and *stokje* ('stick$_{\text{DIM}}$'). Depending on the base form assumed for the suffix, either of the rules in (15) can be used.

(15) a. Insert *tje* in env. [N__]$_{\text{NOUN.+Diminutive}}$
b. Insert *je* in env. [N__]$_{\text{NOUN.+Diminutive}}$

If we assume that -*tje* is the base form both in *vogeltje* and in *stokje*, we can use (15a) in both cases, but we have to explain how the suffix become -*je* in the latter case. An alternative would be to have both rules in (15), with phonological conditions attached to them to ensure that *vogel* is assigned to (15a) and *stok* to (15b). Dutch diminutives are at level 2 as the attachment of the diminutive suffix does not affect stress or changes in the phonology of the base. The question why (15) operates at level 2 and (14) at level 3, i.e. the distinction between derivation and inflection, is not answered within the theory.

Lexical Morphology

Table 6.2 *Examples of Slovak diminutives*

Base form	Diminutive	Base form	Diminutive
vankúš ('pillow')	vankúšik	vlak ('train')	vláčik
strom ('tree')	stromček	prst ('finger')	prštek
káva ('coffee')	kávička	stuha ('ribbon')	stužka
kladivo ('hammer')	kladivko	brucho ('belly')	bruško

What the rules in (15) do not cover either is the specialized meaning of *stokje*. As noted in section 4.2, it can refer not only to a small stick, but also to salty sticks as a snack. Semantic peculiarities of this type can hardly be captured by morphological rules such as (15). LMP explains how words are formed, but cannot always account for semantic aspects of words, especially in the case of semantic specialization. Such cases are assigned to lexicalization. The fact that such lexicalized items are formed is not in the scope of the theory.

The position of diminutives in Slovak in LMP is somewhat different from their Dutch counterparts. Some examples illustrating the complications of the formation of diminutives in Slovak are presented in Table 6.2.

In Table 6.2 we can see a set of examples of Slovak diminutives derived by different suffixes and variants. The examples on the left have the base unchanged in the derived form. The suffixes are *-ik, -ček, -ička, -ko*.[4] The examples on the right display a number of morphophonological changes, consonantal alternations k/č, st/šť,[5] h/ž, ch/š and the vowel change a/á. For a more detailed account of morphonological changes triggered by diminutive suffixes in Slovak, see Gregová (2015). Because of the morphophonological changes, in LMP at least some Slovak diminutives should be formed at level 1. A decision whether all diminutives result from derivation at level 1 or some are formed at level 2 would require a more elaborate analysis. This does not mean that diminutives are not regular. Katamba and Stonham (2006: 100) emphasize that 'it is vital not to equate "root-changing" or "non-neutral" with "irregular"'. They mention the irregular formation of the plural in *ox-oxen*, which does not apply to phonologically similar nouns **fox-foxen* or **box-boxen*. Compared with the English plural, however, Slovak diminutives have a much more systematic alternation. They are root-changing but not irregular.

In sum, it is not problematic to formulate rules for the plural and the diminutive in Dutch and in Slovak in LMP. The distinction between the levels is primarily phonologically determined as far as level 1 is concerned, but for the distinction between levels 2 and 3, which is the

---

[4] The final vowels in *-ička* and *-ko* are markers of the declension and gender class. As such, they are part of the suffix in a word formation analysis. In a morphological analysis, they can be separated from the suffixes as markers of the nominative singular.
[5] In Slovak spelling, the palatalized ť is written t when it is followed by e.

distinction between derivation and inflection, LMP does not give a systematic solution.

6.2.3 Paradigms

Kiparsky (1982, 1983) does not mention paradigms. The concept is brought up in later work in the context of Stratal Optimality Theory (SOT). This model is inspired on one hand by LMP, on the other by Optimality Theory (OT).

OT was first proposed by Prince and Smolensky (1993).[6] OT is a formalism for evaluating ranked constraints in the mapping from an underlying input form to the output produced. Constraints fall into two major classes, faithfulness constraints and markedness constraints. Faithfulness means that the output corresponds closely to the input. Markedness constraints imply that more marked forms of output are dispreferred. OT was proposed first of all for phonology, but was also applied to morphology and syntax from an early date (cf. Archangeli and Langendoen 1997).

A problem in the use of OT is the phenomenon of opacity. Opacity occurs when the context that triggers a phonological change is not visible in the surface form, because it has been changed by a rule applying later. In LMP, opacity can be dealt with by exploiting the different levels. In SOT, proposed by Bermúdez-Otero (1999) and Kiparsky (2000), levels are used to differentiate the ordering of constraints.

SOT is first of all a theory of sound structure. Katamba and Stonham (2006: 216–217) demonstrate the usefulness of SOT in the discussion of (de-)gemination of consonants in examples such as the ones given in (16).

(16) a. innocuous [ɪˈnɒkjuəs]
     b. unknown   [ˈʌnnəʊn]

In both examples in (16), we have a prefix ending in [n] and a base starting with [n], but in (16a), there is no gemination whereas in (16b) there is. This difference corresponds to the difference that *in-* is a level 1 prefix and *un-* a level 2 prefix. In OT, the evaluation of constraints is represented in tableaux. An example of a tableau for (16a) is Table 6.3.

In Table 6.3, the first column lists the possible outputs, one with and one without gemination. The other columns represent constraints with the higher ranked constraints more to the left. DEP-IO and MAX-IO are faithfulness constraints. DEP-IO prohibits the insertion of segments and MAX-IO the deletion of segments in the output. The first constraint is a markedness constraint which prohibits gemination. In OT all constraints are interpreted as

---

[6] First circulated in April 1993, this text is now available in its ROA version of August 2002, to which we will refer.

Lexical Morphology

Table 6.3 *The analysis of* innocuous *in SOT*

innocuous	*CC	DEP-IO	MAX-IO
☞ ɪˈnɒkjuəs			*
ɪˈnnɒkjuəs	*!		

preferences and the optimal output is the one that violates the minimum of high-ranked constraints. Conventionally, ☞ is used to indicate the optimal output variant. The geminated variant violates *CC. Violations are marked by *. If the violation is fatal, it gets a ! The non-geminated variant does not violate *CC. It only violates MAX-IO, because one of the [n] is lost. However, as MAX-IO is ranked lower than *CC, the variant in (16a) still is the optimal one. The shaded cells do not play a role in the evaluation.

Although OT can explain (16a), it would predict that in *unknown*, the gemination would also be undone. Here the strata of LMP are invoked. Katamba and Stonham (2006: 217) give the tableaux presented here in Table 6.4. At level 1, we do not have the prefix *un-*, because it only appears at level 2. We do have irregular inflection, e.g. *known*, at this level. Which forms are output candidates is to some extent arbitrary, as long as the best one is among them. Therefore, it does not harm to have the output of (16b) here, as it will always lose against the more faithful output candidate. At level 2 the constraints are reranked. Faithfulness is now more important than the prohibition of gemination. This means that the degeminated form, which violates faithfulness, violates a higher-ranked constraint than the geminated form. Therefore, (16b) is selected as the optimal output.

It is in this context that Kiparsky (2005: 115) introduces the notion of *paradigm*, making the statement in (17).

(17) Paradigms emerge through blocking from the competition between expressions. We can say that a morphological feature F is intrinsically PARADIGMATIC if there is a morpheme which is specified only for F (a 'default' morpheme), and that a paradigm is COMPLETE if there is a default morpheme for every feature.

The reference to blocking in (17) highlights the idea of a paradigm as a set of output candidates in tableaux such as Table 6.3. In this sense, a morpheme can be seen as a paradigm of competing allomorphs. Kiparsky (2005: 115) calls a morpheme a 'micro-paradigm'. Blocking as referred to in (17) is the result of constraints applied in a tableau. It results from two constraints, *economy* and *expressiveness*. Economy is a markedness constraint, excluding needlessly complex forms, and expressiveness corresponds to MAX-IO in Table 6.3.

As an example, Kiparsky (2005) discusses the formation of the comparative of *bad*. The paradigm of forms he considers is (18).

Table 6.4 *The analysis of* unknown *in SOT*

Level 1			
known	*CC	DEP-IO	MAX-IO
☞ nəʊn			
ʌnəʊn		**!	
ʌnnəʊn	*!	**	
Level 2			
ʌn - nəʊn	DEP-IO	MAX-IO	*CC
nəʊn		**!	
ʌnəʊn		*!	
☞ ʌnnəʊn			*

(18) a. worse
      b. badder
      c. more bad
      d. bad

The forms (18a) and (18d) are listed in the lexicon, (18b) is generated in morphology and (18c) in syntax. The competition between (18b) and (18c) is resolved by economy, because (18b) is one word and (18c) two. The competition between (18a) and (18d) is decided by expressiveness, because the feature comparative is not expressed in (18d). Kiparsky (2005) does not compare (18a) and (18b), but we can assume that this competition is also resolved by economy, because (18a) has only one morpheme. That (18b) can be used as the comparative of *bad* in the sense 'tough, mean' is then explained by the fact that (18a) does not have this meaning specified in the lexicon. Therefore, (18a) does not block (18b) in this sense.

With this background, we can now turn to the paradigm of Slovak *gitara* we presented in section 4.3. This paradigm, giving the different forms for case and number values of the same noun, is of a very different nature to the one in (18). Each combination of case and number values has a specified form assigned to it. It also contrasts with the notions of *paradigmatic* and *complete* as used in (17). In agglutinative languages such as Turkish, case and number features are expressed by separate morphemes, as illustrated in Table 6.5, giving the inflectional paradigm for *el* ('hand').

The Turkish accusative plural *elleri* in Table 6.5 consists of the stem *el*, the suffix *-ler* for the plural and the suffix *-i* for the accusative. These suffixes have a consistent meaning throughout the paradigm, as shown by forms such as *eli* and *eller*. Although there are different realizations of these suffixes for other stems, Lewis (1967: 28–34) explains all of these as phonologically conditioned adaptations. The selection of the variants is largely determined by rules of vowel harmony. Therefore, case and number endings in Turkish fulfil the conditions of paradigmaticity and completeness in (17).

Table 6.5 *Paradigm of the Turkish noun el ('hand'), from Lewis (1967: 29)*

	Singular	Plural
Absolutive	el	eller
Accusative	eli	elleri
Genitive	elin	ellerin
Dative	ele	ellere
Locative	elde	ellerde
Ablative	elden	ellerden

In Slovak, the situation is different. The accusative plural *gitary* can be decomposed into the stem *gitar-* and the suffix *-y*, but *-y* expresses both accusative and plural. Moreover, *-y* is also used for the nominative plural and the genitive singular. Finally, for other nouns, other endings are used. Thus, *ulica* ('street') and *hrdina* ('hero') have the accusative plural forms *ulice* and *hrdinov*. This means that the Slovak nominal paradigm is not paradigmatic and complete in the sense of (17).

The discussion of (17) and (18) shows that in SOT, paradigms are interpreted in a rather different way than we presented the notion in section 4.3. For us, inflectional paradigms are first of all united as a single naming unit. Once the name *gitara* has been assigned to a concept, the inflected forms follow without a further naming act. Derivational paradigms such as (19) extend this idea beyond inflection.

(19) a. blog ('blog$_N$')
    b. blogovať ('blog$_V$')
    c. blogový ('blog$_A$')

Whereas (19a) is the result of naming, (19b) and (19c) are determined by (19a) in a way similar to how the inflected forms of *gitara* follow from the citation form. This notion of *paradigm* has no direct link to competition. It is not covered by Kiparsky's (2005) treatment of what he calls *paradigms*.

6.2.4 Naming and transposition

Kiparsky (1982, 1983) does not explicitly discuss transposition. The relationship between examples such as *explore* and *exploration* can be accounted for in LMP by a level 1 rule. The verb *explore* enters level 1 as an underived item and the non-neutral suffix *-ation* attaches at level 1. That it is a level 1 suffix can be seen in that it causes a stress shift from the second syllable to the penultimate one. The contrast between transposition and word formation as a naming process is more difficult to capture in LMP. In section 4.4, we used the examples repeated in (20) to illustrate this contrast.

(20) a. the installation in their territory of foreign military bases
b. [they] were taken to a Salvadorean military installation

The noun *installation* in (20a) refers to the process of installing whereas in (20b) it refers to the result of this process. In LMP, the noun as used in both (20a) and (20b) must be formed at level 1. The question is how to account for the difference in specific meanings and the relation between them. Kiparsky (1983: 11–12) discusses verbs derived from nouns referring to instruments, e.g. *to hammer, to brush, to paddle*. He demonstrates that their meaning does not necessarily imply the use of the specific instrument denoted by the base noun as in (21).

(21) a. He brushed his coat with his hand.
b. I paddled the canoe with a copy of the New York Times.

In (21a) we can see that a brush is not necessary as the instrument for brushing a coat. Similarly, in (21b) a copy of the *New York Times* can function as an instrument used for paddling. Kiparsky (1983: 12) analyses the denominal verbs in (21) as derived at level 1. He understands the loss of specificity of meaning of the verbs in (21), so that the instrument can be something else than an instance of the underlying noun, as a clear sign of their lexicalization. This means that these N/V pairs must be listed. For the relationship between (20a) and (20b), it seems that an analogical analysis can be applied. The result meaning in (20b) is based on the process meaning in (20a) in the same way as the compositional meaning of the verbs *brush* and *paddle* underlies the more general meaning in (21). The only way to encode this difference is to list both meanings.

6.2.5 Onomasiological coercion

In section 4.5, we discussed *doorman* and its equivalents in German, Dutch and Slovak, repeated in (22), as an example of onomasiological coercion.

(22) a. Türsteher ('door_stander') DE
b. uitsmijter ('out_thrower') NL
c. vyhadzovač ('throw_out-er') SK

Based on the dictionary definition in COBUILD (2023), we demonstrated in section 4.5 that the four languages selected different elements for the lexicalization. English and German use the location whereas Dutch and Slovak the function of the person. In LMP the formation of all examples in (22) takes place at level 2. However, the lexicalized aspects of the meanings must be listed. Although LMP is useful in explaining how the words are formed, the correspondence between the form selected in order to name a particular

Lexical Morphology 105

concept and the meaning of the selected form, designating the concept that is being named, is not covered in the theory.

6.3 Word formation and naming in LMP

In contrast to Distributed Morphology as discussed in Chapter 5, LMP places word formation in the lexicon. The model makes a clear distinction between the two components, lexicon and syntax. As affixes do not have entries in the lexicon, they must be part of a rule. Therefore, the word rather than the morpheme is the key unit in LMP. The lexicon is organized in levels and the ordering of morphological processes guides the order of affixes in a word form. For Kiparsky (1982), morphological processes at level 1 tend to be more irregular, both formally and semantically, than the processes at later levels.

The distinction between the lexical component and the syntactic component gives us a tool to distinguish the naming expressions in (23) from the syntactic structures in (24).

(23) a. Hartkäse ('granular cheese')
b. čajová lyžička ('teaspoon')
c. (a) bird's nest (in a low branch)
d. commuter suburb

(24) a. harter Käse ('hard cheese')
b. čistá lyžička ('clean spoon')
c. (lays its eggs in another) bird's nest
d. Chicago suburb

Kiparsky's (1982) LMP model makes it possible to treat the examples in (23) as expressions formed at level 2 in Figure 6.1. The expressions in (24) can be treated as syntactic phrases. A more detailed discussion of the individual examples is found in section 6.2.1. Although Kiparsky himself applies LMP only to English, his model can account equally for other languages such as German and Slovak in (23a–b) and (24a–b). The formation of the examples in (23) occurs in the lexicon and the result is characterized by having a naming function. The formation of the expressions in (24) is post-lexical and they do not have a naming function.

The distinction between inflection and derivation is covered in the LMP model as given in Figure 6.1. Derivational and inflectional processes with a + boundary take place at level 1, derivational # boundary processes are placed at level 2. Finally, inflectional # boundary processes occur at level 3. The distinction between level 2 and level 3 is actually the distinction between inflection and derivation. As such, this distinction is formally represented in LMP. The success of this representation is only partial, because level 1 includes examples of both and does not distinguish them. Another problem is that the distinction between levels 2 and 3 is understood as given or preset. In (25), we repeat the rules for the Dutch plural and diminutive of the noun *vogel* ('bird').

(25) a. Insert *s* in env. [N__]$_{\text{NOUN.+Plural}}$
 b. Insert *tje* in env. [N__]$_{\text{NOUN.+Diminutive}}$

The rule in (25a) produces *vogels* ('birds'), the one in (25b) *vogeltje* ('bird$_{\text{DIM}}$'). In LMP, regular plural formation as in (25a) occurs at level 3, whereas the diminutive formation as in (25b) is placed at level 2. Kiparsky's LMP model does not give any reason or criterion on what basis (25a) should be at level 3 and (25b) at level 2.

In the discussion of paradigms in section 6.2.3, we discovered that LMP has a different interpretation to the one we adopted in section 4.3. In Kiparsky (2005), paradigms are understood as emerging from the competition of expressions. Two constraints apply, economy and expressiveness. A comparison of the inflectional paradigm of the Turkish noun *el* ('hand') and the Slovak noun *gitara* in 6.2.3 revealed that the former meets the conditions of paradigmaticity and completeness whereas the latter does not. The notion of derivational paradigm as presented in (19) for Slovak *blog* falls outside of the scope of Kiparsky's treatment of paradigms due to the absence of a direct link to competition.

Transposition is not mentioned by Kiparsky (1982, 1983) and the contrast between process and result readings of the noun *installation* discussed in section 6.2.4 can only be encoded by listing both of them. This also means that there is no mechanism to distinguish transposition from word formation as a naming process.

For onomasiological coercion, we discussed *doorman* and its counterparts in some other languages in section 6.2.5. LMP gives a solution for the formation of all of these at level 2. Differences in lexicalized meanings must be listed. This means that LMP does not always cover the naming aspect.

In sum, naming is treated in LMP in most cases by listing the form with the specialized meaning. There is a limited scope for identifying expressions used for naming from other expressions by the distinction between the lexicon and syntax, but the lexicon also contains forms that are not used for naming. This indicates that naming is not a major concern in the design of the model.

CHAPTER 7

The Lexical Semantic Framework

The Lexical Semantic Framework (LSF) is a framework presented originally by Lieber (2004). It was further developed by Lieber (2009, 2016a). Because of its strong link to the author, it is a much more homogeneous framework than the ones we discussed in Chapters 5 and 6. A concise overview is provided by Andreou (2020). Here we will briefly introduce the main assumptions adopted in LSF in section 7.1 and consider how the data presented in Chapter 4 can be accounted for in section 7.2. Section 7.3 summarizes which aspects of the data the theory covers, which theoretical mechanisms it uses, and how successful it is in its coverage.

7.1 LSF as a framework

Lieber (2004) is a monograph devoted to a number of specific research questions. When it was published, Rochelle Lieber was already a recognized morphologist with a number of influential publications, but the 2004 monograph presented a break from her earlier work. Thus, in her overview of the treatment of compounding, Lieber (2016b) refers only to one of her publications from before 2004 and this only to correct a claim she made there.[1] An example of an idea taken over from Lieber (1992) is her analysis of conversion as relisting (2004: 90).

Lieber (2004) does not set out to develop a new theoretical framework. In fact, the name *Lexical Semantic Framework* and its abbreviation are introduced only by Lieber (2016a: 5). Instead, Lieber (2004: 2) starts with a number of research questions that can be formulated as in (1).[2]

---

[1] The publication in question is Lieber (1983). Lieber (2016b: 43) includes it in a list of sources that contain a generalization which is contradicted by corpus data.
[2] The formulations in (1) are our own. They are more concise than Lieber's (2004: 2) and specify elements that emerge from her later discussion. Andreou (2020: 1017) gives a different reformulation.

(1) a. Polysemy: why do derivational affixes often have several different meanings?
b. Multiple-affix: why are there often several derivational affixes for expressing the same meaning?
c. Zero-derivation: how should change of meaning without corresponding change of form be analysed?
d. Semantic mismatch: why is there in a particular word not always a single meaning element corresponding to a single morpheme?

The four research questions in (1) have a rather precise focus. They are all concerned with derivation and they all address the correspondence between semantic and formal aspects of derived words. Whereas (1a) and (1b) constitute converse paradigmatic perspectives on the mapping between form and meaning, (1c) and (1d) address syntagmatic problems in this mapping. As such, they constitute a systematic way to investigate possible mismatches in the correspondence between form and meaning.

From the selection of questions and Lieber's treatment of them, a number of assumptions about the structure of the grammatical system and the nature of linguistic units can be deduced. We summarize them in (2).

(2) *Basic assumption in LSF*
a. Word formation takes place in the lexicon.
b. Lexical entries describe morphemes.
c. Morphemes have a form and a meaning.

In (2a), we see the Lexicalist Hypothesis as proposed by Chomsky (1970). Lieber proposes a theory of the lexicon. When she proposes mechanisms that are only operative in the lexicon, she presupposes that the lexicon and phrasal syntax are distinct. From the reference to affixes as having a meaning in (1a–b), we can infer the assumption in (2b). The problematic nature of the observations underlying (1c–d) only arises when (2c) is assumed. In terms of Hockett's (1954) distinction between Item-and-Arrangement (IA) and Item-and-Process (IP) models of morphology, Lieber adopts an IA model in which the items correspond to Saussurean signs in the sense that they consist of a form and a meaning.[3]

The theory Lieber (2004) proposes consists of a representation of the meaning of lexical entries and a mechanism for their combination in complex words. Concise presentations of the formalism are given by Lieber (2009: 79–87; 2016a: 94–100) and Andreou (2020: 1017–1023).

---

[3] Saussure (1916) does not propose signs corresponding to morphemes, but the binary nature of the sign as he assumes it also makes cases where units of meaning do not correspond to units of form problematic.

The semantic representation of a lexical entry consists of a skeleton and a body. The skeleton uses a number of semantic features, selected from a universal list. Lieber (2009: 85) gives a list of eighteen such features. The selection of features from this set that make up the skeletons is language-specific and reflects the syntactic role of these features. Lieber (2016a: 98) adds two features to the list and makes the point that the list is determined by what various languages need in syntax. For English, Lieber (2009: 80) gives a list of seven features that determine the skeleton: [material], [dynamic], [IEPS], [Loc], [B], [CI], [scalar].[4] Lieber (2016a: 95) adds [animate]. The features that a language does not select for the skeleton can be used to characterize the systematic part of the body. Other aspects of the meaning constitute the encyclopedic elements of the meaning. Thus, for *author*, Lieber (2009: 87) gives [+material] as a feature of the skeleton, ⟨+human⟩ as a systematic feature of the body, and {writes for publication} as an encyclopedic element of the body.

The skeleton is formalized as a predicate-argument structure. The predicate is characterized by means of features. Lieber uses features both in a privative sense and with binary values. This means that for a predicate, there are three possibilities for [material]: [+material], [–material] and the absence of the feature. The number of arguments for a predicate does not depend on the features it has. This is illustrated by the examples from Lieber (2009: 81) in (3).

(3) a. chef   [+material, dynamic ([ ])]
    b. author   [+material, dynamic ([ ], [ ])]

The single argument in (3a) refers to the entity classified as *chef*. In (3b), a second argument is added, because one cannot be an author without being the author of something. The use of [dynamic] in (3) indicates what Lieber (2009: 81) describes as that 'they are processual in nature'. The fact that [dynamic] is not specified as [+dynamic] or [–dynamic] suggests that features actually introduce four possibilities, with the fourth being the lack of specification.

Lieber uses the features [material], [dynamic] and [scalar] to characterize the syntactic categories of nouns, verbs and adjectives. For [material] she states that '[t]he presence of this feature defines the conceptual category of SUBSTANCES/THINGS/ESSENCES, the notional correspondent of the syntactic category Noun' (2009: 80). Furthermore, '[t]he presence of the feature [dynamic] without [material] defines the class of SITUATIONS, the notional equivalent of both verbs and adjectives' and 'adjectives are differentiated from verbs by the presence of the feature [scalar]' (2009: 81).

---

[4] The abbreviation IEPS stands for 'Inferable Eventual Position or State', Loc for 'Location', B for 'Bounded', and CI for 'Composed of Individuals'.

The structure of a skeleton and a body is used for all lexical entries. Affixes have a regular lexical entry which specifies their skeleton (Lieber 2004: 36). Although for many affixes the skeleton may be the only part of the meaning that is specified, prepositional affixes such as *over* also have a body (Lieber 2004: 128).

Complex words arise by the combination of lexical entries. In derivation the combination is implemented as the addition of the affixal skeleton as an outer layer to the skeleton of the base (Lieber 2004: 36). This means that the affix selects the base rather than the reverse. In compounding, the two components are concatenated. Coindexation then links arguments of the two components. An example of derivation is given in (4), based on Lieber (2004: 68).

(4) a. *write*   [+dynamic ([ ], [ ])]
    b. *-er*   [+material, dynamic ([ ], ⟨base⟩)]
    c. *writer* [+material, dynamic ([$_i$], [+dynamic ([$_i$], [ ])])]

The semantic specification for the base *write* in (4a) characterizes it as a verb with two arguments. The entry for *-er* in (4b) specifies that it produces nouns of a processual nature and has two arguments. In its syntactic specification, it must be stated which categories of base it attaches to. In the semantic specification of *writer*, the base in (4a) is inserted in the position reserved for the base in (4b). In order to interpret the result, the first argument of the affix must be coindexed with the first argument of the base, as indicated in (4c). This makes *writer* an agent noun. The selection of arguments to be coindexed is governed by the Principle of Coindexation (Lieber 2004: 61).

Characteristic of LSF is the focus on the internal structure of lexical meaning. In at least two respects, however, Lieber's approach subordinates this structure to phonology and syntax. On one hand, she assumes that the basic elements are morphemes consisting of a non-null phonological and semantic representation. This restricts the degree of semantic analysis, because smaller units are not possible. Thus, it is not possible to separate the potentiality and the passive in the English suffix *-able*, because the suffix cannot be meaningfully divided. It is reflected in Lieber's analysis of conversion. On the other hand, Lieber takes syntactic categories as being encoded in the semantic representation. We will postpone a more detailed discussion of this point to section 7.2.4.

A final point we want to mention here concerns the use of corpus data. This is not inherent in LSF, but it is prominent in Lieber's (2016a) study of nominalization. Corpora can provide important data for linguistic research, but as is well known, they have limitations that have to be taken into account. Three types of limitation are listed in (5).

(5) a. When an expression appears in the corpus, it may be an error.
    b. When an expression does not appear in the corpus, it may be an accident.
    c. The interpretation of expressions is not included in the corpus.

The problems in (5a) and (5b) were recognized by Chomsky in his early work and led to the distinction between competence and performance. They were also discussed in Post-Bloomfieldian linguistics.[5] The problem in (5c) was excluded from consideration in Post-Bloomfieldian linguistics, because it required reference to the interpreting mind, but it is closely related to Chomsky's (1957) levels of adequacy. Without taking into account the meaning of expressions, it is not possible to reach beyond observational adequacy.

Lieber (2016a) proposes her use of corpus data as a contribution to the linguistic debate, because they falsify claims. A careful formulation of this idea is (6).

(6) [I]ntuitions about the forms and possible readings of complex nouns are often surprisingly unreliable: morphological and syntactic configurations that theorists, on the basis of intuitions, have deemed unacceptable often turn out to be easy to find and quite unproblematic in ordinary contexts. (Lieber 2016a: 7)

Crucial about (6) is that it does not oppose intuitions to corpus data, but proposes to use corpus data to enhance intuition.[6] By adding 'quite unproblematic', Lieber excludes (5a). It is not just the occurrence in a corpus, but its subsequent acceptance (on the basis of an intuitive judgement) that may override an initial intuitive judgement. In other places, Lieber's description is more problematic, e.g. (7).

(7) I concentrate here on claims of unacceptability of some pattern or reading. In such cases, it is clear how the claim in question can be falsified – we have only to find attested examples in the corpus. (Lieber 2016a: 155)

If taken at face value, (7) is simply wrong. Thus, COCA (2008–2020) contains 35 occurrences of *langauge* and 6 of *inforamtion*, but this does not make them expressions of English. Finding an expression in the corpus cannot by

---

[5] For a discussion of the research programme of Post-Bloomfieldian linguistics and the role of the problems in (5a–b) in the Chomskyan revolution, see ten Hacken (2007: 130–135).
[6] It is rather unfortunate, however, that (6) and (7) use *unacceptable* where *ungrammatical* would be the correct qualification. On the distinction, cf. Chomsky (1957: 15) and ten Hacken (2011).

itself falsify a claim, because of (5a). We take it that in formulations such as (7), it is intended to add the intuitive judgement that the relevant examples are unproblematic before reaching a conclusion about their interpretation. In fact, this is supported by Lieber's (2016a: 11) explicit restriction of the scope of her research to English, because as she states, this is the only language she knows well enough to be confident in her judgements on finer semantic nuances.

7.2 The treatment of relevant contrasts in LSF

In this section, we will go over the data we presented in Chapter 4 and indicate how they can be treated in LSF. The structure of the section follows the structure of Chapter 4.

7.2.1 Words and phrases

In developing LSF, Lieber assumes a distinction between the lexicon and the syntax. The position of word formation is made explicit in (8).

(8) [N]oninflectional word formation – derivation, compounding, and conversion – serves to create lexemes and to extend the simplex lexicon. (Lieber 2004: 9)

According to (8), word formation creates new lexemes rather than phrases. This makes it trivial to distinguish the two German examples in (9).

(9) a. Hartkäse ('granular cheese')
    b. harter Käse ('hard cheese')

The formal mechanism covering the integration of the two components in the compound (9a) is the Principle of Coindexation. Lieber (2009: 96–97) formulates different versions of this principle without choosing one, but in any case it is an operation that applies when semantic skeletons are composed. In (9b), we have a syntactic construction, marked by a phrasal category and not governed by the Principle of Coindexation. Although the morphemes *hart* and *Käse* are the same, the way they are combined is not. This difference is represented in (10).

(10) a.   hart   Käse
          [–dynamic, –scalar ([$_i$])]   [+material ([$_i$])]
    b. [$_{NP}$ [$_{AP}$ [$_A$ hart er]] [$_N$ Käse]]

Whereas (9b) has a syntactic structure of the type in (10b), following a version of X-bar theory, (9a) has a lexical representation as a word with coindexation of the two components. Syntactically *Hartkäse* is just a noun.

The German pair in (9) contrasts with the Slovak pair in (11).

(11) a. čajová lyžička ('teaspoon')
     b. čistá lyžička ('clean spoon')

Both (11a) and (11b) are syntactically NPs consisting of A+N. The difference between them is that *čajová* in (11a) is a relational adjective whereas *čistá* in (11b) is a qualitative adjective. The question is whether this difference can be and should be represented in the structure. To our knowledge, Lieber does not discuss the representation of RAs in LSF. One obvious difference between the Slovak (11a) and its English translation is that *čajová* is an adjective, so that it must have [scalar] in its skeleton. All relational adjectives have [–scalar]. The adjective is derived from the noun *čaj* ('tea') and has the inflectional ending for the nominative singular of the feminine to agree with *lyžička*. This gives skeletons such as (12).

(12) a. čaj   [+material ([ ])]
     b. -ov-   [–dynamic, –scalar ([ ], ⟨base⟩)]
     c. čajov-   [–dynamic, –scalar ([$_i$], +material ([$_i$]))]
     d. lyžičk- [+material ([ ])]

In (12) we leave out the representation of the inflectional endings. We will return to the representation of inflection in sections 7.2.2 and 7.2.3 below. The formation of *čajov(á)* as represented in (12a–c) is parallel to the one of *writer* in (4). Making *čajová lyžička* into a compound means coindexing the arguments in the skeleton in (12c) with the argument in the concatenated skeleton in (12d). As with other compounds, the interpretation of the meaning of the coindexation has to proceed on the basis of the other available information, in particular elements from the body. For (11b), there is no reason to coindex the adjective and the noun. They are a syntactic combination.

The approach to the contrasts in (9) and (11) can be extended to the contrast between the two contexts of *bird's nest* in (13).

(13) a. She points to a bird's nest in a low branch.
     b. The mother cuckoo lays its egg in another bird's nest.

Coindexation can be used to make *bird's nest* a word in (13a), whereas (13b) has a noun phrase *[[another bird]'s nest]*. The genitive marker 's can be analysed as a linking element in (13a), parallel to German *Arbeitsmarkt* ('job market'), which has an -s- as a linking element between *Arbeit* ('work') and *Markt* ('market'). In (13b), it should rather be analysed as a clitic, attaching to the noun phrase rather than the noun, as is visible in examples such as *the Duchess of Cambridge's picture*.

We can also use this technique for the contrast in (14).

(14) a. a commuter suburb of Charleston
b. the Chicago suburb of Cicero

We can express the different roles of the modifiers of *suburb* by coindexation in (14a), which makes *commuter suburb* a compound and therefore a word, but not in (14b), which makes *Chicago* a syntactic modifier of *suburb*.

Summarizing this section, we can conclude that coindexation is the crucial operation that distinguishes words from phrases. Some formal matters, such as the inflectional ending of the relational adjective in (11a) and the representation of the *'s* in (13a) remain to be solved, but it is generally possible to express the contrast between words and phrases by means of coindexation, which applies in words, but not in phrases.

7.2.2 The borderline between inflection and derivation

Lieber's statement quoted in (8) not only distinguishes word formation from syntax, but also hints at a distinction from inflection. The formulation 'noninflectional word formation' is somewhat unusual, but the reference to the creation of lexemes makes it clear that there is a relevant borderline between inflection and derivation. What we call *word formation*, following what we perceive as common practice, is what Lieber (2004: 9) calls *noninflectional word formation*.

The data we take as our example for the distinction between inflection and derivation are Dutch plural and diminutive nouns such as the ones in (15).

(15) a. vogel   sg
b. vogels   pl
c. vogeltje   dim-sg
d. vogeltjes   dim-pl

As Lieber (2004: 9) excludes inflection from the scope of her monograph, it is obvious that we cannot expect a full account of it. She does consider it as a potential extension for future work (2004: 181), but we do not know of any full-fledged treatment of inflection in LSF.

In a brief discussion of inflection, Lieber (2004: 151) gives the entry in (16) for the English regular plural ending.

(16) -s   [–B, +CI (⟨base⟩)]

In Dutch, as illustrated in (15b) and (15d), -s is also used as a plural ending, although it is in competition with -en. The entry in (16) can be compared to other entries for suffixes, (4b) for English -er and (12b) for Slovak -ov-.

Similar to these entries, the suffix is modelled as a function over the base, adding features. In (16), these features are [–B] and [+CI]. Lieber (2004: 136–139) introduces these as *quantity features*. They are among the features that determine the skeleton in English. B stands for *Bounded* and CI for *Composed of Individuals*. For nouns, Lieber (2004: 137) gives the four classes in (17).[7]

(17) a. [+B, –CI] *person, pig, fact*
      b. [–B, –CI] *furniture, water*
      c. [+B, +CI] *committee, herd*
      d. [–B, +CI] *cattle, sheep*

In (15b), the base *vogel* is of the type in (17a). This means that the plural suffix in (16) changes the sign of both [B] and [CI]. Lieber does not indicate that [+B] serves as a condition, but [CI] not. It is usually assumed that only singular and group nouns (17a, c) have plurals, mass nouns (17b) and plural nouns (17d) not. For *water*, the plural form is used, e.g. *international waters*, but arguably it does not have the regular meaning.

The main difference between (16) and the derivational suffixes in (4b) and (12b) is that the suffix in (16) does not have an argument of its own. This is a property that can be used deliberately to encode the contrast between derivation and inflection.

As we have seen, there are two regular plural endings in Dutch, which for some nouns are both possible, as illustrated in (18).

(18) a. vogel   vogels   ('bird')
      b. huis   huizen   ('house')
      c. methode methodes/methoden   ('method')

This type of competition between different suffixes is an instance of the multiple-affix problem in (1b). As such, it only extends an observation about word formation to inflection.

Conversely, the idea that the diminutive suffix illustrated in (15c) has a meaning that can range over small size, positive evaluation and a number of specialized meanings, such as the focus on the event for nouns expressing a time period (e.g. *dagje*, 'day$_{DIM}$') or a quantity for mass nouns (e.g. *biertje*, 'beer$_{DIM}$'), is not surprising in the context of LSF. It is an instance of the polysemy problem in (1a). Lieber (2016a: 149–151) suggests that for English suffixes with an evaluative meaning component, e.g. the negative connotation in *conventioneer* and *hipster*, this component is encoded in the body, but that in languages with regular evaluative morphology, the skeleton must be

---

[7] Lieber refers to what she calls the semantic equivalent of nouns, substances/things/essences. We doubt that *furniture* should be conceived of as not composed of individuals.

involved. For Dutch *-tje*, we can assume that it is a full derivational suffix with a skeleton and a body. The binding of the argument of the suffix with an argument of the base triggers the interaction of the information encoded for the base and the suffix to come up with an interpretation.

Summarizing, we note that the analysis of derivational affixes by Lieber (2004, 2016a) can be extended to Dutch diminutives. For inflectional affixes such as the one marking the nominal plural, the same set of features can be used. The distinction between derivation and inflection is expressed by the presence or absence of an argument apart from the base, as illustrated by the contrast between (4b) and (16).

7.2.3 Paradigms

The position of inflectional paradigms in LSF is implied by the statement in (8), at the start of section 7.2.1. When (non-inflectional) word formation creates lexemes, we can assume that the unit taken as input is also a lexeme. This means that the case and number forms for Slovak *gitara* are taken together as one unit, for instance when forming *gitarista* ('guitarist').

As Lieber (2004) uses the statement in (8) in the delimitation of the domain of her study and excludes inflection from it, it is understandable that she does not present a theory of inflectional paradigms. As we saw in section 7.2.2, she distinguishes inflectional affixes from derivational affixes by the absence of the inherent argument. However, she points out that not all of inflection can be represented along the pattern of (16), making the distinction between inherent and contextual inflection (2004: 152). This distinction is based on a classification by Kuryłowicz (1964: 15–17), but the names are from Booij (1994: 30–31). Inherent inflection produces forms that are semantically different, such as the plural for nouns. Contextual inflection yields oppositions between forms that are semantically identical but syntactically different. Kuryłowicz (1964: 17) gives the example of the nominative and the accusative for Latin nouns.

In the paradigm for *gitara*, we have a combination of inherent and contextual inflection. For number, the contrast belongs to inherent inflection. For case, the different values appear on different sides of the divide. The contrast between nominative and accusative is among the prototypical examples of contextual inflection. However, locative and instrumental cases are rather inherent, because they have a fairly clearly determined meaning. This means that the distinction between inherent and contextual inflection is in conflict with a systematic representation of nominal paradigms. If this distinction is the basis for the coverage of number and case for Slovak *gitara*, it is individual forms that are treated, not their paradigmatic organization.[8]

---

[8] Booij (1996) uses this as an argument to keep both types of inflection in the same component of grammar.

The notion of *derivational paradigm* is referred to by Booij and Lieber (2004), but not in the same sense as we used it in section 4.3. They refer to 'a kind of basic paradigmatic structure for affixal semantics' (2004: 343) which consists of a series of classes into which affixes may fall. They propose a set of six classes defined in terms of the features [dynamic] and [material] that determine the class of the output of the affixation process. Lieber (2004: 39) adds three further classes and one more feature, [IEPS], to characterize them. She draws the parallel with the verbal paradigm defined by person and number features. The idea is that the features create 'the cells of a semantic paradigm into which particular derivational affixes might be placed' (2004: 38). Lieber (2016a: 56–59) proposes to replace this model by that of a so-called *derivational ecosystem*. In her elaboration of this idea, she refers to semantic field theory.[9] As an example of a derivational ecosystem, she gives a table with on one axis the affixes and on the other a set of semantic classes (2016a: 60–61). The idea behind such a table is to account for the different readings an affix may have. Instead of assigning a fixed number of specific meanings to an affix, the ecosystem describes the environment in which an affix is chosen for a particular meaning.

The difference to the notion of *derivational paradigm* we introduced in section 4.3 can be illustrated by the Slovak examples in (19) and (20).

(19) a. blog ('blog$_N$')
b. blogovať ('blog$_V$')
c. blogový ('blog$_A$')

(20) a. bloger ('blogger$_N$')
b. blogerka ('blogger$_{FEM}$')
c. blogerský ('blogger$_A$')

In (19), we have a paradigm consisting of an inanimate noun and a corresponding verb and relational adjective. In (20), we have another paradigm, consisting of an animate noun, the feminine counterpart of the noun and a relational adjective. The central point of these two paradigms is that (19a) and (20a) are the result of naming acts, whereas (19b–c) and (20b–c) are largely determined by these naming acts. The availability of *blog* in (19a) requires naming, but once *blog* is accepted, *blogovať* in (19b) is available for use without requiring an additional naming act.

In sum, we can say that Lieber's writings do not give an account of inflectional paradigms because they do not fall into the scope of her theory. For

---

[9] Semantic field theory is usually linked to the work on *Wortfeldtheorie* by Jost Trier (1894–1970). Van der Lee and Reichmann (1973) give an overview of the theory and its reception. Trier (1973) is a collection of foundational articles, mainly published in the 1930s. Lieber (2016a: 58) does not refer to Trier, but to Lehrer (1974). Lehrer (1974: 15–19) describes the relationship to Trier's work.

derivational paradigms, she has a different interpretation of their role in a theory than we assume here. For Lieber, they are a way of organizing affixes into a semantic system. For us, a derivational paradigm organizes a number of related complex words into a structure that requires only one main naming act. In this sense, Lieber's theory does not cover derivational paradigms.

7.2.4 Transposition and the formation of names

In section 4.4, we defined *transposition* as in (21).

(21) Transposition is a process that
 a. changes the syntactic category of a word,
 b. does not change its semantic category, and
 c. does not modify, add or delete any semantic features.

In section 7.1, we noted that Lieber uses the semantic features [material], [dynamic] and [scalar] to characterize the semantic equivalents of nouns, verbs and adjectives. She characterizes transposition in (22).

(22) [D]erivational morphology is transpositional when the only meaning change it induces on its base is that which is entailed by the change in syntactic category it effects. (Lieber 2004: 38)

Lieber attributes (22) to Beard (1995) without indicating a page, but she presents it as a view she fully supports. Clearly, this view of transposition stands in direct opposition to the one underlying the definition in (21). By assigning meaning change directly to the change of syntactic category, Lieber denies the existence of transposition in the sense of (21).

An example of transposition we discussed in section 4.4 is the contrast in (23).

(23) a. an issue open to empirical exploration
 b. an issue open to being explored empirically

To us, (23a) and (23b) are semantically equivalent. The difference exists only in syntax, where *exploration* is a noun modified by an adjective, whereas *explore* is a verb modified by an adverb. For Lieber, *exploration* must have a different meaning to *explore*, because its nominal status is marked by having the feature [material] in the first position in its skeleton. In a discussion of -*ness*, Lieber (2004: 158) observes that 'adjectives bear different semantic features from nouns'. To us, this is a purely artificial importation of syntactic information into the semantic representation. It is not falsifiable in the sense that the presence or absence of [–material] cannot be distinguished empirically. In our view, *explore* refers to a process and *exploration* refers to exactly the same process. As such, they are semantically indistinguishable and any changes of the type exemplified in (23) are due to syntax.

Following Borer (2013), Lieber (2016a) introduces the term *ATK nominalizations*, where *ATK* stands for '-*ation* and kin'. She describes them as 'E/R nominals derived from verbal bases with affixes other than -*ing*' (2016a: 16) and devotes a substantial part of her monograph to their analysis. For -*ation* and other ATK nominalizers, Lieber (2016a: 101) introduces the skeletons in (24).

(24) a. [–material, α dynamic (⟨base⟩)]
     b. [α material, β dynamic ([ ], ⟨base⟩)]

The idea is that (24a) represents the process reading, which Lieber calls the event reading, and (24b) the result reading, which Lieber calls the referential reading. The variables α and β can be specified as + or –, but they can also be left unspecified. The resolution of these variables depends on what Lieber (2016a: 8) calls *Contextual Coercion*. We will return to this notion in section 7.2.5.

The main difference between the skeletons for the process and result readings in (24) is that the suffix has an argument of its own in (24b), but not in (24a). We encountered this distinction in section 7.2.2. There, the plural suffix has the skeleton (16) without the extra argument, whereas regular noun-forming suffixes such as -*er* in (4b) have such an argument. The argument in (24b) can be coindexed with one of the arguments of the base. In the case of -*er*, coindexation selects the verbal argument that is highlighted by the resulting noun. The application of this procedure can be illustrated with our example of an ambiguous nominalization in (25).

(25) a. the installation in their territory of foreign military bases
     b. [they] were taken to a Salvadorean military installation

In (25a), *installation* refers to the process. Compared with the verb *install*, there is no reduction in the arguments that can be realized. Although the argument corresponding to the verbal subject is left unspecified here, the object *foreign military bases* is realized in the sentence. In (25b), *installation* refers to the result. This means that the noun itself corresponds to the verbal object, which can no longer be realized externally. Using the lexical entries in (24), we can express this contrast in (26).

(26)   -ation   install
     a. [–material, α dynamic ([+dynamic ([ ], [ ])])]
     b. [+material, α dynamic ([$_i$], [+dynamic ([ ], [$_i$])])]

In (26a), no coindexation takes place, because the affix does not have an argument of its own. In (26b), the argument of the suffix is coindexed with the object of the verb. Presumably, the subject is not available for coindexation, because the subject of *install* must be animate and the argument of the suffix excludes this. Therefore, the Principle of Coindexation selects the object of the verb to coindex it with the argument of the suffix and the meaning can be described as 'that which is installed'.

In (26), we did not resolve the [α dynamic]. We have no intuitions about the use of the feature [dynamic] for nouns and the specification of this feature does not affect the aspects of the analysis we are interested in here. For the feature [material], the value in (26a) stems from the skeleton in (24a). In (26b), we know that an installation must be [+material], but the precise origin of this value is less clear. Lieber invokes Contextual Coercion, whereas we would propose to attribute it to onomasiological coercion. The difference between them is that whereas Contextual Coercion evokes a performance context, onomasiological coercion occurs in naming.

Two aspects of this analysis deserve to be highlighted. First, by assimilating the skeleton of the E reading to the skeletons of inflectional suffixes, Lieber takes what we call *transposition* as defined in (21) out of word formation. This is a consequence we fully agree with. Second, the systematic relation between the skeletons in (24) is not directly expressed. There is no directionality in the relation, because it is not clear from the skeletons whether the E reading is derived from the R reading or the reverse. In fact, the two readings are juxtaposed and they can be thought of as homonyms.

Let us now turn to the German and Slovak equivalents. As we noted in section 4.4, both languages have a corresponding form, *Installation* and *inštalácia*, as well as an alternative formation, *Installierung* and *inštalovanie*. We repeat here the German examples we gave in (27).

(27) a. die Installation der Heizungsanlage
'the installation of_the heating_system'
b. veraltete Installationen erneuern
'outdated installations renew', i.e. replace outdated installations
c. die Installierung der Heizungsanlage
d. *veraltete Installierungen erneuern

In (27a) we have the process reading and in (27b) the result reading of *Installation*. As (27c–d) show, only the process reading is available for *Installierung*. We noted in section 4.4 that *Installierung* is significantly less frequent than *Installation*. For Slovak, the relation between *inštalácia* and *inštalovanie* is similar.

Although Lieber (2004, 2016a) restricts her research to English, she does so only for practical reasons of language competence and there is no reason to assume that LSF should not apply to German and Slovak. In fact, Lieber (2009: 91, 100–103) discusses examples from Georgian and from Japanese for phenomena that do not occur in English. Given the similarities in the

The Lexical Semantic Framework

behaviour of -*ation* in English, -*ation* in German and -*ácia* in Slovak, it seems reasonable to assume that the proposal to use the skeleton in (24) can be extended to these suffixes. This raises the question of how to account for -*ung* in German and -*nie* in Slovak.

One question to be asked is whether -*ung* and -*nie* are also in the class of ATK. As we saw, Lieber (2016a: 16) explicitly excludes -*ing* in English. This suffix behaves differently, because it exists for all non-modal verbs and also has a function as a participle. German -*ung* is historically related to -*ing*, as Marchand (1969: 302) notes, but it is a noun-forming suffix. Fleischer and Barz (2012: 226) give several examples of verbs that do not have a nominalization in -*ung*, including the one in (28).

(28) a. die Seminararbeit abgeben
  'the seminar_paper off_give', i.e. hand in the seminar paper
 b. *die Abgebung der Seminararbeit
 c. die Abgabe der Seminararbeit
  'the handing_in of_the seminar_paper'

The verb *abgeben* ('hand in') in (28a) is not in the scope of the rule for -*ation*. Instead, it has an affixless form with ablaut, *Abgabe*, as in (28c) as a nominalization. This form blocks the formation with -*ung* as seen in the ungrammaticality of (28b). This illustrates that -*ung* is involved in a competition with other nominalization rules in a way comparable to ATK. Unlike English -*ing*, German formations with -*ung* are not automatically acceptable. The Slovak suffix -*nie* in *inštalovanie* behaves more like English -*ing*.

A solution that would apply to *Installierung* in (27) is to assume that -*ung* only has the skeleton (24a). However, this assumption is not compatible with the data in (29), from Duden (2021: *Bildung*).

(29) a. die Bildung der Jugend
  'the education of_the youth'
 b. eine umfassende Bildung besitzen
  'a comprehensive education possess',
  i.e. have a comprehensive education

The noun *Bildung* can have a process reading as in (29a) and a result reading as in (29b) in a way that is typical of ATK in English. As such, we must assume that -*ung* has both readings in (24). This leaves the ungrammaticality of (27d) unexplained. As Fleischer and Barz (2012: 227) state, the pattern in (27) is typical of the way -*ation* and -*ung* are used for verbs where both are possible. Whereas -*ation* only attaches to verbs with an infinitive in -*ieren*, -*ung* has a much broader domain of application.

One way to approach these data is to assume that the result reading is derived from the process reading. In case a noun has a result reading that is more prominent, a new form can be used to emphasize the process reading.

This is a solution that appeals to naming needs. However, it is unclear how such a solution could be expressed in the formalism of LSF.

To sum up, Lieber (2004) denies the possibility of transposition in the sense of (21), because for her the change of syntactic category must be encoded in the semantic representation. As (24) shows, however, Lieber distinguishes transposition from derivation by assigning a referential argument only to the latter. As such, transposition is in LSF formally similar to inflection. The account of the relationship between the process and result readings in a case such as *installation* is not strongly developed and there is no explanation for the lack of a result reading for German *Installierung* and Slovak *inštalovanie*. The idea that they are formed in response to the need to emphasize the process reading is difficult to express in LSF.

7.2.5 Onomasiological coercion

As an example of onomasiological coercion, we discussed *doorman* and gave the COBUILD (2023) definition in (30).

(30) a. A doorman is
 b. a man who stands at the door
 c. of a club,
 d. prevents unwanted people from coming in, and makes people leave if they cause trouble.

Whereas the components *door* and *man* are mentioned in (30b), the relationship between them is implicit in *doorman*. Moreover, the information in (30c–d) is not expressed in the compound at all.

Lieber (2009: 98) discusses the example of *dogbed*, which has the same structure as *doorman*. She proposes that the referential arguments of the two nouns are coindexed, leading to a skeleton structure as in (31), which will be supplemented by elements of the bodies as specified in the lexical entries for *door* and *man*.

(31)   *door*   *man*
        [+material ([$_i$])] [+material ([$_i$])]

In the same way as in (10a), we need an interpretation for the coindexation of the two arguments in (31). Lieber makes the statement in (32) about this.

(32) [T]he relationship between the head and the non-head of an N + N compound is free to be fixed by context. Although individual endocentric attributive compounds may be lexicalized with specific meanings and although specific combinations of nouns may be predisposed pragmatically towards particular interpretations, [. . .]

the relationship between the compounding elements is not fixed by formal rules. (Lieber 2004: 98)

In (31), Lieber identifies three procedures by which the meaning in (30) can emerge for *doorman*. First it can be 'fixed by context', which Lieber (2016a: 8) calls *Contextual Coercion*, then it can be 'lexicalized with [a] specific meaning' and finally it can be 'predisposed pragmatically towards [a] particular interpretation'. Let us consider each of these in more detail.

For the use of context to determine the interpretation of coindexation in (31), we need to consider examples of use. In (33), we have two examples from BNC (2007).

(33) a. Bennett had been doorman at the Garrick Club for twenty-three years and had developed a way with unpleasantness.
b. Charles leant against the wall. The doorman watched his visitor as if he expected him to steal the light fittings.

From (33a), we can infer (30c) fairly straightforwardly. The reference to *unpleasantness* gives a hint of the tasks of a doorman, but nothing as specific as (30d). In (33b), we do not have any indication of (30c) and the hint as to (30d) remains quite vague. The specific meaning of *doorman* remains unclear with examples such as (33).

The concept of *pragmatic predisposition* is a rather vague one. We can think of the body of the entries for *door* and *man* and of the meaning of related words. In (34), we give the definitions from COBUILD (2023) for the two words.

(34) a. A door is a piece of wood, glass, or metal, which is moved to open and close the entrance to a building, room, cupboard, or vehicle.
b. A man is an adult male human being.

The definitions in (34) are the first ones for each entry. None of the other definitions is particularly relevant to the interpretation of *doorman*. As related words, (35) lists the entries for N+N compounds with *door* as a first and *man* as a second noun in the frequency bands 5 and 6 in OED.[10]

(35) a. doorway, doorstep, doorbell
b. chairman, businessman, policeman, fisherman, Congressman, workman, clergyman, countryman, seaman, horseman, fireman, headman, serviceman, watchman, airman, journeyman

---

[10] Search performed 8 August 2022. Excluded were cases such as *statesman* with an -s- as a kind of linking element.

The information in (34) does not contribute much to finding elements in (30). The list in (35b) includes several compounds where the non-head indicates the task, e.g. *chairman, fireman*. However, this provides only a very small part of (30d).

This leaves lexicalization as the main source of the meaning of *doorman*. Here the question is how this lexicalization is achieved.

It seems to us that the elephant in the room is naming. What Lieber proposes in (32) is mainly oriented towards the interpretation of a word perceived in performance. Interpretation is the effort to reconstruct the meaning intended by the speaker. In the case of a new word, the speaker chooses the word for a concept. The speaker has the meaning of the word as a starting point. Naming is the action of selecting a word (or, more generally an expression) for this meaning. The degree of freedom of this choice is indicated by the different expressions corresponding to *doorman* in German, Dutch, and Slovak, repeated here as (36).

(36) a. Türsteher ('door_stander') DE
 b. uitsmijter ('out_thrower') NL
 c. vyhadzovač ('throw_out-er') SK

The components, the ways they are combined and the coindexation are different for the expressions in (36). The resulting meaning is more or less the same.

7.3 Word formation and naming in LSF

Like Lexical Morphology and Phonology discussed in Chapter 6, LSF assumes a clear distinction between morphology and syntax. However, like Distributed Morphology discussed in Chapter 5, LSF takes the basic units of the lexicon to be morphemes. In LSF, rules in the lexicon combine morphemes into word forms. Word formation is covered by such rules. Word forms are inserted into syntactic structures afterwards.

Lexical mechanisms in LSF include the distinction between skeleton and body, predicate-argument structures, features and coindexation. These mechanisms are used to describe morphemes as they are listed as well as word forms as they are formed in the lexicon.

When two structures are combined by a morphological rule, their predicate-argument structures are integrated and arguments of the two structures are coindexed. This coindexation only takes place in morphology. Therefore, we can use coindexation to encode an expression as a morphological structure.

The use of coindexation gives us a transparent and flexible method to distinguish morphological structures from syntactic structures. We can use it to treat the expressions in (37) as morphological and the ones in (38) as syntactic.

The Lexical Semantic Framework 125

(37) a. Hartkäse ('granular cheese')
 b. čajová lyžička ('teaspoon')
 c. (a) bird's nest (in a low branch)
 d. commuter suburb

(38) a. harter Käse ('hard cheese')
 b. čistá lyžička ('clean spoon')
 c. (lays its eggs in another) bird's nest
 d. Chicago suburb

The contrasts between the four examples in (37) and their counterparts in (38) were discussed in section 7.2.1. We are not sure whether it is Lieber's intention, but it is definitely possible within the LSF formalism to use coindexation for all of (37) and not to use it for the examples in (38). The most salient cases are the relational adjective in (37b) and the deictic compound in (38d). The flexibility of the mechanism allows for this treatment. When we adopt this analysis, coindexation indicates that the expressions in (37), but not the ones in (38), are formed in the lexicon and are expected to have a naming function.

For the distinction between inflection and derivation, Lieber uses the argument structure. In (39), a generic representation of the distinction is given.

(39) a. [features (⟨base⟩)]
 b. [features ([ ], ⟨base⟩)]

In (39), *features* is used as a placeholder for the feature specification in the skeleton of a morpheme. Inflectional affixes have a representation of the type in (39a). An example is the entry for the plural in (16). Such morphemes only apply to a base and add their features to the resulting word form. Derivational affixes have a representation of the type in (39b). An example is the entry for Slovak -*ov*- in (12b). Here, an argument is introduced, so that when a morpheme of this type is combined with a base, coindexation is possible.

In a similar way to coindexation, this use of argument structure gives us a transparent and flexible method to distinguish complex expressions that are used for naming from those whose complex nature is used only to satisfy syntactic constraints. It is clear that all cases of inflection should get a structure of the type in (39a). However, in this case we can be sure that Lieber does not want to restrict the contrast in (39) to the opposition between inflection and derivation. As we saw in section 7.2.4, she proposes a distinction of this type, illustrated in (22), to account for the two readings of nouns in -*ation*. This means that affixes marking transpositions also get a skeleton of the type in (39a). In this way, we can restrict skeletons of the type in (39b) to expressions used for naming.

With coindexation and the contrast in argument structure in (39), we have a powerful set of mechanisms to distinguish expressions that result from word formation and are used for naming from other expressions. Formulated concisely, word formation as a naming device involves coindexation and this implies that affixes must have an argument as in (39b) that can be coindexed. In this way, LSF allows for a more precise characterization of the set of naming units than Distributed Morphology and Lexical Morphology and Phonology.

In the discussion of paradigms in section 7.2.3, we observed a profound difference of interpretation. Lieber interprets paradigms as a way of organizing affixes into a system to explain how a particular affix is chosen for a particular meaning. She restricts the scope of her discussion of paradigms to derivational paradigms and, in a later stage, replaces these by derivational ecosystems. We interpret paradigms as units that are chosen in a naming act. In this sense, inflectional paradigms are basic and derivational paradigms are extensions. This sense of paradigm is not covered in LSF.

In the discussion of onomasiological coercion in section 7.2.5, we identified a clear distinction in the approach taken. Lieber (2004: 98), as quoted in (32), identifies different ways in which the actual meaning of an expression resulting from word formation can arise. However, she avoids any reference to naming in this context. It seems that this is a consequence of her focus on the interpretation of an expression by the hearer. For the hearer, clues leading to the interpretation of a complex expression can be taken from the context of use, from the pragmatic predisposition of the components and from its being stored in the hearer's mental lexicon. The success of the interpretation by the hearer is measured, however, by the degree of correspondence to the speaker's intended meaning. That is to say, the naming process performed by the speaker sets the standard for the hearer's interpretation. In naming, onomasiological coercion determines the ultimate result. Therefore, we cannot ignore onomasiological coercion in an account of word formation as a naming device.

CHAPTER 8

Construction Morphology

Construction Morphology is a theory of morphology presented by Booij (2010). By its name it evokes a link to Goldberg's (1995) Construction Grammar. At the same time, it is linked to Jackendoff's (2002) Parallel Architecture. The edited volume of Booij (2018) shows that the theory has been used by a range of other researchers and applied to various languages. Concise representations in handbooks are presented by Booij (2013, 2016, 2020) and by Masini and Audring (2019). Here we will briefly outline the main theoretical assumptions and tools in section 8.1 and then consider in section 8.2 how they can account for the data presented in Chapter 4. In section 8.3, we evaluate the success in the coverage of naming and compare the theory with the frameworks we discussed in previous chapters.

8.1 Construction Morphology as a theory

Booij (2010) intends to present and establish a new theory of morphology. When it was published, Geert Booij was already a recognized authority in morphology. His 1977 PhD dissertation is in the generative tradition. Together with Jaap van Marle he had edited the *Yearbook of Morphology* since 1988 and he was one of the editors of the two-volume handbook of morphology published in the *HSK* series, Booij et al. (2000, 2004). Many of his colleagues perceived Booij's (2010) monograph as a break with his earlier work. In fact, Booij (2020) only refers to his work from 2005 onwards. Masini and Audring (2019: 365) give a list of publications on Construction Morphology by Booij starting in 2002.

Booij (2010) is a monograph consisting of ten chapters with a brief conclusion and outlook in chapter 11. The first three chapters are mainly devoted to presenting the theory, with the remaining seven chapters giving case studies and extensions. Several of these are based on articles published separately.

The name *Construction Morphology* is a clear reference to the theory of Construction Grammar proposed by Goldberg (1995). The notion of *construction* is taken over from Goldberg. It bridges the classical division between grammar and lexicon. The idea is that a construction can specify lexical material as well as syntactic constraints. The version of Construction Grammar most frequently referred to by Booij is that of Croft (2001). Croft (2001: 18) presents a construction as consisting of a set of form-related properties, a set of meaning-related properties, and a symbolic correspondence between them. The form-based properties are syntactic, morphological and phonological. The meaning-based properties are semantic, pragmatic and discourse-functional.

Before referring to Goldberg and Croft, however, Booij (2010: 5–9) introduces Jackendoff's (2002) Parallel Architecture (PA). In PA, phonological, syntactic and conceptual representations of an expression are generated each by their own rules and subsequently linked to each other. This model of grammar stands in opposition to Chomsky's models, in which syntactic structure is the central generative structure, from which phonological and semantic representations are derived by interpretation rules.

In earlier writings about Construction Morphology, Booij uses the abbreviation *CM* (2010: 1; 2016: 425). Later he uses *CxM* (2020: 1004). The latter aligns it with Construction Grammar, which, as *CG* had already been taken by Categorial Grammar,[1] uses *CxG*. Masini and Audring (2019: 365) highlight the 'programmatic name' of Construction Morphology as well as the connection with CxG, while mentioning Jackendoff's work only in passing. In any case, CxM adopts Jackendoff's (1975) Full Entry Theory and the three levels of representation in PA.

Lexical entries in CxM encode constructions. A word is a construction. The lexical entry of a word specifies its phonology, syntax and meaning. Idioms are also constructions. The only difference to words is that they have more structure in their specification of phonology and syntax. It is only on the basis of words that word formation patterns can emerge, as Booij (2016: 425) states in (1).

(1) a. Language users first acquire words, and only once they have acquired a sufficiently large set of words of a certain type can they conclude by abstracting morphological patterns.
   b. This pattern will be memorized beside the set of memorized words on which it is based,
   c. and the abstract pattern serves as a recipe for coining new complex words.

---

[1] The abbreviation CG is also used by Langacker (1987a) for Cognitive Grammar (cf. Chapter 10). However, the term *Categorial Grammar*, abbreviated CG, was already in use earlier (cf. Bar-Hillel et al. 1960). Steedman (1993) gives a historical overview of the emergence of Categorial Grammar.

Construction Morphology

We divided the quotation in (1) into three parts, because three different claims are made here. In (1a), we have a claim about the origin of word formation rules in a speaker. Speakers infer the rule from a set of words with certain similarities. This is a traditional view, which Booij (2010: 3) links to Hermann Paul (cf. section 2.2). In (1b–c), two different uses of word formation rules are indicated. On one hand, word formation rules serve to structure the lexicon, as hinted at in (1b), on the other hand they can be used to produce new words, as stated in (1c). Booij (2016) gives the example in (2).[2]

(2) a. dancer, fighter, singer, walker
 b. dance, fight, sing, walk
 c. [$_N$ [$_V$ danc] er], [$_N$ [$_V$ fight] er], [$_N$ [$_V$ sing] er], [$_N$ [$_V$ walk] er]
 d. <[$_N$ [$_V$ x]$_i$ er]$_j$ ↔ [Agent of SEM$_i$]$_j$>

In (2a) and (2b), two sets of corresponding words are listed. Together they are a 'set of words' in the sense of (1a), but it would probably be better to conceptualize them as a set of word pairs. On the basis of the similarities in these pairs, the structures in (2c) can be inferred. In a further step, the pattern in (2d) can be formulated. The words in (2a–b) are lexical entries. The structured words in (2c) replace the entries for (2a) once this reanalysis has been made. The pattern in (2d) is also a lexical entry. All entries are constructions. The one in (2d) is also a schema. By the unification of a schema and a base word, a new complex word can be created.

It is worth exploring the nature of the schema in (2d) a bit further. First, a schema is not an entry for a morpheme. Booij (2010: 15) explicitly excludes lexical entries for morphemes such as *-er*, because they are not signs. Second, a schema is not a word formation rule. Word formation rules are procedural, but schemas are declarative (Masini and Audring 2019: 369). Therefore, they do not overgenerate non-existing words and word forms. By listing the entries, the lexicon states that *walker* but not **stander* is an existing word of English (2019: 372). As Booij (2013: 271) states, the lexicon includes what 'belong[s] to the lexical convention of the language involved'.

Masini and Audring (2019: 365) identify *construction*, *schema* and *constructicon* as the central concepts of CxM. A construction is a conventionalized pairing of a form and a meaning. It corresponds to a lexical entry. A schema is a construction that is partly or entirely abstract. An example is (2d). The name *constructicon* is basically equivalent to *lexicon* in the sense that it refers to the set of constructions. It is sometimes used to emphasize the nature of lexical entries as constructions.

An important consequence of the idea that all lexical entries are constructions is that there is no clear distinction between grammar and lexicon.

---

[2] Non-matching brackets in (2d) corrected (cf. Booij 2016: 430). In order to avoid the collision of subscripts indicating syntactic category and coindexation, we shifted the syntactic category markers to the opening bracket.

This explains the emphasis placed in CxM on constructions that are in between the two. Idioms are an obvious case, but Booij (2010: 12–13) also gives the example of (3).[3]

(3) a. $<[_{NP} [_N x]_i [_{PP} [_P van] [_{NP} [_D een] [_N x]_j]]]_k \leftrightarrow$
$[SEM_j \text{ with } SEM_i\text{-like property}]_K>$
b. een *kast van een huis*, dat nodig geverfd moet worden
'a cupboard*$_i$ of a house$_i$ that$_i$ urgently painted must be'
(i.e. a big house that urgently needs to be painted)

In (3a) we have the schema of the N_1+*van een*+N_2 construction in Dutch. It is exemplified in the italicized part of (3b). Semantically, N_2 is the head, because a *kast van een huis* is a kind of *huis*. Syntactically the structure has N_1 as its head, modified by the PP headed by *van*. Nevertheless, the gender marking of the relative pronoun *dat* in (3b) excludes a coindexation with *kast* and only allows one with *huis*. As Masini and Audring (2019: 276) observe, CxM does not use *head* as a structural notion.

Another phenomenon that received special attention in CxM is that of affixoid. As an example Booij (2020: 1007) gives the use of Dutch *pracht* ('beauty, splendour') in (4).

(4) a. prachtvrouw ('great woman')
b. prachtkans ('great opportunity')
c. $<[_N [_N \text{pracht}]_k N_i]_j \leftrightarrow [\text{great}_k SEM_i]_{SEMj}>$

The noun *pracht* can be used as the first component of N+N compounds. However, in (4a–b), the meaning has become more abstract and can be described as a very positive evaluation. The schema in (4c) generalizes over this possibility. Here it is the boundary between compounding and derivation that is blurred. Along these lines, constituents of compounds may develop into affixes. Hüning and Booij (2014) argue for an analysis in which this is not grammaticalization but constructionalization. The difference between these two terms is that the former implies a distinction between lexicalization and grammaticalization, whereas the latter emphasizes the unified nature of the two. In CxM, each level of construction is a lexical entry and the transition from word to syntactic rule is a matter of degree.

The lexicon, or constructicon, is organized as an inheritance hierarchy. It is marked by multiple inheritance and default inheritance. The effect of multiple inheritance can be illustrated with the examples in (2). A complex word, in this case one of the agent nouns in (2a), inherits from the base

---

[3] Compared with Booij's example (12), we added the angle brackets. In line with Culicover and Jackendoff's (2005: 135–148) argument for a flat structure of the NP, we used NP instead of N' as the highest category in (3a).

word, here the corresponding verb in (2b), as well as from the pattern, here (2d). Default inheritance is seen, for instance, in the case of compounding. There are different types of compounding. More specific types of compounding add more information to the structure. However, this additional information can also override information inherited from higher nodes in the hierarchy. Booij (2010: 18) gives the schema in (5) for nominal compounds in Dutch.

(5) <[$_N$ [$_X$ a]$_k$ [$_N$ b]$_i$]$_j$ ↔ [SEM$_i$ with relation R to SEM$_k$]$_j$>
        | |
     [αF] [αF]

The schema in (5) specifies that a nominal compound in Dutch has a noun as the second component. The category of the first component is unspecified (X). The headedness of the compound is expressed by the agreement in the features F between the right-hand component and the compound. In the semantic specification, the compound is described as a hyponym of the right-hand noun and the nature of the relation to the left-hand noun is left open. The schema in (5) is quite high in the inheritance hierarchy. Other schemas may specify the information further. There may, for instance, be separate schemas for compounds where a is a noun, a verb or an adjective. The schema in (4c) is further down in the hierarchy. It narrows down the nature of a to a single noun and overrides the semantic specification of the relation in (5). At the bottom of the hierarchy, we have constructions corresponding to individual compounds.

Unification is the operation that applies when a word is created on the basis of a schema. In the case of *dancer*, the entry for the verb *dance* is unified with the schema in (2d) adding *-er*. If we have two affixation processes, the two affixes may be added one after the other or they may first be unified to form a complex affixation schema. This is illustrated in (6) and (7).

(6) a. onverwoestbaar ('indestructible')
      b. verwoesten   ('destroy')

(7) a. [$_A$ *on* [A]]
      b. [$_A$ [V] *baar*]
      c. [$_A$ *on* [$_A$ [V] *baar*]]

The adjective in (6a) has a prefix *on-* and a suffix *-baar*. They correspond more or less to English *un-* and *-able*. The underlying verb is (6b). However, the intermediate adjective *verwoestbaar* does not occur. In (7a–b), the form-side of the schemas for *on-* and *-baar* are given. Instead of first unifying (7b) with the entry for (6b) to form *verwoestbaar* and then unifying this with (7a), we can also start by unifying (7a) and (7b) to form (7c). Booij (2010: 43) proposes that the schema unification in (7c) explains the non-occurrence of *verwoestbaar* despite the occurrence of (6a).[4]

Another way of combining two schemas is a so-called *second order schema*. Booij (2010: 31–36) introduces the basic mechanism. Booij and Masini (2015) introduce the name and discuss it in more detail. A good example is the English correspondence in (8).

(8) a. altruism   altruist
    b. pacifism   pacifist
    c. communism   communist
    d. abolitionism abolitionist

As noted by Booij (2010: 33), there the pairs in (8) are related to each other, but this relationship cannot always be expressed in terms of a word that serves as the base for two different suffixation rules, one with *-ism* and one with *-ist*. There is no word **altru* for (8a) or **pacif* for (8b). For *commune* in (8c) it would be left unexplained why both words have a very specialized development of its meaning in exactly the same way. Only in (8d) is there an underlying word *abolition* that the two nouns can be derived from.

In a morpheme-based theory of morphology, it would be possible to solve (8a–b) by positing *altru-* and *pacif-* as bound stems. However, this does not solve the meaning specialization in (8c). In a word-based theory, Aronoff (1976: 88) proposes a truncation rule. In this way, the nouns in *-ist* in (8) can be derived from the nouns in *-ism*. Booij (2010: 33) proposes a direct correlation between the schemas for the two suffixes, as in (9).

(9) <[$_N$ x-*ism*]$_i$ ↔ SEM$_i$> ≈
    <[$_N$ x-*ist*]$_j$ ↔ [person with property Y related to SEM$_i$]$_j$>

The schema in (9) is an entry in the lexicon alongside separate entries for schemas introducing *-ism* and *-ist*. It applies to all cases in (8). The variable x is only referred to in the form-side of the schemas. This means that in the case of (8a–b), the schema in (9) can be used to derive the form in *-ist* from the one in *-ism* without referring to non-existing stems. The operator ≈ is non-directional, so that (9) does not state that one form is derived from the other. For (8c) it is better to use (9) as a way of relating the derived nouns to each other than to relate each of them to *commune* and assume a parallel specialization in their meaning. In the case of (8d), the relationship to *abolition* is not stated by (9), but by the separate schemas for *-ism* and *-ist*. These schemas exist alongside (9). The nouns in (8d) illustrate multiple inheritance in the sense that their full interpretation involves a number of different schemas.

---

[4] We intentionally do not say that *verwoestbaar* is ungrammatical. Ten Hacken (2019a: 81) gives an alternative account of such cases based on naming. We will return to this in Chapter 13.

Construction Morphology

In sum, CxM is a theory of morphology in which the lexicon is reinterpreted as a constructicon. This means that a lexical entry is a construction. Constructions may be words, rules or generalizations. In a construction, a relation between phonological, syntactic and semantic information is specified in a way that is compatible with Jackendoff's PA.

8.2 The treatment of relevant contrasts in CxM

In this section, we will go over the data we presented in Chapter 4 and indicate how they can be treated in CxM. The structure of the section follows the structure of Chapter 4.

8.2.1 Words and phrases

About the difference between words and phrases in CxM, Booij (2016) makes the two statements in (10).

(10) a. [T]here is no sharp demarcation of grammar and lexicon. (Booij 2016: 437)
b. This does not mean that we give up the difference between syntax and morphology. (Booij 2016: 444)

At first sight, the two statements in (10a) and (10b) seem to contradict each other. After all, morphology is concerned with words and words are associated with the lexicon. By contrast, phrases are associated with syntax and grammar is usually seen as focused on syntax. It is therefore interesting to consider how they are implemented in a number of borderline cases between words and phrases. Our first example is the German pair in (11).

(11) a. Hartkäse ('granular cheese')
b. harter Käse ('hard cheese')

The two expressions in (11) use the same adjective and noun, but (11a) names a concept and (11b) is a description. For a related contrast pair, Booij (2010: 177) suggests that a crucial difference lies in the syntactic categories assigned to the various constituents. We have used this suggestion in our constructions in (12).

(12) a. $<[_N [_A a]_k [_N b]_i]_j \leftrightarrow$
[type of SEM_i characterized by $\text{SEM}_k]_j>$
b. $<[_{NP} [_{AP} [_A a+\alpha F]]_k [_N b+\alpha F]_i]_j \leftrightarrow$
[SEM_i that has the property of $\text{SEM}_k]_j>$

In (12a), we took the schema for nominal compounds in (5) as a starting point. On the form-side, the difference is that the first component, *a*, is specified as an adjective. This triggers a slightly different semantic interpretation with a more specific relation between the two components. In (12b), we propose a schema for the syntactic rule combining adjectives and nouns. The projection of A to AP makes it possible to add a modifier to the adjective, e.g. *zeer* ('very'). Such modification of the adjective is not possible in (11a). We labelled the outer brackets NP, assuming that determiners and other modifiers of the noun can be inserted.[5] The two occurrences of αF indicate the agreement between adjective and noun.

The two schemas in (12) express the contrast in (11) and implement the two statements in (10). We have two schemas of the same basic type, both of which are part of the constructicon. Still, (12b) can be recognized as syntactic because of the projections, which are absent from the morphological schema in (12a).

Let us now turn to the Slovak contrast in (13).

(13) a. čajová lyžička   ('teaspoon')
      b. čistá lyžička   ('clean spoon')

As Booij (2020: 1010) states, '[t]he set of lexical expressions also comprises lexical idioms of various types.' In this context, he refers to Cetnarowska (2015), who discusses Polish counterparts to (13a) such as (14).

(14) a. dział finansowy   ('finance department')
      b. ogród zoologiczny ('zoological garden')

As the examples in (14) show, relational adjectives in Polish generally follow the noun they modify, but otherwise they behave very similarly to Slovak *čajový* in (13a). Cetnarowska (2018: 308) proposes the schema in (15) for the expressions in (14).

(15) $[N^0_i \ A^0_j]_k \leftrightarrow$
      [NAME for SEM$_i$ with some relation R to entity E of SEM$_j$]$_{\text{SEM}k}$

Cetnarowska (2018: 308) closely follows Booij (2010: 187), who proposes a similar schema for Dutch relational adjectives. Compared with the schemas in (12), the agreement is not expressed and the projections are not labelled. A crucial point, however, is that the relational adjective does not project

---

[5] In (12b), we use NP where Booij (2010: 177) uses N'. Using NP is in line with the flat structure of NP, as argued for by Culicover and Jackendoff (2005: 135–148). Also in mainstream generative syntax, we have an NP in positions such as these. In Abney's (1987) proposal for the structure of noun phrases, the NP in (12b) would be embedded in a DP as the complement of a determiner.

to an AP. This explains a number of well-known properties of relational adjectives such as their inability to take intensifiers, e.g. *bardzo finansowy ('very financial'). Another point to note is the description of the meaning, which starts with NAME. This is of course one way of making the distinction between naming and descriptive expressions explicit, but it is not used systematically.

For relational adjectives such as in (13a) and (14), an alternative approach would be to encode the information about the relational adjective as a schema for the suffix that forms it. After all, čajový is based on čaj ('tea') in a regular way. In (16), we propose such a schema for -ový.

(16) <[$_{NP}$ [$_A$ [$_N$ a]$_k$+ov+αF]] [$_N$ b+αF]$_i$]$_j$ ↔ [SEM$_i$ with relation R to SEM$_k$]$_j$>

In (13a), the noun čaj instantiates a and the noun lyžička instantiates b. The suffix -ov- is attached to the first noun to turn it into an adjective that agrees with the second noun in the features F. The -ý is the inflectional ending for nominative singular masculine. This adjective does not project to an AP. The semantic value of the full expression is calculated in exactly the same way as for Dutch compounds in (5). In our view, this constitutes an advantage over (15), which, when adapted to Slovak, would not relate to the noun čaj, but only to some 'entity E of' the meaning of čajový.

If we adopt (16) for (13a) and use a general adjective-noun rule like (12b) for (13b), the semantic distinction between (13a) and (13b) is triggered by the suffix -ový. This makes sense, but it misses the generalization that čajový is a relational adjective. Slovak relational adjectives are formed by a number of suffixes. The two main alternative suffixes are illustrated in (17).

(17) a. nočný stolík ('night$_{ADJ}$ table$_{DIM}$', i.e. bedside cabinet)
     b. školská lavica ('school$_{ADJ}$ bench')

In (17a), the relational adjective is formed by affixing -ný to noc ('night') and in (17b) by affixing -ský to škola ('school'). The choice between these suffixes is not determined by a specific rule. The generalization could be expressed as a further schema which leaves the form of the suffix unspecified. Such a schema would serve as a redundancy rule in the sense of Jackendoff (1975).

Another aspect of the contrast in (13) is that RA+N combinations such as (13a) are generally used for naming a concept, whereas (13b) describes an object. In individual cases, two mechanisms are available to encode this difference, the lack of projection and the use of NAME. Both are illustrated in (15). In (16), we used the first mechanism only, but it would be trivial to insert 'NAME of' at the start of the semantic description.

Booij (2010: 169–190) sets up an extensive argument to defend the decision not to distinguish constructions for naming and constructions for description. His point is that constructions can generally be used in both ways. It is generally assumed that A+N phrases are descriptive and N+N compounds are names for concepts. However, he gives examples of A+N phrases that serve as names and N+N compounds that serve as descriptions. Examples of A+N names include (18).

(18) a. vrije trap ('free kick')
b. donkere kamer ('dark room')

In (18), the adjectives are qualitative and they are inflected as regular adjectives. In the same way as the English translations, they are in principle ambiguous. In the case of (18b), this ambiguity is also plausible in the sense that it can refer to any room that is dark. The fact that the adjectives cannot be modified and cannot be used predicatively without losing the naming sense can be accounted for by the lack of projection in the same way as for relational adjectives.

For compounds, the expectation is the opposite, but we have already come across the pair in (19) in section 4.1.

(19) a. a commuter suburb of Charleston
b. the Chicago suburb of Cicero

For Booij, there is no sense that compounds should result in names any more than A+N combinations. This means that the contrast in (19) is similar to the one in (13) in the sense that the same construction may or may not result in a lexical entry. The difference is that syntactically the two examples in (19) behave in the same way. We can use a schema like (5) for both of them. We would need two schemas in order to encode that compounds may or may not be used as names for a concept. Whereas *commuter suburb* in (19a) would be the result of the schema with 'NAME of' in it, (19b) would use the schema without this addition.

Let us now turn to the genitive construction. As our examples, we used the contrast in (20).

(20) a. She points to a bird's nest in a low branch.
b. The mother cuckoo lays its egg in another bird's nest.

Cetnarowska (2018: 309) proposes a schema for Polish genitive constructions. On the basis of that schema, we propose the schema in (21) for the English genitive construction in (20a).

(21) <$[_{NP} [_N [_N a]_j+s]] [_N b]_i]_k$ ↔
[NAME for SEM$_i$ with some relation R to SEM$_j$]$_{SEMk}$>

Compared with Cetnarowska's schema, we only changed the order of the two nouns to reflect the difference in word order between English and Polish and adapted the notational conventions. In (20a), *bird* instantiates *a* in (21) and *nest* corresponds to *b*. The lack of an NP projection for the first noun restricts the syntactic behaviour and the use of 'NAME for' expresses the naming function. For (20b), we can add the projection and take away 'NAME for' to get the basis for the appropriate schema. Adding the projection immediately changes the structure so that *[another bird]* can be a constituent.

In exploring the borderline between words and phrases, we looked at constructions with a nominal head and various types of modifier. CxM uses the absence of a phrasal projection of the modifier as a way to preclude an expansion of this modifier as a constituent. Cetnarowska (2018) also uses 'NAME for' in the semantic description to identify names.

8.2.2 The borderline between inflection and derivation

As examples of phenomena at the borderline between inflection and derivation, we took the opposition between plural and diminutive in Dutch, as illustrated for *vogel* ('bird') in (22).

(22) a. vogel   sg
     b. vogels   pl
     c. vogeltje dim-sg
     d. vogeltjes dim-pl

In CxM, there is no distinction between inflection and derivation. In section 4.2, we gave two reasons why plural and diminutive are different. One is that plural triggers agreement and diminutive does not. The morphological effects of the diminutive can be explained by the fact that it assigns neuter gender to the resulting noun. The other difference is that the diminutive refers to a new concept, whereas the plural does not. The question to ask, then, is how CxM accounts for these differences.

On the basis of the discussion so far, we could propose the schemas in (23) for the suffixes expressing Dutch plural and diminutive.

(23) a. $<[_N [_N x]_i s]_j \leftrightarrow$ [two or more instances of $\text{SEM}_i]_j>$
     b. $<[_N [_N x]_i en]_j \leftrightarrow$ [two or more instances of $\text{SEM}_i]_j>$
     c. $<[_N [_N x]_i tje]_j \leftrightarrow$ [diminutive of $\text{SEM}_i]_{\text{SEMj}}>$

In (22a) and (22c), the schema in (23a) is used for the plural. The alternative suffix in (23b) is found in *huizen* ('houses'), the plural of *huis* ('house').

Booij (2016: 439–440) gives the schemas in (24) for the English singular–plural contrast.

(24) a. $<[(x_i)_{\omega\text{-}j} \leftrightarrow [N_i, +\text{sg}]_j \leftrightarrow [\text{SG} [\text{SEM}_i]]_j>$
     b. $<[(x_i\text{-}z)_{\omega\text{-}j} \leftrightarrow [N_i, +\text{pl}]_j \leftrightarrow [\text{PL} [\text{SEM}_i]]_j>$
     c. $<[(x_i)_{\omega\text{-}j} \leftrightarrow [N_i, +\text{sg}]_j \leftrightarrow [\text{SG} [\text{SEM}_i]]_j> \approx$
        $<[(x_i\text{-}z)_{\omega\text{-}j} \leftrightarrow [N_i, +\text{pl}]_j \leftrightarrow [\text{PL} [\text{SEM}_i]]_j>$

In (24b), we find the schema for the plural. It separates the phonological and syntactic representations, so that we distinguish between the syntactic feature [+pl] and its realization /z/. In the phonological structure, ω stands for a phonological word. In (24a), we have the schema for the singular. It does not have a suffix in the phonological structure, but does have a feature in syntax. The semantic representation is rather rudimentary, as it only repeats the syntactic feature. The schema in (24c) is a second-order schema. It states that if there is a singular form of a noun with the properties specified in the part before ≈, there is also a corresponding plural form as specified in the part following ≈ and vice versa.

When we compare the treatment of the English plural in (24) with the one for Dutch in (23a–b), there are two significant differences. First, (24a) treats the singular as the result of a schema that is parallel in structure to the one for the plural. Second, (24c) treats the singular and the plural as two connected forms. If we assume that neither of these has a parallel in the treatment of the diminutive, these mechanisms can be seen as an expression of the difference between inflection and derivation. This raises the question of how we should interpret the statement that CxM does not distinguish inflection and derivation. We will return to this question in 8.2.3.

A question that does not arise in English is the contrast between (23a) and (23b). Booij (2002: 24) proposes the generalization that in Dutch a plural noun ends in a trochee. This is exemplified by the contrast between *vogels* and *huizen*. Although there are some complications, as explained by Booij (2002: 24–34), this generalization is largely correct. In CxM, such generalizations can be expressed as schemas themselves. In the hierarchy of constructions, the schema for the phonological generalization functions as a default. More specific rules and individual exceptions can be stated to override this default.

A final point to note is the specification of the meaning. In (23) and (24), the contribution of the plural and diminutive suffixes to the meanings of the entire word is treated rather schematically. There is an important difference, however. Whereas a diminutive of a noun in Dutch denotes a new concept, a plural of a noun does not. In (23c), this is encoded by adding SEM to the final bracket of the conceptual structure, whereas (23a–b) do not have this.

Although CxM proclaims not to distinguish inflection and derivation, it has several mechanisms for expressing the contrasts that are usually associated with this distinction. One of these concerns agreement. Agreement is typical of inflection. It is the result of an operation on features in syntax. A second contrast is that derivation tends to result in a name of a new concept, whereas inflection does not. The availability as a name is expressed by adding a SEM marker to the outermost bracket. A final contrast concerns the treatment of the unmarked value. As Dutch plural is inflectional, the absence of plural can be marked as singular. By contrast, the absence of diminutive in Dutch is not marked.

Construction Morphology

8.2.3 Inflectional and derivational paradigms

In Chapter 4, we used the Slovak paradigm of the noun *gitara* as an example of an inflectional paradigm. The idea is that the features of number and case have a specific range of values and for each slot the paradigm specifies the form that fills it.

In the context of CxM, second-order schemas are used to encode inflectional paradigms. The general idea is illustrated in (24c). For the Slovak paradigm of *gitara*, twelve separate statements about the formation of individual forms are made, all of them juxtaposed with the ≈ sign between them. Booij (2016: 442) suggests such a treatment for Latin nouns, which behave similarly to their Slovak counterparts, and suggests that there may be further statements on the relation between the forms. In verbal paradigms of Romance and Slavic languages and Greek, it is in most cases sufficient to specify a limited number of forms from which all other forms can be derived. For French, the three forms in bold in Table 8.1 take this role for the verb *recevoir*.

In French, verbs have a fairly elaborate inflection. The verb *recevoir* ('receive') is one of a rather large class of verbs that do not belong to one of the regular inflection classes.[6] In Table 8.1, three combinations of mood and tense are given, with their forms for the six person and number combinations. The three forms in bold can be used to derive all the other forms in the table. For Ancient Greek, Bornemann and Risch (1978: 78) list forms that constitute the *Stammformenreihe* ('principal parts') determining the entire verbal paradigm. For Slovak, dictionaries give the infinitive, the first person singular and the third person plural of the present tense.

In our example of *gitara*, we may use the second-order schema in (25) for the paradigm.

(25) $<[(x_i\text{-a})_{\omega\text{-}j} \leftrightarrow [N_i, +\text{nom} +\text{sg}]_j \leftrightarrow [\text{SG }[\text{SEM}_i]]_j> \approx$
        $<[(x_i\text{-y})_{\omega\text{-}j} \leftrightarrow [N_i, +\text{gen} +\text{sg}]_j \leftrightarrow [\text{SG }[\text{SEM}_i]]_j> \approx$
        $<[(x_i\text{-e})_{\omega\text{-}j} \leftrightarrow [N_i, +\text{dat} +\text{sg}]_j \leftrightarrow [\text{SG }[\text{SEM}_i]]_j> \approx$
        $<[(x_i\text{-u})_{\omega\text{-}j} \leftrightarrow [N_i, +\text{acc} +\text{sg}]_j \leftrightarrow [\text{SG }[\text{SEM}_i]]_j> \approx$
        $<[(x_i\text{-e})_{\omega\text{-}j} \leftrightarrow [N_i, +\text{loc} +\text{sg}]_j \leftrightarrow [\text{SG }[\text{SEM}_i]]_j> \approx$
        $<[(x_i\text{-ou})_{\omega\text{-}j} \leftrightarrow [N_i, +\text{inst} +\text{sg}]_j \leftrightarrow [\text{SG }[\text{SEM}_i]]_j> \approx$
        $<[(x_i\text{-y})_{\omega\text{-}j} \leftrightarrow [N_i, +\text{nom} +\text{pl}]_j \leftrightarrow [\text{PL }[\text{SEM}_i]]_j> \approx$
        $<[(x_i)_{\omega\text{-}j} \leftrightarrow [N_i, +\text{gen} +\text{pl}]_j \leftrightarrow [\text{PL }[\text{SEM}_i]]_j> \approx$
        $<[(x_i\text{-ám})_{\omega\text{-}j} \leftrightarrow [N_i, +\text{dat} +\text{pl}]_j \leftrightarrow [\text{PL }[\text{SEM}_i]]_j> \approx$
        $<[(x_i\text{-y})_{\omega\text{-}j} \leftrightarrow [N_i, +\text{acc} +\text{pl}]_j \leftrightarrow [\text{PL }[\text{SEM}_i]]_j> \approx$
        $<[(x_i\text{-ách})_{\omega\text{-}j} \leftrightarrow [N_i, +\text{loc} +\text{pl}]_j \leftrightarrow [\text{PL }[\text{SEM}_i]]_j> \approx$
        $<[(x_i\text{-ami})_{\omega\text{-}j} \leftrightarrow [N_i, +\text{inst} +\text{pl}]_j \leftrightarrow [\text{PL }[\text{SEM}_i]]_j>$

---

[6] French has two main conjugation classes. Mauger (1968: 202–230) lists 102 verbs with basic inflectional irregularities and 196 verbs that follow one of these patterns.

Table 8.1 *Partial conjugation of French* recevoir *('receive')*

	indicatif présent	indicatif imparfait	subjonctif présent
1 sg	**reçois**	recevais	reçoive
2 sg	reçois	recevais	reçoives
3 sg	reçoit	recevait	reçoive
1 pl	**recevons**	recevions	recevions
2 pl	recevez	receviez	receviez
3 pl	**reçoivent**	recevaient	reçoivent

In (25), we adopt the conventions from (24c) and divide the form specification into information for phonological and syntactic structures. In the genitive plural, a different schema will have to bring about the vowel lengthening in the stem to result in *gitár*. The paradigm in (25) applies to a large set of feminine nouns in Slovak.

In Booij's writings, inflection generally has a less important place than word formation. In fact, Booij and Masini (2015) only discuss second-order schemas for derivational paradigms. However, in discussing derivational paradigms, Štekauer (2014: 362–364) makes a distinction between Booij's treatment of derivational paradigms as a way of treating individual cases and the much more systematic approach adopted by Dokulil (1962), Horecký et al. (1989) and Furdík (2004). Whereas Booij (2010) concentrates on the formation of word pairs of the type illustrated in (8) in section 8.1, Horecký et al. (1989: 44) describe a derivational paradigm as consisting of an ordered set of all words directly related to the same motivating word.[7]

The examples of the Slovak anglicisms *blog* and *bloger* and their derivations show that a single naming action may result in several related words. Also in these cases, derivational paradigms can be encoded as second-order schemas. We repeat the triple for *blog* in (26) and propose a second-order schema in (27).

(26) a. blog
b. blogovať
c. blogový

(27) a. <N_i ↔ [Thing]$_i$> ≈
b. <[$_V$ N_i ovať] ↔ [Action related to [Thing]$_i$]> ≈
c. <[$_A$ N_i ový] ↔ [Thing]$_i$>

The division into *a*, *b*, *c* in (27) is only for convenience of reference, it is not intended as part of the formalism. In (27b), the specification of *ovať* is

---

[7] In fact, Horecký et al. (1989: 44) use the term *slovotvorná paradigma* ('word formation paradigm') rather than *derivačná paradigma* ('derivational paradigm').

intended as a reference to the verbal inflection class that is marked by this infinitival ending. Similarly, (27c) uses *ový* to refer to the adjectival inflection class by means of the nominative masculine singular. These form specifications constitute the connection with the second-order schema for the inflectional endings. The suffix in (27c) is the same that is addressed in (16). In principle, it would be possible to insert (16) instead of (27c). However, because of the possibility of multiple inheritance, (16) and (27c) can also be taken as different pieces of information about the same set of words.[8]

As we saw in this section, inflectional and derivational paradigms are encoded as second-order schemas. This encoding does not depend on the distinction between inflection and derivation.

8.2.4 The distinction between transposition and the formation of names

In his overview of CxM, Booij (2020: 1005) gives (28) as a first example of a constructional schema for derivation.

(28)   <[$_N$ [$_A$ x]$_i$ ness]$_j$ ↔ [Property of SEM$_i$]$_{SEMj}$>

The schema in (28) is intended to account for 'English deadjectival nouns in *-ness* that denote the property expressed by the corresponding adjectives' (Booij 2020: 1005). An example is *sloppiness*. Clearly, the form-side relates *sloppiness* to *sloppy*. The meaning-side of (28) hides a problem in the way it is formalized. As Booij (2020: 1006) explicitly adopts Jackendoff's PA, we can use Jackendoff's (1990) formalism for Conceptual Structure to encode the meaning of *sloppy* as in (29a).

(29)   a.   [$_{PROPERTY}$ SLOPPY]
       b.   [Property of [$_{PROPERTY}$ SLOPPY]$_i$]$_{SEMj}$

When we replace SEM$_i$ in (28) by (29a) we get (29b). However, in (29b) we have the same property referred to twice. We can avoid this problem by encoding the noun and the adjective as having the same meaning, as in (30).

(30)   <[$_N$ [$_A$ x]$_i$ ness]$_j$ ↔ [Property]$_{SEMi,j}$>

The specification of the meaning as a property is justified because it is only for qualitative adjectives designating a property that nominalization with *-ness* is possible. We can see this when we consider the examples in (31).

---

[8] In (27b–c), we did not coindex the semantics of the entire expression with the outer bracket of the form. In the case of (27c), this would interact with the question of transposition, which we discuss in section 8.2.4.

(31) a. presidential office
    b. the presidentialness of the office

Whereas in (31a) *presidential* is normally interpreted as a relational adjective along the lines of (16), the nominalization with (30), as shown in (31b), excludes this reading. We may either reject (31b) as ungrammatical or attempt to come up with an interpretation in which *presidential* refers to a property.

One of the examples of transposition we introduced in section 4.4 is the German pair *Installation* and *Installierung*. We repeat the examples illustrating their difference in (32).

(32) a. die Installation der Heizungsanlage
       'the installation of_the heating_system'
    b. veraltete Installationen erneuern
       'outdated installations renew', i.e. replace outdated installations
    c. die Installierung der Heizungsanlage
    d. *veraltete Installierungen erneuern

Whereas *Installation* has both a process reading, as in (32a), and a result reading, as in (32b), *Installierung* only has the process reading in (32c), as the ungrammaticality of (32d) shows. There are several questions related to these data. First, there is the question of how to relate the two readings of *Installation*. Then there is the question of how the two nouns are related to each other and to the verb *installieren*. A third question is why *Installierung* has only one reading, the process reading.

The relation between process and result readings is found in many languages. Masini and Audring (2019: 379) give a schema for Italian *-ita* as in *crescita* ('growth') from the verb *crescere* ('grow') along the lines of (33).

(33) $<[_N [_V x]_i \text{ ita}]_j \leftrightarrow [\{\text{EVENT} | \text{RESULT}\} \text{ of } \text{SEM}_i]_{\text{SEM}_j}>$

In (33), we adapted the formalism to make it compatible with other examples discussed here. The curly brackets indicate an alternation. For EVENT, this leads to the same problem as we noted in (28). However, as the schema in (33) is actually used to illustrate the use of conditions on the input restricting the productivity of the schema (which we omitted in (33)), we should perhaps not put too much weight on this aspect.

More pertinent may be the discussion of Dutch *-er* by Booij (2010: 76–84). Some examples of it are given in (34).

(34) a. schrijven – schrijver   ('write – writer')
    b. kloppen – klopper   ('knock$_V$ – knocker')
    c. Amsterdam – Amsterdammer
    d. apotheek – apotheker   ('pharmacy – pharmacist')

Apart from the deverbal uses in (34a–b), expressing agent or instrument, there are also the denominal uses for inhabitant in (34c) and person with a relation to the base noun (34d). Booij (2010: 84) proposes a hierarchy of schemas and subschemas to account for the relation between the different uses of *-er*. This solution exploits the possibility of default inheritance in an inheritance hierarchy. At the highest level, the meaning of *-er* is described as 'entity with relation R to SEM', where SEM stands for the meaning of the base. At the next level, a further specification is based on the syntactic category of the base. The third level specifies the distinction between personal agent and impersonal agent (2010: 80) for (34a–b). At this level, the type in (34c) with a place name is also specified as a subschema of the denominal use.

The data in (32) are different in the sense that the two readings of *-ation* must be hierarchically related, but cannot be distinguished in terms of the base. As argued by ten Hacken (2019a: 80–82), the process reading is more basic than the result reading. Both readings are also in principle available for *-ung*, as illustrated in (35).

(35) a. Die Fälschung von Banknoten ist strafbar.
 'the counterfeiting of banknotes is punishable'
 b. Diese Banknote ist eine Fälschung.
 'this banknote is a counterfeit'

A result reading of the type we see for *Fälschung* ('counterfeit') in (35b) is not available for *Installierung* in (32d). This means that the result reading is a more specific use, but where it appears, it usually appears alongside the process reading. We can encode this by making the result reading a subschema of the process reading. Alternatively, we may opt not to encode this, but then we cannot explain why (32d) is not good.

For the relation between nouns in *-ation* and underlying verbs in *-ieren*, Hüning (2018: 349) gives a second-order schema as in (36).

(36) $\langle [_V [x]_i \text{ ier}]_j \leftrightarrow [\text{to undertake SEM}_k]_{\text{SEMj}}\rangle \approx$
 $\langle [_N [x]_i \text{ ation}]_k \leftrightarrow [\text{the event/action of SEM}_j]_{\text{SEMk}}\rangle$

The second-order schema in (36) is based on Booij's (2010: 34) schema for the Dutch counterpart of these verbs and nouns. The index i is only used in the form-side. It correlates the two bases in the entries related in (36), but it does not require that x has a lexical entry of its own. In our case, *install* is not a German word. By this use of x, Booij avoids making an entry for *install* and similar bound stems. As noted in section 8.1, Booij (2010: 15) claims that morphemes are not signs and should not be lexical entries. The index j stands for the verb in *-ieren* and the index k for the noun in *-ation*. The way they are related displays a circularity that is in general not accepted in a dictionary. Whereas *installieren* is described as 'to undertake (an) *Installation*', *Installation* is described as 'the event/action of *installieren*'. As a way to relate these two words, however, (36) is not problematic. A second-order schema is used to relate two (or more) entries, not to generate one from the other.

In (36) it is worth noting that only the process reading is referred to. As we argued, the choice of the process reading as the underlying one is correct. We can derive the result reading in the lexical hierarchy as described above. In the same way as (28), however, the transpositional nature of the nominalization is encoded by a redundant specification. As the meaning of *installieren*, as captured in SEM_j, is already an event or action, adding 'the event/action of' is pleonastic.

In sum, we can say that transposition can be expressed in CxM, but in published accounts a redundant specification of the type illustrated in (28) is found. There is no formal problem in replacing such representations by more accurate ones along the lines of (30). For the relation between the German verb *installieren* and the corresponding noun *Installation*, a second-order schema can be used. The relation between process and result readings can be encoded by a hierarchical relationship. No explanation is offered why *Installation* can have both readings and *Installierung* only the process reading.

8.2.5 Onomasiological coercion

As an example of onomasiological coercion, we gave *doorman* in section 4.5. In CxM, *doorman* is first of all a compound. As such it is in the scope of a construction that is similar to the Dutch one repeated here in (37) in a simplified form.

(37) $<[_N [_X a]_k [_N b]_i]_j \leftrightarrow [SEM_i \text{ with relation R to } SEM_k]_j>$

In the case of *doorman*, *door* instantiates a and *man* is b. The construction therefore only specifies that a doorman is a man with some relation to (a) door. Booij does not seem to be interested in the naming process as such, because we did not find any explicit statement about it. Booij (2016: 429) explains that '[h]olistic properties of a construction can be observed in coercion effects', but this does not refer to onomasiological coercion. Booij's sense of coercion is rather concerned with interpretation than with naming. A good example of what Booij means by coercion is (31b). Booij (2016: 429) gives the example of comparatives and superlatives of non-gradable adjectives. The difference is that in Booij's sense of coercion, the meaning of a base is extended to fit the requirements of a construction, whereas in onomasiological coercion, the meaning of the output is constrained to fit the concept that is to be named. In Booij's sense, coercion is something remarkable that only happens in some contexts of use. It may happen in naming, but not in such regular cases as *doorman*, where the two components fit with (37) without any problem. By contrast, onomasiological coercion occurs in all instances of naming.

Construction Morphology

One way to cover a larger part of the meaning of *doorman* in CxM is to exploit the inheritance hierarchy as an organization of the constructicon. In a way similar to the Dutch affixoid *pracht* in (4), we might propose (38) as a construction for compounds with *man* as a second component.

(38) <[$_N$ [$_X$ a]$_k$ [$_N$ man]$_i$]$_j$ ↔ [SEM$_i$ whose task is determined by SEM$_k$]$_j$>

The problem with this approach becomes clear when we compare (38) with the definition of *doorman* from COBUILD (2023), presented in section 4.5 and repeated here in (39).

(39) a. A doorman is
 b. a man who stands at the door
 c. of a club,
 d. prevents unwanted people from coming in, and makes people leave if they cause trouble.

The progress from (37) to (38) in determining the meaning of *doorman* is minimal. The verb in (39b) remains unexpressed as does (39c). The task referred to in (38) relates to (39d), but there remains a considerable gap in the degree of specification between having a task determined by *door* and preventing unwanted people from coming in.

At this point, it is worth returning to the concept of *constructionalization*, discussed in the context of (4). As elaborated by Hüning and Booij (2014), constructionalization is on one hand distinguished from grammaticalization, on the other from lexicalization. Specifying that *doorman* has the meaning in (39) is a case of lexicalization, whereas (38) illustrates constructionalization. CxM has something to say about constructionalization, because it refers to regularities, but not about lexicalization, because it refers to individual expressions. The same point can be made about the German, Dutch and Slovak translations of *doorman*. They involve different constructions, but evoke naming problems of the same type.

8.3 Word formation and naming in CxM

In CxM, the semantic interpretation of expressions is an important consideration. As such, it can be compared with Lieber's Lexical Semantic Framework (LSF) we discussed in Chapter 7. A major difference between LSF and CxM is that LSF takes morphemes as the basic units, whereas CxM denies that bound morphemes are signs. This means that affixes have a lexical entry in LSF, but not in CxM. In this respect, CxM is more similar to Kiparsky's Lexical Morphology and Phonology we discussed in Chapter 6.

In our view, the difference should not be exaggerated. CxM includes schemas that represent generalizations about lexical entries. Schemas are used for affixes in a way we saw, for instance, in (2d), repeated here as (40), for the English agent forming suffix -er.

(40) $<[_N [_V x]_i \text{ er}]_j \leftrightarrow [\text{Agent of SEM}_i]_j>$

The information specified in (40) includes the phonological shape of the suffix, the environment it can appear in and the meaning of the full expression containing it. This is the same amount of information that is contained in a lexical entry for -er in LSF. Schemas such as (40) are lexical entries in CxM. The main difference is that (40) is not a word formation rule. It does not give an input and output. Schemas are purely declarative in the same way as lexical entries for words. They do not overgenerate. As Masini and Audring (2019: 372) state, although (40) is compatible with both *walker* and **stander*, only the former is listed in the lexicon and (40) will not generate the latter. In principle, this assigns an important place to naming as an act of extending the lexicon, but this is not elaborated in the CxM literature. In this sense, one might be reminded of the place of the Encyclopedia in Distributed Morphology, as discussed in Chapter 5.

In section 8.2, we found a number of mechanisms for distinguishing complex expressions that serve as naming units. In the contrast with descriptive phrases, three main mechanisms are used. They can be illustrated with the schemas in (12a) and (15), repeated here in (41).

(41) a. $<[_N [_A a]_k [_N b]_i]_j \leftrightarrow$
[type of SEM$_i$ characterized by SEM$_k$]$_j>$
b. $[N^0_i A^0_j]_k \leftrightarrow$
[NAME for SEM$_i$ with some relation R to entity E of SEM$_j$]$_{SEMk}$

In (41a) we see the schema for German A+N compounds, e.g. *Hartkäse* ('granular cheese'), based on Booij's (2010: 18) schema for nominal compounds. In (41b), we have Cetnarowska's (2018: 308) schema for Polish relational adjective constructions such as *dział finansowy* ('finance department'). The first mechanism is the projection of the non-head. We see this most clearly in (41a), where A is not embedded in an AP. This precludes the realization of complements and modifiers of the adjective. The second mechanism is visible in the formulation of the semantics. In (41a), we have 'type of' and in (41b) 'NAME for'. The latter formulation especially makes it explicit that we are dealing with a naming unit. The third mechanism is the assignment of a separate SEM to the complex unit. This is only done in (41b), but this may be because (41a) is from a stage of the development of the formalism where this was not implemented yet. We can compare the latter two mechanisms to the idea pursued by Borer (2014) in the context of Distributed Morphology and mentioned in section 5.3, namely to identify structures that serve as naming units.

Booij (2010: 169–190) argues extensively against a distinction between constructions for naming and constructions for describing. This seems to be in conflict with the use of the mechanisms shown in particular in (41b). Perhaps Booij's original argument can be understood as targeting a crude distinction. He gives examples like *vrije trap* ('free kick') in (18a) to illustrate that A+N phrases can serve a naming purpose. Conversely, we saw *Chicago suburb* in (19b) as an example of a deictic compound with a descriptive function. We should therefore not state that A+N phrases are always descriptive and N+N compounds always naming expressions. As long as the mechanisms in (41b) are used carefully, this is not a problem.

The use of SEM at the outer bracket can also be used to identify naming expressions in contrast to inflection. We saw this in the contrast in (23), repeated here partially in (42).

(42) a. $<[_N [_N x]_i s]_j \leftrightarrow$ [two or more instances of $SEM_i]_j>$
 b. $<[_N [_N x]_i tje]_j \leftrightarrow$ [diminutive of $SEM_i]_{SEMj}>$

In (42a), we have the schema for the plural of Dutch *vogel* ('bird') and in (42b) the one for the diminutive. The fact that the plural in *vogels* ('birds') constitutes a separate piece of information, whereas the diminutive *vogeltje* ('bird$_{DIM}$') creates a new prototype, is expressed by the presence of SEM at the outer bracket of (42b) as contrasted with its absence in (42a). Another mechanism to achieve this is suggested by Booij (2016: 439–440). It is illustrated by the entries for the English plural in (24), repeated here as (43).

(43) a. $<[(x_i)_{\omega\text{-}j} \leftrightarrow [N_i, +sg]_j \leftrightarrow [SG [SEM_i]]_j>$
 b. $<[(x_i\text{-}z)_{\omega\text{-}j} \leftrightarrow [N_i, +pl]_j \leftrightarrow [PL [SEM_i]]_j>$
 c. $<[(x_i)_{\omega\text{-}j} \leftrightarrow [N_i, +sg]_j \leftrightarrow [SG [SEM_i]]_j> \approx$
    $<[(x_i\text{-}z)_{\omega\text{-}j} \leftrightarrow [N_i, +pl]_j \leftrightarrow [PL [SEM_i]]_j>$

Corresponding to the plural schema in (42a), we have (43b). However, the singular also has a separate schema in (43a) and the two schemas are connected in the second-order schema in (43c). For the diminutive, there is no separate value for the non-diminutive, so that there is also no scope for any second-order schema that would connect them.

As we saw in section 8.2.3, second-order schemas of the type in (43c) are the result of any generalization about two schemas. They are most intuitive for simple cases such as the English singular–plural contrast. For inflectional paradigms of the type we find in Slovak, they are possible but fail to catch the systematic nature. This is also the case for derivational paradigms.

The discussion of transposition in section 8.2.4 showed a problem in the perception of the data. The idea that a transposition does not change the meaning is not expressed in the examples of schemas found in the literature. Booij (2020: 1005) gives a schema for *-ness* that includes the property of a property in (28). We can correct this, leading to (30), where the adjective and the noun with *-ness* have the same semantic index. However, this perception of transposition hampers the analysis of our example of German *Installation* and *Installierung*. It is difficult to encode and impossible to explain that both are possible with a process reading, but only *Installation* also has a result reading.

Finally, in the discussion of onomasiological coercion, we found that CxM's emphasis on constructionalization shifts attention away from the naming perspective. Constructionalization is opposed both to grammaticalization and to lexicalization. It reduces the barrier to encode aspects of meaning in a construction, but the type of coercion that goes along with naming is not covered. Booij (2016: 429) mentions coercion only in the perspective of interpretation. This raises problems of the same type as we found in the context of LSF in Chapter 7.

In sum, although CxM differs from LSF in adopting a word-based view of the lexicon, its degree of success in the coverage of naming is very similar. With the assignment of SEM, it has a powerful mechanism for identifying naming expressions, supplemented by a number of specific mechanisms that can be used in a more restricted set of cases. The coverage of paradigms is less systematic than desirable and onomasiological coercion is neither discussed nor properly covered.

CHAPTER 9

Relational Morphology

Relational Morphology (RM) is the name introduced by Jackendoff and Audring (2016: 468) for the approach to morphology developed by Ray Jackendoff in the framework of Parallel Architecture (PA). The start of the use of RM as a name coincides with Jackendoff's collaboration with Jenny Audring. The main reference for RM is Jackendoff and Audring (2020). As Booij's CxM also adopts PA, a question that poses itself is how RM is related to CxM. Jackendoff and Audring (2016: 468) state that they 'draw freely on Construction Morphology (Booij, 2010)'. In their preface, Jackendoff and Audring (2020: ix) state that 'Geert [Booij] has been a constant source of inspiration, advice, and encouragement.' Nevertheless, there are certain differences not only of emphasis, but also of substance between RM and CxM. In section 9.1, we will present RM as a framework for research and in section 9.2, we will consider how the data we presented in Chapter 4 can be covered in RM. In section 9.3, the success of the coverage of these data is evaluated and compared with that of some related frameworks discussed in previous chapters.

9.1 Relational Morphology as a framework

Ray Jackendoff did his PhD in the context of what Newmeyer (1986a) called the *Linguistic Wars*. In the discussion between interpretive and Generative Semantics, he sided with Chomsky. An indication of the prominent role he played is that in Huck and Goldsmith's (1995) account of the events, Jackendoff is one of the four linguists interviewed, the only one defending interpretive semantics. In Chapter 3, we came across Jackendoff's (1975) elaboration of Chomsky's (1970) Lexicalist Hypothesis. Jackendoff (1975) proposes a theory of the lexicon based on the Full Entry Theory. In this theory, the lexicon has fully specified entries that are linked by redundancy rules. This organization of the lexicon is a constant feature of Jackendoff's theorizing. Jackendoff (2010), a collection of articles with the title *Meaning and the Lexicon*, has the 1975 article at the start.

Jackendoff is not primarily a morphologist. His emphasis is rather on semantics. Jackendoff (1983) presented the foundation of a theory of Conceptual Structure, which Jackendoff (1990) elaborated in more detail. Several articles about details of the formalism and its application to various phenomena appear in Jackendoff (2010).

The framework of Parallel Architecture was first presented by Jackendoff (1997). PA is Jackendoff's solution to the problem that his Conceptual Structure does not match the system of assumptions that Chomsky had meanwhile developed about syntactic representation. The central difference is that, whereas Chomsky assumes that semantic interpretation is based on and derived from syntactic representation, Jackendoff proposes that phonological, syntactic and conceptual representations are each generated by rules and linked to each other without one of them taking priority over the others. Jackendoff (1997) uses compounds and fixed phrases as a central argument for his PA.

Jackendoff (2002) presents a general theory of language based on PA. In his chapter on lexical storage (2002: 152–195), he also addresses the representation of morphology. A first elaboration of the formalism to be used in word formation appears in Jackendoff's (2009) chapter in the *Oxford Handbook of Compounding*. A revised version of this chapter constitutes the final chapter of Jackendoff (2010).

Jenny Audring completed her PhD at the Free University of Amsterdam in 2009. She worked on grammatical gender, but also published on CxM together with Geert Booij, e.g. Booij and Audring (2017). As they say in their preface, Jackendoff and Audring met in 2012 and started working together on morphology, thus developing RM (2020: ix).

Despite its name, RM is not adequately characterized as a theory of morphology. Jackendoff and Audring (2020: 4) present RM as a 'reconceptualization of linguistic theory' based on 'interweaving themes at three levels: morphology, the structure of the lexicon, and the place of the language capacity in the human mind'. One could say that RM is primarily a theory of the organization of the lexicon. This may seem a less ambitious scope than a reconceptualization of linguistic theory, but it should not be forgotten that in PA, lexical entries are not only entries for words, but also entries for rules and anything in between words and rules.

Jackendoff (2002: 167–182) argues in detail that there is a gradual transition between lexicon entries for prototypical words and syntactic rules. In between the two, we find, for instance, lexicon entries for idioms and for syntactic constructions with partially specified lexical material. An example of the latter is what Jackendoff (1997) calls the 'time'-*away* construction, exemplified in *Bill slept the afternoon away*. Jackendoff (2002: 182) concludes that the entire spectrum from words to syntactic rules should be covered by lexical entries of the same basic type. The only difference is what type of information is specified. In an entry for a prototypical word, it is mainly the phonological and conceptual information that is specified, with the syntax reduced to a syntactic category. In an entry for a typical syntactic rule, it is the syntactic structure that is specified, with the phonology empty and the conceptual structure minimal. The 'time'-*away* construction will have *away* specified in phonology, syntactic conditions in a partially specified syntactic tree, and the contribution to meaning in a partial conceptual structure. In this way, all of a speaker's knowledge of their language is specified in the lexicon.

As a central hypothesis of RM, Jackendoff and Audring (2020: 52) propose the Relational Hypothesis in (1).[1]

(1) *Relational Hypothesis*
All schemas can be used relationally. A particular subset of them, the productive ones, can *also* be used generatively.

The 'schemas' in (1) correspond to schemas in Booij's (2010) CxM, but as Jackendoff and Audring (2020: 39) mention, (1) is also an activation of Jackendoff's (1975) idea of redundancy rules. The fact that *redundancy rule* has *rule* in it should not distract from the observation that they operate as constraints, not as procedural rules. As explained by Jackendoff and Audring (2020: 31–32), a rule-based theory depends on a sequence of operations performed in a particular order. Instead, RM assumes a constraint-based theory. Lexical entries provide information. This information can be used to determine whether a particular entry is applicable and to extend the information content of an expression that is being formed. The system working with the lexical entries produces expressions that comply with the constraints they impose and combine the information they provide.

A central issue addressed in (1) is the question of productivity. In his introduction to a collection of his articles, Jackendoff (2010: 28–34) identifies this *semi-productivity* as a crucial issue for further research. Jackendoff and Audring (2016: 473) replace the name *semi-productivity* by *non-productivity*, without changing the view of the nature of the phenomenon. RM can be seen as the elaboration of a theory of semi- or non-productivity, including its position in the lexicon and its relation to productivity. Jackendoff and Audring (2020: 46) explain their interpretation of productivity in (2).

(2) By a productive pattern, we mean one that speakers use freely and systematically in novel instances, and that hearers interpret without particular attention.

The formulation in (2) is reminiscent of the well-known definition of productivity by Schultink (1961).[2] Central in Schultink's definition are the

---

[1] Emphasis as in original.
[2] For a critical discussion of Jackendoff's use of *productivity* in relation to Schultink's (1961) definition, Corbin's (1987) analysis and Baayen's (1992) notions, see ten Hacken (2019a: 48–58).

conditions of unintentionality and an in principle uncountable number of instances. In (2), the former is rendered by 'freely' and 'without particular attention', the latter by 'systematically'. As Jackendoff and Audring (2020: 46–50) note, there is no direct correlation with frequency, although frequency does play a role. As further factors they identify transparency and generality. They correspond to two types of predictability, on one hand of the intended interpretation and on the other of the acceptability of the expected result. It is interesting that they also mention 'that the freedom to produce novel instances of a pattern is partly a matter of fashion' (2020: 49). Here, naming must be understood as what is subject to fashion, i.e. which pattern is chosen. However, there is no explicit mention of naming in their text.

In interpreting (2), we have to take into account that for Jackendoff and Audring (2020: 41), it is not a schema that is productive, but a variable in a schema. The idea is that a schema specifies information at phonological, syntactic and conceptual structure. This information can be expressed by a constant or a variable. For each variable, it is specified separately whether it is productive. In this sense, the formulation in (2) is somewhat misleading, because it refers to a productive pattern. We may say that a productive variable is one that speakers may instantiate with new material, i.e. with items that are not stored as instantiations of the variable in their mental lexicon.

An important consequence of the hypothesis in (1) is that schemas can be used to encode generalizations that are not usually related to word formation. Jackendoff and Audring (2020: 50–52) discuss gender assignment to nouns. In many languages there are phonological, morphological or semantic generalizations, often in the form of defaults. Thus, in Slovak, nouns with a nominative singular in *-o*, e.g. *mesto* ('city'), are neuter. They propose to encode such generalizations as redundancy rules, i.e. schemas. In the same way as non-productive schemas, they serve to organize the lexicon.

Both CxM and RM assume PA as the basic infrastructure for the storage of linguistic information. A difference between the two is that, whereas CxM uses inheritance hierarchies, RM uses relational links instead. Jackendoff and Audring (2020: 68–70) point out a number of problems that are caused by the directional nature of inheritance. They give the examples in (3).

(3) a. ambition ~ ambitious
    b. flirt ~ flirtation ~ flirtatious
    c. assassin ~ assassinate

In (3a), it is difficult to determine which word inherits from the other. In (3b), we can say that both the noun *flirtation* and the adjective *flirtatious* inherit from the verb *flirt*. In (3a), however, there is no corresponding lexical item **ambit*, so we would have to hypothesize an abstract or virtual item (Jackendoff and Audring 2020: 70). In (3c), the noun is semantically based on the verb, but morphologically it is the other way round. The relational links should be distinguished from interface links. Whereas interface links connect constituents of phonological, syntactic and conceptual structures of a single expression, whether a lexical entry or not, relational links connect constituents at the same level of structure from different lexical entries. The interplay between different types of link can be illustrated with the entries for *bake*, *baker* and *-er* in (4) to (6), based on Jackendoff and Audring (2020: 89).[3]

(4) a. $bake_1$
    b. V_1
    c. $[BAKE\ (Agent: X, Patient: Y)]_1$

(5) a. $[bak_1\ er_2]_3$
    b. $[V_1\ aff_2]_3$
    c. $[PERSON^\alpha;\ [BAKE\ (Agent: \alpha, Patient: INDEF)]_1]_3$

(6) a. $[\ldots_x\ er_2]_y$
    b. $[V_x\ aff_2]_y$
    c. $[PERSON^\alpha;\ [F\ (Agent: \alpha, \ldots)]_x]_y$

The index *1* is an interface index when it links (4a), (4b) and (4c). In (5), it has the same function, but it links the stem in (5a) to the verb in (5b) and the meaning of the verb in (5c). At the same time, *1* is a relational index when it links *bake* in (4a) and (5a), when it links V in (4b) and (5b), and when it links the meaning of the verb in (4c) and (5c). In (5), we see the indices *2* and *3* as well. They are only interface links here, correlating with the suffix and the derived word, respectively.

The meaning represented in (5c) includes the meaning in (4c). However, whereas in (4c) the two arguments are variables, *X* and *Y*, in (5c) neither of these variables is available for binding. Instead of *X* in (4c), we have α in (5c). The difference is that, whereas *X* is a variable that can be instantiated in the context of use of the word, α is bound by PERSON within the conceptual structure. Instead of *Y* in (4c), we have 'INDEF' in (5c), which is simply a statement that this argument cannot be instantiated. This should not be interpreted so as to exclude *a baker of delicious cakes*, however, where the object is introduced by a preposition.

In (6), we have the schema for *-er*. The index *2* is an interface index within (6), linking (6a) and (6b), but at the same time a relational index establishing the relation with the corresponding element in (5). The index α in (6c) works in the same way as in (5c). The ... in (6a) and (6c) encode underspecified material. In (6a), it means that the base to which *-er* is attached is not

---

[3] In the representation of entries in this chapter, we use a threefold division, where *a* stands for the phonological structure, *b* for the syntactic structure and *c* for the conceptual structure. As we are not interested in phonological details, we use orthographic representation, which also makes it easier to identify the entries.

phonologically restricted. In (6c), we do not know the argument structure of the verb. The only constraint is that there is an agent. The two instances of ... in (6) are independent of each other. The subscripts *x* and *y* in (6) are variables that are instantiated as *1* and *3* in (5).

The nature of RM as a theory about the structure of the lexicon is also illustrated by Jackendoff and Audring's (2020: 71) contrast of *baker*, *butcher* and *king*. All three are nouns with an agentive interpretation. In the case of *butcher*, we have a suffix -*er*, but no verb. In the case of *king*, there is no suffix. For *butcher* and *king*, we can describe the meaning in a way parallel to (5c). For *butcher*, we can also set up relational links with the schema in (6) and an interface link between -*er* and *aff*. For *king*, no such links are available. In a similar way, they account for the pairs in (3).

In sum, RM does not have word formation rules in the sense of rules for the formation of new words on the basis of existing ones. What is usually treated as the input and output of such rules is used in RM as a way of structuring the lexicon by establishing links between entries. The starting point is then a list of fully specified entries. The result is an intricately organized network of entries with relational links between them.

9.2 The treatment of relevant contrasts in RM

In this section, we will go over the data we presented in Chapter 4 and indicate how they can be treated in RM. The structure of the section follows the structure of Chapter 4.

9.2.1 Words and phrases

In the genesis of PA, the relationship between words and phrases takes a special position. As mentioned in section 9.1, Jackendoff (1997) originally used the observation that phrasal expressions can also be stored in the mental lexicon as a motivation to propose a parallel architecture.[4] Therefore, it is interesting to consider how the contrasts we introduced in section 4.1 can be dealt with. As a first example, we used the German examples in (7).

(7) a. Hartkäse ('granular cheese')
 b. harter Käse ('hard cheese')

---

[4] Jackendoff (1997: 209–215) gives a list of expressions that were used as solutions in a television game show. Many of them are compounds. There are also A+N expressions, e.g. *blue cheese*, proper names, idioms, book and film titles, and clichés. They have in common that they are multi-word expressions for which it can be argued that they are stored in the mental lexicon.

The base components in (7a) and (7b) are the same, but (7a) is a compound and (7b) a phrase. In German, the contrast is visible in the form, where the adjective is stressed in (7a) and inflected in (7b), and in the meaning, where (7a) designates a type of cheese and (7b) describes a cheese.

Jackendoff's (2009) proposal for the treatment of compounds was an important step in the development of RM, but it only treats N+N compounds. Building on this proposal, Schlücker (2016) develops an account of German A+N compounds.

Jackendoff (2009) proposes a number of different mechanisms to account for the meaning of compounds. The first is the compound schemas (2009: 122). For N+N compounds, he proposes an argument schema for compounds where the non-head is an argument of the head and a modifier schema for all other cases. In the modifier schema, there is an underspecified function F relating the two components of the compound. In a second step, he proposes a list of basic functions that can instantiate F (2009: 123–124). The list of functions varies slightly in other presentations of the account (cf. Jackendoff 2010: 436–442; 2016: 27–31). Finally, the basic functions interact with each other and with general cognitive mechanisms to produce a fairly precise description of F for individual compounds.

Schlücker (2016: 182–184) argues against one of the basic functions proposed by Jackendoff in all variants of his list, CLASSIFY. Jackendoff (2016: 27) gives the examples in (8).

(8) a. beta cell
    b. X-ray
    c. Leyden jar
    d. Molotov cocktail

For examples such as (8), Jackendoff states that the first noun 'plays only a classificatory role' (2016: 27). As Schlücker observes, however, 'this classificatory function of the first constituent is not a characteristic of this particular kind of noun-noun compounds but is rather a common property of all nominal compounds' (2016: 182). That is to say, the compounds in (8) are special only because they do not have a more specific relation. From a naming perspective, one can doubt this, because it would imply that the name has no motivation. Thus, in the case of (8c), we have an object that has the shape of a jar and was invented in Leiden. Even in the case of (8a), the naming took place when two types of cell had to be distinguished, the other one being named *alpha cell*.[5]

Instead of CLASSIFY as a basic function, Schlücker proposes to have a function IS A SUBTYPE OF, which is included in the basic schema for

---

[5] Ceranowicz et al. (2015: 3) attribute the first distinction to Lane (1907), who used *A cells* and *B cells*. Hellman et al. (1962) distinguished two types of A cells and called one of them *alpha cells*. Lane's B cells were then called *beta cells*.

compounding. This is important for the analysis of (7), because it distinguishes (7a) from (7b). She proposes the schema in (9) for A+N compounds such as (7a).

(9) $[A_1 \ N_2]$ =
[IS A SUBTYPE OF $([[Y_2^\alpha; [X_1 \ (\ldots \alpha \ldots)]]; \text{TYPE}], [Y_2; \text{TYPE}])$]

The notation in (9) gives the syntactic and the conceptual structure, separated by the = sign. Applied to (7a) and starting from the back, (9) says first of all that *Käse*, which instantiates *Y*, is a type. Then it establishes a subtype relation between the type of *Käse* modified by *hart*, which instantiates *X*, and the general type *Käse*.

For a full account of the contrast in (7), we also have to ensure that (9) does not apply to (7b). In (7b), we have an NP and the meaning is of an intersective nature. That is to say, (7b) refers to *Käse* which has the property *hart*, but without implying that the result is a type of cheese. We can use (10) to encode this.

(10) $[_{NP} A_1 \ N_2]$ = [THING$_2$; [PROPERTY]$_1$]

In (10), it is specified that the syntactic constituent combining A and N is a phrase. In (9), we could add the information that the corresponding constituent is a noun to make the contrast more explicit. In the conceptual structure, the semicolon marks restriction, which matches the intersective interpretation of the A+N combination.

Our next example is the Slovak contrast in (11).

(11) a. čajová lyžička ('teaspoon')
     b. čistá lyžička ('clean spoon')

Whereas *čajový* in (11a) is a relational adjective, *čistý* in (11b) is a qualitative adjective. Schlücker (2016: 189–190) discusses relational adjectives in German. She proposes the schema in (12).

(12) $[[_A N_1 \ \text{AFF}_3] \ N_2]$ = $[Y_2^\alpha; [F \ (\ldots X_1, \ldots, \alpha, \ldots)]]$

Although (12) is for German, we can equally apply it to Slovak. In (11a), *čaj* is N_1, *-ový* is AFF$_3$ and *lyžička* is N_2. The meaning is then a spoon (*Y*, coindexed with *lyžička*) such that there is a function *F* linking it to tea (*X*, coindexed with *čaj*). The precise nature of *F* is determined in naming. In (11b), the schema in (12) cannot apply because there is no noun in *čistý* that would match N_1. Instead, (11b) uses the rule in (10).

As a third example of a contrast straddling the division between words and phrases, we discuss the Saxon genitive in English. In section 4.1, we gave the contrast in (13).

Relational Morphology 157

(13) a. She points to a bird's nest in a low branch.
   b. The mother cuckoo lays its egg in another bird's nest.

In (13a), *bird's nest* refers to a type of nest, in (13b) *another bird's nest* to the nest of another bird. For *bird's nest* in (13a), we can adapt the compound schemas for Dutch compounds proposed by Jackendoff and Audring (2020: 101) as in (14).

(14) a. $[\ldots_x s \ldots_y]_z$
   b. $[_N N_x N_y]_z$
   c. $[Y_y^\alpha; [F(\ldots, X_x, \ldots, \alpha, \ldots)]]_z$

In (14a), *s* is phonologically in between two words that are unspecified. It is not linked to syntactic or conceptual information. Syntactically and conceptually, (14b) and (14c) are identical to the representations of compounds without the linking element. For a discussion of the role of linking elements in compounding, see Koliopoulou (2014).

The use of (14) for *bird's nest* is in principle possible for both sentences in (13). In both cases, it competes with a reading in which the genitive marker is attached to an NP and makes the larger NP definite. That the compound reading is more plausible in (13a) and less so in (13b) depends on knowledge about the world and about the context that is activated in interpreting these sentences.

Our final example in this section concerns two different interpretations of compounds illustrated in (15).

(15) a. Mount Pleasant is a charming historic seafood village that, thanks to the bridge, is now a commuter suburb of Charleston.
   b. She writes of her pilgrimage to the Eastern Orthodox Church of St. George in the Chicago suburb of Cicero.

In (15a), *commuter suburb* refers to a type of suburb, whereas in (15b), *Chicago suburb* does not. In Schlücker's (2013) terminology, *commuter* has a classifying function in (15a) and *Chicago* an identifying function in (15b). The most plausible solution to representing this contrast in RM is to assume that *commuter suburb* is a lexical entry whereas *Chicago suburb* is not. This means that, although naming is not addressed in RM, at least the result of it is represented.

For the examples we discussed in this section, it is plausible to assume that the contrast between words and phrases coincides with the distinction between expressions stored in the mental lexicon and expressions produced in performance. The boundary between these two classes is somewhat fluid in the sense that for regularly formed expressions it can vary between speakers. Ten Hacken (2019a: 13–15) makes this point in more detail. Descriptive expressions may also be stored if they are used frequently enough. Whether they are stored is a subconscious decision in the brain of an individual speaker.

9.2.2 Lexemes and word forms

For the distinction between lexemes and word forms, we used the example of the plural and the diminutive for nouns in Dutch and in Slovak. The idea is that the plural characterizes word forms within the same lexeme, whereas the diminutive constitutes a new name and produces a new lexeme.

Jackendoff and Audring (2020: 132–167) address the representation of inflection in RM in some detail. They start by characterizing the difference between inflection and derivation and identify two relevant properties, listed in (16).

(16) a. [I]nflection comes in *paradigms*. (Jackendoff and Audring 2020: 133, emphasis in the original)
b. [I]nflection has a much richer interaction with phrasal syntax. (Jackendoff and Audring 2020: 134)

In Chapter 4, we distinguished the paradigmatic nature of inflection from cases where such paradigms are less obvious. In Dutch, the distinction between the plural and the diminutive cannot be made on the basis of a paradigm. As elaborated in ten Hacken (2013a), in both cases, we have only the contrast between two relevant forms. In section 4.2, we used the examples of *vogel* ('bird') and *huis* ('house') in (17).

(17) a. vogel   huis
b. vogels   huizen   pl
c. vogeltje   huisje   dim
d. vogeltjes   huisjes   dim-pl

In (17), we present plural and diminutive as privative features. They contrast with non-plural and non-diminutive. In order to highlight this, (17a) and (17c) are not marked as singular. In this way, plural is perfectly parallel to diminutive. This is justified by the fact that both plural and diminutive are marked by a suffix that is added to the unmarked stem. Because of the parallelism, (16a) cannot be used to distinguish plural and diminutive in Dutch. Without other evidence, it would be arbitrary to classify the contrasts (17a–b) and (17c–d) as paradigmatic, but the ones between (17a) and (17c) and between (17b) and (17d) not.

Although Jackendoff and Audring (2020) do not mention the regularity of the formation as a separate criterion, it is worth noting that the formation of the diminutive is more regular than that of the plural. As illustrated in (17a–b), there are two phonologically unrelated suffixes for the plural in Dutch. Although their distribution is partly determined by the phonology of the stem (cf. section 5.2.2), they can hardly be seen as allomorphs. By contrast, the differences between the forms of the diminutive, as seen in (17c–d), can largely be explained as phonological adaptations. Also, the predictability of the possibility of pluralizing and diminutivizing is very similar. Restrictions concern, for instance, mass nouns, but we observe such cases as (18).

(18) a. suiker ('sugar')
b. suikers ('sugars')
c. suikertje ('sugar$_{DIM}$')

As a mass noun, *suiker* does not normally take a plural or a diminutive. It is also not normally compatible with an indefinite article. The plural form in (18b) triggers a meaning that can be pluralized, e.g. types of sugar. The diminutive tends to trigger a meaning as a small quantity. Thus, (18c) may refer to a sugar cube.

Traditionally, the plural is taken to be inflection and the diminutive derivation. There is some evidence that can be collected under the category of (16b). The plural triggers agreement in some determiners and in the verb, whereas the effects of the diminutive can be accounted for as changing the gender of the noun. However, a much more fundamental factor is the difference in the effect on the meaning. Whereas the plural does not change the concept, diminutive creates a name for a new concept. Ten Hacken (2013a: 65, 67) gives the entries for the plural in (19) and the diminutive in (20).

(19) a. $[_{Wd}\ Wd_p\ [_{Cl}\ en]]_q$
b. $[_N\ N_p\text{<+plural>}]_q$
c. $[\text{PLURAL}\ ([X]_p)]_q$

(20) a. $[_{Wd}\ Wd_p\ [_{Cl}\ tje]]_q$
b. $[_N\ N_p\text{<+dim>}]_q$
c. $[\text{DIM}\ ([X]_p)]_q$

The entry for *-en* as in *huizen* in (19) is based on Jackendoff's (2002: 160) entry for English past tense *-ed*, but with some adaptations it can also be used in RM. The main difference would be that the *p* index in (19) would be changed to α. The Greek index is used to link the entries of the singular and the plural. RM would set up a corresponding entry for the other main plural ending, *-s*. Any generalizations about the choice of one ending or the other can be encoded as further schemas, i.e. lexical entries. The actual plural forms are also listed directly, so that they are retrieved faster than any attempt to construct the competing alternative online.

The entry for *-tje* in (20) is constructed so as to cover (17c) in a way precisely parallel to (19). As ten Hacken (2013a: 67–68) notes, this highlights the problems arising from a treatment of the diminutive in the same way as the plural. A first problem is that the syntactic feature <+dim> has no actual role in syntax. Diminutive determines the gender, but this should rather be indicated by a feature <+neut>, which is actually active in Dutch syntax. The second problem concerns DIM in (20c). Whereas plural is something that can be chosen separately from the base, diminutive is not a separate category. The diminutive can affect the meaning of the base broadly on a spectrum from small size to positive evaluation. However, as we saw in section 4.2, there are also many cases where the meaning cannot be derived compositionally. Ten Hacken (2013a) uses this as an argument to introduce a separate word formation component in PA. However, this is not the road taken in RM.

In RM, the relationship between lexical entries is encoded by indices that link elements of their specification. For the plural we can use paradigmatically related entries for the singular and the plural as in (21) and (22).

(21) a. $[\ldots]_\alpha$
     b. $[N]_\alpha$
     c. $[X]_\alpha$

(22) a. $[\ldots_\alpha \, en_1]_x$
     b. $[_N \, N_\alpha \, PL_1]_x$
     c. $[PLURAL \, ([X]_\alpha)]_x$

The representation of the singular and the plural follows Jackendoff and Audring (2020: 119, 136). In (21), we have the singular, which has no phonological reflection and no specific syntactic or semantic representation. The only reason for having this entry is that the index α links it to the plural in (22). The entry in (22) is an adaptation of (19). Note that the suffix is also represented as a syntactic entity, in contrast to the representation as a feature on the noun in (19).

The fact that there are two regular entries for the plural means that the entry for the singular also has to be doubled. We may, for instance, use β for the class of nouns with a plural in -s. This is the solution Jackendoff and Audring (2020: 140–147) propose for the contrast between weak and strong verbs in English.

As diminutive is not inflectional, the entry for -*tje* will not have a Greek index. Most of the examples given by Jackendoff and Audring (2020) have an argument structure that the derivational process acts upon, but this does not apply here. As -*tje* is not ambiguous between a size reading and an evaluative reading, the best representation is some vague characterization of its general contribution to the meaning of the suffixed word. This leads to (23).

(23) a. $[\ldots_x \, tje_1]_y$
     b. $[_N \, N_x \, aff_1]_y$
     c. $[SMALL \, OR \, POSITIVELY \, EVALUATED \, ([X]_x)]_y$

It should be kept in mind that (23) is first of all a redundancy rule. It exists in addition to entries for individual diminutive nouns. The idiosyncratic aspects of the meaning of idiosyncratic diminutive nouns are specified in these entries. The predictable aspects are not counted in full as a burden on the memory, because (23) catches them.

Relational Morphology 161

In Slovak, the plural is part of the nominal paradigm, which we will discuss in section 9.2.3. The diminutive is similar to the Dutch diminutive, except that there are several competing suffixes. This means that there are several entries of the type in (23), one for each suffix. This reduces the predictability of diminutive forms and increases the memory load, which includes the information which suffix combines with a particular noun. Otherwise, the solution is not different from the one for Dutch diminutives.

It is important to insist on the origin of plural and diminutive words. RM specifies that the schemas in (22) and (23) are productive. This means that the formation aspect of new entries is accounted for. The naming aspect, however, is not directly addressed.

9.2.3 Paradigms

As noted in (16), in RM paradigms play a central role in the distinction between inflection and derivation. Jackendoff and Audring (2020: 140–156) present accounts of verbal paradigms in English and German that can also be used as a basis for the nominal paradigms in Slovak, which we took as our example in section 4.3.

The basic mechanism for the representation of paradigms is the coindexation with Greek variables linking the entries for the individual word forms, as illustrated in (21) and (22). In the case of the Slovak noun *gitara*, the stem *gitar-* can be encoded as a bound stem (24) (cf. Jackendoff and Audring 2020: 149). Each slot in the paradigm expressing a case–number combination is encoded as a schema of the type in (25).

(24) a. $[gitar]_1$
 b. $[N]_1$
 c. $[GUITAR]_1$

(25) a. $[\ldots{}_\alpha y_2]_x$
 b. $[_N N_\alpha \text{ NOM}_2, \text{PL}_2]_x$
 c. $[\text{PLURAL }([X]_\alpha)]_x$

In (25), α stands for the paradigm of feminine nouns with a 'hard' final consonant and an *-a* ending in the nominative singular.[6] The mappings of the index 2 in (25a–b) indicate the cumulative exponence. We did not include the gender. As an inherent feature, it would be expected that it is part of (24b). The Slovak grammatical tradition sees it as one of the features expressed by *-a*, which would suggest it is in (25b).

---

[6] The class of consonants actually includes the hard consonants {d, t, n, g, k, ch, h} as well as the neutral consonants {p, b, f, v, s, z, m, l, r}. There are three other inflection classes for feminine nouns.

RM is very flexible in the expression of generalizations. There are four paradigms for feminine nouns. In each of them, the genitive singular, the nominative plural and the accusative plural are identical in form. Which ending appears in these three slots depends on the paradigm, but they are always the same. There is no grammatical or semantic reason for this. Jackendoff and Audring (2020: 154) indicate how such morphomic patterns can be expressed. For our case, we can propose the schemas in (26–28).

(26) a. $[\ldots_\beta \ldots_\gamma]_\delta$
  b. $[N_\beta \text{ FEM, GEN}_\gamma, \text{SG}_\gamma]_\delta$
  c. ∅

(27) a. $[\ldots_\beta \ldots_\gamma]_\delta$
  b. $[N_\beta \text{ FEM, NOM}_\gamma, \text{PL}_\gamma]_\delta$
  c. ∅

(28) a. $[\ldots_\beta \ldots_\gamma]_\delta$
  b. $[N_\beta \text{ FEM, ACC}_\gamma, \text{PL}_\gamma]_\delta$
  c. ∅

In (26–28), the conceptual structure is empty. This does not imply that the nouns do not have a meaning, but that these schemas do not contribute to their meaning. The index β stands for the noun stem, γ for the ending, and δ for the entire word form. These indices connect the schemas in the lexicon. The phonological information is limited to the fact that the form consists of a stem and an affix, or more precisely, a part coindexed with N and a part coindexed with the case and number features. As expressed here, the gender is only a condition. If desired, it can receive another copy of γ to specify it as realized by the ending.

Another problem in our paradigm of *gitara* is the genitive plural *gitár*. The general rule is that for feminine nouns the genitive plural has a zero ending and lengthening or diphthongization of the final stem vowel. Jackendoff and Audring (2020: 147) propose a mechanism for ablaut in English strong verbs that can also be used here. In the phonological representation, a part of the form is enclosed between ** and this can then be related to another schema with a corresponding different specification for this part of the form. As the morphophonological aspects are not our main concern, we will not propose a detailed elaboration of this idea.

In our discussion of paradigms in section 4.3, we also addressed derivational paradigms. As an example, we used the Slovak triples in (29) and (30).

(29) a. blog   ('blog$_N$')
  b. blogovať   ('blog$_V$')
  c. blogový   ('blog$_A$')

(30) a. bloger   ('blogger$_N$')
  b. blogerka   ('blogger$_{FEM}$')
  c. blogerský ('blogger$_A$')

The idea is that the borrowing of (29a) triggers the formation of (29b–c). Similarly, (30b–c) are triggered by (30a). The relation between (29a) and (30a) is not one of word formation in Slovak. Both are borrowings from English.

In RM, paradigms constitute one of the two distinctive properties of inflection, as listed in (16). Each of the six words in (29) and (30) has an inflectional paradigm of its own, whose categories are determined by the syntactic category of the lexeme. We do not want to give up the idea that (29a), (30a) and (30b) are nouns inflected for case and number. It would be wrong to include, for instance, *blogerka* as a part of the (inflectional) paradigm of *bloger*. Similarly, *blogujem* is the first person singular present tense of *blogovať* (29b). It would be wrong to analyse it as the first person singular present tense verb of *blog* (29a).

Jackendoff and Audring (2020: 107–109) discuss the well-known example of English pairs of nouns in *-ism* and in *-ist*. In cases such as *pacifism* and *pacifist*, there is no underlying word. In cases such as *behaviourism* and *behaviourist*, both nouns have the same idiosyncratic relationship to *behaviour*. They trace this observation to Di Sciullo and Williams (1987: 20–21). In RM, the mechanism for expressing the relationship is called *sister schemas*. It corresponds to what Booij (2010) calls *second-order schemas*.

A derivational paradigm is a relation between lexemes, not between word forms of the lexeme. In a language such as Slovak, which has extensive inflectional paradigms, it is important to distinguish them from derivational paradigms. By using the same mechanism for both, we would not be able to preserve this distinction. In (30a–b), *bloger* and *blogerka* name different concepts. The consequences are most obvious when we consider oblique forms such as (31).

(31) a. blogera ('blogger$_{\text{N.ACC.SG}}$')
     b. blogerku ('blogger$_{\text{FEM.ACC.SG}}$')

The treatment of the forms in (31) has to attribute them to the correct lexeme. The form in (31b) is not part of the lexeme (30a), but of the related lexeme (30b). Therefore, (31a) and (31b) should be related to (30a) in different ways. In order to maintain this distinction, we need different sets of variables. As we already have letters, numbers and Greek letters, we might take a different script, e.g. Cyrillic, Hebrew or Devanagari. What is decisive, however, is that the indices are recognizable as being from non-overlapping sets. For (29), the schemas generalize over nouns, verbs in *-ovať* and adjectives in *-ový*. By coindexing these three, we can encode the statement that if there is a noun, we can expect there to be a corresponding verb in *-ovať* and a corresponding adjective in *-ový*. Similarly, for (30), we can state that for a noun designating a human role, we can form a noun for a female in this role by adding *-ka* and an adjective in *-ský*. More precise restrictions of the meaning and the conditions under which the formation is possible can be inserted.

9.2.4 Naming and transposition

In their discussion of the differences between inflection and derivation, Jackendoff and Audring observe that 'some derivational patterns are meaningless too, for instance verbs vs. their derived process nominals' (2020: 133). They give the pair in (32) as an example.

(32) a. They constructed the building rapidly.
     b. the rapid construction of the building

In this context, they even mention the term *transposition*. Although this is not a proposed treatment, it at least acknowledges the concept. In a different context, Jackendoff and Audring (2020: 188–191) propose schemas for *-ness* and *-ity*. However, here the focus is on the opposition between the phonological effects of these suffixes. As they note candidly, '[w]e omit semantics for convenience' (2020: 188).

In section 4.4, we discussed German *Installation* and *Installierung* in the context of the examples in (33).

(33) a. die Installation der Heizungsanlage
       'the installation of_the heating_system'
     b. veraltete Installationen erneuern
       'outdated installations renew', i.e. replace outdated installations
     c. die Installierung der Heizungsanlage
     d. *veraltete Installierungen erneuern

What needs to be accounted for is that *Installation* and *Installierung* are both possible process nouns corresponding to the verb *installieren*, as in (33a) and (33c), but that only *Installation* has an additional reading referring to the result, as in (33b), whereas for *Installierung*, (33d) shows that this reading is not available.

A first point to consider is the position of *Installation* and *Installierung* in the lexicon. In RM, we can assume that there are entries for these nouns and for the verb *installieren*. The schema for *-ation* is then related to that for verbs in *-ieren* by means of indices, as in (34) and (35).

(34) a. $[\ldots _\alpha \text{ation}_1]_x$ (35) a. $[\ldots _\alpha \text{ier}_2]_y$
     b. $[_N - \text{aff}_1]_x$ b. $[_V - \text{aff}_2]_y$
     c. $[F (\ldots, \ldots)]_{\alpha, x}$ c. $[F (X, Y)]_{\alpha, y}$

The schemas in (34) and (35) have three types of index. The numbered indices are for specified material. In (34), this is 1 for the affix *-ation* and in (35) it is 2 for the affix *-ier*. In both cases, these affixes attach to something that is not a stem, notated –, corresponding to *install* in our example. The verb stem entry in (35) corresponds to Jackendoff and Audring's (2020: 149) entry for the stem *mach-* ('make'). The use of – follows Jackendoff and Audring's (2020: 108) schemas for *-ism* and *-ist*. However, in the case of German *-ation* and *-ier(en)*, the two meanings are the same. We use α to link the identical parts in phonology and the meanings between the two schemas, and x and y to link the three levels of representation within each schema. In the meaning of the noun in *-ation*, we replaced the variables by ... to account for the fact that nouns do not have arguments in the same way as verbs (cf. Jackendoff and Audring 2020: 133n2).

In (34), we account for the reading of *Installation* in (33a). The next task is to add the reading in (33b). The conceptual structure of (34) has the two-place function F. The result reading focuses on the second argument. We can encode this by the schema in (36).

(36) a. $[\ldots_\alpha \text{ation}_1]_x$
     b. $[_N - \text{aff}_1]_x$
     c. $[\text{THING}^\beta; F(\ldots, \text{Patient}: \beta)]_{\alpha, x}$

The schema in (36) is based on Jackendoff and Audring's (2020: 89) schema for *-er* as an agent noun suffix. It should be noted that we have a fourth type of index here. Whereas α links (36) to (34) and (35), β makes THING in (36c) a kind of quantifier binding the Patient. Jackendoff and Audring use Greek letters for both purposes, but not in the same schema. As long as we are aware of the different status, there is no formal problem with this.

In order to account for the contrasts in (33), we also have to cover *-ung*. The suffix *-ung* applies to a wide range of verbs (see Fleischer and Barz 2012: 225–229). For verbs in *-ieren*, it is in competition with *-ation*, but unlike *-ation*, it attaches after the full stem, as in *Installierung*. Therefore, we can state the relationship of nouns with *-ung* to their corresponding verbs as in (37) and (38).

(37) a. $[\ldots_\gamma \text{ung}_3]_z$ (38) a. $[\ldots_\gamma]_w$
     b. $[_N V_\gamma \text{aff}_3]_z$ b. $[V_\gamma]_w$
     c. $[F(\ldots, \ldots)]_{\gamma, z}$ c. $[F(X, Y)]_{\gamma, w}$

The schemas in (37) and (38) are very similar to the ones for *-ation* in (34) and (35). We are here interested only in transitive verbs, so we used the same semantic specification in (38c) as in (35c). The starting point is a full verb stem, so that V in (37b) and (38b) is also coindexed with γ. The competition between (37) and (34) is resolved by specifying the resulting entries in the lexicon. RM is a theory of the relations between entries in the lexicon more than of the formation of new words.

A problem the schemas in (34) to (38) do not solve is illustrated by the sentences in (39).

(39) a. Die Sammlung des Roten Kreuzes [...] findet am 16. April statt.
'the collection of_the Red Cross [...] takes on 16 April place'
b. Seit knapp zwei Jahren ist die Sammlung als öffentliches Museum für jeden zugänglich.
'since almost two years has_been the collection as public museum for everyone accessible'

For nouns such as *Sammlung* ('collection'), derived from *sammeln* ('collect'), we have the same contrast between two readings as for *Installation* in (33a–b). In (39a), it refers to the process of collecting, in (39b) to the result of such a process. Although the object of *sammeln* is not specified, contextual clues and world knowledge suggest that it is money or clothes in (39a) and art in (39b).

In (37), we have the schema for *Sammlung* in the sense of (39a), but we need another schema for (39b). We propose one in (40).

(40) a. $[\ldots_\gamma \text{ung}_3]_z$
b. $[_N V_\gamma \text{aff}_3]_z$
c. $[\text{THING}^\delta; F(\ldots, \text{Patient}: \delta)]_{\gamma, z}$

The schema in (40) is closely parallel to the one in (36). In the same way as (36), it involves four types of index, with γ and δ belonging to different types. We need (40) in order to account for the result reading of *Sammlung* in (39b) and for many other similar examples. However, with (40) we lose the explanation we had for the ungrammaticality of (33d). We need to stipulate that this reading does not occur.

The discussion of the data in (33) and (39) and their treatment in RM shows both the possibilities and the limitations of the approach. Because RM has a bottom-up approach, starting from fully specified entries, the schemas work as generalizations over these entries. The two readings of German *Installation* can be stated in the lexicon as two entries and related to each other by a schema. The same approach can be taken for the two readings of *Sammlung*. What remains problematic is that *Installierung* is possible in only one reading. The schemas would predict that either it is not possible at all or it is possible in both readings.

9.2.5 Onomasiological coercion

As an example of onomasiological coercion, we took the English compound *doorman* and gave COBUILD's (2023) definition in (41).

(41) a. A doorman is
b. a man who stands at the door
c. of a club,
d. prevents unwanted people from coming in, and makes people leave if they cause trouble.

As *doorman* is a compound, Jackendoff's (2009) discussion of the system for expressing the meaning of compounds in PA is relevant here. A first relevant element of this system is action modality. In (41), it is not specified whether *doorman* is an occupation or a stage-level predicate. The difference can be illustrated on the basis of (42).

(42) a. On the beach, he met a doorman who was on holiday.
b. We talked to the doorman who turned out to be the owner's brother helping out for the day.

In (42a), *doorman* is used in the sense of occupation and stage-level is denied. In (42b), the opposite is true. As both seem to be equally acceptable, we can conclude that *doorman* does not have a lexical specification for action modality. This is the same as for Jackendoff's (2009: 119) example of *violinist*.

Then we turn to the compound schemas. As *man* does not have arguments, we use the modifier schema as in (43).

(43) $[[_N \text{door}]_1 [_N \text{man}]_2] = [\text{MAN}_2^\alpha; [\text{F} (\ldots, \text{DOOR}_1, \ldots, \alpha_2, \ldots)]]$

The question raised by (43) is how to specify F, the function that expresses the relation between *door* and *man*. The only usable basic function Jackendoff (2009: 123–124) gives is LOC. Jackendoff (2016: 28) reorganizes it as BE (X, AT/IN/ON Y). This develops (43) into (44).

(44) $[[_N \text{door}]_1 [_N \text{man}]_2] = [\text{MAN}_2^\alpha; [\text{BE} (\alpha_2, \text{AT/IN/ON} [\text{DOOR}_1])]]$

The meaning of *doorman* is then reduced to (41b). Whereas Jackendoff (2009: 127–128) envisages an elaboration of complex interacting functions, in compounds such as *doorman*, there is no evidence for any of them. The meaning components in (41c–d) are only accessible when we consider the naming process.

It is interesting to see to what extent the situation of *doorman* is peculiar. We can get some information about this by considering the translations we discussed in section 4.5. They are repeated in (45).

(45) a. Türsteher ('door_stander') DE
b. uitsmijter ('out_thrower') NL
c. vyhadzovač ('throw_out-er') SK

In (45a), we have a synthetic compound involving the verb *stehen* ('stand'). Using the version of the argument schema from Jackendoff (2016: 25), we can arrive at the representation in (46).[7]

---

[7] In representing the meaning of German words, we use English translations as functions in Conceptual Structure. The use of English is determined by the fact that

(46) $[[_N \text{ Tür}]_1 [_N [_V \text{ steh}]_3 \text{ er}]_2] =$
   $[\text{PERSON}_2^\alpha; [\text{STAND}_3 (\alpha_2, \text{AT/IN/ON } [\text{DOOR}_1])]]$

The difference between (46) and (44) is mainly in the degree of specification following from the form. Instead of MAN in (44), it is STAND that is specified in (46). The function AT/IN/ON in (46) must be found in the generally available repertoire, because *stehen* is intransitive. Again, (41c–d) are not specified.

In (45b–c), we have a different naming pattern. Both Dutch and Slovak have the form of an agent noun based on a verb which is preceded by a particle, but in Dutch *uit* is a preposition, whereas in Slovak *vy-* is a prefix to the verb. In line with this contrast, there is no verb **uitsmijten* corresponding to (45b), but for (45c) there is a verb *vyhadzovať* ('throw_out'). For the semantic contribution of the components, this does not make a big difference. In (47), we give the representation for (45b).

(47) $[[_P \text{ uit}]_1 [_N [_V \text{ smijt}]_3 \text{ er}]_2] =$
   $[\text{PERSON}_2^\alpha; [\text{PF } (\text{THROW}_3 (\alpha_2, \text{INDEF}, [_{\text{Path}} \text{ OUT}_1])]]$

In (47), we introduce an action modality. PF stands for *proper function*. The point is that an *uitsmijter* has the task indicated in (41d), but does not have to perform this action in order to be an *uitsmijter*. The verb *smijten* is transitive, but the object is indefinite and cannot be specified for (45b). The particle *uit* is here analysed as an intransitive preposition indicating a path. In (47), a large part of (41d) is expressed, but (41c) and most of (41b) remain unexpressed. This leads to a similar situation as for (44) and (46).

In RM, the generalizations are formulated from a bottom-up perspective. This means that the full meaning of *doorman* is specified in the entry for *doorman*. The function of (44) is not to replace this information, but to express generalizations that reduce the storage load in the lexicon. RM does not ask the question of how *doorman* enters the lexicon with the meaning it has. At most, it specifies that certain variables in schemas are productive. The question of naming, illustrated by the different naming patterns of *doorman* and its translations in (45) for the concept described in (41b–d), is not addressed.

9.3 Word formation and naming in RM

In RM, Jackendoff's framework of Parallel Architecture (PA) serves as a background. As this background is shared with Construction Morphology

---

our text is in English. The approximation that is necessarily involved in translation at word level is in our view not problematic when it is understood that these functions only serve to generalize over a meaning that is not further analysed here. In this sense, we adopt the same approach as Jackendoff does in his writings.

Relational Morphology

(CxM), which we discussed in Chapter 8, it is legitimate to ask to what extent they are variants of the same theory. In devoting separate chapters to RM and CxM, we follow Audring and Masini's (2019) handbook. As both editors are co-authors of the relevant chapters, we can assume that in RM and CxM, the two theories are perceived as clearly distinct. Lieber and Štekauer's (2009) handbook also has separate chapters for the two theories, Jackendoff (2009) and Booij (2009). At the same time, Booij (2010) refers to Jackendoff's work and Jackendoff and Audring (2020) to Booij's work as an important source of inspiration and without explicit criticism.

The foundational difference between the two theories is that CxM is a theory of morphology and RM is a theory of the organization of the lexicon. As a consequence, in RM word formation is not primarily considered as a rule-based mechanism for the formation of new words, but rather as a mechanism for relating lexical entries, as formulated in the Relational Hypothesis in (1). This hypothesis can be seen as an elaboration of Jackendoff's (1975) Full Entry Theory.

An original property of RM based on (1) is the idea that coindexation takes place between lexical entries at the level of individual components of their specification. This is formalized in relational links. Relational links constitute a way of implementing the idea that the main function of word formation rules is the structuring of the lexicon, not the formation of new lexical entries. As pointed out by Jackendoff and Audring (2020: 68–70), relational links differ from inheritance hierarchies as used in CxM, because they are non-directional.

The Relational Hypothesis also highlights the importance of productivity. As discussed in section 9.1 and shown in (2), Jackendoff and Audring (2020: 46) understand productivity in a way that is reminiscent of Schultink's (1961) definition with its references to unintentionality and in principle unlimited numbers. The tension this creates with the idea of specifying all entries as a starting point leads Jackendoff and Audring (2020: 49) to refer to 'fashion' as a factor in the production of novel instances of a rule.

In section 9.2, we found two main mechanisms for distinguishing word formation as a naming device from syntax and from inflection. One is focused on the borderline with syntax and uses syntactic categories. It is illustrated in the analysis of the Slovak contrast in (11), repeated here as (48).

(48) a. čajová lyžička   ('teaspoon')
      b. čistá lyžička   ('clean spoon')

In (48a), we have a relational adjective and the expression has the function of naming a concept. In (48b), the modifying adjective is used to describe a property of the item referred to by the noun. The schemas in (49) and (50) can be used to encode this difference.

(49) a. $[[\ldots_x \text{ov}_1] [\ldots_y]]_z$
 b. $[_N [_A N_x \text{aff}_1] N_y]_z$
 c. $[Y_y{}^\alpha; [F (\ldots X_x, \ldots, \alpha, \ldots)]]_z$

(50) a. Ø
 b. $[_{NP} A_x N_y]$
 c. $[_{THING} Y_y; [_{PROPERTY} X_x]]$

The schema in (49) encodes the suffix -*ov(ý)*, one of the main Slovak suffixes for relational adjectives and the one used in (48a). It follows Schlücker's (2016: 190) analysis of relational adjectives in the schema in (12) and the formalism for suffixes illustrated in (6), taken from Jackendoff and Audring (2020: 89). The subscripts *x*, *y* and *z* encode connections between different levels within an entry. The subscript *1* connects the phonological realization of the suffix to the affix in syntax. It is understood that inflectional affixes are covered by other schemas that will add information mainly to the phonological and syntactic representation. The schema in (50) encodes A+N phrases of the type in (48b), where the noun represents a thing and adjective a property of this thing. It may be useful to formulate this more generally for other semantic categories of nouns, but for (48b), (50) expresses the required information. The main difference that shows that (49) is a schema for naming concepts and (50) for descriptive expressions is that in (49b) the highest structure is labelled N, whereas in (50b) we have NP.

The other mechanism we found focuses on the distinction between word formation and inflection and is based on the observation that 'inflection comes in *paradigms*' (Jackendoff and Audring 2020: 133). In a section entitled 'Formalization of inflection vs. derivation', Jackendoff and Audring (2020: 135–139) use the device of sister schemas to encode paradigms as a way of distinguishing inflection from derivation. In section 9.2.2, we showed how this mechanism can be used to make the formation of Dutch plural nouns inflectional, but of Dutch diminutives derivational. Sister schemas correspond to Booij's (2010) second-order schemas. The idea of sister schemas is to introduce a new type of index that combines lexical entries into a paradigm.

In our discussion of derivational paradigms in section 9.2.3, we also encountered these sister schemas. This creates a problem that can be illustrated with the derivational paradigm in (29), repeated here as (51).

(51) a. blog ('blog$_N$')
 b. blogovať ('blog$_V$')
 c. blogový ('blog$_A$')

From a naming perspective, it is important to distinguish the way the verb in (51b) is related to the noun in (51a) from the way that different inflected forms of the noun in (51a) are related to each other. This point concerns word forms such as the ones in (52).

(52) a. blogu ('blog$_{\text{GEN.SG}}$')
      b. bloguje ('blog$_{\text{3.SG.PRES}}$')

Whereas (52a) is a form of the noun (51a), (52b) is not. The relationship of (52b) to the noun (51a) is indirect. It is a form of the verb in (51b) and as such belongs to its paradigm. Although the verb in (51b) is paradigmatically related to the noun in (51a), this does not make (52b) a part of the paradigm of the noun. In order to maintain the distinction between inflectional paradigms and derivational paradigms, we proposed in section 9.2.4 to use two types of index. We are not sure whether this is in line with Jackendoff's and Audring's conception of RM, but in our view it is the only way to ensure that expressions for naming and expressions for description are distinguished.

In the same way as we have seen for CxM in Chapter 8 and for LSF in Chapter 7, in RM too there is a contrast between on one hand the success in distinguishing between complex expressions used for naming and those that have a descriptive function, and on the other the lack of attention paid to the actual naming process. In RM, the starting point is that the fully specified lexical entries exist. The question is how they are organized. Although productivity is an important issue, the discussion turns on the question of how the new entry is formed, not why. This restricts the possibilities of explaining certain observations.

In our discussion of transposition in section 9.2.4, we showed that it is necessary to take into account the reason for forming a new word in order to explain why German *Installierung* can only have the process reading. We need both the process and the result reading of *-ung* in order to account for the two readings of *Sammlung* ('collection') in (39). We cannot use blocking of the application of the schema for *-ung* to the verb *installieren* ('install'), because *Installierung* occurs. Only on the basis of naming can we explain that *Installierung* fulfils the function of highlighting the process reading in contrast to *Installation*.

Another case where the limitations of approach taken in RM become visible is in onomasiological coercion. As explained in section 9.2.5, the mechanism for compounding in Jackendoff (2016) can only cover a part of the meaning of *doorman* and its German equivalent *Türsteher*. It is limited to an account of the relationship between the elements that are expressed. How these elements are chosen from the meaning of the concept and where the rest of the meaning of the complex word comes from is beyond the scope of the theory. Ten Hacken (2019a) argues that it is only by adding a separate word formation component that these aspects of naming can be accounted for in PA. Another proposal for a separate word formation component in PA is Benavides (2022a). Jackendoff (2022) rejects this idea, but Benavides (2022b) does not accept his argumentation.

CHAPTER 10

Cognitive Grammar

Langacker (1987a, 1991) developed the framework of Cognitive Grammar (CG) as an alternative to the models developed in the generative tradition. An updated presentation of the theory can be found in Langacker (2007, 2008). Langacker sees CG as unique in the sense that it neither derives from any other theory, 'nor is it particularly close to any' (2007: 421). The leading idea is that language is shaped and constrained by the functions it serves. The central task is to account for the link between form, as encoded in phonological units, and meaning, as encoded in semantic units. The key concept is the symbolic unit, which is an association of a phonological and a semantic unit. Heyvaert (2009) elaborates the consequences for the modelling of word formation. Langacker (2019) shows how CG treats morphology. Here, in section 10.1 we will introduce the main theoretical assumptions of CG. Then, in section 10.2 we will consider how it can account for the data given in Chapter 4. Finally, in section 10.3 we will evaluate to what extent CG covers these data adequately.

10.1 Cognitive Grammar as a framework

Langacker developed the framework of CG from 1976, in response to the discussion in generative linguistics in this period. As described in sections 3.1.3 and 3.1.4, this period was marked by the 'linguistic wars' between Generative Semantics and Interpretive Semantics (cf. Newmeyer 1986a). Langacker (2007: 421) viewed the disputes as 'vacuous and sterile' and realized a necessity to approach language from a completely new perspective.

At that time, Langacker already worked at the University of California, San Diego, where he stayed until his retirement in 2003. He received his PhD at the University of Illinois Urbana-Champaign in 1966 and his dissertation was in generative linguistics. In response to his dissatisfaction with developments in generative theory at the time, Langacker (1982) proposed a new theory under the label *Space Grammar*. The new name *Cognitive Grammar* appeared in Langacker (1987a, 1991), a work in two volumes with a full presentation of the theory. As Langacker (2007: 421) notes in a historical overview, this version does not have any substantial modifications compared with earlier work. Langacker (2008) is a textbook overview of CG. At present it has been more than forty years since the theory was presented. Meanwhile it has become influential and has been elaborated further by a number of cognitive linguists, e.g. Taylor (2000, 2002), Radden and Dirven (2007) and Giovanelli et al. (2020).

As Langacker argues for a different approach to language, the central assumptions about language from the perspective of CG are presented in (1).

(1) a. Language is shaped and constrained by the functions it serves. (Langacker 2008: 7).
b. CG is a nonmodular view of language. (Langacker 2008: 14)
c. The two basic functions of language are *symbolic* (allowing conceptualizations to be symbolized by sounds and gestures) and *communicative/interactive*. (Langacker 2007: 422)

In the elaboration of (1a) Langacker emphasizes the semiological function of language, which means that the main aim of the linguistic sign is to symbolize a conceptualization. Langacker (2008: 14–15) understands the main role of the semiological function as 'permitting meanings to be symbolized phonologically'. In line with (1b), lexicon, morphology and syntax are not viewed as separate modules or components in CG. On the contrary, they represent a continuum that can be described fully by a set of symbolic structures. The idea is developed further in (1c) where two functions of language are highlighted: first the symbolic function, which assumes that only symbolic structures are used for the description of lexicon, morphology and syntax, second the communicative/interactive function involving many aspects of communication such as expressiveness, manipulation or social communion (Langacker 2007: 422). The communicative/interactive function indicates another basic assumption of CG, that linguistic units are abstracted from the actual pronunciations and contextual understandings termed as *usage events*. Langacker (2007: 422) calls this approach *strongly functional*, contrasting it with various other functional approaches.

The notion of *symbolic structure* is crucial in CG and requires a more detailed description. An instance of the most basic type is represented in Figure 10.1. The symbolic structure Σ contains a link between a semantic structure (S) and a phonological structure (P). The phonological structure includes not only sound, but also the orthographic representation and gestures. It is important to mention that either of S and P can evoke the other. This means that a symbolic structure is bipolar, with a semantic and a phonological pole, which is illustrated in (2).

(2) [[SHRINK]/[shrink]]

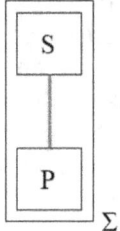

Figure 10.1 *Diagrammatic representation of a symbolic structure in CG*

In the symbolic structure of the morpheme in (2), [SHRINK] represents its semantic pole or its conceptualization, and its phonological structure is represented orthographically as [shrink]. In CG, a morpheme is a unit whose symbolic complexity is zero. This means that it cannot be analysed into smaller symbolic components. As shown in Figure 10.1, a morpheme such as (2) consists merely of a single symbolic relationship.

It is possible to combine two symbolic structures to form a higher-level symbolic structure as in Figure 10.2. In Figure 10.2 we see a lower-level structure and a higher-level structure which together represent a so-called *symbolic assembly*. It shows a greater symbolic complexity, illustrated as in (3).

(3)   [[[SHRINK]/[shrink]] - [[ABLE]/[able]]]

As a result of the higher degree of symbolic complexity in (3), a complex lexical item is formed through the process of affixation.

An example of a diagram representing multiple affixation is given in Figure 10.3. Figure 10.3 illustrates one of the basic claims of CG, namely that the same process of composition is active in the semantic and phonological structures of an expression. This can be seen in (4).

(4)   [[[NON]/[non]] - [[[SHRINK]/[shrink]] - [[ABLE]/[able]]]]

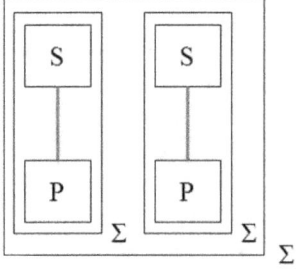

Figure 10.2 *Diagrammatic representation of a higher-level symbolic structure*

Cognitive Grammar

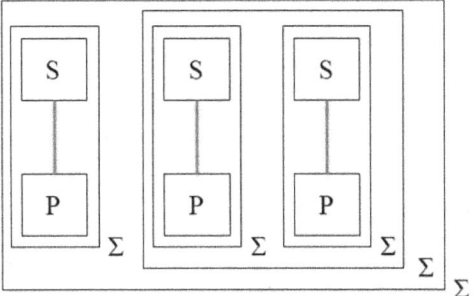

Figure 10.3 *Diagrammatic representation of a combination of symbolic structures*

The example in (4) corresponds to the diagram in Figure 10.3 and shows how multiple affixation can be covered in CG. The examples in (2), (3) and (4) are all lexical items used conventionally in English.

This brings us to Langacker's understanding of the lexicon. Langacker (2008: 16) defines the lexicon as 'the set of fixed expressions in a language'. Fixed expressions can be units larger than words, for instance *sunny day*. CG does not make a clear-cut distinction between the lexicon and non-lexical expressions. On the other hand, there may be lexical expressions that are rather novel than conventional. Langacker (2008: 16) gives the example of *dollarless*. As Langacker (2019: 347) states it, conventionality or well-formedness is understood as a matter of degree.

Langacker (2008: 16) distinguishes four basic phenomena in the lexicon: association, automatization, schematization and categorization. Association is understood as a psychological link between items in the mind. The association between a mental conceptualization and phonological structure, for instance in (2), defines a basic symbolic structure.

The second phenomenon, automatization, results in the entrenchment of combinations of linguistic items as units such as in (3) and (4). Entrenchment is an important notion, which means that the lexical items become established units. For Langacker (2008: 16–17), lexical items are only such expressions 'that have achieved the status of units for representative members of a speech community'. Langacker (2008: 16–17) illustrates the difference between a unit and non-unit in (5).

(5) ([[DOLLAR]/[dollar]] - [[LESS]/[less]])

The lexical item in (5) is a possible word, but it is less familiar and less conventionally established. Therefore, (5) is not an established unit, which is marked by the round brackets. This contrasts with the components *dollar* and *-less* in square brackets that have the status of units. Automatization or entrenchment of a structure is a matter of degree. In the case of *dollarless*, a higher frequency may increase its entrenchment. At the moment, this does not seem to be the case, as the frequency in COCA (2008–2020) is 1. It is in the section fiction. Automatization takes place only when it is possible to access knowledge without conscious effort.

Schematization is 'the process of extracting the commonality inherent in multiple experiences to arrive at a conception representing a higher level of abstraction' (Langacker 2008: 17). Schematization is also a matter of degree; for example, *ring* can be 'circular piece of jewellery worn on the finger'. However, rings can also be worn in other places, e.g. an earring, which brings us to a more schematic value 'circular adornments worn on the body'. An even higher degree of schematization is possible: *ring* as 'circular object', e.g. the rings in gymnastics.

Finally, categorization is understood as 'the interpretation of experience with respect to previously existing structures' (Langacker 2008: 17). Langacker gives a straightforward example of categorization when A is schematic for B, so B elaborates or instantiates A. This is captured in A → B. The arrow means that B is compatible with A but it is characterized more precisely. This is illustrated in (6).

(6) a. CIRCULAR ENTITY → CIRCULAR ARENA
    b. CIRCULAR ARENA ⇢ RECTANGULAR ARENA

In (6a) we see an example of categorization when *ring* applies to circular arenas such as in circuses and bullfighting rings. This contrasts with (6b) illustrating the extension of the use of *ring* to rectangular arenas, such as in boxing. Here, A stands for a prototype and B for an extension from it. The relation between them is represented by a dashed arrow. B is in conflict with the specifications of A, but it is assimilated to the category on the basis of perceived similarity or association.

Some crucial claims about the relationship between lexicon and grammar in CG are presented in (7).

(7) a. A clear demarcation between lexicon and grammar is far from evident (Langacker 2008: 18).
    b. Lexicon is best characterized as the unit expressions of a language, irrespective of complexity: morphemes, stems, words, fixed phrases, idioms, proverbs, even longer passages (Langacker 2019: 347).
    c. Grammar comprises structures that are more schematic, hence immanent in both lexical items and novel expressions (Langacker 2019: 347).

In (7a) Langacker rejects a sharp distinction between lexicon and grammar based on a set of primitives without intrinsic meaning. This was the conception of the distinction that was current in the discussion in generative linguistics in the 1970s. CG takes rather a continuum approach with fuzzy boundaries. In line with (7b), the lexicon can be described by assemblies of symbolic structures. Lexical units can be ordered depending on their degree of symbolic complexity, as shown in (2), (3) and (4). The ordering can be even more complex, including items larger than words. Langacker (2008: 19) gives the example in (8).

(8) a. moon
    b. moonless
    c. moonless night
    d. a moonless night
    e. on a moonless night

Each of the expressions in (8) is an expansion of the preceding one. The point in (7c) is that structures of grammar tend to be more schematic and lexical ones more symbolic. Whereas for (8a), a symbolic representation of the type in Figure 10.1 is appropriate, (8e) can be described by a schema as in (9).

(9) a. PREP a N_1+less N_2
    b. PP

The schema in (9a) includes lexical and grammatical components. The same expression can be represented more schematically as in (9b). To sum up, in CG language contains maximally schematic grammatical elements, highly specific lexis, and multi-word units that are both schematic and specific.

10.2 The treatment of relevant contrasts in CG

In this section, we will present how the data from Chapter 4 can be covered in CG. The structure of the section follows the structure of Chapter 4.

10.2.1 Words and phrases

In section 10.1, we saw that morphology and syntax are not independent components in CG, but together with the lexicon they form 'a continuum fully reducible to assemblies of symbolic structures' (Langacker 2008: 15). In (10) and (11), Langacker makes two statements about the relationship between words and phrases.

(10) Morphology and syntax are not delimited in any precise or consistent way such as productivity, regularity, and lexical status (Langacker 2019: 347).

(11) a. If we wish to make a distinction, we can do no better than follow the tradition of drawing the line at the level of word.

b. Morphology is described by schematic assemblies (like *N+less*) whose instantiations are no larger than words, and syntax by assemblies (like N_1+*less* N_2) with multi-word instantiations.
c. Even so the boundary is fuzzy, if only due to expressions such as compounds that are intermediate between single words and multi-word expressions (Langacker 2008: 24).

The claim in (10) demonstrates that CG views morphology and syntax as a continuum, without any necessity for a sharp distinction between the two. This claim is elaborated in (11), which we divided into three parts for convenience of reference. In (11a), Langacker aligns the distinction with the distinction between words and phrases. In (11b), the schematic assembly *N+less* represents a derivational pattern illustrated by *moonless, childless, hopeless*. The same schematic assembly is then one component of N_1+*less* N_2, e.g. *moonless night, childless couple, hopeless situation*. The schematic assembly N_1+*less* N_2 is then available 'to sanction the occurrence of novel expressions like *moonless world, dollarless surgeon*, and *ireless dwarf*' (Langacker 2008: 24). The same is valid for morphological patterns and syntactic patterns. Therefore, any distinction between morphology and syntax would be only arbitrary.

In (11c), Langacker places compounds somewhere between words and larger expressions. Compounds are examples of what is called *composite structures* in CG, i.e. structures which integrate two or more component structures (Langacker 1999: 94). Langacker uses the term *component* instead of *constituent*. The reason is that compositionality is not viewed from the perspective of building blocks. Composition is understood as 'a matter of combining component structures in accordance with the correspondences holding between their elements at the semantic and phonological poles' (Langacker 2008: 163). Compositionality refers then to the degree of regularity of the composite structure (Langacker 1987a: 457). In a structure that is compositional, the meaning and form correspond to the meanings and forms of its component parts.[1]

Langacker (1987a: 450) gives the examples of degrees of composition in Table 10.1. The phrase *black bird* is fully compositional. The expression inherits the profile of *bird* and its content is exhausted by its components. This contrasts with the compound *blackbird*, which designates a specific type of bird and is more precise in content than anything that is deducible from *black* and *bird*. The content not contributed by the individual

---

[1] The concept of compositionality is commonly linked to the work of Gottlob Frege (1848–1925). Janssen (2012) gives a systematic overview of its use in linguistics, logic and computer science. The principle of compositionality is usually formulated so as to apply to constituents and refer to the meaning of the constituents as well as the rules that combine them. Heyvaert (2009: 236–238) motivates why Langacker prefers *component* to *constituent* in discussing compositionality.

Table 10.1 *Degrees of composition according to Langacker (1987a: 450)*

Composite structure	Example
[C]=[AB]	black bird
[C]=[ABX]	blackbird
[C]=[A'B']	blackboard

components is represented by X in Table 10.1. Finally, the composite structure of the compound *blackboard* is even in conflict with some specifications of both components as it is not a board in the most usual sense, i.e. a plank, and not always black. As discussed in section 4.5, we tend to think of these specifications in terms of onomasiological coercion. We will come back to this in section 10.2.5.

An important distinction that CG makes is the one between *compositionality* and *analysability*, applicable to 'the extent to which speakers are cognizant (at some level of processing) of the contribution that individual component structures make to the composite whole' (Langacker 1987a: 457). Both compositionality and analysability are seen as a matter of degree in CG. Speakers can be aware of individual components of a composite structure that is only partially compositional, e.g. *blackboard*. There are also cases where one component may be more salient than another, e.g. *screwdriver*, where *screw* is much more prominent than *driver* (Langacker 1987a: 465). Heyvaert (2009: 238) points out that 'Cognitive Linguistics does not view this as an argument in favour of seeing compounding as a morphological rather than syntactic phenomenon'. As noted in (10), the demarcation of morphology and syntax is not central in CG. Therefore, it is interesting to consider how borderline cases between words and phrases can be covered in CG.

Our first example to show the contrast is from German, presented in section 4.1 and repeated for convenience in (12).

(12) a. Hartkäse ('granular cheese')
b. harter Käse ('hard cheese')

The contrast between (12a) and (12b) is traditionally seen as the former being a compound whereas the latter is a phrase. In CG, each expression is an example of a composite structure. For (12a), we could use a structure of the type in Figure 10.2. However, Langacker (2019: 357) gives a different representation, leading to a diagram as in Figure 10.4.

In Figure 10.4, we use Langacker's representation of *thigh bone* as a basis. The difference between this structure and the one in Figure 10.2 is that here the complex expression has a semantic and phonological representation of its own, represented at the centre. Both components in Figure 10.4 are autonomous and can occur independently. Not only is the composite whole independent, but both components *hart* and *Käse* are also independent.

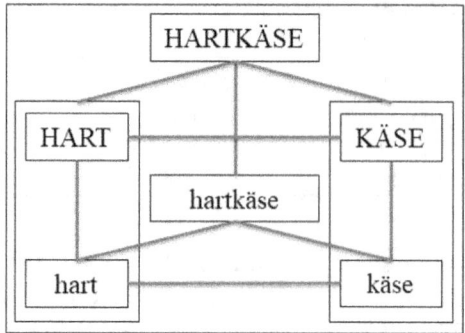

Figure 10.4 *Structure of* Hartkäse *in CG*

The continuum from autonomy to dependence is a key factor in the prototype of compounds, which is the juxtaposition of roughly co-equal elements that normally occur independently (Langacker 2019: 355).

In (12b), we have as an additional element the inflection of *hart*. Based on Langacker's (2019: 357) representation of the plural *bones*, we can use the diagram in Figure 10.5 for *harter*.

The key difference between Figure 10.5 and Figure 10.4 is that there is no box around the semantic and phonological representations of the second element. If we compare this with Figure 10.2, this suggests that the affix is not a full Σ. This may be connected to the fact that Figure 10.2 is for a clearly derivational affix, whereas *bones* is an inflected form. However, Langacker denies that there is a categorical distinction between inflection and derivation. For the full representation of (12b), we need a structure with three basic components. Because Langacker's examples are mainly from English, he does not devote much explicit discussion to the issue of adjectival inflection. We may use a structure along the lines of Figure 10.3, but it may be more appropriate to omit the box around the S and P for the inflectional

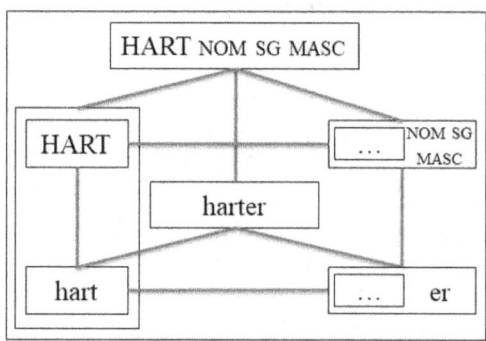

Figure 10.5 *The structure of* harter *in CG*

Cognitive Grammar

ending, as in Figure 10.5. In either case, the contrast between (12a) as the name of a concept and (12b) as a description is not expressed.

Let us now turn to the Slovak examples of A+N combinations repeated here as (13).

(13) a. čajová lyžička ('teaspoon')
 b. čistá lyžička ('clean spoon')

From the perspective of CG, in both examples in (13), we can see composite structures with agreement in number, gender and case between the noun *lyžička* ('spoon') and the modifying adjective. The noun itself ends in a grammatical morpheme -*a* indicating that the expression is a feminine noun in the nominative singular. In the terminology used in CG, the grammatical morpheme contributes to profiling things. Langacker (1987b) makes the point that nouns refer to a semantically coherent class. In CG, this is used to construct such grammatical markers as meaningful. The agreement is displayed in the modifying adjective resulting in a so-called *conceptual overlap* (Langacker 2008: 347) of the same type as for the agreement in (12b). In both expressions in (13) we deal with multi-word expressions which combine specific and schematic information. In CG, a precise delimitation whether an expression is a phrase or a compound is irrelevant despite the fact that semantically, the relational adjective in (13a) has a meaning corresponding to the meaning of a modifying noun in a compound. The difference with the qualitative adjective *čistý* ('clean$_{ADJ}$') in (13b) can be captured by different focusing, prominence and specificity. In line with Langacker (2008: 98), we can say that the relational adjective in (13a) has a relational profile whereas the qualitative adjective in (13b) has a qualitative profile.

As another instantiation of the contrast between words and phrases, we discuss the possessive *'s* in English. In section 4.1, we presented the examples repeated here as (14).

(14) a. She points to a bird's nest in a low branch.
 b. The mother cuckoo lays its egg in another bird's nest.

Genitive constructions as in (14a) are treated in CG as a *reference-point relationship* (Langacker 1995: 58–61). This relationship is based on the idea 'that we commonly invoke the conception of one entity for purposes of establishing a mental contact with another' (Langacker 1995: 58). In (14a), we first focus on *bird* and then on *nest*, relegating *bird* to the background. From the perspective of information structure, in (14b) what is given is described as *another bird* and *nest* is introduced as a new discourse referent. The fact that there is a reference-point relationship is the shared feature. The fact that the possessor functions as a reference point providing mental access to the entity possessed, its target, is valid for all instances (Langacker 2008: 505). The direction follows natural paths (hierarchies) including whole > part, concrete > abstract, and human > animate > inanimate. The expressions in (14) are seen as units in CG without the need to make an explicit distinction between their status as a word or a phrase.

The last contrast to be discussed here involves the combinations in (15).

(15) a. a commuter suburb of Charleston
 b. the Chicago suburb of Cicero

As was shown in earlier chapters, *commuter suburb* in (15a) names a concept of a suburb where people live who typically commute to their work, whereas *Chicago suburb* in (15b) only specifies the location. One of the basic assumptions of CG is that 'our mental universe subsumes everything we are capable of conceptualizing' (Langacker 2008: 276). Usually when we conceptualize something, we then want to talk about it and therefore we need to know how to refer to it. CG offers several grounding strategies for achieving nominal reference, of which the *descriptive strategy* and the *deictic strategy* are the essential ones. *Description* refers to the ability to construct an expression that describes any sort of what we imagine using the lexical and grammatical means of a language. A minimal description is represented by a simple lexical specification, e.g. *suburb*. Then novel descriptions can be produced that can be of any level of structural complexity and any level of semantic specificity. This can be illustrated in (15a) by *suburb* > *commuter suburb* > *a commuter suburb of Charleston*. Similarly, in (15b) the descriptions include *Cicero* > *the suburb of Cicero* > *the Chicago suburb of Cicero*. The deictic strategy uses a reference to the context of a discourse. In (15a), identification relative to the discourse is carried out by grounding the elements, through which the speaker directs the hearer's attention to a referent. A combination of descriptive and deictic strategies is usually sufficient for singling out the intended referent. In (15a), *of Charleston* is a grounding element that identifies precisely which *commuter suburb* is referred to in a context. In (15b), *Chicago* is a clarification explaining to the hearer where the suburb of Cicero is located.

The treatment of words and phrases in CG is given by its non-modular view of language. As there are no separate components for lexicon, morphology and syntax, there is no possibility of drawing a line between words and phrases. Lexicon, morphology and syntax form a continuum where any unit can be accounted for using different degrees of structural and semantic complexity without distinguishing naming and description. Of the contrasts we discussed, only the one in (15) can be adequately described in CG, using the distinction between descriptive and deictic strategies. In the pairs in (12) to (14), both members are descriptive, not deictic, so that this distinction does not affect them.

10.2.2 Lexemes and word forms

CG can account for inflection and derivation, without, however, making a strict distinction between them. Langacker (2008: 346) motivates his view that such a distinction is not necessary in (16).

(16) The very notion that there is a specific line of demarcation rests on theoretical assumptions (e.g. a categorical distinction between lexicon and grammar) viewed in CG as being both gratuitous and empirically problematic.

Langacker acknowledges that there is a traditional distinction, but for CG it would be beside the point to transform it into a categorical one. The view in (16) is entirely compatible with ten Hacken's (2014) discussion of the distinction, because whether the contrast is a continuum or a matter of two clearly delineated concepts depends on their use in a theory. For Langacker, many affixes are inflectional in some respects and derivational in others, or somewhere between inflectional and derivational for a given parameter. Langacker (2008: 347) illustrates this with an example of gender markers, which are considered inflectional because they take part in agreement. However, gender endings can be 'internal and derivational even in the strong sense of being responsible for its categorization as such' (Langacker 2008: 347), illustrated for Spanish in Table 10.2.

Table 10.2 shows that with animate nouns, the suffix -o serves to designate male creatures and -a specifies female creatures. CG treats such morphemes as schematic for the entire class they derive. The endings -o and -a schematically represent nouns profiled as referring to males or females while stems are genderless (Langacker 1991: 185). However, for inanimate nouns, the same endings -a and -o do not mean [MALE] or [FEMALE]. Langacker (1991: 185) suggests that their meaning is [THING]. As Langacker (1987b) argues, nouns designate concepts in the category [THING] and the suffixes can be interpreted as assigning a stem to the class of nouns. Harris (1991) gives a more elaborate discussion of the role of these markers in Spanish that goes in the same direction. In CG, the role of the markers is based on the fact that the theory recognizes highly abstract grammatical meanings. The semantic value of the markers -o and -a in inanimate nouns is that of the noun-class schema. Langacker (1991: 185) motivates it by the fact that -o and -a are noun-forming suffixes.

Table 10.2 *Examples of gender markings in Spanish nouns*

Animate nouns		Inanimate nouns	
alumno ('male student')	alumna ('female student')	cerro ('hill')	mesa ('table')
muchacho ('boy')	muchacha ('girl')	techo ('roof')	casa ('house')

For English, Langacker (2019: 353–354) treats irregular past tense forms from the perspective of their analysability. The past tense form *went* is semantically analysable, but morphologically it is opaque. Semantically, it has the components GO and PAST, but phonologically, only the whole form can be said to have a symbolizing function. An example of the opposite is *understand* where the semantic poles of the elements *under* and *stand* do not contribute to the meaning of the whole unit, but they invoke phonological poles of *under* and *stand*. The past tense form *went* is well entrenched, which means that it blocks the regular form **goed*. In *understand*, the composite meaning of the whole unit blocks the emergence of a compositional meaning based on *under* and *stand*.

Although CG does not make a principled distinction between inflection and derivation, we can still investigate how it can account for the differences between the plural and the diminutive in Dutch we presented in section 4.2. In (17), we give the schematic representations of the plural forms *vogels* ('birds') and *huizen* ('houses') and the diminutive *vogeltje* ('bird$_{DIM}$') in CG.

(17) a. (vogel)$_A$ ---> (vogels)$_{A'}$ = ((vogel)$_A$ s)$_{A'}$
     b. (huiz)$_A$ ---> (huizen)$_{A'}$ = ((huiz)$_A$ en)$_{A'}$
     c. (vogel)$_A$ ---> (vogeltje)$_{A'}$ = ((vogel)$_A$ tje)$_{A'}$

In (17), (A) qualifies an autonomous element and (A') a derived element. Langacker (2019: 357) calls (A') 'the actual composite form'.[2] In CG, it is possible to start from an autonomous symbolic element, e.g. a stem, to which dependent elements can apply repeatedly. The resulting output is a higher-order autonomous structure. In (17a), the initial stem is *vogel*. At the same time it is a root, which cannot be further analysed. It should be noted that in CG the status of a root is a matter of degree and it depends on the threshold. For instance, in *propellers*, the root can be *propeller*, *propel* or *pel* (Langacker 2019: 358). The plural -*s* in (17a) is less substantial than the root and it also depends on the root. A similar process takes place in (17b) with the plural marking -*en* dependent on the root *huiz*-. In CG, it is possible to make a distinction between compounding and affixation as shown in Figure 10.4 and Figure 10.5. The structure of compounds as in Figure 10.4 includes two autonomous structures. This is the key difference between compounding and affixation. From the perspective of autonomy and dependence, no clear-cut line between the inflectional plural markers in (17a–b) and the derivational diminutive marker in (17c) can be drawn. What is not accounted for in (17) is the fact that *vogeltje* designates a concept with a different prototype to *vogel*, whereas *vogels* is simply the combination of the concept of *vogel* with the plural. This property is presented in section 4.2 and further illustrated in section 5.2.2.

---

[2] In (17b), *huiz* is given as the underlying form of *huis*, which is the result of final devoicing.

Apart from regular cases such as (17c), in section 4.2 we gave the example of the Dutch diminutive *stokje* ('stick$_{DIM}$'), which can refer not only to a small stick, but also to salty sticks as a snack. This type of semantic specialization can be explained by an extension from a prototype in a way similar to (6). In order to account for the contrast in (17), we would have to assume that all diminutives follow this path, not only the ones that have a clearly different meaning.

In sum, affixation is not strictly divided into inflection and derivation in CG. This is then reflected in their treatment. In CG, it is not necessary to differentiate between the two and similar schematic representations can account for all affixal phenomena. Any semantic specialization effects must be covered by the general mechanism illustrated in (6).

10.2.3 Paradigms

In the CG framework, Langacker (2019: 363) gives his understanding of a morphological paradigm as in (18).

(18) A morphological paradigm [...] is a complex frame with a substantial degree of systematicity: the component schemas represent multiple dimensions [...] each with multiple values, ideally allowing any combination.

The frame as described in (18) comprises multiple component schemas that stand for patterns of morphological composition. In some cases, each value is symbolized by a distinct element, for instance in Spanish *perros* ('dogs'), *-o-* represents masculine and *-s* plural. In other cases, for instance in Slovak form *ženám* ('women$_{DATIVE}$'), *-ám* marks both plural and dative. The values are represented as the complex meaning of one element. In section 4.3, we presented the inflectional paradigm of the Slovak noun *gitara* ('guitar'). In Table 10.3, nominative and accusative singular forms of some nouns following the same pattern are given.

Table 10.3 illustrates the pattern for accusative and instrumental forms for all Slovak feminine nouns in *-a*. The stems in the accusative and instrumental forms are *gitar-*, *knih-* and *žen-*. The inflectional marker is *-u* in the accusative singular and *-ou* in the instrumental singular. CG explains how a speaker of Slovak has access to all inflected forms of any feminine noun from the same class including the ones in Table 10.3. Each form can be represented by a scheme as in Figure 10.6.

Table 10.3 *Selected case forms of some feminine nouns in Slovak*

Feminine noun	Accusative singular	Instrumental singular
gitara ('guitar')	gitaru	gitarou
kniha ('book')	knihu	knihou
žena ('woman')	ženu	ženou

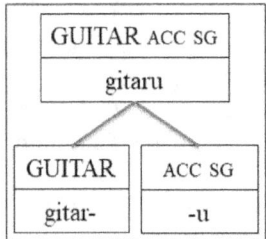 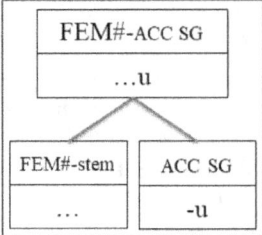 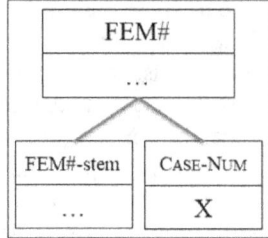

Figure 10.6 *Three levels of schematic construction of the Slovak accusative form* gitaru

Langacker (2008: 252–255) discusses the inflectional paradigm of Spanish verbs of the first conjugation class. In Figure 10.6, we use this to present three levels of generalization for the accusative singular form *gitaru*. The first is specific for this form of this lexeme. The semantic specification gives the translation of the stem and the syntactic interpretation of the ending. The ending *-u* evokes the accusative singular. In the second schema, we generalize to the entire class exemplified in Table 10.3. We use FEM# to delimit this class. It is a subset of the feminine nouns, usually characterized as having a nominative singular in *-a*.[3] All nouns of this class have an accusative singular in *-u*, but we cannot specify the form of the stem. In the third schema, we abstract further and generalize over all case–number combinations for the FEM# class. Here we can characterize phonologically neither the stem nor the ending.

Idiosyncratic forms like irregular plurals in English, e.g. *leaves, wives, knives*, are well-entrenched units and form a category 'just by virtue of the schema being immanent to them' (Langacker 2019: 362). The specificity of these units and strong entrenchment then block the regular forms **leafs, *wifes, *knifes*. This is in general Langacker's solution for irregular forms.

Derivational paradigms are not explicitly mentioned in CG, at least not in Langacker (1987a, 2008). CG covers derivational and inflectional phenomena without making clear-cut distinctions between them. Therefore, in principle, if CG can account for what are traditionally labelled inflectional paradigms, it can also account for derivational paradigms. In section 10.1, we saw how lexical units can be ordered depending on their degree of symbolic complexity. In CG, it is possible to expand the ordering to more complex structures including items larger than words, as in (8). Derivational paradigms in Slovak, e.g. *blog < blogovať < blogový*, as presented in section 4.3, can also be covered in CG.

---

[3] A more precise delimitation is that the consonant preceding the *-a* should also be hard. This is a phonological class specified in Slovak. Other feminine nouns in *-a*, e.g. *ulica* ('street'), have a different inflection pattern. However, the two case forms in Table 10.3 are the same in both classes.

CG offers a formalism for the hierarchical organization of word forms into paradigms. This can also be used for derivational paradigms, because inflection and derivation are not strictly separated. The contrast between dependent and autonomous units discussed in the context of Figure 10.4 and Figure 10.5 is neutralized in the schemas used for paradigms in Figure 10.6.

10.2.4 Naming and transposition

In section 4.2, we presented a concept of transposition that is illustrated by the verb-noun pair *explore* and *exploration*. This concept is relevant to naming, because the noun does not have a different meaning from the verb, only a different syntactic category. Therefore, the nominalization *exploration* is not used for naming a new concept. Langacker (1987b: 90–91) discusses such cases on the basis of the examples in (19).

(19) a. Something exploded!
     b. There was an explosion!

In (19a) we have the verb *explode* that describes the event, whereas in (19b) the nominalization is used to refer to the same event. Although Langacker (1987b: 90) admits that a possible conclusion may be that the verb and noun are semantically identical, he argues for a semantic contrast between *explode* and *explosion*. For Langacker (1987b: 90), the basis for the distinction is that the verb and noun use different images to structure the same conceptual content. The verb *explode* 'imposes a processual construal on the profile event, while *explosion* portrays it as an abstract region' (Langacker 1987b: 90). The verb designates a process. The process consists of a series of component states that are sequentially scanned in time. Sequential scanning then leads to a higher-order conception forming a set of interconnected entities, and a region. Langacker emphasizes that every process defines an implicit region that consists of component states. The nominalization *explosion* raises the region to a higher level through profiling of the composite predication.

Langacker (1987b: 90) gives a schematization of this contrast as in Figure 10.7. In the representation of the verbal expression of the process, we have a sequence of states extended along a temporal axis. The time flow is represented by the arrow, with the thicker part for the actual process. There is an entity passing through this process. This entity is represented by three combinations of semantics and phonology. It is the same entity at three different points in time. These points in time stand for the duration of the process. The representation of the nominalization contains the same basic components. The difference between the verbal and the nominal representation is a matter of profiling. In the verb, the process in its temporal sequence is profiled. In the nominalization, the thick lines of the entity and the thicker part of the arrow have been slimmed down. Instead, the ellipse

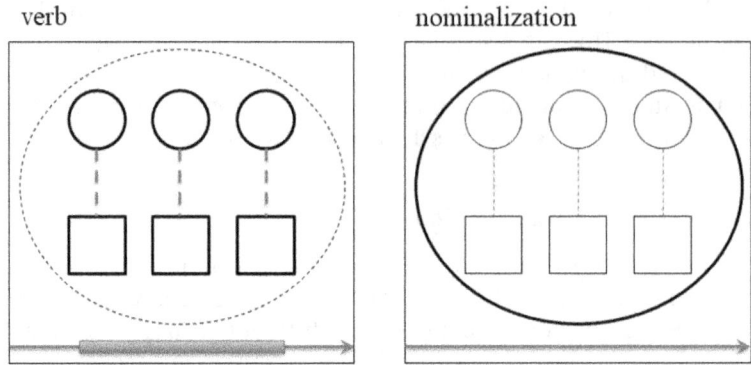

Figure 10.7 *Semantic contrast between a verb and its nominalization in CG*

surrounding the three states of the entity passing through the process is thick. It represents what Langacker calls the higher-order region. This region is composed of the component states. In the nominalization, this higher-order region is profiled. In the verbal representation, the region is marked by a broken line, because it is only implicitly present.

Langacker (1987b: 91) divides nominalizations into two classes. The first includes count nouns, e.g. *explosion, jump, yell, kick*, the second mass nouns, e.g. *jumping, yelling, procrastination, sleep*. As we saw in section 5.2.4, this distinction correlates to some extent with the process–result distinction we illustrated in section 4.4 with the examples repeated here as (20).

(20) a. the installation in their territory of foreign military bases
 b. [they] were taken to a Salvadorean military installation

The main contrast in (20) is that the noun *installation* in (20a) refers to the process of installing whereas in (20b) it refers to the result of this process. For us, this means that (20a) is a transposition, but (20b) not. For Langacker (1987b: 91) the only relevant distinction is between deverbal nominalizations that designate a single perfective process denoted by the verb stem and are count nouns, e.g. *explosion, jump*, and perfective processes producing nominalizations that are mass nouns, e.g. *jumping*. The count noun *jump* is considered as a bounded instance of the abstract substance *jumping*, because it refers to the base process in a generalized or even generic way. Langacker's distinction is made on the basis of a higher-level abstraction, but it does not explain the difference between process and result readings.

The difference between our account in terms of transposition and Langacker's modelling is prominent in the German and Slovak translations of *installation*. German *Installation* and Slovak *inštalácia* have the same ambiguity as installation in (20). The alternative forms, *Installierung* in German and *inštalovanie* in Slovak, only have a process reading, i.e. the

Cognitive Grammar

reading in (20a). From a naming perspective, we can explain this by the fact that they were introduced to avoid ambiguity. There is no parallel explanation in CG, because naming is not used to motivate forms.

Langacker (1987b) does not use the term *transposition* at all. He makes a semantic distinction between verb-noun pairs such as *install* and *installation*. However, he does not address the question whether one or the other is the result of naming. He rejects the definition of *transposition* we give in section 4.4. In fact, in claiming that the pair of representations in Figure 10.7 expresses a semantic distinction between verbs like *explode* and corresponding nouns like *explosion*, he denies the existence of the concept.

10.2.5 Onomasiological coercion

In section 4.5 we presented the notion of onomasiological coercion, which ensures that when a form is chosen to name a concept, it will correspond to the concept we want to assign a name to. The example we used to illustrate it is the meaning of *doorman*, repeated in (21).

(21) a. A doorman is
 b. a man who stands at the door
 c. of a club,
 d. prevents unwanted people from coming in, and makes people leave if they cause trouble.

The definition in (21) is taken from COBUILD (2023). The meaning is divided into three parts, marked (21b–d). The part in (21b) includes the meanings of both components of the compound, *door* and *man*. The parts in (21c–d) are not expressed in *doorman*.

In CG analysability and compositionality are essential in the interpretation of novel composite expressions. Novel composite structures are claimed to be fully analysable. After the novel structure becomes well established, it loses its ability to evoke the activation of its components. The result is that the composite structure is opaque and unanalysable. Langacker (1987a: 297) argues that although it is natural to think of *printer* as meaning 'something that prints', *computer* is less likely as 'something that computes'. Finally, *propeller* is not 'something that propels'. It is possible that *propeller* might have been analysable once it was a novel expression, but with the loss of novelty it became lexicalized.

In fact, this analysis cannot be extended to *doorman*. The point is that *doorman* in the relevant sense was formed to denote the concept described in (21). This is not a specialization of a more general meaning it had earlier. Langacker's examples can be analysed similarly. The mechanical device used to propel a ship or a plane was named *propeller* because of its function. This does not mean that anything propelling something must be a propeller.

This is the same for *computer* and *printer*. The lack of attention for naming makes this point inaccessible in CG.

10.3 Word formation and naming in CG

In presenting Cognitive Grammar, Langacker (2007: 421) emphasizes its distance from other theories. Its coverage of word formation is integrated in a more general attempt to account for the link between form and meaning. The account starts from the symbolic unit, an association of a phonological and a semantic unit. Complex units are the result of composition.

A guiding principle is that CG focuses on the functions of language. As stated in (1), Langacker insists that language is shaped by the functions it serves. He distinguishes symbolic and communicative functions. It seems reasonable to connect these two functions with the contrast between naming and description, which offers a promising starting point for an account of the naming function of word formation.

In naming, a speaker creates a link between an expression and a concept. However, Langacker (2007: 422) takes the abstraction from usage events as the origin of linguistic units. Logically, this cannot be the only source for the speaker, because this would preclude any new expressions. It may be interpreted as a procedure to be followed by the linguist, which would bring CG close to a behaviourist approach. Alternatively, we can assume that abstraction from usage events is one of the types of origin of linguistic units, alongside naming.

The four basic phenomena in the lexicon Langacker (2008: 16–17) describes are more immediately usable in an account of naming. He calls them association, automatization, schematization and categorization. Here, association is most directly linked to the action of naming. Automatization is then the storage in the mental lexicon of the new name. Schematization and categorization are processes in organizing the lexicon. In the context of naming, they can reorganize the lexicon to accommodate new names.

In order to assess the way a theory treats naming, our approach is to start with a number of contrasts that illustrate the borderlines of the set of expressions used in naming. This approach clashes with the general approach in CG, because as stated in (1b), Langacker (2008: 14) assumes a non-modular view of language. As we saw in the quotations in (7) and (11), CG models all contrasts as a matter of degree. As a consequence, there are no definite borderlines between lexicon and grammar, between words and phrases, or between inflection and derivation. As Langacker (2019: 347) states, conventionality and well-formedness are also a matter of degree.

From a cognitive perspective, we would expect that there is a distinction between expressions stored in the mental lexicon of a speaker and expressions that are constructed on the basis of lexical entries. Of course, this distinction is not identical for all speakers and it changes over time, but in principle there must be such a distinction. Taken in this sense, the only way in which the borderline between the scope of the lexicon and of the grammar can be fuzzy is if we take the perspective of linguistic expressions in a community of speakers instead of that of the mental lexicon of an individual speaker. The fuzziness arises only through the differences between speakers. However, whereas the mental lexicon of an individual speaker is an empirical object, there is no empirical object corresponding to a word (or another expression) in a speech community. The word in a speech community only exists as an abstraction.

Nevertheless, Langacker sometimes uses specific mechanisms to account for contrasts that we discuss. Langacker (2019: 357) proposes that the plural marker of *bones* is not a full sign. We used this in Figure 10.5 to represent the inflectional ending in German *harter* as used in (12b). It is not obvious, however, that this should be intended as a general mechanism for inflection in contrast to derivation. Another mechanism occurs in the case of the deictic compound *Chicago suburb* in (15b). We used what Langacker (2008: 276) calls the *deictic strategy* to achieve reference, whereas the naming counterpart *commuter suburb* in (15a) uses the *descriptive strategy*. It is not clear, however, to what extent such mechanisms are intended to be applied generally. In any case, they only cover a small part of the data we considered.

For paradigms, we saw the different levels of generalization in Figure 10.6, which can be used to organize lexical entries. In Figure 10.6, it is used for a Slovak nominal paradigm. However, the same mechanism can be used for derivational paradigms, so that the mechanism cannot be used to model the distinction between derivation and inflection.

For transposition, we saw that Langacker (1987b: 90–91) admits that the verbal expression with *explode* and the nominal expression with *explosion* in (19) describe the same event. As we saw in section 8.2.4, Booij (2020) tends to deny that there is semantic equivalence and proposes a semantic characterization of the distinction between, for instance, *sloppy* and *sloppiness*. In importing a syntactic distinction into the semantic analysis, Langacker's solution represented in Figure 10.7 may remind one of Lieber's (2016a) approach in section 7.2.4. However, whereas Lieber proposes a feature [±material] that marks nouns in semantics in general, Langacker proposes a tailor-made solution for the presumed change of perspective that should reflect the distinction between the verbal and the nominal representation.

The approach to all of these contrasts seems to be driven by the urge to incorporate the data rather than to use them for systematic distinctions. In view of this approach, it seems likely that Langacker would come up with tailor-made solutions for the contrasts we did not find a way to express in his formalism. CG does not aim for a distinction between naming expressions and descriptive expressions.

After the characterization of the set of naming expressions by a number of relevant contrasts, we discussed two phenomena that directly relate to the process of naming. One is the contrast between on one hand German *Installation* and Slovak *inštalácia*, which have both a process and a result reading, and on the other hand German *Installierung* and Slovak *inštalovanie*, which only have a process reading. In English, they all correspond to *installation*. The other phenomenon is the specialized meaning of *doorman* in (21) and its equivalents in German, Dutch and Slovak.

The approach that is uniformly adopted in CG for all such phenomena is based on the interaction of semantic specialization and the sequence of association, automatization, schematization and categorization. The use of round brackets for *dollarless* in (5) is a way of marking the lack of automatization. The result reading of German *Installation* is treated as a semantic specialization. It remains unclear, however, why *Installierung* should not go through the same process of semantic specialization. The idea that *Installierung* is needed to highlight the process in opposition to the result reading of *Installation* is hard to express in CG. It cannot be expressed without referring to naming.

Another illustration of the potential and the limitation of semantic specialization is the treatment of Dutch diminutives. For *stokje* ('stick$_{DIM}$'), it is quite plausible that the special meaning of salty sticks as a snack is the result of semantic specialization. As it is rather difficult to describe the base meaning of the diminutive in a way that is appropriate for all its uses, this means that semantic specialization has to take place immediately. This is clear, for instance, in the case of *weekendje* ('weekend$_{DIM}$'), discussed in section 5.2.2, which cannot have the purely temporal meaning, as in *volgend weekend(*je)* ('next weekend$_{(*DIM)}$').

The problem with semantic specialization as a basis for the account of naming is most strikingly illustrated with our example of *doorman*. For similar examples, Langacker (1987a: 297) proposes that there is a gradual loss of the ability to evoke the activation of the components. This would imply that *doorman* is first formed as a compound and only afterwards gradually starts meaning 'a man who stands at the door of a club, prevents unwanted people from coming in, and makes people leave if they cause trouble'. In fact, it is the need to name this concept that triggers the formation of *doorman*. This road into the lexicon, which is the main one for expressions resulting from word formation, is not covered by the sequence of association, automatization, schematization and categorization.

CHAPTER 11

Štekauer's onomasiological theory

Building on insights from the Prague School, Štekauer (1998) proposed a theory pursuing a different set of questions to the ones determining the agenda of generative linguistics. The theory focuses primarily on explaining the naming process as it occurs in response to the need of a speech community. Conceptualization of meaning is the first step and the selection of formal markers follows from it. The model, developed further by Štekauer (2005, 2016), has a separate word formation component where naming takes place. This component consists of four levels that gradually narrow down the choice of a form to correspond to the concept. Once a new word is formed, it is stored in the lexicon. Alternative naming strategies, including sense extension and borrowing, are linked more directly to the lexicon. In section 11.1, we will present Štekauer's onomasiological model of word formation and the main claims associated with it. In section 11.2, we will discuss how this theoretical model can treat the data given in Chapter 4. Finally, in section 11.3 we will consider to what extent the onomasiological theory covers different aspects of these data.

11.1 Štekauer's onomasiological theory as a framework

The onomasiological theory of word formation in English developed by Štekauer (1998) was inspired by the work of Miloš Dokulil (1912–2002) and Ján Horecký (1920–2006) which we presented in section 3.2. Unlike other theories we discuss, Štekauer's theory does not have a specific name. More broadly, the onomasiological approach 'emphasizes the cognitive-semantic component of language and the primacy of extra-linguistic reality in the process of naming' (Fernández-Domínguez 2019: abstract). This assumption also underlies other recent onomasiological models, proposed by Blank (1997), Koch (2001, 2002) and Grzega (2004). Grzega (2009) gives a comparative overview of their application to compounding.

Štekauer (1998) presents his model of word formation as distinct from purely formal generative approaches. The main distinguishing feature is captured in (1).

(1) There is hardly a work which is built on the 'referent-concept-meaning-form' scheme which, in this book, will be denoted as the *onomasiological approach to word-formation*. (Štekauer 1998: 2)

The quotation in (1) emphasizes that the process of naming begins with an object of extra-linguistic reality, which is conceptualized and needs a name. In line with the functionalist tradition of the Prague School, naming is taken to be initiated by the language users, i.e. the speech community. After the selection of a referent as a starting point, conceptualization takes place followed by semantic analysis. Only then are the formal means selected to name a new concept. The direction of the naming process goes from meaning to form. Semantics provides options which are then mapped into the form. This means that 'semantics is not a mere "tag" attached to formal patterns' (Štekauer 1998: 2), which is in direct contrast to the position taken in Chomsky's theory of interpretive semantics. The process of naming is a driving force in Štekauer's onomasiological model. His model has three independent components: the Word-Formation Component, the Lexical Component and the Syntactic Component. Figure 11.1 shows how individual components interact with each other.

In Figure 11.1 we can see that naming starts from the referent and language users conceptualize it in terms of its characteristic properties.

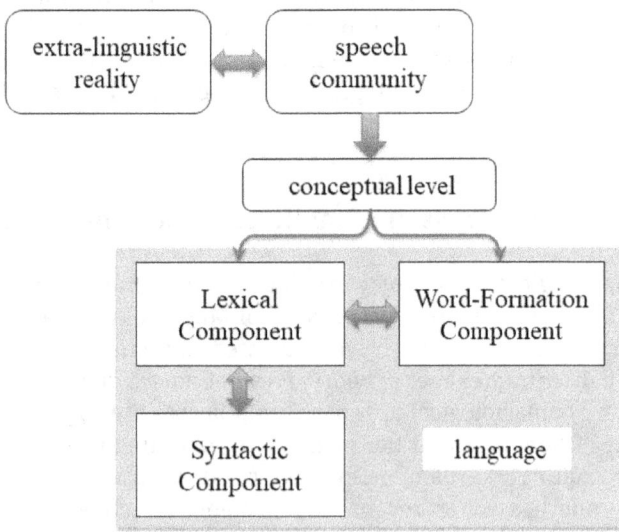

Figure 11.1 *Štekauer's model of naming*

The model highlights the importance of the speech community in naming. In line with the model in Figure 11.1, the next step leads to the linguistic components. A speaker decides whether a name can be retrieved from the Lexical Component or requires the activation of the Word-Formation Component. The former occurs when an existing name has been stored, but also in meaning extension and borrowing, which take place in the Lexical Component. In the latter case the processes in the Word-Formation Component result in a new name. When a new name has been formed in the Word-Formation Component, it moves to the Lexical Component. This connection between the two components is represented by an arrow. A newly formed naming unit can enter the Lexical Component and it can move back to serve as input in the Word-Formation Component for another process to search for a new name. The way in which the Lexical Component in Figure 11.1 is organized becomes more obvious in (2).

(2) Given my paradigmatic approach to Lexicon, I prefer to replace the term 'list' with the term 'component', that is to say, the Lexical Component. (Štekauer 1998: 69).

Two crucial observations are expressed in (2). First, for Štekauer, the Lexical Component is not primarily a list of words. The component includes monomorphemic words, all regularly coined naming units, borrowings and other irregular coinages. Furthermore, it has a separate subcomponent with 'all the affixes including their subcategorization frames, i.e. specifications of their combinability, restrictions on their use, phonological properties, etc.' (Štekauer 1998: 3). In addition to this, (2) observes that the Lexical Component is organized in paradigms. When a new naming unit passes from the Word-Formation Component to the Lexical Component, it is assigned to the corresponding paradigm and receives morphosyntactic features. In fact, it is only the category of word class that is specified in the Word-Formation Component (Štekauer 1998: 56). All other features are added in the Lexical Component. The units there take part in a number of lexical, paradigmatic relations. The onomasiological model in Figure 11.1 determines the scope of word formation as in (3).

(3) [N]aming units are *bilateral signs*, including the meaning and the form. This determines the scope of word-formation: there are no naming units in the Word-Formation Components that are pure forms or pure meanings. (Štekauer 1998: 4)

The formulation in (3) is based on some of the main principles of the Prague School. It is understood that not only the naming units formed in the Word-Formation Component are signs in the Saussurean sense, but also the morphemes that constitute them. Therefore, naming units such as *perceive, conceive, receive, contain, retain, cranberry, possible* or *Monday*, for which no decomposition into morphemes is possible, are treated as monemes and placed in the Lexical Component (Štekauer 1998: 4). However, such naming units can move to the Word-Formation Component where they can take part in a naming process resulting in the formation of words such as *container* and *retainable*. This is in line with the claim that 'a new naming unit is related to at least one naming unit, stored in the Lexicon, through the latter's word-formation base' (Štekauer 1998: 22).

In Figure 11.1 there is no arrow between the Word-Formation Component and the Syntactic Component, which means that there is no direct connection between these two components. It is only the Lexical Component that is linked to the Syntactic Component. The distinction between word formation and syntax is summarized in (4).

(4) A crucial difference between word-formation and syntax consists in the fact that they operate at two different levels: while the generation of naming units is a matter of the system of language (*langue*), with no direct connection to speech, or to specific communication situations (*parole*), sentences are generated in close relation to speech (Štekauer 1998: 36).

The statement in (4) is rooted in the functional principle of the Prague School, which assumes that lower-level units function as building blocks for higher-level units. Phonemes build up morphemes, morphemes build up words, words build up phrases, phrases build up sentences and sentences build up texts. Therefore, 'no use is made either of the speech level (*parole*) or syntactic constructions (*langue*) as possible sources of new, productively coined naming units' (Štekauer 1998: 4). It is only the Lexical Component that provides the input for the Syntactic Component, but not vice versa. The Word-Formation Component is the only one feeding the Lexical Component directly.

A more detailed structure of the Word-Formation Component is given in Figure 11.2. In Figure 11.2, the naming process in the Word-Formation Component follows a trajectory through four levels. The input is a concept. The semantic level specifies semantic properties and the onomasiological and onomatological levels gradually specify form classes. The phonological level determines the name as it can be pronounced. The output is a new complex word. The individual steps of a naming process in Figure 11.2 are illustrated in Table 11.1.

In Table 11.1 we can follow a trajectory towards finding a new name for a concept. The starting point of the process of word formation in Štekauer's onomasiological model is the extra-linguistic reality or, to be more precise, a linguistic demand arising from the needs of a speech community to name a concept based on a particular object found in the external world. In our example in Table 11.1, we search for a name for 'a person who consumes food in an attempt to alleviate feelings of anxiety, boredom, negativity, etc., rather than to satisfy hunger'. The particular object is conceptualized as a

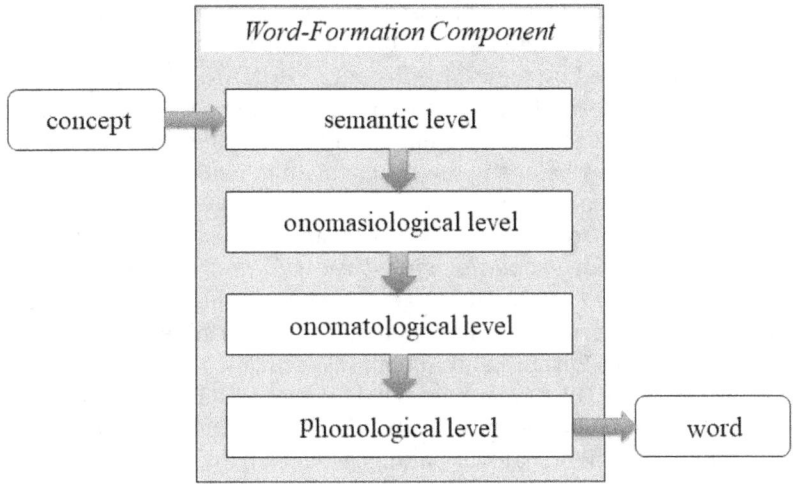

Figure 11.2 *Internal structure of the Word-Formation Component in Štekauer's model*

Table 11.1 *Naming process resulting in* comfort eater *in Štekauer's model*

Levels/stages of naming process	Example
Extra-linguistic reality/speech community	A need to name a new concept in the speech community
Conceptual level	It is a SUBSTANCE. It is HUMAN. The HUMAN carries out ACTION.
Semantic level	+HUMAN, +AGENT, +ACTION, +PURPOSE
Onomasiological level	Onomasiological mark ⇒ Purpose – Action + Onomasiological base ⇒ Agent
Onomatological level	Purpose ⇒ comfort Action ⇒ eat Agent ⇒ -er
Phonological level	/kʌmfət ˌiːtə/

representative of a class that is named, which means that the same object can belong to various classes.

Once such a naming demand exists, the object or a class of similar objects is analysed at the *conceptual level*. The class of objects is abstracted and generalized in terms of logical predicates or *noemes*, which constitute a *logical spectrum*. The most general conceptual categories of SUBSTANCE, ACTION, QUALITY and CONCOMITANT CIRCUMSTANCE are used. The conceptual level is not part of the word formation component itself. Not only is it not confined to a particular language, but it is independent of language.

Next is the *semantic level*. As opposed to the conceptual level, the semantic level forms part of the linguistic sign proper. This means that logical predicates are represented by semes, for instance ±HUMAN, ±AGENT, ±ACTION, ±PURPOSE, which form the semantic structure of the new naming unit, i.e. of the new linguistic sign. The inventory of semes is in principle language-specific, because they belong to the system of an individual language.

From the semantic level, the process moves to the *onomasiological level*. At this level, semes from the semantic level are selected to produce a structure consisting of an *onomasiological base* (OB) and an *onomasiological mark* (OM). In Table 11.1, the OB is Agent. In general, the OM may be further divided into the determining constituent and the determined constituent. In Table 11.1, they are Purpose and Action, respectively. The main role of the OM is to specify the OB, here represented by Agent. The OB and the OM are connected by the *onomasiological connective*, here Purpose – Action – Agent, which determines the semantic relations between them. Together they constitute the onomasiological structure.

At the *onomatological level*, individual morphemes are assigned to the onomasiological structure specified at the previous level in Table 11.1 on the basis of the Morpheme-to-Meaning-Assignment Principle. This is also illustrated by the naming unit *comfort eater*, 'a person who consumes food in an attempt to alleviate feelings of anxiety, boredom, negativity, etc., rather than to satisfy hunger'. The choice is made by the members of the speech community from several available options. For example, the Agent can be expressed in English not only by -*er*, but also by -*ist*, -*man*, etc. The new naming unit then reaches the final *phonological level* of the Word-Formation Component. Here, relevant phonological rules apply. The result is a sign that is stored in the Lexical Component.

In Štekauer's onomasiological model, the relationship between the onomasiological level and the onomatological level takes a central position. It is first of all this relationship which results in replacing the traditional terminology of word formation processes, such as affixation, derivation, blending and compounding, by the so-called *Onomasiological Types* (OTs). Štekauer (1998, 2005) distinguished five OTs in his model. In the later development of his theory, Štekauer (2016) elaborates on his original classification of naming processes in OTs and proposes an extended version with eight OTs. The OTs differ in the onomasiological structure and their morphematic expression at the onomatological level. The structure of OT1 is illustrated in (5).

(5)   OT1   DingM - DedM - Base
                 Purpose - Action - Agent
                 comfort - eat   - er

In (5) we present the onomasiological structure for *comfort eater* given in Table 11.1. The OB is represented by Agent, morphematically expressed by -*er*.

The OM is composed of two constituents, the determined constituent is represented by Action (here *eat*) and determining mark by Purpose (here *comfort*). OT1 in (5) displays a high degree of semantic transparency. Only the relationship between *eater* and *comfort* needs to be determined. Therefore, this type is listener/reader-friendly.

OT2 is illustrated in (6) for the concept meaning 'a tool which enables a user to use the internet anonymously'.

(6) OT2 DingM   - DedM   - Base
          Purpose - Action   - Instrument
          0   - anonymize - er

The onomasiological structure for this concept in (6), resulting in the name *anonymizer*, lacks one of the constituents of the OM. The determining constituent is not expressed. The OB is realized by Instrument and represented by *-er*. The OM corresponds to Action, here expressed by *anonymize*. The degree of semantic transparency in (6) is slightly lower than in (5). This type is more economical and therefore speaker/writer-friendly than OT1, but it requires more effort from the hearer, who has to interpret the 0.

The structure of OT3 is exemplified in (7) for the concept meaning 'a person who is knowledgeable about or keenly interested in food'.

(7) OT3 DingM   - DedM   - Base
          Object - Action - Agent
          food   - 0   - ist

In (7) we can see the onomasiological structure for this concept, resulting in the name *foodist*. The agentive OB is expressed by *-ist*. The action constituent of the OM is not made explicit. It is only the determining constituent of the OM that is represented by *food*, which is the Object of the implicitly understood Action carried out by the Agent. Like OT2, OT3 is also more economical and speaker/writer-friendly than OT1. On the other hand, it allows for more interpretations such as 'a person who knows a lot about food', 'a person who is enthusiastic about preparing food', 'a person who is enthusiastic about consuming food' or 'a person who approaches food on the basis of science'. Therefore, this requires even more effort from the hearer than in the case of OT2.

The three OTs in (5) to (7) are the same in Štekauer (1998, 2005) and in the more recent classification proposed in Štekauer (2016). The earlier classification used a label OT4 for the naming units with a binary onomasiological structure where the OM is simple and cannot be divided further in the way we saw in OT1, OT2 and OT3. Štekauer (2016) reclassifies the original OT4 as OT7. The change of number of the OT is only a formal modification; the internal structure remains the same as that of the original OT4 given in (8).

(8) OT4/new OT7 Mark   - Base
                  Negation - Quality
                  un   - vaccinated

In (8) we have the onomasiological structure for the concept meaning 'that has not undergone vaccination'. A division of the OM into two meaning components, as we saw in (6) and (7), is not possible in this case. The OM in (8) is not further structured.

The new OT4, OT5 and OT8 represent what Štekauer (1998, 2005, 2016) calls conceptual recategorization, i.e. conversion in more traditional terminology. In the earlier classification, all instances were included in one OT that was originally labelled as OT5. The new OT6 covers exocentric compounds. It is economical and speaker/writer-friendly, as only the determining constituent of the OM is lexically expressed. For a more detailed account with examples, see Štekauer (2016: 60–61).

In summary, Štekauer's onomasiological theory makes the act of naming central. His theory explains the whole process of searching for a name for a new concept. New names are formed on the basis of a need that arises in the speech community. The separate component for word formation in Štekauer's model allows not only the meaning of naming units to be described, but also the decision steps preceding their formation to be expressed.

11.2 The treatment of relevant contrasts in Štekauer's onomasiological theory

In this section, we will present how the data from Chapter 4 can be covered in Štekauer's onomasiological theory of word formation. The structure of the section corresponds with the structure of Chapter 4.

11.2.1 Words and phrases

In Figure 11.1, we saw that Štekauer's model has a Word-Formation Component and a separate Syntactic Component. This has direct consequences for the distinction between words and phrases. In (9), Štekauer expresses the difference in the main function between word formation and syntax.

(9) The main function of word-formation is to meet the requirements of a speech-community by coining new naming units for objects, actions, qualities, and circumstances, real or imaginary, if an absence of such naming units is felt to hamper (for various reasons) the process of communication among the members of a speech community. On the other hand, syntax combines already existing naming units into sentences in the process of communication. (Štekauer 1998: 37)

The quotation in (9) is in line with a clear demarcation of word formation and syntax. As formulated in (4), it is based on the functionalism of the Prague School, which does not allow higher-level units to become building blocks for the units at a lower level. Štekauer's onomasiological model rejects the idea of relating word formation directly to syntax. This is reflected in the analysis of our first borderline example from German, repeated in (10).

(10) a. Hartkäse   ('granular cheese')
     b. harter Käse ('hard cheese')

In Štekauer's onomasiological model, the distinction between (10a) and (10b) is in agreement with a traditional view of the former being a compound whereas the latter is a phrase. The compound in (10a) is formed in the Word-Formation Component and its onomasiological structure is given in (11).

(11) OT4/new OT7   Mark   - Base
                        Quality - Substance
                        Hart   - käse

The onomasiological structure of the German expression for 'granular cheese' is binary. It consists of an OB, expressing Substance, and an unstructured OM for Quality. Substance is then expressed by *Käse* ('cheese') and is specified by Quality *Hart* ('hard'). The meaning 'granular cheese' is there, because it is the starting point of the naming process. This contrasts with the combination of units in (10b), which includes an inflected form of *hart* ('hard') modifying the noun *Käse* ('cheese'). The expression in (10b) is formed in the Syntactic Component of Štekauer's model.

In the Slovak examples repeated here as (12), the distinction between processes in syntax and word formation is somewhat different.

(12) a. čajová lyžička ('teaspoon')
     b. čistá lyžička ('clean spoon')

In (12) we have expressions with a noun and a modifying adjective that agrees with the noun in number, gender and case. In Štekauer's onomasiological model, the adjective and noun in (12a) and (12b) are combined in the Syntactic Component. The difference between them is that (12a) names a concept using two words, whereas (12b) is a free syntagmatic combination. In the Slovak linguistic tradition, expressions such as (12a) are classified as multi-word naming units called *združené pomenovania* (cf. section 4.1). According to Furdík (2004: 34), such units are not the object of word formation analysis. Combinations such as (12b) are the object of syntactic analysis. Jarošová (2000a, 2000b) presents a more fine-grained classification of multi-word naming units in Slovak. She divides multi-word units labelled as *združené pomenovania* into lexicalized expressions and multi-word terms. In (12a), we have a lexicalized expression. An example of a multi-word term is *dutá žila* (lit. 'hollow vein', i.e. vena cava). In the case of (12), this means that the borderline between word formation and syntax does not coincide with the one between naming units and syntactic combinations.

Another example of the contrast between words and phrases we discuss involves the possessive 's in English. In section 4.1, we presented the examples repeated here as (13).

(13) a. She points to a bird's nest in a low branch.
 b. The mother cuckoo lays its egg in another bird's nest.

In (13a), *bird's nest* names a concept, whereas in (13b) it is not even a constituent. The Saxon genitive in English presents some well-known theoretical problems. Zwicky (1987) demonstrates that the possessive marker behaves more like an affix when it simplifies to a single formative in cases when the possessive follows the homonymous plural marker, for instance *the cats' favourite places, the crocuses' bright blossoms* (Zwicky 1987: 140). On the other hand, according to Spencer (2019: 246–247), the genitive case marker 'shows typical clitic properties [. . .]: promiscuous attachment (the property of being hosted by a word of the "wrong" category: *[the book we're talking about]'s title*) and wide scope over coordinated phrases: *[the cat and the dog]'s owners*'. Spencer highlights the fact that when the second coordinate is a personal pronoun, for instance **[Kim and you]'s children*, a wide-scope reading is not possible. Payne (2011: 380) suggests that there are two types of Saxon genitive. The first is a head marking genitive which inflects nouns and pronouns as in (13a), the second is a phrase marking genitive which marks words of any category appearing at the end of a noun phrase. This is the one we have in (13b). Only Payne's first type is used for naming.

Štekauer does not explicitly discuss the treatment of examples of the type in (13). However, Štekauer (1998: 144–146) gives the analysis of naming units with the onomasiological mark in the plural. The onomasiological analysis of the compound *excess profits tax* by Štekauer (1998: 146) is given in (14).

(14) DingM   - DedM   - Base
 Stative [+ PLURAL] - Action - Patient
 excess profits   - 0   - tax

In (14) we can see the onomasiological structure for the concept 'tax which pertains to excess profits'. For this concept, the conceptual level already includes the notion of plural. Although the onomasiological mark in (14) is structured, its structure does not correspond to the one in OT1.

Štekauer's onomasiological theory

Unlike our example in (5), the second element, *profits*, does not express an Action. Instead, the predicate connecting *excess profits* with *tax* is not expressed. Therefore, it is an example of OT3, parallel to (7). The determining constituent of the OM is structured into the specifying element *excess* and the specified element *profits*. The marker for the plural is contained in this specified element. It corresponds to the seme [+PLURAL] at the semantic level, which is selected to be realized at onomatological level and is realized as /s/ at the phonological level.

For (13a), we can assume that the concept is described as 'a home built by birds for their eggs'. At the semantic level, the semes [HOME] and [BIRD] are selected. At the onomasiological level, they are inserted in OT3 to give (15).

(15) DingM   - DedM   - Base
      Object [+POSS] - Action - Patient
      bird's   - 0   - nest

The determining constituent of the OM in (15) is not complex in the same way as the one in (14), but does have the marker [+POSS]. In the same way as [+PLURAL] in (14), [+POSS] is selected for realization at onomatological level and realized as 's at phonological level. Having a word formation base with a possessive morpheme is not a problem in Štekauer's onomasiological model, because naming units are stored in paradigms of the Lexical Component. The Saxon genitive form of the naming unit *bird* is retrieved from the corresponding paradigm.

The expression *another bird's nest* in (13b) is analysed as a syntactic constituent in Štekauer's onomasiological model. It is not produced in the Word-Formation Component, but in the Syntactic Component.

The final contrast to be discussed here in the light of Štekauer's theory involves the combinations in (16).

(16) a. a commuter suburb of Charleston
      b. the Chicago suburb of Cicero

As our analysis in section 4.1 shows, *commuter suburb* in (16a) names the concept of a suburb where people live who typically commute to their work, whereas *Chicago suburb* in (16b) only specifies the location. In Štekauer's model, (16a) is the output of operations in the Word-Formation Component. We can represent the onomasiological structure for *commuter suburb* in (16a) as in (17).

(17) DingM   - DedM   - Base
      Object   - Action - Location
      commuter   - 0   - suburb

The interpretation of the onomasiological structure in (17) is a place or location of an unexpressed Action by the Object represented by *commuter*. The OM is complex although only its determining constituent is assigned a formal expression. The determined constituent of the OM is not represented by a morpheme, it only implicitly indicates the action of the people towards the place where they live. This contrasts with the combination in (16b), which is formed in the Syntactic Component. Thus, *Chicago suburb* is a free combination of elements in syntax. In (16), as in (13), the borderline between naming and syntactic combinations coincides with the one between the scopes of the Word-Formation Component and the Syntactic Component.

11.2.2 Lexemes and word forms

In Štekauer's onomasiological theory a principled distinction between inflection and derivation is made. Štekauer (1998: 49) characterizes the relationship between them in (18).

(18) Word-formation is divided, though not separated, from inflectional morphology.

The statement in (18) depends on the recognition that new naming units are produced in the Word-Formation Component. This is not the case for inflection. The Word-Formation Component is linked to extra-linguistic reality in a way inflection is not. As shown in section 11.1, inflection is included in the Lexical Component, where lexemes are organized in paradigms. The selection of a form from the paradigm of a lexeme depends on information from the Syntactic Component. Morphosyntactic features get their value in the Syntactic Component and their form from the paradigm in the Lexical Component.

In section 4.2 we introduced the examples of Dutch plural, repeated here as (19).

(19) a. vogel ('bird') → vogels ('bird$_{PL}$')
    b. huis ('house') → huizen ('house$_{PL}$')

In (19), the two main endings for the plural of nouns in Dutch, *-s* and *-en*, are illustrated. The choice between the plural form in (19a) and (19b) is partly determined by prosodic and other phonological factors. In Štekauer's onomasiological model, the Dutch plurals in (19) are formed in the Lexical Component. Each plural word form belongs to a corresponding paradigm. The Syntactic Component can retrieve any of the forms in (19) whenever it is required by the syntactic context.

As a contrast to the plural, in section 4.2 we used the diminutive. We introduced the Dutch examples repeated here in (20).

(20) a. vogel ('bird')   → vogeltje ('bird$_{DIM}$')
     b. huis ('house')   → huisje ('house$_{DIM}$')

The diminutive in (20a) is marked by the suffix -tje. In (20b), the -t- is elided. In Štekauer's onomasiological model, the formation of diminutives takes place in the Word-Formation Component. In Dokulil's classification, diminutives belong to the modificational onomasiological category. This category differs from the other two, the mutational (relational) category and the transpositional category, in the fact that a modifying feature is added to a concept of a particular semantic category (cf. section 3.2.2). In the case of (20), the modifying feature is diminutive. According to Dokulil (1962: 46–47), the modification can be of several types including not only diminutive but also augmentative, collective and change of gender. Dokulil's approach is also the basis for the cross-linguistic research into evaluative morphology by Körtvélyessy (2012) and Grandi and Körtvélyessy (2015). An onomasiological analysis of the diminutives in (20) based on Štekauer's model is given in (21).

(21) Mark   - Base
     Object - Diminutive
     vogel   - tje
     huis   - je

The onomasiological structure in (21) shows that the suffixes -tje and -je represent a class of diminutives. In terms of the onomasiological structure they stand for the OB. The OB is specified by the OM, which is represented by *vogel* and *huis* in (21). As the OM is unstructured, (21) belongs to OT7 (formerly OT4), shown in (8).

Apart from regular cases such as (20), in section 4.2 we gave the example of the Dutch diminutive *stokje* ('stick$_{DIM}$'), which can refer not only to a small stick, but also to salty sticks as a snack. This type of semantic specialization can be explained by an extension of meaning that takes place in the Lexical Component of Štekauer's model. Another example is the diminutive *kaartje*. Its meaning can be related to one of the meanings of *kaart*, e.g. geographical map or playing card, but it can also have other meanings, e.g. ticket (for a theatre, train, etc.), business card. It should be noted that meanings of the latter type are not generally available for *kaart*. This type of semantic specialization takes place in the Lexical Component. As such, it contrasts with the formation of regular diminutives.

Štekauer's onomasiological model can account for the distinction between the formation of plurals as in (19) and the formation of diminutives as in (20). The former takes place in the Lexical Component, the latter in the Word-Formation Component. Extension of meaning and semantic specialization occur in the Lexical Component. We noted earlier that *vogeltje* designates a concept with a different prototype to *vogel*, as evidenced by the fact that a *meeuw* ('seagull') is a normal instance of *vogel* but a marginal instance of *vogeltje*. This effect is accounted for by the interaction of the Lexical and Word-Formation Components in Štekauer's model.

11.2.3 Paradigms

Paradigms are of great importance in Štekauer's onomasiological model. In (2), we saw that the Lexical Component is organized in paradigms. The prototypical paradigm is the inflectional paradigm. We already mentioned that as soon as a new naming unit moves from the Word-Formation Component to the Lexical Component, it becomes part of the corresponding paradigm. When a naming unit is borrowed, it is immediately stored in the Lexical Component and is also assigned to the corresponding paradigm as illustrated by the inflectional paradigm of *bloger* ('blogger'), sometimes also written *blogér*.

Table 11.2 gives the paradigm of *bloger* ('blogger'). It demonstrates that this word was adapted and fully integrated into the Slovak grammatical system. It is assigned to the declensional paradigm of [+human] masculine nouns ending in a consonant. Morphosyntactic features of number, gender and case are realized cumulatively. All word forms in singular and plural are actively used by Slovak speakers, as can be documented by data from the Slovak National Corpus (SNK 2022).

Štekauer's onomasiological approach to word formation also gives space to accommodate derivational paradigms. Štekauer (2014: 368) states that the similarity between inflectional and derivational paradigms is greater than had earlier been assumed. In (22), Štekauer (1998: 49) gives his generalized understanding of paradigmatic relations.

(22) Word-formation is about naming units coined as signs, and analyzed as units existing in paradigmatic relations in the vocabulary. The process of word-formation is not that of asserting something. It is the process of naming.

In (22), the naming function of word formation is emphasized. In addition, newly formed naming units enter paradigmatic relations with other naming units once they pass into the Lexical Component. This suggests that the units in the Lexical Component are organized not only in inflectional paradigms

Table 11.2 *Paradigm of the borrowed noun* bloger *('blogger') in Slovak*

	Singular	Plural
Nominative	bloger	blogeri
Genitive	blogera	blogerov
Dative	blogerovi	blogerom
Accusative	blogera	blogerov
Locative	blogerovi	blogeroch
Instrumental	blogerom	blogermi

as in Table 11.2, but also in derivational paradigms. Körtvélyessy et al. (2020: 10) treat the derivational paradigm 'as a system of complex words derived from a single word-formation base'. This then includes two dimensions, a vertical and a horizontal one. The vertical dimension is defined by all direct derivatives from a single word formation base. Körtvélyessy et al. (2020: 10) give the examples in (23).

(23) a. dom ('house')
 b. dom-ov ('home')
 c. dom-ček ('house$_{DIM}$')
 d. dom-isko ('house$_{AUG}$')
 e. dom-ov ('towards one's house$_{ADV}$')

The derivatives with the same base in (23) illustrate the paradigmatic capacity of word formation. The horizontal or syntagmatic dimension of the derivational paradigm is shown in (24).

(24) a. dom ('house')
 b. dom-ov ('home')
 c. dom-ov-ina ('homeland')
 d. dom-ov-in-ový ('related to homeland$_{ADJ}$')

The horizontal dimension exemplified in (24) makes it possible 'to identify the number of affixation operations available for a given basic underived word' (Körtvélyessy et al. 2020: 11). In (24b–d), each suffixation process corresponds to one order of derivation; for instance, in (24d) there are three orders of derivation. This also means that the paradigmatic capacity can be investigated for each order of derivation separately or it can include all orders of derivation together. For the horizontal dimension, Štekauer (2014: 368) states that 'a single cognitive category may include several paradigms'. For AGENT, we can find the realizations in (25).

(25) a. teach → teacher
 b. journal → journalist
 c. library → librarian
 d. escape → escapee
 e. milk → milkman

As (25) illustrates, AGENT is not only related to verbs and it can be realized by different suffixes. In (25e), we have a compound. For the example of *bloger*, which we used in section 4.3, the representation of the derivational paradigm is as in (26).

(26) a. bloger → blogerka ('bloger$_{FEM}$')
 b. bloger → blogerský ('blogger$_{A}$')

The notation with arrows in (26) highlights the syntagmatic dimension, even though there is only one derivation at the time. The two examples in (26a–b) can of course also be listed as in (23) to highlight the paradigmatic dimension.

Štekauer (2014: 357) relates the discussion of the difference between inflectional and derivational paradigms to the distinction between inflection and derivation. In (18), Štekauer describes word formation as 'divided, though not separated', from inflection. This is compatible with the recognition that the precise boundaries between inflection and derivation are difficult to determine. The similarities between inflectional and derivational paradigms listed in Štekauer (2014: 357–361) and Körtvélyessy et al. (2020: 7–12) represent a good basis for parallels between inflection and derivation.

For Štekauer (2014: 369) another crucial notion in the concept of derivational paradigm is potentiality, which ensures a high degree of predictability and regularity also typical of inflectional paradigms. It is important that the empty slots in a paradigm can be filled by actual words, even if at present they are not. From this perspective, a derivational paradigm represents a closed system in the sense of a finite set of potential derivatives, which makes derivational paradigms very similar to inflectional paradigms. In Štekauer's onomasiological model, both types of paradigms can be accommodated in a natural way.

11.2.4 Naming and transposition

As mentioned in section 3.2.2, the transpositional onomasiological category is one of the three basic categories distinguished by Dokulil (1962: 43), alongside the mutational and modificational ones.

Dokulil distinguishes three types, illustrated with his Czech examples in Table 11.3. In the first type, a quality is abstracted. Whereas a quality expressed by an adjective, e.g. *hravý*, is attributed to a noun, the abstraction, expressed by a noun, is no longer dependent on any object having the quality. In the second type, we see a similar abstraction for an action. The verb *padat* is predicated of a subject, but the abstraction *pád* does not need a specified subject. In the third type, we start from a descriptive phrase. The prepositional phrase *na stěně*, used as an adverbial, becomes an adjective, which makes the participle unnecessary. In the descriptive phrase, the participle and the adverbial together constitute the mark. The adverbial on its own is the determination of the mark. When *nástěnné* is an adjective, it constitutes the mark by itself.

As Dokulil (1962: 43) points out, transposition is not a typical onomasiological category. In the case of *hravost* ('playfulness'), it is not naming a property, but making an abstraction that differentiates it from *hravý* ('playful'). On the other hand, there are also cases such as *sladkost*, a transposition of *sladký* ('sweet$_A$'). In some contexts, *sladkost* can mean 'sweetness' and behaves like *hravost*. In other contexts, however, it means 'sweet$_N$',

Štekauer's onomasiological theory

Table 11.3 *Dokulil's types of transpositional onomasiological category*

Type of transpositional onomasiological category	Example
Objectivization of QUALITY	*hravý* ('playful') → *hravost* ('playfulness')
Objectivization of ACTION	*padat* ('fall$_V$') → *pád* ('fall$_N$')
Change of the determination of the mark into the mark itself	*noviny visící na stěně* ('newspaper hanging on [the] wall') → *nástěnné noviny* ('on-wall$_A$ newspaper')

i.e. an object that has the property of being sweet. As Dokulil (1962: 46) points out, in the latter case, the formation of *sladkost* is an onomasiological act. In terms of the definition of transposition we use, cf. (14) in section 4.4, *sladkost* is only a transposition if it means 'sweetness'.

In Štekauer's onomasiological theory, we find references to transposition in the treatment of *representation* by Štekauer (1998: 57). He gives two analyses corresponding to the process and the result readings, which we adapt in (27).

(27) a. DingM - DedM - Base
        Object - Action - Process
        0 - represent - ation
   b. DingM - DedM - Base
        Object - Action - State
        0 - represent - ation

The contrast between the two different onomasiological structures for *representation* (27a) and (27b) is that the former refers to the action itself as a process, whereas the latter refers to the state resulting from the action. The structures in (27) suggest that *-ation* changes the meaning of the verb it attaches to in both cases. For (27b) this is not a problem. In the context of (27a), Štekauer states that Process is 'Abstract Action'. We are not sure about the exact interpretation of this difference, but if there is a change of meaning, (27a) is not strictly a transposition in our definition. Panocová (2015: 25) analyses the ambiguity of *body scan*. She proposes that the process and result readings reflect different OTs.

In section 4.4 we illustrated the process–result ambiguity of such nouns with the examples repeated here as (28).

(28) a. the installation in their territory of foreign military bases
     b. [they] were taken to a Salvadorean military installation

The analysis of *installation* in (28) follows the same pattern as that of *representation* in (27). The only difference is that in (28b), we have an Object instead of a State. In German and Slovak, we noted that there are two nouns corresponding to *installation*. The German examples are repeated here in (29).

(29) a. die Installation der Heizungsanlage
 'the installation of_the heating_system'
 b. veraltete Installationen erneuern
 'outdated installations renew', i.e. replace outdated installations
 c. die Installierung der Heizungsanlage
 d. *veraltete Installierungen erneuern

The point about the examples in (29) is that *Installierung* only has a process reading, not a result reading. Štekauer does not discuss such cases in detail, but the onomasiological approach he adopts provides a straightforward explanation for this state of affairs. We can refer to Figure 11.1. When *Installation* has been formed in the Word-Formation Component and added to the Lexical Component, it will normally take precedence over any new word formation. It is more efficient to retrieve a word stored in the lexicon than to form a new word for the same concept. However, if *Installation* is ambiguous, as in (29a–b), it may be preferable to form a new word for the process reading, especially if the result reading is prominent for *Installation*. This explains, therefore, that *Installierung* only occurs in a process reading. It also explains that in a corpus analysis, it is much rarer than *Installation*, as we documented in section 4.4.

In the onomasiological approach, transposition is recognized as a separate category of formations. Štekauer still points to a sense of abstraction that applies between *representation* as a process noun and the verb *represent*. For our German examples of *Installation* and *Installierung*, the onomasiological perspective renders a straightforward explanation for the possibility of the latter, as well as for its limited semantic scope and its reduced frequency.

11.2.5 Onomasiological coercion

In section 4.5 we introduced *doorman* as an example of onomasiological coercion. The coercion ensures that when a form is chosen to name a concept, its meaning will correspond to the concept we want to assign a name to. For *doorman* we also presented equivalents in German, Dutch and Slovak, repeated in (30).

(30) a. Türsteher ('door_stander') DE
 b. uitsmijter ('out_thrower') NL
 c. vyhadzovač ('throw_out-er') SK

In section 4.5 we showed that the four languages select different elements of the conceptualization for the final output of the naming process. English and German (30a) use the location whereas Dutch (30b) and Slovak (30c) use the function of the person. Štekauer's model treats the differences by starting from conceptualization and moving towards the selection of morphemes that represent the onomasiological structure. The German example is presented in (31).

(31) DingM   - DedM   - Base
     Location - Action   - Agent
     Tür ('door') - steh ('stand$_V$') - er

In (31) we can see the onomasiological structure of the German equivalent of *doorman*. The literal meaning of (31) is '[a] man who stands [at a/the] door'. The structure in (31) belongs to OT1, with all three components of the onomasiological structure lexically expressed. The OB in (31) is an Agent, morphematically expressed by *-er*. The OM is composed of two constituents: the determined constituent is Action (here *steh* 'stand$_V$') and the determining constituent Location (here *Tür* 'door'). As noted in section 11.1, OT1 scores high on semantic transparency and is listener/reader-friendly, but requires more effort from the speaker/writer. In (32), we give the onomasiological analysis of the Dutch equivalent in (30b).

(32) DingM   - DedM   - Base
     Goal   - Action   - Agent
     uit ('out') - smijt ('throw$_V$') - er

The onomasiological structure in (32) represents the meaning '[a] person who throws [people who cause problems] out'. As in (31), all three components are morphematically expressed. However, a different Action is chosen, which results in a different function of the determining constituent of the OM. In terms of transparency for the hearer/reader and effort from the speaker/writer, (31) and (32) are similar.

For the Slovak equivalent in (30c), the onomasiological structure is of a different type. It is given in (33).

(33) DingM   - DedM   - Base
     Object   - Action   - Agent
     0   - vyhadzov ('throw_out')   - ač

In (33) we see that in Slovak the same basic naming strategy is used as in Dutch (32), but the realization is different. The Agent OB is represented by the suffix *-ač*. The OB is specified by the determined constituent of the OM *vyhadzovať* ('throw_out$_V$'). Although *vy-* is a prefix, there is no verb **hadzovať*. In terms of OTs, (33) belongs to OT2, which shows a slightly lower degree of semantic transparency than OT1 in the German and Dutch equivalents in (31) and (32). Although particles or prepositions often combine with verbs in Dutch, there is no verb *uitsmijten*. Finally, in (34) we present the analysis of *doorman*.

(34) DingM   -   DedM   -   Base
      Object -   Action -   Agent
      door   -   0   -   man

In (34) the meaning is '[a] man [who stands at the] door'. The OB is assigned the Agent morpheme *man*. The determining constituent of the OM *door* specifies the OB. The verbal element remains unexpressed. The onomasiological structure belongs to OT3, which is higher in economy and lower in semantic transparency. Therefore, it is more friendly towards the speaker/writer than OT1 and OT2. It should be noted that in all expressions lexicalized in (31) to (34), only a selection of the conceptual structure is expressed. In this sense, there is a significant amount of work involved for the hearer/reader.

Štekauer's onomasiological model starts from the concept and gradually selects meaning elements and specifies linguistic elements in moving towards the name. Language-specific elements include both the selection of semantic elements and the specification of formal elements. In this way, the effect we called *onomasiological coercion* is ensured from the start, because the concept to be named is fully specified before the naming process begins.

11.3 Word formation and naming in Štekauer's onomasiological theory

Štekauer's onomasiological theory takes as its starting point the referent-concept-meaning-form scheme evoked in (1). As such, it is radically different from the other theories and frameworks we have seen in Chapters 5–10. It takes word formation first of all as a mechanism for finding new names for concepts.

The theory is based on the Prague School tradition of linguistics, which elaborates ideas from Saussure (1916). Both complex words and the morphemes they are composed of are taken to be signs in Saussure's sense. As highlighted in (4), word formation is distinguished from syntax by assigning it to the *langue*. Word formation creates new signs that become part of the language system. Syntax combines signs into sentences and utterances that belong to the *parole*.

As discussed in section 2.3, Saussure (1916) takes the *langue* to be realized in a speech community. At various places, Štekauer mentions the speech community as the driving force behind word formation. Ten Hacken and Panocová (2011) argue that it is only individual speakers who can carry out the word formation, but the acceptance of a new word in the speech community depends on the degree to which the perception of the need and the felicity of the new word is shared.

In converting the referent-concept-meaning-form scheme into a theory of word formation, Štekauer analyses the process of naming in a way that we modelled in Figure 11.1 and Figure 11.2. The former illustrates the position of the Word-Formation Component in the system of language, the latter the internal structure and the direct input and output of the Word-Formation Component.

In the actual analyses proposed in the literature, the onomasiological level and its mapping to the onomatological level take centre stage. Štekauer developed a system of Onomasiological Types to classify the way elements from a conceptual specification are selected and realized.

In the discussion of the contrasts in section 11.2, we found that in comparison with the models we discussed in earlier chapters, the fact that the model makes the act of naming central increases the potential to express the contrasts precisely. The distinction between word formation and syntax is directly reflected in the model of Figure 11.1, where they are different components. This makes a very natural account of the opposition in (16), repeated here as (35).

(35) a. a commuter suburb of Charleston
 b. the Chicago suburb of Cicero

Whereas *commuter suburb* in (35a) is a result of word formation, *Chicago suburb* in (35b) is formed in syntax. This immediately explains why the former is the name of a concept and the latter is not. This approach is emblematic of most of the contrasts we used for the borderline between word formation and syntax. The only exception is the Slovak contrast in (12), repeated here as (36).

(36) a. čajová lyžička ('teaspoon')
 b. čistá lyžička ('clean spoon')

Because *čajová* in (36a) is an inflected adjective, Štekauer considers the expression in (36a) a syntactic construct. In this, he follows the Slovak tradition, which makes (36a) a *združené pomenovanie* (cf. section 4.1 and section 11.2.1). Štekauer mostly discusses examples from English, but in English we also find relational adjectives, as in *presidential office* (cf. section 8.2.4). Levi (1978) considers such examples equivalent to N+N compounds. In this case, Štekauer's decision to assign structures such as (36a) to the domain of syntax seems based more on the grammatical tradition of Slovak than on the contrast between naming and description.

The contrast between naming expressions and affixed expressions that are not used for naming takes the form of delimiting naming from inflection and transposition. In Štekauer's model, inflection is in the Lexical Component and as such clearly distinguished from affixation that serves naming. In the Lexical Component, inflection is further removed from the extra-linguistic reality. Where information that can be expressed by inflection plays a role in naming, we actually also find it in the word formation process. An example is the occurrence of [+POSS] in (15), repeated here as (37).

(37) DingM   - DedM   - Base
     Object [+POSS] - Action - Patient
     bird's   - 0   - nest

The reason why [+POSS] can be realized in *bird's nest* is that it is part of the information in the concept that was used as input to the Word-Formation Component. It belongs to the information selected at the Semantic Level in Figure 11.2. Parallels between inflection and derivation are visible in the fact that we have both inflectional and derivational paradigms. Štekauer takes paradigms as an important organizational principle of the Lexical Component.

For transposition, we adopt a definition that excludes semantic differences between the two words concerned (cf. section 4.4). Štekauer takes a slightly different position. In his discussion of *representation*, he assumes that the noun is semantically an abstraction from the verb *represent*. According to our definition, this would make *representation* not a transposition.

As for the set of expressions used for naming, we find that Štekauer's onomasiological theory identifies a set that is almost the same as what we started with in Chapter 4. The only exceptions are the relational adjective construction in (36a) and perhaps transpositions. The latter depends on a different analysis of the data.

The fact that Štekauer's onomasiological model takes naming as the starting point for its organization raises expectations about its ability to account for the phenomenon we called *onomasiological coercion*. These expectations are not disappointed. As shown by the examples in section 11.2.5, the way in which *doorman* and its equivalents in German, Dutch and Slovak get their meaning is explained in the sense that the meaning is there from the start. It is represented in the conceptualization that serves as the input for the Word-Formation Component and guides the steps to the choice of a word as a name in Figure 11.2.

In other theories and frameworks, we found that instead of onomasiological coercion it is semantic specialization that is proposed as the main factor in determining the meaning of a word resulting from word formation. An example where this type of explanation is plausible is the Dutch diminutive *stokje* in the sense of salty stick. In Štekauer's onomasiological theory, such a specialization is not analysed as the output of a word formation rule. Instead, the word *stokje* ('stick$_{DIM}$') is formed in the Word-Formation

Component and sent to the Lexical Component. When the need to name the 'salty sticks' comes up, *stokje* is taken in the Lexical Component and receives an additional meaning. This means that whether *stokje* ('salty stick') is a word formation result or not depends on whether *stokje* ('stick$_{DIM}$') had been formed and added to the Lexical Component before or after the need for naming 'salty stick' arose.

Finally, let us turn to the German example with *Installierung* in (29). The issue here is first, that the formation of *Installierung* is not blocked by the existence of *Installation*, and second, that *Installierung* can only have a process reading, whereas *Installation* can have both a process and a result reading. In section 9.2.4, we saw that it is not possible to explain the second fact by assuming that *-ung* does not have a result reading. Other German nouns in *-ung*, e.g. *Sammlung* ('collection'), have both process and result readings. By using naming needs as a starting point, Štekauer's onomasiological theory can explain the observations very elegantly. The ambiguity of *Installation* creates a space for the formation of *Installierung* when it is necessary to exclude the result reading.

In conclusion, we can say that by taking naming as a starting point, Štekauer's onomasiological theory of word formation offers a powerful means of explaining onomasiological coercion and the partial blocking we observed in the context of the process–result alternation.

CHAPTER 12

Natural Morphology

Natural Morphology (NM) is a theory based on Dressler et al. (1987), with as its central notion *naturalness*. Dressler (2005a: 267) understands *natural* as cognitively simple and easily accessible and thus universally preferred. *Marked* is the polar opposite of *natural*. Naturalness and markedness can be considered from universal and language-specific perspectives, giving rise to a certain tension that is resolved in different ways in actual cases. Naturalness is a key term in three subtheories of NM, covering complementary issues: the theory of universal preferences elaborated by Mayerthaler (1981), the theory of typological adequacy (Dressler 1985, 1988) and the theory of system adequacy (Wurzel 1984; Dressler and Ladányi 2000). Each of these is relevant to word formation. In section 12.1, we will present the main tenets of the theory of NM. Then, in section 12.2 we will focus on the data given in Chapter 4 and their accommodation in the framework of NM. Finally, in section 12.3 we will evaluate the degree of coverage of different aspects of these data by the theory of NM.

12.1 Natural Morphology as a framework

The history of NM can be traced back to 1979, when the summer school of the Linguistic Society of America took place in Salzburg and Wolfgang Dressler and a number of other linguists founded a common platform (Dressler 2006: 1).[1] Eight years later a joint volume by Dressler et al. (1987) appeared, based on work in this platform. The theory of NM is functionalist in its nature. Dressler (2005a: 267) highlights the two main functions of language, the communicative and the cognitive functions, and relates them to word formation in (1).

---

[1] Dressler (2020: 963) gives 1977 as the date of the summer school, but the *LSA Bulletin* 78: 12–14 from October 1978 announces the Linguistic Institute hosted by the University of Salzburg for 23 July to 31 August 1979.

Natural Morphology

(1) The specific main functions of word formation are partially shared with inflectional morphology, i.e. semantic and formal motivation of a complex or derived word by its parts or, in a rule format, by its base(s) and the word-formation rules deriving the complex word. Only word formation, but not inflectional morphology, has the lexical function of lexical enrichment.

The statement in (1) emphasizes that word formation serves both the communicative and the cognitive function. The functional difference between word formation and inflection is that the former expands the vocabulary on the level of the system, whereas the latter has a relational function among words in phrases and larger units.

Dressler (2005a: 267) uses naturalness as an umbrella term for other more specific terms that are defined in three subtheories of NM as represented in Figure 12.1. The first is a universal markedness theory, which includes system-dependent morphological naturalness. It mainly concerns universal preferences. The second component covers a theory of typological adequacy, which covers more specific preferences based on morphological types, e.g. inflectional and agglutinative languages. The third component is a theory of system-dependent naturalness, which covers more language-specific preferences. Dressler (2005a: 267) points out that 'these subtheories function as subsequent filters on possible and probable words of a language: what is allowed or even preferred universally, may be rendered dispreferred or even disallowed by typological adequacy and then by language-specific system adequacy'.

For Dressler (1999), the subtheory of universal markedness is a *preference theory*. In this context, he refers to the work of Vennemann (1983) in historical linguistics. Naturalness is viewed as a matter of degree in each of several naturalness parameters that follow from universal markedness theory. Dressler (2005a: 268–277) discusses a number of such parameters. In (2), we list the most relevant parameters for our discussion here.

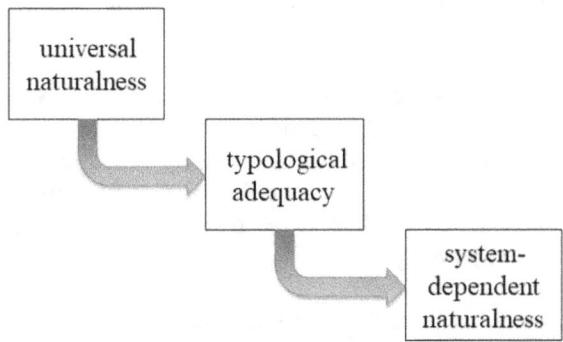

Figure 12.1 *A model of NM*

(2) a. Preference for iconicity
    b. Preference for indexicality
    c. Preference for morphosemantic transparency
    d. Preference for morphotactic transparency
    e. Preference for biuniqueness
    f. Figure-ground preferences

The parameter in (2a) is based on Peirce's classification of signs. Iconicity occurs when form directly reflects meaning. In morphology, an important manifestation is the subparameter of *constructional iconicity* or *diagrammaticity*. The quantity of form and meaning tend to correspond. If more meaning is added, it should be reflected in more form or material. For instance, the noun *blogger* derived from the verb *blog* is constructionally iconic or diagrammatic, because the added meaning of agent noun corresponds to the added form *-er*. The verb *house* derived from the noun *house* is less iconic, because the additional meaning is not reflected in additional form, but in the change from /s/ to /z/. The conversion of $book_N$ to $book_V$ is non-iconic as the addition of meaning is not accompanied by any addition of form. Cases of subtraction are marginal in English, but these are considered anti-iconic. A possible example is *Turk* from *Turkey*. Research in NM suggests that children tend to prefer a greater extent of iconicity than adults. Dressler (2005a: 270) states that the first morphological rules acquired by children are constructionally iconic suffixation rules.

The parameter in (2b) is also based on Peircean semiotics. Indexicality in morphology covers all cases when a morphological marker refers to the base of the rule that introduces it. In Peirce's theory, an index deictically refers to a nearby object. This suggests that affixation is more natural than base modification, and conversion is the least natural as it lacks an overtly expressed signans.

In (2c) we have the parameter of morphosemantic transparency. Full transparency equals full compositionality of the meaning. This is a typical property of inflectional meanings, which we will return to in section 12.2.3. The situation in word formation is different, as Dressler (2005a: 271) describes in (3).

(3) Thus we must differentiate between transparent word formation meaning (G. Wortbildungsbedeutung; cf. Corbin's 1987 notion of *sens construit*) and lexicalized word meaning. Hence word formation rules can only predict word formation meaning but not the opacifying differences between word meaning and word formation meaning.

As suggested in (3), the parameter of morphosyntactic transparency is also gradient. Dressler (2005a: 272) claims that compounds tend to be more semantically transparent than derivations. The reason is that compounds are more descriptive. He gives the example of the compound *dishwashing machine*, which should give a hearer/reader more semantic details than the derivation *dishwasher*.

Another parameter is morphotactic transparency in (2d), presented by Dressler (2005a: 273). On this parameter, the most natural forms include resyllabification, e.g. *teach → teacher*. Less natural or morphotactically less transparent are cases such as *decide → decision*, which has a vowel change as well as a change of the final consonant of the base. Suppletion is extremely weak on morphotactic transparency. An important aspect of the preference for morphotactic transparency is the preference for continuous morphs, which means that suffixation and prefixation are preferred over, for instance, infixation or circumfixation, as in Dutch *gebergte* ('mountain range') from *berg* ('mountain').

In (2e) the preference for biuniqueness is listed. This principle is valid if there is a one-to-one correspondence between the form and the meaning such as in the case of the suffix *-less*. Less natural are examples of one-to-many correspondences between form and meaning, e.g. the suffix *-er* in English, which can form comparative adjectives and agent nouns. Even less natural are cases representing many-to-many correspondences, such as the suffix *-en* serving as a plural marker (alongside *-s*) and forming adjectives (e.g. *golden*, alongside *-ful* as in *successful*) and verbs (e.g. *whiten*, alongside *-ify* as in *glorify*).

Finally, at least for our discussion here, figure-ground preference in (2f) is a parameter that highlights, as Dressler's (2005a: 274) states, the contrast between the head, which in word formation represents the figure, and the non-head, which represents the ground. The consequence is that the non-head is subordinated to the head, which is reflected in particular in suffixation and compounding. Dressler (2005a: 276–278) discusses further preferences and alternative parameters, but they are not relevant for the data we chose in Chapter 4.

Typological adequacy as shown in Figure 12.1 is the second subtheory of NM. Dressler (1985, 1988, 2005a) was inspired by Skalička's approach to language types as an ideal construct, summarized in Skalička (1958). The idea is that the ideal types are found in natural languages to different degrees. In NM, language types are seen as 'sets of consistent *responses to naturalness conflicts*' (Dressler 2005a: 278). In the inflecting-fusional type, one finds a combination of optimal values of the universal parameters of indexicality (2b) and figure-ground preferences (2f). On the other hand, less optimal values are in the parameter of iconicity (2a), morphosemantic transparency (2c), morphotactic transparency (2d) and biuniqueness (2e). In agglutinating languages the situation is rather the opposite. Dressler (2005a: 279) considers typological naturalness as relational, i.e. relating different universal natural parameters to individual language components.

The third component in Figure 12.1 is system-dependent naturalness, which concerns the morphology of specific languages. Wurzel (1984) describes it for systems of inflectional morphology. When there are two or more competing system-defining structural properties, Wurzel claims that the most dominant one is the most adequate. Dressler (2005a: 279) illustrates it by means of the property [±Latinate] pertaining to the stratification of derivational morphology. The suffix *-ity* selects bases of Latinate origin, whereas *-ness* can be added to non-Latinate bases. Non-Latinate derivation is dominant, which explains that *-ness* can also attach to Latinate bases such as in *opaqueness* as a variant of *opacity*. It is in this context that NM treats productivity.

Within system-dependent naturalness a distinction is made between static morphology and dynamic morphology. Static morphology refers to the storage of morphological forms including derivations and compounds and their organization. Dynamic morphology covers morphological rules and is connected with productivity. This opposition corresponds to the one between *Wortgebildetheit* and *Wortbildung* by Dokulil (1968) we discussed in section 3.2.2. Dressler (2005a: 280) assumes a competition between static and dynamic morphology for all morphological constructions formed by rules and direct lexical access.

As a third system-dependent contrast of naturalness, Dressler (2005a: 281) gives the contrast between on one hand universal naturalness and typological adequacy and on the other hand system-dependent naturalness. Typological adequacy is considered 'as a filter and elaboration on universal naturalness', as represented in Figure 12.1, whereas language-specific system adequacy, i.e. system-dependent naturalness, is viewed 'as a filter and elaboration on typological adequacy' Dressler (2005a: 281).

Much of the literature in NM tries to support the model of naturalness with the three levels in Figure 12.1, and the different kinds of parameters and preferences by the use of data from the morphology of various languages. As a result, NM does not propose a full account of morphology, but rather a system that is founded on the data they select. The underlying idea of naturalness is appealing, but NM is sometimes attacked as not sufficiently rigorous in its formulation of its claims, e.g. by Bauer (2003: 265).

12.2 The treatment of relevant contrasts in NM

In this section, we aim to present how the data from Chapter 4 can be covered in NM. In pursuing this aim, we encountered problems of a different type to the ones we had in earlier chapters. As Bauer (2003: 265) notes, 'very little descriptive work has been done using natural morphology'. We will nevertheless propose a treatment of the phenomena we introduced in Chapter 4 in line with what we found in the literature for those phenomena where we are reasonably confident that we understand the prevailing intention in NM and can extrapolate from the examples discussed. The structure of the section corresponds with the structure of Chapter 4.

12.2.1 Words and phrases

The notion of prototype is important in NM (cf. Dressler 1990). Therefore, the fuzziness of boundaries between individual components of language and categories is more characteristic of the theory of NM than clear-cut boundaries. Dressler (2005b: 36) makes the claims concerning compounds and phrases given in (4).

(4) a. A prototypical compound is a word which consists of two prototypical lexical words.
 b. Prototypically all members of a compound recur as free forms (i.e. autonomous words).
 c. Prototypically, compound members belong to major lexical categories, with a preference for nouns.
 d. The core of prototypical compounds is surrounded by non-prototypical compounds in transition to syntax, derivation, and the lexicon.

In (4) Dressler gives an overview of the properties relevant for prototypical compounds. In line with (4a) a combination of a lexical word with a clitic is not a prototypical compound, for instance the Italian example *darlo* '[to] give-it' (Dressler 2005b: 36). The statement in (4b) makes formations such as *cranberry* less prototypical. According to (4c), the combination of function words, which Dressler (2005b: 36) illustrates with *wherever, within, onto*, as well as the combination of a noun with a function word, e.g. German *Ich-sucht* ('ego-mania'), are less prototypical. Dressler calls them 'rare and unproductive'.

In (4d), Dressler evokes less prototypical compounds surrounding the prototype. As an example he gives juxtapositions. The criterion which juxtapositions share with compounds is non-separability, or in other words the impossibility of changing the linear order of elements and of inserting another word between the members of a compound in contrast to a phrase. On the other hand, Dressler (2005b: 36) explains that phonologically and morphologically, juxtapositions may have properties of syntactic phrases. He gives the German example *Hohepriester* ('the (Jewish) high-priest'). This is an A+N combination, which unlike A+N phrases in German has main stress on the first member (modifier) and secondary stress on the second (head). This stress pattern is typical of German compounds. There are two ways in which the word can be inflected. One option is that only the final part is inflected, so that the genitive singular is *des Hohepriesters*. An alternative is that both members are inflected, yielding *des Hohenpriesters*. There is no difference in meaning between the two combinations. Dressler (2005b: 36) concludes that 'the second variant is more phrase-like, the first more compound-like and the corresponding prototypical compound would be (potential) *Hoch-priester*'.[2]

With this background we will turn to the contrasts between words and phrases from section 4.1. The German examples of A+N combinations are repeated as (5).

(5) a. Hartkäse ('granular cheese')
b. harter Käse ('hard cheese')

From the perspective of prototypicality, (5a) is a more prototypical compound, whereas (5b) is less prototypical. In contrast to the German example with the two genitive forms for *Hohepriester*, however, in (5) the absence or presence of the inflectional ending reflects a difference in meaning.

The preference for morphosemantic transparency, as in (2c), is another parameter operating in NM that can be used to contrast words and phrases. As mentioned above, full transparency means full compositionality. Dressler (2005a: 271) points out that '[i]n word formation, morphosemantic transparency can never be complete, because Frege's principle of semantic compositionality can hold only for syntax.' Thus, the meaning of the phrase in (5b) is fully compositional, whereas the meaning of (5a) is not. On the other hand, Dressler (2005a: 271) admits that the compound *high-school* may also be classified as a morphosemantically transparent compound. This is based on the fact that first, the meaning of the head is fully transparent and second, the semantic modification by its first member (non-head) is still obvious. *High-school* is high in a metaphorical sense in contrast to elementary school. In (5a), the meaning of the head *Käse* ('cheese') is fully transparent. The meaning of the modifier *hart* is slightly less transparent, because it is used to identify a particular type of cheese that has this property, rather than any cheese with this property. The parameter of morphosemantic transparency in NM is a matter of degree. The scale of transparency assumes that transparency of the head is more important than of the non-head. Therefore, the compound in (5a) is still relatively high in morphosemantic transparency. As mentioned, the phrase in (5b) is fully compositional.

The distinction between our Slovak A+N examples is analysed slightly differently in NM. We repeat the examples in (6).

(6) a. čajová lyžička ('teaspoon')
b. čistá lyžička ('clean spoon')

---

[2] In fact, DeReKo (2023) gives 11 occurrences of *Hochpriester* in the W-corpus, compared with 3,771 for *Hohepriester*. The genitive *Hohepriesters* has 381, *Hohenpriesters* 225 occurrences. Dressler inserts hyphens to separate all morphemes, but they are not written in German orthography.

The examples in (6) are fairly similar. In both cases the noun is modified by an adjective that agrees with it in number, gender and case. The difference is that in (6a) *čajový* ('tea$_{ADJ}$') is a relational adjective, whereas *čistý* ('clean') in (6b) is a qualitative adjective. As we noted in section 4.1, relational adjectives are syntactically adjectives, but have a meaning that is identical to that of a noun in non-head position of a compound. Semantically, the difference between the two adjectives in (6) is that (6a) names a concept using two words, whereas (6b) is a free phrasal combination. Both examples in (6) are placed further from the prototype of a compound, but it is hard to find any criterion in NM to make a distinction between them. The parameter of morphosemantic transparency leads to similar results. The meaning of (6a) and (6b) is fully compositional and transparent.

Another example for the distinction between words and phrases we discussed involves the possessive *'s* in English. In section 4.1, we presented the examples repeated here as (7).

(7) a. She points to a bird's nest in a low branch.
    b. The mother cuckoo lays its egg in another bird's nest.

In (7a), *bird's nest* names a concept, whereas in (7b) it does not. Dressler (2005b: 32) discusses the parameter of morphotactic transparency of English compounds with a pluralized non-head such as *sportsman, sales tax*. Inflected words which are not identical with citation forms are universally less preferred bases. This also applies to (7a). In the German examples *Frauenfeind* ('woman hater'), *Friedensvertrag* ('peace treaty'), Dressler (2005b: 33) treats the elements *-en-* and *-s-* as interfixes which 'do not contribute to the meaning of the compound and [. . .] reduce morphotactic transparency'. The name for a concept in (7a) is considered less natural than the construction in (7b).

The final contrast we describe in section 4.1 covers the combinations in (8).

(8) a. a commuter suburb of Charleston
    b. the Chicago suburb of Cicero

The contrast in (8) is that the expression *commuter suburb* in (8a) names the concept of a suburb where people live who typically commute to their work, whereas *Chicago* in (8b) only gives more precise information about the location of the suburb. The application of the parameter of morphosemantic transparency gives very similar results for (8a) and (8b); both expressions are transparent and compositional. Both (8a) and (8b) meet the prototype criteria valid for compounds in (4a–c).

To sum up, the theoretical principles of NM make it possible to distinguish words and phrases, but they do not impose clear-cut boundaries. In practice, this means that some of the contrasts we presented can hardly be differentiated. Both the compound and the phrase in the contrasts in (6) and (8) fulfil all the optimal conditions in (4a–c).

12.2.2 Lexemes and word forms

For the distinction between inflection and word formation, NM takes the same general approach as in the one between word formation and syntax. Dressler et al. (1987: 5) takes inflection and word formation to be prototypes and characterizes the distinction as in (9).

> (9) A differentiation of inflectional and derivational morphology cannot result in two disjunctive classes. Rather we conceive of 'prototypical' inflection and 'prototypical' derivation as opposite poles of a morphological scale.

The statement in (9) clearly shows that inflection and derivation in NM represent a cline with individual cases positioned along it depending on the degree of how prototypical they are. Dressler et al. (1987: 4) emphasizes that there are no universally valid definitions characterizing the contrasts of inflection vs derivation and derivation vs compounding. On the other hand, he considers word formation and inflectional morphology 'more similar to each other than to any other component of language' (Dressler et al. 1987: 4).

We used the Dutch plural and diminutive to illustrate the contrast between inflection and derivation. The examples of the Dutch plural from section 4.2 are repeated here as (10).

> (10) a. vogel ('bird') → vogels ('bird$_{PL}$')
> b. huis ('house') → huizen ('house$_{PL}$')

The word forms in (10) display the two main plural endings in Dutch. In (2c), we presented as one of the central claims of NM that morphosemantic transparency is preferred, which should make it a typical property of inflectional meanings. This is the case for (10a) and (10b), because the endings -s and -en have a clear meaning. For the ending in (10b), there are minor irregularities in distribution which can reduce morphosemantic transparency, because -en can also be used to mark the infinitive and the plural of verbs. For the one in (10a), there are some nouns where the -s can also be used as a genitive marker, e.g. *vaders* ('father's' or 'fathers'), creating an actual ambiguity.

In section 4.2, we contrasted the Dutch plural forms in (10) with the Dutch examples of diminutives repeated here in (11).

> (11) a. vogel ('bird') → vogeltje ('bird$_{DIM}$')
> b. huis ('house') → huisje ('house$_{DIM}$')

Evaluative morphology is treated as non-prototypical word formation in NM, e.g. by Dressler (1994) and Dressler and Merlini Barbaresi (1994). The diminutive in (11a) is derived by the suffix -*tje*. The -*t*- is elided in the second example in (11b). As mentioned above, morphosemantic transparency plays a more important role in inflectional morphology than in word formation. Dressler (2005a: 277–278) explains this idea on the basis of *flutist* as a more prototypical case of derivation. Here, we have the entire word as well as its component parts *flute* and -*ist* that should ideally be biunique. However, the entire word has semiotic priority over its component parts. Therefore, derived words are more likely to develop specialized meanings. In inflection, this specialization does not occur, because an inflected word is not a lexical entry.

The diminutives in (11) are derivational, but less prototypical than *flutist*. Therefore, we expect that they tend to develop specialized meanings to a larger degree than the plurals in (10), but less so than typical derivations. In fact, we noted that there are some diminutives with specialized meanings, e.g. Dutch *kaartje* ('business card') in relation to *kaart* ('map') and Slovak *stromček* ('tree$_{DIM}$') which is also used in the sense of Christmas tree. To the extent that such cases are less common than for other derivational rules, such data support Dressler's argument. However, this means that there is no clear boundary between naming expressions and other expressions.

12.2.3 Paradigms

Whereas the distinctions between morphology and syntax and between inflection and word formation we discussed in sections 12.2.1 and 12.2.2, respectively, draw on universal naturalness, the organization of inflection into paradigms is an example of system-dependent naturalness. As represented in Figure 12.1, system-dependent naturalness is a separate theory of naturalness, subordinate to universal and typological naturalness. Wurzel (1989: 63) emphasizes that unlike phonological classes, which have a universal basis, inflectional classes are strictly language-specific. This means that inflectional categories are not taken from a universal inventory. At the same time, inflectional classes in a particular language present a uniform paradigm of realization for these inflectional categories. This is illustrated by the paradigm of Slovak *gitara* we gave in section 4.3. The endings in the table for *gitara* are the same for all feminine nouns with an -*a* in the nominative singular and a stem ending in a hard or neutral consonant.

Wurzel (1989: 239) makes it clear that a paradigm is not just a list, but a structure. In the case of the nominal paradigm for *gitara*, we have the case–number combinations that can be adequately represented in a table. For verbs, the structure is more complex, because person, number, tense and aspect each have an influence on the overall realization of the forms. The structure of paradigms is supported by implicational relations. Wurzel (1987: 78) calls these *implicational paradigm structure conditions* and notes that they are essential for the learnability of the paradigm. An example in the paradigm for *gitara* is that the genitive singular, nominative plural and accusative plural are all realized as *gitary*. This can be formulated as in (12).

(12) For all feminine nouns in Slovak, if the form for the genitive singular is {X}, the form for the nominative plural is {X} and the form for the accusative plural is {X}.

Another implicational condition can be used for the relationship between the nominative singular and the accusative singular. It is formulated in (13).

(13) For all feminine nouns in Slovak, if the nominative singular is {X-a}, the accusative singular is {X-u}.

The difference between (12) and (13) is that in (12), we only have a relationship between unspecified forms, whereas in (13), the actual endings are correlated. The generalization in (12) has a broader scope, because it holds for all feminine nouns, whereas in (13) we have a more specific condition referring to the ending. Gaeta (2019: 259) proposes a formalism for expressing such generalizations for Latin, which has a similar organization of nominal inflectional patterns.

Wurzel (1987: 76–78) discusses the correlation between generalizations over paradigms and extramorphological properties of words. We find these, for instance, in the phonology, the syntax and the semantics of the words. Phonological generalizations are pervasive in the Slovak paradigm structure, because in general the ending of a noun gives a clear indication of its paradigm. Thus, all Slovak nouns whose nominative singular ends in *-o* are of neuter gender and have the same paradigm. For nouns in *-a*, there are more options. There are two feminine paradigms, distinguished by the class of the phoneme preceding the *-a*. There is also a masculine paradigm, which only applies to nouns designating a person, e.g. *hrdina* ('hero') and *kolega* ('colleague'). Because of the implicational generalizations, the system of paradigms remains learnable.

Gaeta (2019: 261–263) explains how naturalness and markedness are used in NM by looking at the historical development of inflectional paradigms. When paradigms change, this should be a move towards a less marked structure. However, the complexity of paradigm structure makes it possible that different later stages are each less marked than the starting point. Therefore, dialects can diverge and develop in different directions. In this connection, McMahon (1994: 106) assesses NM's contribution to historical linguistics as a step forward in the sense that it integrates the interaction between the universal and the language-specific into the historical development of morphology.

For our purposes, the treatment of paradigms is interesting in the sense that lexemes as naming expressions should be distinguished from the adaptation of a lexeme to the syntactic context in which it is used. As Wurzel (1987: 76) observes, membership in an inflectional class is not a constitutive property. Unlike the *signifiant* and *signifié* in a Saussurean sign, the inflectional class does not determine the sign. This means that once we have the form and the meaning of a lexeme, its inflectional paradigm is determined. Therefore, NM accepts the idea that there is a difference between inflected forms, which do not have their own sign, and lexemes, which are a sign.

Derivational paradigms are not usually addressed in NM. In characterizing the contrast between inflection and derivation, Dressler et al. (1987: 5) also mention paradigms. In this context, they refer to derivational paradigms in quotation marks. They give a reference for it, so the quotation marks may be interpreted as an actual quotation, but as they only quote these two words, it suggests they do not accept the concept as one that is valid in their theory.

12.2.4 Naming and transposition

In NM, the phenomenon of transposition as we defined it in section 4.4 is not discussed under this name. However, there are studies of individual cases that we would classify under this label. As we took *installation* and its German and Slovak equivalents as an example in section 4.4., we will focus here on the study by Gaeta and Ricca (2006), who address the competition between five Italian suffixes that produce action nouns from verbs. They give the examples in (14) for these suffixes (2006: 66).

(14) a. cambiare → cambiamento ('change')
     b. trasformare → trasformazione ('transform')
     c. mappare → mappatura ('map')
     d. lavare → lavaggio ('wash')
     e. decadere → decadenza ('decay')

In (14), the glosses refer to the verb. The suffix in (14b) is the one corresponding to *installation*. In contrast to German and Slovak, Italian has several Latin-based suffixes, as can be expected in a Romance language. The focus of Gaeta and Ricca's study is to describe and explain the shift in productivity that can be observed on the basis of historical data. Gaeta (2019: 253–256) summarizes the results and offers an interpretation in NM. Radimský and Štichauer (2021) give an alternative account focused on (14a–b).

As explained in ten Hacken and Panocová (2022: 30–31), the suffix that emerges as *-ation* in English and as *-azione* in (14b) Italian is based on the Latin *-io*, attached to the *-t*-stem, or 'third stem' as Aronoff (1994: 37–39) calls it. Gaeta and Ricca (2006) use -(z)ione as the base form of the suffix and distinguish two possible stems in Italian it can attach to, the verbal theme and the past participle. In (14b), it is not possible to distinguish the two, because they yield the same result. Gaeta and Ricca (2006: 76) give the examples in (15) to illustrate the difference.

(15) a. fondare → fondazione ('found')
     b. deludere → delusione ('disappoint')

In (15a), the past participle of the verb is *fondato*, so that it is the verbal theme *fonda-* that serves as a base. In (15b), the verbal theme would lead to *deludizione, but it is the past participle *deluso* that is used as a base. Therefore, both bases occur.

The focus of Gaeta and Ricca's (2006) study as far as this suffix is concerned is how the choice of one or the other base has developed diachronically. Reasoning from markedness in NM, they predict that the type of formation in (15a) should be more productive than the one in (15b), because it is more natural. In (15b), more phonological rules have to be applied, so that it goes up the scale of markedness. They formulate this in terms of morphotactic transparency (2006: 75). On the evidence of a corpus-based study of the productivity of nouns in -(z)ione, they claim that this prediction was confirmed. Gaeta (2019: 254–255) summarizes this point and connects it to Dokulil's (1968) contrast between *Wortbildung* and *Wortgebildetheit*. The idea is that the less natural type in (15b) is available as *Wortgebildetheit*, i.e. it occurs in the form of connections between structurally related items in the lexicon, but the more natural type in (15a) is the one we find in actual *Wortbildung*. This corresponds to Dressler's (2005a: 280) notion of the competition between static and dynamic morphology we presented in section 12.1.

A striking point about the analysis of Italian -*azione* in NM is the diachronic focus. Gaeta (2019: 256) highlights the dynamic dimension as a factor in language change. Such a research focus connects with, for instance, the work of Paul (1886) we discussed in section 2.2, in the sense that it aims to explain the direction of language change. In NM, language change must be a reduction in markedness.

When we compare the discussion of -*azione* in NM with our presentation of the data for *installation* in English, the most striking difference is that NM is first of all interested in explaining the form of the resulting noun, whereas we are interested in determining the set of naming expressions. In section 4.4, we took an interest in *installation* because of the ambiguity in (16).

(16) a. the peoples reject the installation in their territory of foreign military bases
     b. The soldiers were taken to a Salvadorean military installation.

Natural Morphology 229

The point is that in (16a), *installation* has the same meaning as the verb *install* and in (16b) it refers to a concrete object resulting from the action designated by the verb. This contrast is not addressed in NM, because NM focuses on explaining formal differences, which are not extant in *installation* in (16). A very similar point can be made about the contrast between German *Installation* and *Installierung*. We repeat the relevant examples in (17).

(17) a. die Installation der Heizungsanlage
'the installation of_the heating_system'
b. veraltete Installationen erneuern
'outdated installations renew', i.e. replace outdated installations
c. die Installierung der Heizungsanlage
d. *veraltete Installierungen erneuern

In (17a–b), we have the same type of contrast for German *Installation* as in (16) for English *installation*. In (17c–d), we see that the alternative *Installierung* is possible, but only in the process reading. In NM, lexicalization plays an important role, because it affects the degree of morphosemantic transparency. Lexicalization is understood in two ways. Dressler (2005b: 30) mentions on one hand that every stored expression is lexicalized because it is stored. On the other hand, he mentions that some expressions are more lexicalized than others, because they are less transparent (2005b: 31). In (17), we have rule-based meanings, so that the transparency is high. Whether they are stored in the mental lexicon depends on individual speakers, but it is likely that *Installation* in both senses and *Installierung* as used in (17c) are stored for many speakers of German.

For (17), the questions that NM does not address is how it is possible that *Installierung* is formed, although *Installation* is already in many speakers' mental lexicon, and why *Installierung* only has a process reading, not a result reading.

12.2.5 Onomasiological coercion

For the issue of onomasiological coercion, we used the example of *doorman* in English in section 4.5. COBUILD (2023) gives the definition in (18).

(18) a. A doorman is
b. a man who stands at the door
c. of a club,
d. prevents unwanted people from coming in, and makes people leave if they cause trouble.

In NM, what is interesting about examples such as *doorman* is their degree of iconicity. In order to study this, we have to compare it with other words.

In section 4.5, we presented the equivalent expressions in German, Dutch and Slovak in (19).

(19) a. Türsteher ('door_stander') DE
b. uitsmijter ('out_thrower') NL
c. vyhadzovač ('throw_out-er') SK

When we compare *doorman* with *Türsteher* in (19a), we note that *doorman* consists formally of two elements and *Türsteher* of three. As the meaning is the same, the one described in (18b–d), we can say that *Türsteher* is more iconic than *doorman*. Both focus only on (18b), but whereas *doorman* leaves out the predicate, *Türsteher* expresses it. Arguably, *man* is more expressive than the agentive *-er*, but the difference does not make up for the unexpressed predicate in *doorman*. In Dressler's (2005a: 272) ranking, based on work by Libben (1998), *doorman* and *Türsteher* are both in the highest category of morphosemantic transparency.

We can also compare Dutch (19b) and Slovak (19c). The difference between their structures is only that in Dutch, *uit* ('out') is a separate word, whereas in Slovak, the verb is *vyhadzovať* ('throw_out'). There is no Dutch verb **uitsmijten* and no Slovak verb **hadzovať*. In Slovak, *vy-* is a common verbal prefix, which can often be paraphrased as 'away' or 'out'. In this pair, it is not so clear which one is more iconic. They consist of the same number of morphemes that express corresponding meanings.

When we compare German *Türsteher* and Dutch *uitsmijter*, it is difficult to determine a ranking for iconicity. The two expressions in (19a–b) have the same number of morphemes. In terms of morphosemantic transparency, we also find it difficult to differentiate them. We might approach this by determining which of (18b) or (18d) is more important as a part of the meaning of the word. This assessment is speaker-dependent. There is no communicative pressure to reach the same judgement, so that speakers may well have different opinions without noticing it. As the discussion of (18) and (19) shows, the ranking of iconicity and morphosemantic transparency shows a strong correlation.

NM does not address the issue of onomasiological coercion directly. Although they are also involved in naming, iconicity and morphosemantic transparency do not focus on the same properties. The difference is that onomasiological coercion explains why *doorman* has the meaning in (18b–d), whereas iconicity and morphosemantic transparency aim to characterize the degree of markedness of *doorman* as a name for this concept.

12.3 Word formation and naming in NM

NM is a functionalist theory. As such, it puts the functions of language in a central position. As a functionalist theory, it has relationships to Cognitive

Grammar (CG) and to Štekauer's onomasiological theory we discussed in Chapters 10 and 11. Dressler (2005a: 267) takes the communicative and the cognitive functions as the main ones. The cognitive function corresponds to what Langacker (2007: 422) calls conceptualization. For naming, it is conceptualization that is the most important.

Among the three functionalist theories we discussed, NM shares with CG its emphasis on the gradual nature of linguistic contrasts. Whereas Štekauer sets up a Word-Formation Component that is at the same time distinct from the Lexical Component and from the Syntactic Component, NM and CG do not want to make such clear-cut distinctions. Research in NM differs from both CG and Štekauer's theory in that it does not propose formalizations of its observations. Gaeta (2019: 259) is exceptional in at least stating his Paradigm Structure Conditions formally.

Delimiting the set of naming expressions from inflected word forms and syntactic phrases is dependent on formal mechanisms that determine precise boundaries. In NM, it is difficult to find any positive reference to formal mechanisms and to precise boundaries. In section 12.2.3, we saw that Wurzel (1987: 76) makes a distinction between inflected forms, which do not have their own signs, and lexemes, which are signs. However, we saw that this reference to a borderline is quite isolated. In (4), Dressler (2005b: 36) denies the existence of a sharp borderline between compounds and phrases by making all relevant properties gradual. At the same time, Wurzel does not propose any mechanisms by which the borderline between inflection and word formation might be formally expressed.

The main research questions in NM are not related to the opposition between naming and description. Instead, they focus on markedness. Whereas the opposition between naming and description can be conceptualized as a binary one, markedness is typically a gradual feature. Therefore, markedness is a property that comes to life in a comparison. One expression is more or less marked than another. This attitude directs research away from a formal account of the nature of language and towards the explanation of diachronic developments. In this sense, NM has a similar view of linguistics as Paul (1886) (cf. section 2.2). Wurzel refers to Paul on many occasions.

It is perhaps surprising that a functionalist theory like NM is so form-oriented. The study of naturalness and markedness focuses on the question to what extent one form is more natural as an expression of a given meaning than another form. It does not ask how the meaning is associated with this form or why the form was selected for this meaning. NM is, for instance, not particularly interested in the way *installation* as a process is related to *installation* as an object resulting from this process. The question NM wants to answer about *installation* is only how this form is chosen. As a further consequence of this research direction, NM has no explanation for the corresponding German data. The question why German *Installierung* is not blocked by *Installation*, but can only have a process reading, is entirely beyond its scope.

Surprisingly, although NM is a functionalist theory, it has little to say about naming. NM does cover word formation, but does not address the questions about naming that we raised in Chapter 4. If one is interested in the reasons for historical change or the degree of transparency in compounds, NM may have inspiration to offer, but for naming it shies away from any substantial theoretical account.

CHAPTER 13

An assessment of similarities and differences between theoretical frameworks

In this final chapter, we aim to compare the theories and frameworks we discussed in Chapters 5–12 and to evaluate how decisions taken in their design affect the degree to which they can treat the naming function of word formation adequately. The central questions to be dealt with by a theory of word formation as a naming device can be formulated as in (1).

(1) a. Which expressions belong to word formation as a naming device?
 b. What do these expressions mean?

The selection of phenomena in Chapter 4 was oriented towards collecting data pertaining to these questions for the eight theories and frameworks we chose in section 3.3. Question (1a) concerns the delimitation of the set of relevant expressions. We will address this question in section 13.1. Question (1b) concerns the way the meaning of the expressions is determined. This will be addressed in section 13.2. On this basis, section 13.3 gives a general evaluation of which properties of theories are helpful in the adequate treatment of word formation as a naming device.

13.1 The set of naming expressions

In determining the set of naming expressions, we have to be aware of the different borderlines of this set. We distinguish the three contrasts in (2) as the basic ones.

(2) a. Naming expressions as against descriptive expressions
 b. New naming expressions as against formal variation reflecting only syntactic rules
 c. Rule-based naming expressions as against non-rule-based naming expressions

In our discussion, we have focused on (2a) and (2b), because these are the questions that are central in morphology. An answer to (2c) is generally presupposed, but for a complete delimitation of the set of naming descriptions, it is necessary. Before we turn to a more detailed discussion of the first two questions, section 13.1.1 outlines a framework for the discussion of the relation between each of the three questions and the way the mental lexicon is used and extended. Then, sections 13.1.2 and 13.1.3 give an overview of how the different morphological theories and frameworks treat the contrasts in (2a) and (2b), respectively.

13.1.1 A framework for the use and extension of the mental lexicon

The delimitation of the set of naming expressions requires a position on all three of the contrasts listed in (2). These contrasts are in different dimensions, in the sense that they capitalize on mutually independent properties and thus determine what can be considered a three-dimensional space in which phenomena can be placed. Nevertheless, there is a strong core of properties that unites rule-based expressions used for naming concepts. In section 1.3, we discussed the nature of naming and used Figure 1.2 to model the processes involved. In Figure 13.1, we present a slightly different view of this model, adapted so as to focus on the extension and use of the mental lexicon.

We can use the model in Figure 13.1 to clarify the position of each of the contrasts in (2). In (2a), we have a contrast between naming and describing as two communicative functions. In Figure 13.1, they are positioned in entirely different places. Naming expressions are the result of the choice of a name for a concept. This choice is represented by the arrow labelled *naming*. Descriptive expressions are the result of the use of the mental lexicon to produce intended performance. Their formation is placed in the arrow labelled *use*. We deliberately refrain from using labels such as *morphology* or *syntax*, because the rules determining how naming and use

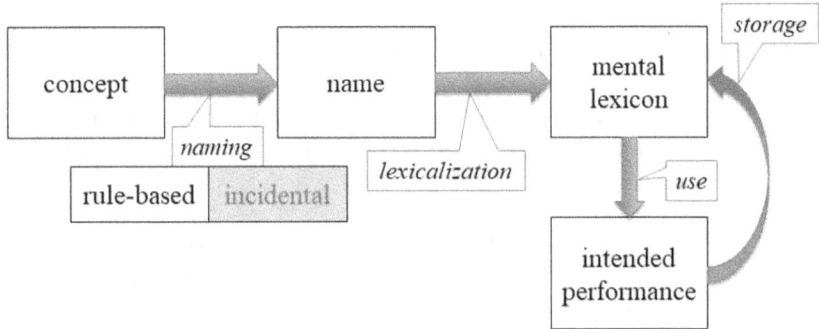

Figure 13.1 *Processes in the extension and use of the mental lexicon*

are carried out depend on the theory or framework. The contrast in (2a) is further discussed in section 13.1.2.

The contrast in (2b) is of a somewhat different nature. New naming expressions are of course still in the scope of the arrow labelled *naming*. The formal variation identified as the contrasting notion concerns forms that are not the result of naming. The choice between these variants does not depend on the concept, but on the formulation of intended performance. We include here inflection as well as transposition. This contrast is further discussed in section 13.1.3.

The contrast in (2c) is of a completely different nature. It distinguishes two types of naming. In Figure 13.1, they are labelled *rule-based* and *incidental*. Here, *rule-based* refers to naming by word formation and *incidental* to naming by borrowing, metaphors, analogy, etc., without the involvement of word formation rules. The class marked *incidental* is only determined by the absence of a rule, not by the presence of borrowing, metaphors, analogy, etc. This contrast is illustrated by the examples in (3) and (4).

(3) a. Computer   DE
     b. neck (of a violin)
     c. underwhelmed

(4) a. Rechner   DE
     b. spaceship
     c. ear witness

In (3a) and (4a), we have two German words for *computer* that we also discussed in section 1.3. Whereas (3a) is a loanword from English, (4a) is the result of analysing the English word and translating the parts into German. In (3b) and (4b), we have two examples of the use of metaphor. In a metaphor, selected properties of a concept are used as a motivation to use its name also for another concept.[1] In (3b), the shape of a human being is taken as a basis for naming a part of a violin. In (4b), the function of a ship is used as a basis for coming up with a name for a vehicle designed to travel in space. The difference is that in (3b), the name is taken over unchanged, whereas in (4b), *ship* is used as the head of a compound. In (3c) and (4c), we have two examples of analogy. In analogy, there is always a word that serves as a model. In (3c), the model is *overwhelmed*, in (4c), *eye witness*. The difference is that *whelmed* is not a common word of English, whereas *witness* is. Therefore, the examples in (4) can be analysed as regular word formation. The English *computer* in (4a), the regular meaning of *ship* in (4b) and the model of *eye witness* in (4c) contribute to the motivation for

---

[1] Ritchie (2013: 3–14) explains the difficulty of defining *metaphor* more precisely. As we do not make any claims concerning the delimitation of the concept, we use a general characterization.

applying a word formation rule, but they do not replace the rule. In (3), we do not have a word formation rule and alternative mechanisms for naming take over the role of word formation. As the contrast in (2c) does not raise any significant theoretical controversies in word formation or morphology, we did not highlight it in our discussion of the individual theories.

A phenomenon that we do discuss in some detail, but that does not have an immediately obvious place in the contrasts in (2), is that of paradigms. The main role of paradigms is to contribute to the organization of the mental lexicon. In terms of Figure 13.1, they are located in the box *mental lexicon*. They do not directly influence the use of the lexicon in producing intended performance, although the organization of the lexicon affects efficiency, for instance by priming. Paradigms do not have a unified role in naming. Inflectional paradigms determine lexemes that serve as names. For derivational paradigms, we can use the Slovak example in (5), which we also used in various earlier chapters.

(5) a. blog   ('$blog_N$')
     b. blogovať ('$blog_V$')
     c. blogový ('$blog_A$')

In (5), we have a noun and two derived words, a verb and an adjective. This constellation with the formation rules used in (5b) and (5c) is quite frequent in Slovak, which is why it is considered a derivational paradigm. The base in (5a) is a borrowing, so it is used for naming but does not belong to word formation. The verb in (5b) has the meaning of an action related to the noun in (5a). It is an example of naming by means of regular word formation. Here the derivational paradigm has a role similar to the rule of analogy in (4c). The adjective in (5c), by contrast, does not name a new concept. It is a relational adjective, used in, for instance, *blogový príspevok* ('blog contribution', i.e. blog post). As such, it is a transposition that does not name a new concept. Therefore, from a naming perspective, (5a) is a borrowing, i.e. non-rule-based naming, (5b) a result of word formation, i.e. rule-based naming, and (5c) a transposition, i.e. no naming.

A final point to note in Figure 13.1 is that it shows two ways the mental lexicon can be extended. One is based on naming and subsequent lexicalization, the other on use in intended performance. The first is triggered by a new concept. In lexicalization, the new name is incorporated into the mental lexicon. The second can apply to any complex expression that has been built up for use in performance and for which it is judged more efficient to store it, so that it can be retrieved from the mental lexicon in future use.[2] It is typical of what Wray (2002) calls *formulaic language*. Some examples from Slovak are given in (6).

---

[2] The judgement that it is more efficient is not a conscious decision. It is determined automatically by our brain.

An assessment of theoretical frameworks

(6) a. dobré rano ('good morning')
 b. dobrý deň ('good day')
 c. dobrý večer ('good evening')

The expressions in (6) are greetings that are used at different times of day. Whereas (6a) can normally only be used until around 9 a.m., (6b) can be used all day until about 6 p.m. and (6c) afterwards. It is clear that these expressions should be stored in the mental lexicon. However, unlike names, they do not refer to any particular concept. We use *storage* to refer to the process that stores these expressions, reserving *lexicalization* for the incorporation of naming expressions.

13.1.2 Naming vs description

For the borderline between naming expressions and descriptive expressions, the most common formal approximation is the distinction between the lexicon and syntax. This is based on the generalization that naming expressions are words. A problem with this generalization is that *word* is a concept whose boundaries are not very sharp. The examples of contrasts we introduced in section 4.1 to illustrate the problems of this boundary are all in some way related to compounding. The main examples are repeated here as (7) to (10).

(7) a. Hartkäse ('granular cheese') DE
 b. harter Käse ('hard cheese') DE

(8) a. čajová lyžička ('teaspoon') SK
 b. čistá lyžička ('clean spoon') SK

(9) a. bird's nest
 b. [another bird]'s nest

(10) a. commuter suburb
 b. Chicago suburb

In each contrast, the *a* example is a naming expression and the *b* example a formally similar descriptive expression. Of these pairs, the one in (7) has a contrastive inflectional marking and the one in (9) can be formulated in terms of syntactic constituency, whereas for (8) and (10) no formal support for the contrast is available.

Compounding is a well-known problematic phenomenon for the boundary between words and phrases, because a compound is typically a complex word with words as its components. In view of these considerations, we can expect that it is important whether a theory or framework makes a principled distinction between syntax and the lexicon. Table 13.1

Table 13.1 *Positions on the distinction between lexicon and syntax*

Different components	No clear distinction	Alternative solution
Lexical Morphology and Phonology (LMP)	Distributed Morphology (DM)	Three lists
Lexical Semantic Framework (LSF)	Construction Morphology (CxM)	Syntactic rules as lexical entries
	Relational Morphology (RM)	
Štekauer's Onomasiological Theory (*Št*)	Cognitive Grammar (CG)	No categorical difference
	Natural Morphology (NM)	

gives an overview of the decisions in the theories and frameworks we discussed in Chapters 5–12. In Table 13.1, abbreviations for each theory or framework are given that are used throughout this chapter. The one in italics (*Št*) is an ad hoc solution, because there is no generally used abbreviation.

Three theories have a clear distinction between a lexical component and a syntactic component. LMP and LSF assume that morphology is a rule system in the lexicon, as proposed by Chomsky (1970) in the Lexicalist Hypothesis. In *Št*, word formation is in a component of its own. In theories of this type, we can assume that complex naming expressions are formed by rules that are not in the syntactic component.

LMP is mainly interested in the phonological impact of morphological rules. Still, we can model each of the contrasts in (7) to (10) as a contrast between a lexical expression and a syntactic (post-lexical) formation. In LSF, the semantic effect of the rules takes centre stage. Coindexation is the mechanism used to distinguish the application of rules in the lexicon from syntactic operations. In both cases, we can use the classification as a naming expression as a criterion for treating the expression in the lexicon. *Št* has a threefold division between syntax, lexicon and word formation. The dedicated Word-Formation Component guarantees that complex naming expressions are distinguished from other expressions.

Five theories have no clear distinction between lexical and syntactic components. The alternatives they propose are different. At least for DM, CxM, RM and CG, we can interpret this as a rejection of the Lexicalist Hypothesis. NM does not take an explicit position, because its conception of the lexicon is based on the European structuralist tradition, not on generative linguistics. The alternatives these five theories propose can be grouped into three types.

First, DM builds up expressions from morphemes. In general, morphemes have a phonological, a syntactic and a semantic specification, but in DM these specifications are each in a different list. The three lists are separate from each other and consulted at different points in the generation of a sentence. There is no mapping of information between items in the lists at the level of the morpheme. The distinction between naming expressions and syntactic expressions is only visible when we are dealing with the semantic interpretation. Idiosyncratic aspects of the meaning of complex naming expressions are encoded in the Encyclopedia, the list with semantic information. In order to distinguish the status of the expressions in (7) to (10), the *a* examples have an entry in the Encyclopedia, the *b* examples do not. The question is to what extent the need for a look-up in the Encyclopedia can be predicted. In section 5.2.1, we saw some mechanisms that construct the contrasts in syntactic terms, e.g. root incorporation for compounds such as (7a), but they do not cover all cases. Thus, although in (8) we can say that there is a contrast between a complex and a simple adjective, this contrast does not generally coincide with the one between relational and qualitative adjectives, which is the one we actually need here. Therefore, in this respect DM is only partially successful.

Both CxM and RM adopt Jackendoff's Parallel Architecture (PA) as their underlying framework. In PA, a lexical entry is a combination of phonological, syntactic and semantic (or conceptual) information. As we saw in section 9.1, Jackendoff (2002) makes the argument that purely syntactic rules can be formalized as lexical entries with extremely reduced phonological and semantic sections. Compared with DM, we have the same types of information, but they are combined. In PA, the mapping between them constitutes a lexical entry and lexical entries encode a speaker's competence, whereas in DM such correlations play hardly any role. Using lexical entries for the full range of stored expressions, PA cannot directly use the contrast between lexical and syntactic constructs as the basis for the distinction between naming expressions and descriptive expressions. In some cases, the projection level can serve as a substitute. Thus, we could use N for (7a), (8a) and (10a) and NP for (7b), (8b) and (10b). In CxM, Booij's use of SEM suggests a more general solution, namely to mark all naming expressions by an unambiguous semantic label.

In the same way as Jackendoff does for PA, in CG too the argument is made that idioms are in a sense in between words and syntactic phrases. CG uses this argument to support an analysis in which there is a continuum between words and sentences without any clear borderline separating lexical and syntactic constructs. This leads to a different approach to the examples in (7) to (10) from the one adopted in PA. For a contrast such as (8), CG assumes that we are not dealing with a naming expression in (8a) and a description in (8b), but with more or less descriptive expressions along a cline. This is not compatible with our conceptualization of the extension and use of the mental lexicon in Figure 13.1.

In NM, there is less explicit discussion of the issue, but it seems that the approach is similar in nature to the one adopted in CG. Thus, in discussing definitions of compounding, Dressler (2006: 24) writes that 'universal definitions are [. . .] cross-linguistically never watertight – in many languages there are exceptions or fuzzy transitions to non-compounding'. In (4) in section 12.2.1, we quoted further statements to the same effect. Dressler et al. (1987: 6) present a diagram of a continuum from syntax to lexicon, where syntax is associated with processing and the lexicon with storage. Inflection and word formation are placed in between syntax and the lexicon, with inflection closer to syntax and word formation closer to the lexicon. This view reflects a similar position to what is assumed in CG. The position taken by NM is equally incompatible with our conceptualization in Figure 13.1.

On this basis, we can conclude that a distinction between different components for the formation of words and the formation of phrases is in general helpful for the distinction between word formation as a naming device and the descriptive use of the mental lexicon. However, it only offers a solution if the assignment to the component covering word formation is flexible enough to distinguish between form and function. In the case of the examples in (7) to (10), it should be possible to include rule-based naming expressions such as (8a) in word formation and exclude incidental use of similar forms without naming value, such as (10b). The use of a formal marker, whether a mechanism like the coindexation in LSF or a label like SEM in CxM, can serve as a good supplementary or alternative method of ensuring the identification of the correct set. A dedicated word formation component, as in Št, is arguably the most principled solution. However, as we saw in section 11.3, Štekauer considers (8a) a syntactic construct, not a product of word formation.

To summarize, the identification of naming expressions in contrast to descriptive expressions can be performed by a mechanism or feature that only applies to naming expressions or by assigning the formation of complex naming expressions to a dedicated component. In the implementation of this idea, it is crucial that the question whether something is labelled or treated as word formation is determined only by its rule-based naming function. From this perspective, it is understandable that ten Hacken (2019a) and Benavides (2022a) independently come up with proposals to add a separate word formation component to Jackendoff's PA.

13.1.3 New names vs adaptation of existing names

Not all word forms are used as names. Some forms are only the adaptation of existing names to the syntactic context. Often, this idea is discussed as a distinction between inflection and derivation. In sections 4.2 to 4.4, we presented different aspects of the contrast between new names and adaptation of existing names. Some relevant contrasting pairs are given in (11) to (13).

(11) a. vogel ('bird') NL
b. vogels ('birds') NL
c. vogeltje ('bird$_{DIM}$') NL

(12) a. Gitara je nová. SK
'[the] guitar is new'
b. Mám novú gitaru. SK
'[I] have [a] new guitar'

(13) a. Sie installieren die Heizungsanlage.   DE
'they install the heating_system'
b. die Installation der Heizungsanlage   DE
'the installation of_the heating_system'
c. veraltetete Installationen erneuern   DE
'outdated installations renew', i.e. replace outdated installations

There are two types of inflection. One is illustrated in (11a–b), the other in (12). They relate in different ways to the concept that is modified. The Dutch plural in (11b) is a separate concept. When we consider the contrast between the singular in (11a) and the plural in (11b), we have the same concept *vogel* in both. In (11b), there is an additional concept of plural. The Slovak contrast in (12) reflects the syntactic use of the noun *gitara*. In (12a), it is nominative and in (12b), it is accusative. The case contrast does not add a separate concept, but only adapts the noun to the syntactic environment. The relevant syntactic environment is determined by government and agreement.[3] The noun *gitara* takes its case from its relationship to the verb. The adjective *nový* ('new') agrees with the noun it modifies in gender, number and case. In both types of inflection, no new names are created.

Distinguishing the type of inflection that is illustrated by (12) from derivation is not so difficult. Agreement and government are external factors that determine the correct form of a lexeme in a particular context. In the case of (11), the problem is more complex. It is important to distinguish the plural in (11b) and the diminutive in (11c). The difference is that the diminutive triggers a new concept. The prototype for (11a) is much more permissive than the one for (11c). Whereas *meeuw* ('seagull') and *adelaar* ('eagle') are good examples of (11a), the former is at best a marginal example of (11c) and the latter is clearly not in its scope.[4] Whereas in (11b) we have two separate concepts, one of them the same as the one in (11a), in (11c) we have a single concept that is not the same as the one in (11a). Therefore, naming is involved in (11c), but not in (11b).

In (13a–b), we have an example of transposition. We defined transposition in section 4.4 as in (14).

(14) Transposition is a process that
   a. changes the syntactic category of a word,
   b. does not change its semantic category, and
   c. does not modify, add or delete any semantic features.

---

[3] We use *government* and *agreement* here in a relatively traditional sense, not in the specialized sense of generative linguistics, e.g. Chomsky (1981) or Pollock (1989).
[4] It is possible to use *vogeltje* for large birds in an ironic sense. However, the irony depends on their not being in the regular scope of the concept *vogeltje*. This is similar to the ironic use of *excellent* to mean 'very bad'.

Transposition is closely connected to the type of inflection we see in (12). The only difference is that inflection is usually taken not to change the syntactic category, whereas transposition does just that. The differences between (13a) and (13b) follow directly from the contrast in syntactic category. The verb in (13a) requires a subject and an accusative object. The noun in (13b) requires a determiner and has an optional subject and object. If they are realized, they appear in the genitive case or with a preposition. The perception of transposition as distinct from naming is complicated by the existence of variants of the type in (13c). The contrast between (13b) and (13c) is in a sense the mirror image of the one between (13a) and (13b). In (13c), we have no change in form or syntactic category, but a change in concept compared with (13b). Therefore, there is no naming involved in the formation of *Installation* in (13b) from the verb *installieren*, but the formation of *Installation* in (13c) from the noun in (13b) is an instance of naming. As the latter formation process is rule-based, we consider it an instance of word formation.

As noted in section 13.1.1, we discussed some of the phenomena covered here in terms of paradigms. However, we do not consider paradigms directly important in the context of naming. Paradigms are important for the organization of the lexicon, but it is the contrast between inflection and word formation that is essential for delimiting the set of naming expressions. In Figure 13.1, paradigms are in the mental lexicon, whereas naming creates a relation between a concept and a name.

An overview of the mechanisms used for the distinction between naming expressions and inflected or transpositional forms in the theories and frameworks we discussed in Chapters 5–12 is given in Table 13.2. The table presents the theories and frameworks in an order that corresponds roughly to the importance they assign to the distinction. We start with theories that

Table 13.2 *Mechanisms for distinguishing naming units from inflection and transposition*

Framework or theory	Mechanisms
Štekauer's Onomasiological Theory (Št)	Separate Word-Formation Component
Lexical-Semantic Framework (LSF)	Argument structure
Lexical Morphology and Phonology (LMP)	Levels
Construction Morphology (CxM)	SEM for naming units Second-order schemas
Relational Morphology (RM)	Productivity central Sister schemas
Distributed Morphology (DM)	f-morphemes vs l-morphemes Encyclopedia
Cognitive Grammar (CG)	No categorical distinctions Some ad hoc mechanisms
Natural Morphology (NM)	Markedness central No categorical distinction

distinguish inflection and derivation, then turn to the theories that make at least some categorical distinctions and end with the ones where categorical distinctions are generally rejected. The order in the table will also be followed in the explanation of our assessment.

That *Št* is at the top is motivated by the fact that it is the only theory that has word formation and inflection in different components of grammar. It is not surprising, therefore, that Štekauer takes a keen interest in the distinction between inflection and derivation (cf. Štekauer 2015). As argued by ten Hacken (2014), the terminological nature of *inflection* and *derivation* makes it possible in principle to set up a definition and take it as the authority for the distinction. However, in the discussion of transposition, Štekauer adopts a different analysis of the data from the one we propose here. In (13), Štekauer takes *Installation* in (13b) as a case of word formation and in (13c) as a case of sense extension in the Lexical Component. We would consider *Installation* in (13b) as the formation of a syntactically different, conceptually identical expression, i.e. on a par with inflection. By contrast, we see *Installation* in (13c) as a rule-based naming unit, i.e. as word formation.

In LSF, inflection and derivation are both in the lexicon, but Lieber distinguishes them. She proposes a mechanism for this in the form of a difference in argument structure. Word formation is based on the coindexation of the morphemes involved. Inflectional morphemes do not have the argument that is used for coindexation. This mechanism is very flexible in the sense that we can use a definition of word formation to determine what belongs to it and then decide to use the extra argument in all cases of word formation. In principle, we can also exclude transposition from word formation in this way. However, for the formation of *Installation* in (13c) by a word formation process, we need a type of rule that is not used by Lieber, namely a rule that changes the meaning, but not the form or the syntactic category. The fact that Lieber (2020) uses a definition of derivation that includes a change of syntactic category as a sufficient condition shows that such an analysis is not her intention.

In LMP too, inflection and derivation are both in the lexicon. As an organizing principle of the lexicon, the type of boundary takes higher priority than the distinction between inflection and derivation. This means that for #-boundaries, derivation is at level 2 and inflection at level 3, but for +-boundaries, both are at level 1. Naming is not recognized as a relevant criterion and transposition is treated as derivation. As LMP is strongly form-oriented, no mechanisms for a systematic treatment of naming expressions are provided.

With CxM, we get to the domain of theories that do not distinguish inflection and derivation. The lack of this distinction is also reflected in the approach to paradigms, because Booij does not distinguish the treatment of inflectional paradigms and derivational paradigms. Both are formalized by second-order schemas, which state the implicational relationship between two or more schemas. However, in the discussion of the distinction between naming expressions and descriptive expressions in section 13.1.2, we already came across the marker SEM. This marker is at the same time very powerful and highly elegant. Its power resides in the fact that we can assign it directly to the expressions used for naming. This means that we are not dependent on approximations based on other criteria. The elegance of this solution lies in the fact that it addresses the naming nature of the expression directly at the semantic level and in the fact that it is used uniformly to distinguish naming expressions from descriptive expressions in syntax and from inflection and transposition.

As RM is also based on PA, its outlook is very similar to what we find in CxM, but there is a difference in emphasis that has a significant impact on the identification of naming units. For paradigms, RM uses sister schemas instead of second-order schemas. The difference is that sister schemas represent a purely relational, symmetric view, whereas second-order schemas determine an inheritance hierarchy. Inheritance is directional, hence inherently asymmetric. RM is more radically interested in the organization of the lexicon at the expense of the process of the creation of new lexical entries. The distinction between inflection and derivation is therefore harder to express. Jackendoff (2002: 156) replaces it by the distinction between productive and semi-productive, later non-productive, rules. Productivity is related to naming in the sense that a word formation rule that is used in naming has to be productive. However, the emphasis on productivity leads us away from the different role inflection and derivation play in naming. Inflection is an automatic response to syntactic requirements, whereas naming is a conscious response to naming needs. Jackendoff and Audring (2020: 133–134) mention paradigms and the interaction with phrasal syntax as the main properties of inflection. However, they also discuss derivational paradigms and PA has lexical entries for words as well as syntactic rules. Therefore, it is not obvious how these properties can be operationalized as criteria for the distinction between naming units and adapted forms.

In DM, the distribution of the lexicon among three lists shows that the representation of lexical entries is not a priority issue. The generation of expressions that correspond to what we labelled 'intended performance' in Figure 13.1 is the main concern. The difference between inflection and derivation is dissolved into different ways of determining the unit that is inserted in a syntactic tree, the information about pronunciation that is accessed after Spell-Out, and the semantic information that is only inspected in semantic interpretation after completion of the syntactic tree. The distinction between l-morphemes and f-morphemes catches some of the syntactic differences between rule-based expressions used for naming and their adaptation to the syntactic context, but does not consider the role of actual naming. Naming expressions must have an entry in the Encyclopedia.

With CG, we get to the theories that view the distinction between inflection and derivation as a matter of degree. Intuitively, we may agree that the inflection of *nový* ('new') in (12) is more typical than the plural marker

An assessment of theoretical frameworks 245

in (11b). However, Figure 13.1 does not have a continuum that stretches between naming and the production of intended performance. In some cases, CG offers mechanisms that can account for the distinction, such as the lack of a sign Σ for inflectional endings, but they do not seem to be used systematically. The transposition in (13b) is modelled as a change of perspective. However, as this perspective is expressed in the meaning, it imports a purely syntactic difference into the semantic representation.

In NM, the continuum from natural to marked is the focus of attention. Perceived degrees of naturalness are the result of the interaction of different factors. Naming can be seen as one of these factors. However, the reduction to the representation on a continuum from natural to marked blurs the distinction between naming and syntactic adaptation.

To summarize, the identification of naming expressions in contrast to variants that adapt the expression to the syntactic context can be performed by a mechanism or feature that only applies to naming expressions or by assigning the formation of complex naming expressions to a dedicated component. *Št* offers an example of a dedicated component. The use of argument structure in LSF and the use of SEM to mark naming units in CxM are examples of a mechanism and a feature that determine the distinction.

13.2 The meaning of new names

In (1) we formulated two central questions to be answered by a theory of word formation as a naming device. The first concerns the set of items used in naming, the second the actual meaning of such an item. As word formation is rule-based, we can expect that compositionality plays a role in determining this meaning. Janssen (2012) gives an overview of the use of compositionality in linguistics. A complex expression that is fully compositional has a meaning that corresponds exactly to the meaning of its constituent parts and the way they are combined by the rule.

Word formation is only partially compositional. The reason is that it is used in naming. In section 1.3, we introduced onomasiological coercion as a central property of naming. The expression chosen as a name will have as a meaning the concept that is being named. In the context of naming, we chose *doorman* as our example. In section 4.5, we used the definition from COBUILD (2023), repeated here as (15), as the description of the concept.

(15) a. A doorman is
 b. a man who stands at the door
 c. of a club,
 d. prevents unwanted people from coming in, and makes people leave if they cause trouble.

In the case of *doorman*, it is two of the three elements of (15b) that are expressed. The predicate linking the two, 'stand' in (15b), and the meaning components in (15c–d) are part of the meaning of *doorman*, but were not used in selecting the elements of its form. We also considered the translations in (16).

(16) a. Türsteher ('door-stand$_V$-er') DE
     b. uitsmijter ('out-throw$_V$-er') NL
     c. vyhadzovač ('throw$_V$_out-er') SK

In German (16a), *steh* expresses the predicate in (15b), but compared with *doorman*, 'man' is generalized to agent. Dutch (16b) and Slovak (16c) take elements from the function in (15d) as a motivation for the selection of elements that serve as input to the word formation rule. Despite these differences, all of (16) have the same meaning as (15). This is caused by onomasiological coercion.

Onomasiological coercion is not limited to word formation. Also, if borrowing is used to name a new concept, the result is a name for this new concept, which may be different, often narrower, than in the donor language. In section 1.3, we gave the example of Slovak *interview*. For English, OED (2023: *interview*) gives three main meanings in current use, labelled 4a–c and listed in (17).

(17) a. A formal session of questioning or interrogation of a person by the police.
     b. A formal meeting in which an applicant for a job, course of study at a college or university, etc., is asked questions in order to assess his or her suitability; [. . .]
     c. A meeting or conversation in which a journalist or (later) radio or television presenter, etc., asks questions of a person of public interest for the purpose of publication or broadcasting [. . .]

For Slovak, KSSJ (2003: *interview*) gives two meanings, listed in (18).

(18) a. rozhovor (publicistu) s význ. osobou určený na zverejnenie
        'conversation ([of a] journalist) with [a] specific person intended for making_public'
     b. rozhovor zisťujúci niekt. informácie
        'conversation [in order to] find_out some information'

The meaning in (18a) corresponds to the one in (17c). The meaning in (18b), labelled as sociological, is based on this. For (17a–b), Slovak has other expressions and *interview* is not used. The reason is that when *interview* was borrowed, it was a response to the need to name the concept in (18a). Onomasiological coercion ensured that *interview* had (only) this meaning. The meanings in (17a–b) were not relevant in the borrowing process.

That the meaning of complex expressions is not entirely compositional is of course not limited to naming expressions. For phrasal expressions too we often find differences between their compositional meaning and their intended meaning. A typical example of a mismatch is (19).

(19) Do you know what time it is?

In (19), the compositional reading asks for an answer with *yes* or *no*, but this is rarely the intended meaning. The non-compositionality of phrasal expressions is studied in pragmatics.[5] There is a clear difference between onomasiological coercion and non-compositional aspects of phrasal meaning that belong to the domain of pragmatics. In Figure 13.1, onomasiological coercion concerns naming and pragmatics concerns use.

Another phenomenon that concerns the meaning of words resulting from the application of word formation rules is the one illustrated by the German examples in (20).

(20) a. die Installation der Heizungsanlage
        'the installation of_the heating_system'
     b. veraltete Installationen erneuern
        'outdated installations renew', i.e. replace outdated installations
     c. die Installierung der Heizungsanlage
     d. *veraltete Installierungen erneuern

The examples in (20a–b) are the same as (13b–c). As noted in the discussion of (13), *Installation* can have two meanings, one where it has the same meaning as the verb *installieren*, here (20a), and one where it refers to the result of the process expressed by the verb, here (20b). Apart from *-ation*, German also has a deverbal nominalizing suffix *-ung*. Whereas *-ation* only attaches to verbs in *-ieren*, *-ung* attaches to a much wider range of verbs. The data in (20) raise two complementary questions. First, why is *Installierung* in (20c) possible? We would expect it to be blocked by *Installation* in (20a). Second, why is *Installierung* in (20d) not possible? How can we explain that *Installierung* has only the process reading?

The concept of blocking was introduced by Aronoff (1976: 43) and defined as in (21).

(21) *Blocking* is the nonoccurrence of one form due to the simple existence of another.

---

[5] Clark (2013: 4–42) gives examples illustrating the range of interpretation that is covered in pragmatics.

Rainer (2020) gives an overview of the historical precedents of the concept and the further development of the discussion of blocking. The problem with blocking as defined in (21) is that Aronoff refers to a 'form'. In this way, it cannot differentiate between (20c) and (20d). As shown in section 9.2.4, it is also impossible to attribute the difference to a property of the suffix *-ung*. We gave the example of *Sammlung* ('collection'), derived from the verb *sammeln* ('collect'). *Sammlung* can have the meaning both of 'action of collecting' and of 'a number of objects collected'.

What we propose instead is to explain (20) on the basis of naming needs. The result reading is based on the process reading.[6] As *Installation* has both readings, there may be situations in which it is necessary to emphasize the process reading. In such a context, the speaker may decide to create a new word, using an alternative word formation rule, in order to avoid ambiguity. We call this effect *onomasiological motivation*. It is in a sense the opposite of blocking. Instead of overgeneration where every rule applies except when it is blocked, we assume that word formation always takes place for a reason. In the absence of a reason, no rule is triggered.[7] Onomasiological motivation is the reason for triggering a naming act.

Onomasiological motivation is not only relevant in the explanation of the data in (20), but also in the Dutch data in (22), elaborating on an example we encountered in section 8.1.

(22) a. verwoesten ('destroy') 12,543
b. *verwoestbaar ('destroyable') 3
c. onverwoestbaar ('indestructible') 1,906

The examples are followed by the frequency in CHN (2021). The suffix *-baar* corresponds to English *-able* and produces adjectives from verbs. The prefix *on-* corresponds to English *un-* and attaches to adjectives. As we saw in section 8.1, Booij (2010: 43) claims that (22b) does not exist. He proposes to derive (22c) from (22a) directly by unification of the two derivation processes into a complex process adding *on-* and *-baar* at the same time. With onomasiological motivation, we can explain (22) as follows. The starting point for the formation of (22c) was the need to name the property of being highly resistant to any force or effort that might result in destruction or serious deterioration. On the basis of (22a), two steps are necessary to create (22c). This is not a problem, because we are interested in naming this concept, not in trying out word formation rules. Once (22c) is lexicalized,

---

[6] Thomas (2013a) shows this for English and French nouns in *-ation*. Ten Hacken (2019a: 79–81) gives a summary of the data she adduced to support the claim.
[7] An interesting parallel with the development in Chomskyan syntax can be observed. Whereas Chomsky (1981) proposes a model with *move α*, i.e. move anything anywhere unless a constraint prohibits it, Chomsky (1993) reverses this and assumes that movement is a Last Resort that occurs only because it is necessary.

it can serve as a further support for the choice of (22b) for the opposite property. However, there is not much need for this, as shown by the low frequency. In this way, onomasiological motivation also explains (22).

Onomasiological coercion and onomasiological motivation are both strongly based on the naming perspective of word formation. They are complementary. Whereas onomasiological motivation determines that a new form is coined, onomasiological coercion determines the meaning of the new form.

In many of the theories we discussed, examples such as *doorman* are treated as semantic specialization. In this scenario, the formation of *doorman* is modelled in two steps as in (23).

(23) *Semantic specialization*
    a. Formation of the compound *doorman*
    b. Specialization of the meaning as in (15b–d)

As we saw in section 10.2.5, this is indeed the scenario that Langacker assumes in CG. The idea of listing lexicalized meanings in LMP and of specifying idiosyncratic aspects of the meaning in the Encyclopedia in DM also assume such a scenario. In DM, the application of merge combines the two morphemes spelled out as *door* and *man* and it is only in the semantic interpretation that the specialized meaning plays a role.

The implausibility of (23) can be shown by the combined force of onomasiological coercion and onomasiological motivation. Speakers do not apply word formation rules without a reason. The application is driven by the need to create a new association of a name and a concept. The perception of this need may be limited to the speaker who applies the rule or be shared by a wider community, but there is no word formation without a perceived need. Moreover, when word formation is applied, it is applied to name a particular concept. The meaning of whichever new form is chosen as a name is the concept to be named. Therefore, the idea that there should be two steps as in (23), with an intermediate stage between (23a) and (23b) is entirely unrealistic.

An approach that seems at first sight more plausible than the semantic specialization in (23) is the one based on the hearer's efforts to interpret a new expression. This focus can be found most clearly in LSF, but also to some extent in CxM and RM. We discussed Lieber's approach in the context of *doorman* in section 7.2.5. Lieber (2016a: 8) introduces the term *Contextual Coercion*. Without giving a real definition of this term, she gives the example of the interpretation of the feature [material] in the process and result readings of the word *construction* in (24).

(24) [T]he feature [material] is fixed on the basis of inferences from the immediate syntactic context in which the noun is found, from its wider syntactic context, from the overall discourse, and from encyclopedic knowledge. (Lieber 2016a: 104)

It is immediately obvious in (24) that the perspective is that of the hearer or reader, because the noun 'is found' in a particular context. At first sight, it seems that Contextual Coercion is the basis of an alternative approach with equivalent explanatory value to our proposal based on onomasiological coercion.

In order to make a motivated choice among the alternative analyses, it is useful to consider how we can determine the actual meaning of a word. When we ask our first-year students, they tend to answer that they look it up in the dictionary. This is the approach that reflects semantic specialization. It considers a language as a system. However, as argued in ten Hacken (2009a, 2020a), named languages are not empirical entities and dictionaries cannot be purely descriptive. As far as there is a system for a named language, it is a generalization over the different competence of individual speakers. The answer we get from a dictionary about the actual meaning of a word is what the lexicographer writing this entry decided to put there.

If meaning resides in the speaker-hearer of a language, the question is which of these two roles is more important in determining the actual meaning of a word. We can evaluate both the speaker's use and the hearer's interpretation of a word, but there is a difference. As a measure for the correctness of a speaker's use, we can only take some authority, e.g. a particular dictionary. This authority is a sociological phenomenon, not a linguistic state. Many lexicographers prefer to defer to language use as reflected in a corpus. As a measure of the correct understanding by the hearer, however, we can take the speaker's intended meaning. If the hearer understands a word in the way intended by the speaker, they have identified the correct meaning. Therefore, Lieber's notion of Contextual Coercion in (24) plays a role in the use of language, as located between the mental lexicon and the intended performance in Figure 13.1, but it is onomasiological coercion that determines the actual meaning of the output of word formation rules.[8]

In view of these considerations, Štekauer's onomasiological theory of word formation has a clear advantage over the other theories we discussed in Chapters 5–12. By its focus on the speaker's perspective, onomasiological motivation and onomasiological coercion are accommodated in a very natural way. Štekauer proposes a theory that explains how a name is chosen for a concept. This means that onomasiological coercion is explained as the effect of the concept being determined before the start of the naming process. Onomasiological motivation is reflected in the fact that the naming process is triggered by the need to name a new concept.

---

[8] Arguably, Contextual Coercion as proposed by Lieber belongs to pragmatics in the sense that the speaker and hearer take into account what they expect the other to know in formulating and interpreting utterances. In this sense, it stands in opposition to onomasiological coercion, which is directly connected to naming.

13.3 Properties of a good theory of word formation as a naming device

In this final section, we will consider which properties of the theories we discussed are beneficial for their account of word formation as a naming device. In section 13.3.1, we will consider some of the traditional ways of classifying morphological theories. Then we look at the relation between morphology and the functions of language in section 13.3.2. In section 13.3.3, we turn to the different ways that new lexical entries can be motivated. On the basis of these three considerations, we will then return to the questions in (1) in section 13.3.4 and propose an answer on the basis of the material we collected and the analysis we carried out.

13.3.1 Traditional distinctions relating to morphology

An issue that has a long history of debate is the question whether morphology is an autonomous component or not. Schultink (1988) gives a historical overview of how ideas on this issue developed in the course of the twentieth century. Among the eight theories we discussed in Chapters 5–12, four make a principled distinction between morphology and syntax and four others do not. In LMP, morphology is covered in the lexicon and organized according to levels, whereas syntax is post-lexical. In Št, there is a separate Word-Formation Component. In LSF and NM, the scope of the theory is restricted to morphology, in the case of LSF word formation, which implies a distinction. Conversely, DM denies a principled difference between morphology and syntax, because they both operate on morphemes. PA, as adopted in both CxM and RM, takes lexical entries to range from words to syntactic rules, with idioms bridging the conceptual space between them. Starting from the idea that all transitions in language are gradual, CG derives a somewhat similar view with idioms in between words and rules.

In the study of naming, the most important distinction is the one between naming expressions and descriptive expressions. For word formation as a naming device, we also have to consider the distinction between rule-based and non-rule-based naming expressions in (2c). We would like to distinguish rules that have the aim of naming from rules that are geared towards the formation of descriptive expressions. This is not fully achieved by separating morphology and syntax, because inflection is not oriented towards naming. Among the theories with an autonomous morphology, LMP and NM do not identify word formation as a separate phenomenon. LSF and Št do.

Another traditional distinction is the one between morpheme-based and word-based theories of morphology. This distinction is related to the one between Item-and-Arrangement (IA) and Item-and-Process (IP) described by Hockett (1954). Both DM and LSF assume that morphemes have lexical entries and that rules combine them, which implies IA. By contrast, LMP and CxM explicitly deny that morphemes have entries of their own. They are introduced as side effects of the application of rules, which implies IP. In RM, not much emphasis is placed on the distinction. We can understand this when we consider (25).

(25) a. $[\ldots_x\ er_2]_y$
 b. $[V_x\ aff_2]_y$
 c. $[PERSON^\alpha; [F\ (Agent: \alpha, \ldots)]_x]_y$

In (25), we see the specification of English -er creating agent nouns, discussed in section 9.1. If we consider (25) as an entry for the morpheme -er, we have a morpheme-based theory. However, if (25) is seen as a redundancy rule making a generalization about where -er can occur and how it affects the structure it applies to, it is compatible with a word-based perspective. Jackendoff consistently rejects an IP approach, supporting a declarative interpretation of rules as contributing information without specifying the procedure for using it.

In our view, the distinctions between morpheme-based and word-based theories and between IA and IP have little bearing on naming. They affect the way a form is produced, but say nothing directly about the way the form is used or the reason it is produced. As such, it is not accidental that these distinctions are discussed mainly in American structuralism and generative grammar, where the study of language is focused on the forms.

13.3.2 Morphology and functions of language

The study of the functions of language has traditionally been linked with European structuralism. There are many brands of functionalist linguistics, but we only considered three theories that are usually classified as such. They all distinguish two main functions of language. The first function is communication. Communication is often seen as the main function of language. In the context of generative grammar, Chomsky (1980: 230) denies that communication is a function of language that is in some way privileged and should determine aspects of its form. In functionalist approaches, we find that there is always a second function that is assumed, although the precise description and the name differ. This is the function that is most directly linked to naming.

As we saw in section 2.3, Mathesius (1936: 97–98) makes a distinction between functional onomatology and functional syntax. The latter corresponds to the communicative function, the former is more closely linked with naming. In section 3.2.1, we saw that Horecký (1959: 29) calls these two functions *pomenúvacia funkcia jazyka* and *usúvzťažňovacia funkcia jazyka* in Slovak. As explained there, these names are difficult to translate, but the functions correspond to the ones Mathesius distinguished. In Štekauer's onomasiological theory these two functions are assigned to different components. In Figure 11.1, functional syntax is located in the Syntactic Component and functional onomatology in the Word-Formation Component.

In NM, the two functions are called *communicative* and *cognitive*. Dressler (2005a: 267) describes the cognitive function as 'the function of supporting cognition'. This is less specific than functional onomatology, but we can also relate it to naming. Although CG emerged in the United States, it belongs rather to the European strand of structuralism in its emphasis on the functions of language. Langacker (2007: 422) distinguishes the two basic functions as *symbolic* and *communicative/interactive*. He explains the former as 'allowing conceptualizations to be symbolized by sounds and gestures'. Here *gestures* should not be taken to refer to gesticulating, but to sign language. Therefore, Langacker connects the symbolic function directly to naming.

We consider *conceptualizing function* a good characterization of the second function of language. The distinction between the communicative and the conceptualizing function can be linked to Figure 13.1. The communicative function is located in the connection between the mental lexicon and intended performance. The conceptualizing function is in the connection between concept and name. This is also the function that Chomsky (1986: 4) refers to when he claims that communication is not the primary function of language.

When we now consider the position of morphology with respect to the communicative function and the conceptualizing function, we see that in both functions, morphology plays a role, but it is not the same morphology. The distinction does not follow the traditional distinction between inflection and derivation, but it is not entirely independent. In section 13.1.3, we noted that there are two types of inflection. One type, illustrated by the Dutch plural *vogels*, leads to the expression of two pieces of information that were selected separately. The other type, illustrated by the Slovak accusative singular *gitaru*, leads to the adaptation of the form of a name to the syntactic environment. Both reflect the communicative function. We group these inflectional categories together with transposition as defined in (14). In the same way as *gitaru*, the choice between a verbal expression with *installieren* or a semantically identical nominal expression with *Installation* does not reflect a new conceptualization, but adapts the form to communicative choices. Chomsky (1970: 190) proposes that there is a single lexical entry corresponding to both *refuse* and *refusal*, which is underspecified for syntactic category. As we saw in section 5.2.1, DM takes up this idea. In the case of transposition, the nature of the choice of nominal or verbal realization is similar to the choice whether to use an active or a passive sentence where both are possible and semantically identical. Mathesius explains the difference involved in this type of contrast in terms of information structure.

The conceptualizing function appeals to word formation rules. Here a new concept is formed and a name is selected for the concept. Alternatively, a concept can be presented as a new one by choosing a new name for it. In the former case, which is common in scientific fields where new concepts emerge frequently, naming contributes to the establishment of the concept. In the latter case, which is common for euphemisms, naming contributes to a new perspective on the concept.

13.3.3 Two roads into the lexicon

The distinction between the communicative and the conceptualizing functions of language is related to the two roads into the lexicon represented in Figure 13.1. These two roads correspond to the two incoming arrows of the box *mental lexicon*. The communicative function focuses on the interaction between the mental lexicon and the intended performance. There are two arrows between them. The one to the intended performance is labelled *use* and represents the common interpretation of the communicative function. The one from the intended performance is labelled *storage*. This is a process that is very well elaborated by Jackendoff (2002). As noted in section 13.1.1, it concerns cases of what Wray (2002) calls *formulaic language*. However, Jackendoff (2002: 160–161) also indicates that it is at work when inflected forms are stored. As an example, we can look at the frequency data from COCA (2008–2020) in (26).

(26) a. circumstance   5,708
     b. circumstances 41,992

As shown by the contrast in (26), the plural of *circumstance* is more than seven times as frequent as the singular. It is therefore likely that many speakers have stored (26b) as an entry in their mental lexicon. Apart from PA, another theory where storage in the sense of Figure 13.1 plays an important role is CG. Langacker uses the term *entrenchment* for the process of storing a complex expression in the lexicon.

An important consideration here is the nature of the lexicon. There is no mental lexicon of English, in which (26b) is stored or not. Whether (26b) is stored can only be determined at the level of the individual speaker. This is not an 'ideal speaker-listener' in the sense of Chomsky (1965: 3), but an actual person. To the extent that different speakers of English have implemented the same decision as to whether (26b) is stored or not, this is the result of independent decisions by their brains. Here *decision* refers to a process that is not consciously controlled by thought but driven by an automatic evaluation of efficiency.

If storage is the only way to create new lexicon entries, new words can only consist of rule-based combinations of stored lexical elements. There are three problems with this view. First, not all new words are rule-based combinations of stored lexical elements. Counterexamples are, for instance, borrowings. Second, the meaning of rule-based word formations is generally not compositional. An example from German is (27).

(27) Anrufbeantworter
'phone-call_answer-er', i.e. answering machine

The German compound in (27) seems quite transparent. It is a synthetic compound with a deverbal head *Beantworter* ('answerer') and an object *Anruf* ('phone call'). The suffix *-er* forms agents without specifying their nature. Therefore, compositionally, (27) could refer to either a person or a machine. However, (27) only refers to a machine. This is not because no person could answer a phone, so specialization is not driven by semantic necessity. It would be empirically random to suppose that (27) is formed first and then speakers consider whether it refers to a person or a machine. What happens instead is that, before (27) was formed, a concept was identified and a name was determined to refer to this concept. This is what we call onomasiological coercion.

The third problem with a storage-only view of lexical extension is illustrated in (20). The questions about (20) are on one hand, why *Installierung* is possible although we already have *Installation*, and on the other hand, why *Installierung* can only have a process reading, not a result reading. In many cases, the non-occurrence of possible words can be explained by blocking, (21), but not in the case of *Installierung*, as it occurs in (20c). At the same time, nominalizations with *-ung* can have both the process and the result reading, but not in this case. The explanation we use here is based on onomasiological motivation. Only if there is a concept to be named will word formation be triggered.

For these three problems, the solution is simple when we assume that storage is not the only road into the lexicon. Naming provides an alternative. Naming is triggered by a naming need. Therefore, it is subject to onomasiological coercion and onomasiological motivation. When the result is lexicalized, in the sense of Figure 13.1, we have a new lexical entry. Lexicalization applies both to rule-based cases, such as (27), and to non-rule-based cases, such as borrowings.

In the same way as for storage, lexicalization also takes place in an individual speaker. This means that a particular speaker determines that there is a need for a new named concept and produces a name for it. The acceptance in the speech community depends on the reception of the new word by other speakers.

13.3.4 Selection criteria for word formation as a naming device

In this concluding section, we will use the argumentation built up in this chapter to evaluate how well different theories can answer the questions we formulated in (1), repeated here as (28), and which of their properties determine this.

(28) a. Which expressions belong to word formation as a naming device?
b. What do these expressions mean?

For the delimitation of the set of rule-based naming expressions, as referred to in (28a), we found solutions of three different types. The first type is to introduce specific mechanisms that apply to all and only rule-based naming expressions. We found an example in Lieber's LSF. She uses coindexation as the relevant mechanism. Coindexation takes place between two arguments of morphemes that are combined to form a naming expression. For syntactic combinations, no coindexation takes place. For inflectional affixes, coindexation is not possible, because there is no argument that can be coindexed. In the entry for derivational affixes, such an argument is available and it is coindexed with the base the affix attaches to. The second type of solution is to introduce a feature that marks all and only naming expressions. We found an example in Booij's CxM. He uses the feature SEM to indicate complex expressions that have a specific meaning. The third type of solution is to set up a special component for rule-based naming expressions. In Štekauer's onomasiological theory, this is the Word-Formation Component.

For these solutions to the problem of identifying rule-based naming expressions to work well, it is of course necessary that they are applied consistently. We saw, for instance, in section 8.2.4, that Booij (2020: 1005) assigns SEM to the noun formed by -*ness*. However, in a case like *sloppiness*, this would lead to two instances of SEM referring to the same property in the same word. In our view, transpositions of this type are not names for new concepts and should not have a SEM of their own. Another example of a problem is the treatment of relational adjectives in Štekauer's onomasiological theory. In the contrast in (8), discussed in section 13.1.2, it is necessary that the RA+N combination is treated as a rule-based naming expression, i.e. formed in the Word-Formation Component. This is not in accordance with the Slovak tradition as represented by Furdík (2004). Conversely, the relational adjective on its own does not refer to a separate concept. As a transposition, it should not be in the scope of the Word-Formation Component.

Finally, we turn to (28b). Here, we found that onomasiological coercion is a crucial factor. Because a new word is formed as a name for a concept, the new word will be a name for the concept. Typically, elements from the concept are selected as a basis for choosing the linguistic realization, but not all of the concept can be expressed. This is illustrated by the meaning of *doorman* in (15) and its translations into German, Dutch and Slovak in (16). At the same time, because a new word is formed as a name for a concept, only if a new name for a concept is necessary will there be a new word. This is what we call onomasiological motivation. It explains why German *Installierung* in (20) occurs as a synonym of *Installation*, but only in the process reading.

Among the eight theories and frameworks discussed in Chapters 5–12, Štekauer's onomasiological theory is the only theory that implements onomasiological coercion and onomasiological motivation. Crucial is that the starting point is the speaker's considerations in choosing a form for a concept. The process is modelled as a gradual specification in Figure 11.2. The concept is fixed at the start and the form of the word at the end of the process.

As we argued at the end of section 13.2, in order to find the actual meaning of a word, we have to take the speaker's perspective. We can evaluate the success of the hearer's interpretation by comparing it with the speaker's intention. If we want to evaluate the speaker's production, there is no empirical standard, only the linguistic norm. Therefore, the onomasiological perspective is better than the semasiological one if we want to account for word formation as a naming device.

The limitation of Štekauer's onomasiological approach is above all one of scope. Whereas, for instance, DM, CxM and RM are embedded in a general theory of language, Štekauer elaborates the Word-Formation Component in detail, but leaves the structure of the other components in Figure 11.1 largely unspecified. His remarks on the Lexical Component and the Syntactic Component are not comparable to, for instance, the elaboration of syntax in the Minimalist Program (e.g. Radford 2004) and Simpler Syntax (Culicover and Jackendoff 2005). This explains the proposals to add a word formation component to Jackendoff's (2002) Parallel Architecture by ten Hacken (2019a) and Benavides (2022a).

Bibliography

Abney, Steven Paul (1987), *The English Noun Phrase in its Sentential Aspect*, PhD dissertation, Massachusetts Institute of Technology.

Alexiadou, Artemis, Gianina Iordăchioaia and Elena Soare (2010), 'Number/Aspect Interactions in the Syntax of Nominalizations: A Distributed Morphology Approach', *Journal of Linguistics* 46: 537–574.

Allen, Margaret Reece (1978), *Morphological Investigations*, PhD dissertation, University of Connecticut.

Amacker, René (1995), 'Geneva School, after Saussure', in E. F. Konrad Koerner and R. E. Asher (eds), *Concise History of the Language Sciences: From the Sumerians to the Cognitivists*, Oxford: Pergamon/Elsevier Science, pp. 239–243.

Anderson, Stephen R. (1992), *A-Morphous Morphology*, Cambridge: Cambridge University Press.

Andreou, Marios (2020), 'Lexical Semantic Framework for Morphology', in Rochelle Lieber (ed.), *The Oxford Encyclopedia of Morphology*, New York: Oxford University Press, pp. 1017–1031.

Archangeli, Diana and D. Terence Langendoen (eds) (1997), *Optimality Theory: An Overview*, Oxford: Blackwell.

Aronoff, Mark H. (1976), *Word Formation in Generative Grammar*, Cambridge, MA: MIT Press.

Aronoff, Mark H. (1994), *Morphology by Itself: Stems and Inflectional Classes*, Cambridge, MA: MIT Press.

Audring, Jenny and Francesca Masini (eds) (2019), *The Oxford Handbook of Morphological Theory*, Oxford: Oxford University Press.

Aufinger, Sara (2022), *Neologismen im Deutschen und Französischen: ein Vergleich*, PhD dissertation, Leopold-Franzens-Universität Innsbruck.

Baayen, Harald (1992), 'Quantitative Aspects of Morphological Productivity', in Geert Booij and Jaap van Marle (eds), *Yearbook of Morphology 1991*, Dordrecht: Kluwer Academic, pp. 109–149.

Bally, Charles (1922), 'La pensée et la langue', *Bulletin de la Société de Linguistique de Paris* 23: 117–137.

Bar-Hillel, Yehoshua, Chaim Gaifman and Eliyahu Shamir (1960), 'On Categorial and Phrase Structure Grammars', *Bulletin of the Research Council of Israel*, 9F (1): 1–16, repr. in Yehoshua Bar-Hillel (1964), *Language and Information:*

Selected Essays on Their Theory and Application, Reading MA: Addison-Wesley, pp. 99–115.

Bauer, Laurie (1983), *English Word-Formation*, Cambridge: Cambridge University Press.

Bauer, Laurie (2003), *Introducing Linguistic Morphology*, 2nd edn, Edinburgh: Edinburgh University Press.

Beard, Robert (1995), *Lexeme-Morpheme Base Morphology: A General Theory of Inflection and Word Formation*, Albany: State University of New York Press.

Beekes, Robert S. P. (1995), *Comparative Indo-European Linguistics: An Introduction*, Amsterdam: John Benjamins.

Benavides, Carlos (2022a), 'Morphology within the Parallel Architecture Framework: The Centrality of the Lexicon below the Word Level', *Isogloss* 8 (1)/7: 1–87.

Benavides, Carlos (2022b), 'Response to "Alternative Theory of Morphology in the Parallel Architecture: A Reply to Benavides 2022"', *Isogloss* 8 (1)/15: 1–15.

Bennis, Hans (1986), *Gaps and Dummies*, Dordrecht: Foris.

Bermúdez-Otero, Ricardo (1999), *Constraint Interaction in Language Change: Quantity in English and Germanic*, PhD dissertation, University of Manchester.

Blank, Andreas (1997), 'Outlines of a Cognitive Approach to Word-Formation', in *Proceedings of the 16th International Congress of Linguists*, Paper No. 0291, Oxford: Pergamon.

Blevins, James P. (2016), *Word and Paradigm Morphology*, Oxford: Oxford University Press.

Bloch-Trojnar, Maria (2006), *Polyfunctionality in Morphology: A Study of Verbal Nouns in Modern Irish*, Lublin: Wydawnictwo KUL.

Bloch-Trojnar, Maria (2013), *The Mechanics of Transposition: A Study of Action Nominalizations in English, Irish and Polish*, Lublin: Wydawnictwo KUL.

Bloomfield, Leonard (1933), *Language*, London: Allen & Unwin.

BNC (2007), *British National Corpus*, XML edn, University of Oxford, http://www.natcorp.ox.ac.uk/.

Bobaljik, Jonathan D. (2020), 'Distributed Morphology', in Rochelle Lieber (ed.), *The Oxford Encyclopedia of Morphology*, New York: Oxford University Press, pp. 976–1004.

Bochner, Gregory (2021), *Naming and Indexicality*, Cambridge: Cambridge University Press.

Bonet, Eulàlia (1991), *Morphology after Syntax: Pronominal Clitics in Romance*, PhD dissertation, Massachusetts Institute of Technology.

Booij, Geert (1977), *Dutch Morphology: A Study of Word Formation in Generative Grammar*, Lisse: Peter de Ridder Press.

Booij, Geert (1994), 'Against Split Morphology', in Geert Booij and Jaap van Marle (eds), *Yearbook of Morphology 1993*, Dordrecht: Kluwer Academic, pp. 27–49.

Booij, Geert (1995), *The Phonology of Dutch*, Oxford: Oxford University Press.

Booij, Geert (1996), 'Inherent versus Contextual Inflection and the Split Morphology Hypothesis', in Geert Booij and Jaap van Marle (eds), *Yearbook of Morphology 1995*, Dordrecht: Kluwer Academic, pp. 1–16.

Booij, Geert, Christian Lehmann and Joachim Mugdan (eds) (2000, 2004), *Morphologie – Morphology: Ein Internationales Handbuch zur Flexion und Wortbildung – An International Handbook on Inflection and Word-Formation*, vol. 1: 2000, vol. 2: 2004, Berlin: Walter de Gruyter.

Booij, Geert (2002), *The Morphology of Dutch*, Oxford: Oxford University Press.

Booij, Geert and Rochelle Lieber (2004), 'On the Paradigmatic Nature of Affixal Semantics in English and Dutch', *Linguistics* 42: 327–357.

Booij, Geert (2009), 'Compounding and Construction Morphology', in Rochelle Lieber and Pavol Štekauer (eds), *The Oxford Handbook of Compounding*, Oxford: Oxford University Press, pp. 201–216.

Booij, Geert (2010), *Construction Morphology*, Oxford: Oxford University Press.

Booij, Geert (2013), 'Morphology in Construction Grammar', in Thomas Hoffmann and Graeme Trousdale (eds), *The Oxford Handbook of Construction Grammar*, Oxford: Oxford University Press, pp. 255–273.

Booij, Geert and Francesca Masini (2015), 'The Role of Second Order Schemas in the Construction of Complex Words', in Laurie Bauer, Lívia Körtvélyessy and Pavol Štekauer (eds), *Semantics of Complex Words*, Cham: Springer, pp. 47–66.

Booij, Geert (2016), 'Construction Morphology', in Andrew Hippisley and Gregory Stump (eds), *The Cambridge Handbook of Morphology*, Cambridge: Cambridge University Press, pp. 424–448.

Booij, Geert and Jenny Audring (2017), 'Construction Morphology and the Parallel Architecture of Grammar', *Cognitive Science* 41 (S2): 277–302.

Booij, Geert (ed.) (2018), *The Construction of Words: Advances in Construction Morphology*, Cham: Springer.

Booij, Geert (2020), 'Construction Morphology', in Rochelle Lieber (ed.), *The Oxford Encyclopedia of Morphology*, New York: Oxford University Press, pp. 1004–1016.

Borer, Hagit (2013), *Structuring Sense III: Taking Form*, Oxford: Oxford University Press.

Borer, Hagit (2014), 'Derived Nominals and the Domain of Content', *Lingua* 141: 71–96.

Bornemann, Eduard and Ernst Risch (1978), *Griechische Grammatik*, 2nd edn, Frankfurt am Main: Diesterweg.

Bosák, Ján and Klára Buzássyová (1985), *Východiská morfémovej analýzy: (morfematika, slovotvorba)*, Bratislava: Veda, vydavateľstvo Slovenskej akadémie vied.

Brinton, Laurel J. and Elizabeth C. Traugott (2005), *Lexicalization and Language Change*, Cambridge: Cambridge University Press.

Brown, Dunstan (2019), 'Network Morphology', in Jenny Audring and Francesca Masini (eds), *The Oxford Handbook of Morphological Theory*, Oxford: Oxford University Press, pp. 305–326.

Butt, John and Carmen Benjamin (2004), *A New Reference Grammar of Modern Spanish*, 4th edn, London: Hodder Arnold.

Carstairs, Andrew (1981), *Notes on Affixes, Clitics, and Paradigms*, Bloomington: Indiana University Linguistics Club.

Carstairs, Andrew (1987), 'Diachronic Evidence and the Affix–Clitic Distinction', in Anna Giacalone Ramat, Onofrio Carruba and Giuliano Bernini (eds) (1987), *Papers from the 7th International Conference on Historical Linguistics*, Amsterdam: John Benjamins, pp. 151–162.

Carstairs-McCarthy, Andrew (1992), *Current Morphology*, London: Routledge.

Carstairs-McCarthy, Andrew (1994), 'Inflection Classes, Gender, and the Principle of Contrast', *Language* 70: 737–788.

ten Cate-Silfwerbrand, Ragnhild (1973), *Zweedse spraakkunst voor iedereen*, Utrecht and Antwerp: Spectrum.

Ceranowicz, Piotr, Jakub Cieszkowski, Zygmunt Warzecha, Beata Kuśnierz-Cabala and Artur Dembiński (2015), 'The Beginnings of Pancreatology as a Field of Experimental and Clinical Medicine', *BioMed Research International* 2015: 128095.

Cetnarowska, Bożena (2015), 'The Lexical/Phrasal Status of Polish Noun+Adjective or Noun+Noun Combinations and the Relevance of Coordination as a Diagnostic Test', *SKASE Journal of Theoretical Linguistics* 12 (3): 142–170.
Cetnarowska, Bożena (2018), 'Phrasal Names in Polish: A+N, N+A and N+N Units', in Geert Booij (ed.), *The Construction of Words: Advances in Construction Morphology*, Cham: Springer, pp. 287–313.
CHN (2021), *Corpus Hedendaags Nederlands*, Leiden: Instituut voor de Nederlandse Taal, http://hdl.handle.net/10032/tm-a2-s8 (13 March 2023).
Chomsky, Noam (1953), 'Systems of Syntactic Analysis', *The Journal of Symbolic Logic* 18: 242–256.
Chomsky, Noam (1957), *Syntactic Structures*, The Hague: Mouton.
Chomsky, Noam (1965), *Aspects of the Theory of Syntax*, Cambridge, MA: MIT Press.
Chomsky, Noam and Morris Halle (1968), *The Sound Pattern of English*, New York: Harper & Row.
Chomsky, Noam (1970), 'Remarks on Nominalization', in Roderick A. Jacobs and Peter S. Rosenbaum (eds), *Readings in English Transformational Grammar*, Waltham, MA: Ginn, pp. 184–221.
Chomsky, Noam (1973), 'Conditions on Transformations', in Stephen R. Anderson and Paul Kiparsky (eds), *A Festschrift for Morris Halle*, New York: Holt, Rinehart & Winston, pp. 232–286.
Chomsky, Noam (1977), *Essays on Form and Interpretation*, New York: North Holland.
Chomsky, Noam (1980), *Rules and Representations*, New York: Columbia University Press.
Chomsky, Noam (1981), *Lectures on Government and Binding*, Dordrecht: Foris, 3rd rev. edn 1984.
Chomsky, Noam (1986), *Knowledge of Language: Its Nature, Origin, and Use*, Westport, CT: Praeger.
Chomsky, Noam (1993), 'A Minimalist Program for Linguistic Theory', in Kenneth Hale and Samuel J. Keyser (eds), *The View from Building 20: Essays in Linguistics in Honor of Sylvain Bromberger*, Cambridge, MA: MIT Press, pp. 1–52.
Chomsky, Noam (2000), 'Minimalist Inquiries: The Framework', in Roger Martin, David Michaels and Juan Uriagereka (eds), *Step by Step: Essays on Minimalist Syntax in Honor of Howard Lasnik*, Cambridge, MA: MIT Press, pp. 89–155.
Clark, Billy (2013), *Relevance Theory*, Cambridge: Cambridge University Press.
COBUILD (2023), *Collins COBUILD Advanced Learner's Dictionary*, New York: HarperCollins, https://www.collinsdictionary.com (12 March 2023).
COCA (2008–2020), *The Corpus of Contemporary American English*, edited by Mark Davies, http://corpus.byu.edu/coca.
COED (2011), *Concise Oxford English Dictionary*, 12th edn, edited by Angus Stevenson and Maurice Waite, Oxford: Oxford University Press.
Collins (1999), *Collins German–English English–German Dictionary, Unabridged*, 4th edn, Glasgow: HarperCollins.
Corbett, Greville G. and Norman M. Fraser (1993), 'Network Morphology: A DATR Account of Russian Nominal Inflection', *Journal of Linguistics* 29: 113–142.
Corbin, Danielle (1987), *Morphologie dérivationnelle et structuration du lexique*, 2 vols, Tübingen: Niemeyer.
Coulmas, Florian (2018), *An Introduction to Multilingualism: Language in a Changing World*, Oxford: Oxford University Press.
Craigie, William A. and C. T. Onions (1933), 'Historical Introduction', *A New English Dictionary on Historical Principles, Supplement*, Oxford: Clarendon, pp. vii–xx.

Creemers, Ava, Jan Don and Paula Fenger (2018), 'Some Affixes Are Roots, Others Are Heads', *Natural Language and Linguistic Theory* 36: 45–84.
Croft, William (2001), *Radical Construction Grammar: Syntactic Theory in Typological Perspective*, Oxford: Oxford University Press.
Culicover, Peter W. and Ray Jackendoff (2005), *Simpler Syntax*, Oxford: Oxford University Press.
van Dale (2022), *Van Dale Groot Woordenboek van de Nederlandse Taal*, 16th edn, edited by Ton den Boon and Ruud Hendrickx, Utrecht and Antwerp: Van Dale Lexicografie.
Depecker, Loïc (2012), 'Les manuscrits de Saussure: une révolution philologique', *Langages* 185: 3–6.
DeReKo (2005–2023), *Deutsches Referenzkorpus*, Mannheim: Institut für Deutsche Sprache, https://www.ids-mannheim.de/digspra/kl/projekte/korpora/.
Di Sciullo, Anna Maria and Edwin Williams (1987), *On the Definition of Word*, Cambridge, MA: MIT Press.
Dokulil, Miloš (1962), *Tvoření slov v češtine I: Teorie odvozování slov*, Prague: Nakladatelství ČSAV.
Dokulil, Miloš (1964), 'Zum wechselseitigen Verhältnis zwischen Wortbildung und Syntax', *Travaux du Cercle Linguistique de Prague* 1: 215–224.
Dokulil, Miloš (1968), 'Zur Theorie der Wortbildung', *Wissenschaftliche Zeitschrift der Karl-Marx-Universität Leipzig, Gesellschafts- und Sprachwissenschaftliche Reihe* 17: 203–211.
Dokulil, Miloš (1994), 'The Prague School's Theoretical and Methodological Contribution to "Word Formation" (Derivology)', in Philip Luelsdorff (ed.), *The Prague School of Structural and Functional Linguistics: A Short Introduction*, Amsterdam: John Benjamins, pp. 123–161.
Downing, Pamela Ann (1977), 'On the Creation and Use of English Compound Nouns', *Language* 53: 810–841.
Dressler, Wolfgang U. (1985), 'Typological Aspects of Natural Morphology', *Wiener linguistische Gazette* 36: 3–26.
Dressler, Wolfgang U., Willi Mayerthaler, Oswald Panagl and Wolfgang Ullrich Wurzel (1987), *Leitmotifs in Natural Morphology*, Amsterdam: John Benjamins.
Dressler, Wolfgang U. (1988), 'Zur Bedeutung der Sprachtypologie in der Natürlichen Morphologie', in Jorn Albrecht, Harald Thun and Jens Lüdtke (eds), *Energeia und Ergon 3: Das sprachtheoretische Denken Eugenio Coserius in der Diskussion*, Tübingen: Narr, pp. 199–208.
Dressler, Wolfgang U. (1990), *Semiotische Parameter einer textinguistischen Natürlichkeittheorie*, Vienna: Österrreichische Akademie der Wissenschaften.
Dressler, Wolfgang U. (1994), 'Diminutivsbildung als nicht-prototypische Wortbildungsregel', in Klaus-Michael Köpcke (ed.), *Funktionale Untersuchungen zur deutschen Nominal- und Verbalmorphologie*, Tübingen: Niemeyer, pp. 131–148.
Dressler, Wolfgang U. and Lavinia Merlini Barbaresi (1994), *Morphopragmatics*, Berlin: Mouton de Gruyter.
Dressler, Wolfgang U. (1999), 'On a Semiotic Theory of Preferences in Language', in Michael Shapiro (ed.), *The Peirce Semiotic Papers: Essays in Semiotic Analysis*, vol. 4, New York: Berghahn, pp. 389–415.
Dressler, Wolfgang U. and Maria Ladányi (2000), 'Productivity in Word Formation (WF): A Morphological Approach', *Acta Linguistica Hungarica* 47: 103–144.

Dressler, Wolfgang U. (2005a), 'Word-Formation in Natural Morphology', in Pavol Štekauer and Rochelle Lieber (eds), *Handbook of Word-Formation*, Dordrecht: Springer, pp. 267–284.
Dressler, Wolfgang U. (2005b), 'Towards a Natural Morphology of Compounding', *Linguistica* 45 (1): 29–40.
Dressler, Wolfgang U. (2006), 'Compound Types', in Garry Libben and Gonia Jarema (eds), *The Representation and Processing of Compound Words*, Oxford: Oxford University Press, pp. 23–44.
Dressler, Wolfgang U. (2020), 'Natural Morphology', in Rochelle Lieber (ed.), *The Oxford Encyclopedia of Morphology*, New York: Oxford University Press, pp. 963–976.
Duden (2011–2023), *Duden Online*, Berlin: Bibliographisches Institut, https://www.duden.de (12 March 2023).
Everaert, Martin, Arnold Evers, Riny Huybregts and Mieke Trommelen (eds) (1988), *Morphology and Modularity*, Dordrecht: Foris.
Fernández-Domínguez, Jesús (2019), 'The Onomasiological Approach', in Mark Aronoff (ed.), *Oxford Research Encyclopedia of Linguistics*, Oxford: Oxford University Press, https://doi.org/10.1093/acrefore/9780199384655.013.579.
Fleischer, Wolfgang and Irmhild Barz (2012), *Wortbildung der deutschen Gegenwartsprache*, vol. 4, Berlin: De Gruyter.
Fudge, Erik C. (1995), 'The Glossematic School of Linguistics', in E. F. Konrad Koerner and R. E. Asher (eds), *Concise History of the Language Sciences: From the Sumerians to the Cognitivists*, Oxford: Pergamon/Elsevier Science, pp. 262–268.
Furdík, Juraj (1978), 'Slovotvorná motivovanosť slovnej zásoby v slovenčine', in Jozef Mistrík (ed.), *Studia Academica Slovaca 7: Prednášky XIV. letného seminára slovenského jazyka a kultúry*, Bratislava: Alfa, pp. 103–115.
Furdík, Juraj (2004), *Slovenská slovotvorba (teória, opis, cvičenia)*, edited by Martin Ološtiak, Prešov: Náuka.
Gaeta, Livio (2019), 'Natural Morphology', in Jenny Audring and Francesca Masini (eds), *The Oxford Handbook of Morphological Theory*, Oxford: Oxford University Press, pp. 244–264.
Gaeta, Livio and Davide Ricca (2006), 'Productivity in Italian Word Formation: A Variable-Corpus Approach', *Linguistics* 44 (1): 57–89.
Garrett, Andrew (2008), 'Biography of Paul Kiparsky', in Kristin Hanson and Sharon Inkelas (eds), *The Nature of the Word: Essays in Honor of Paul Kiparsky*, Cambridge, MA: MIT Press, pp. xv–xvi.
Gilliver, Peter (2016), *The Making of the Oxford English Dictionary*, Oxford: Oxford University Press.
Giovanelli, Marcello, Chloe Harrison and Louise Nuttall (2020), *New Directions in Cognitive Grammar and Style*, London: Bloomsbury.
Goldberg, Adele (1995), *Constructions: A Construction Grammar Approach to Argument Structure*, Chicago: Chicago University Press.
Grandi, Nicola and Lívia Körtvélyessy (eds) (2015), *Edinburgh Handbook of Evaluative Morphology*, Edinburgh: Edinburgh University Press.
Greenberg, Marc L. (2005), 'Serbo-Croatian and South Slavic Languages', in Philipp Strazny (ed.), *Encyclopedia of Linguistics*, 2 vols, New York: Fitzroy Dearborn, pp. 956–958.
Gregová, Renáta (2015), 'Slovak', in Nicola Grandi and Lívia Körtvélyessy (eds), *Edinburgh Handbook of Evaluative Morphology*, Edinburgh: Edinburgh University Press, pp. 296–305.

Grimm, Jacob (1893 [1822]), *Deutsche Grammatik, erster Theil, zweite Ausgabe, neuer vermehrter Abdruck*, edited by Wilhelm Scherer, Gütersloh: Bertelsmann.

Grzega, Joachim (2004), *Bezeichnungswandel: Wie, Warum, Wozu? Ein Beitrag zur englischen und allgemeinen Onomasiologie*, Heidelberg: Winter.

Grzega, Joachim (2009), 'Compounding from an Onomasiological Perspective', in Rochelle Lieber and Pavol Štekauer (eds), *The Oxford Handbook of Compounding*, Oxford: Oxford University Press, pp. 217–232.

de Haas, Wim and Mieke Trommelen (1993), *Morfologisch Handboek van het Nederlands: Een overzicht van de woordvorming*, The Hague: SDU.

ten Hacken, Pius (2007), *Chomskyan Linguistics and its Competitors*, London: Equinox.

ten Hacken, Pius (2009a), 'What is a Dictionary? A View from Chomskyan Linguistics', *International Journal of Lexicography* 22: 399–421.

ten Hacken, Pius (2009b), 'Early Generative Approaches', in Rochelle Lieber and Pavol Štekauer (eds), *The Oxford Handbook of Compounding*, Oxford: Oxford University Press, pp. 54–77.

ten Hacken, Pius (2011), 'Grammaticality', in Patrick C. Hogan (ed.), *The Cambridge Encyclopedia of the Language Sciences*, Cambridge: Cambridge University Press, p. 349.

ten Hacken, Pius and Renáta Panocová (2011), 'Individual and Social Aspects of Word Formation', *Kwartalnik Neofilologiczny* 58: 283–300.

ten Hacken, Pius (2012), 'In What Sense is the OED the Definitive Record of the English Language?', in Ruth V. Fjeld and Julie M. Torjusen (eds), *Proceedings of the 15th EURALEX International Congress*, Oslo: Department of Linguistics, pp. 834–845.

ten Hacken, Pius (2013a), 'Diminutives and Plurals of Dutch Nouns', *Quaderns de Filología: Estudis lingüístics* 18: 61–70.

ten Hacken, Pius (2013b), 'Semiproductivity and the Place of Word Formation in Grammar', in Pius ten Hacken and Claire Thomas (eds), *The Semantics of Word Formation and Lexicalization*, Edinburgh: Edinburgh University Press, pp. 28–44.

ten Hacken, Pius (2014), 'Delineating Derivation and Inflection', in Rochelle Lieber and Pavol Štekauer (eds), *The Oxford Handbook of Derivational Morphology*, Oxford: Oxford University Press, pp. 10–25.

ten Hacken, Pius (2015), 'Transposition and the Limits of Word Formation', in Laurie Bauer, Lívia Körtvélyessy and Pavol Štekauer (eds), *Semantics of Complex Words*, Cham: Springer, pp. 187–216.

ten Hacken, Pius (2019a), *Word Formation in Parallel Architecture: The Case for a Separate Component*, Berlin: Springer.

ten Hacken, Pius (2019b), 'Relational Adjectives between Syntax and Morphology', *SKASE Journal of Theoretical Linguistics* 19 (1): 77–92.

ten Hacken, Pius (2019c), 'Early Generative Grammar', in Jenny Audring and Francesca Masini (eds), *The Oxford Handbook of Morphological Theory*, Oxford: Oxford University Press, pp. 105–121.

ten Hacken, Pius (2020a), 'Norms, New Words, and Empirical Reality', *International Journal of Lexicography* 33: 135–147.

ten Hacken, Pius (2020b), 'Compounding in Morphology', in Rochelle Lieber (ed.), *The Oxford Encyclopedia of Morphology*, New York: Oxford University Press, pp. 683–700.

ten Hacken, Pius (2020c), 'Classical Generative Morphology', in Rochelle Lieber (ed.), *The Oxford Encyclopedia of Morphology*, New York: Oxford University Press, pp. 949–962.

ten Hacken, Pius (2020d), 'Language and Translation', in Lew N. Zybatow and Alena Petrova (eds), *Was ist und was soll Translationswissenschaft – Redefining and Refocusing Translation and Interpreting Studies*, Berlin: Lang, pp. 37–51.

ten Hacken, Pius and Renáta Panocová (2022), 'The Suffix *-ation* in English', *Arbeiten aus Anglistik und Amerikanistik* 47 (1): 29–58.
Haeseryn, W., K. Romijn, G. Geerts, J. de Rooy and M. C. van den Toorn (1997), *Algemene Nederlandse Spraakkunst*, Groningen: Nijhoff and Deurne: Wolters Plantyn.
Halle, Morris (1973), 'Prolegomena to a Theory of Word Formation', *Linguistic Inquiry* 4: 3–16.
Halle, Morris and K. P. Mohanan (1985), 'Segmental Phonology of Modern English', *Linguistic Inquiry* 16: 57–116.
Halle, Morris and Alec Marantz (1993), 'Distributed Morphology and the Pieces of Inflection', in Kenneth Hale and Samuel J. Keyser (eds), *The View from Building 20: Essays in Linguistics in Honor of Sylvain Bromberger*, Cambridge, MA: MIT Press, pp. 111–176.
Hanks, Patrick (1987), 'Definitions and Explanations', in John M. Sinclair (ed.), *Looking Up: An Account of the COBUILD Project in Lexical Computing and the Development of the Collins COBUILD English Language Dictionary*, London and Glasgow: Collins ELT, pp. 116–136.
Harley, Heidi and Rolf Noyer (1998), 'Licensing in the Non-lexicalist Lexicon: Nominalizations, Vocabulary Items and the Encyclopaedia', *MIT Working Papers in Linguistics* 32: 119–137.
Harley, Heidi and Rolf Noyer (2003), 'Distributed Morphology', in Lisa Cheng and Rint Sybesma (eds), *The Second Glot International State-of-the-Article Book: The Latest in Linguistics*, Berlin: Mouton de Gruyter, pp. 463–496.
Harley, Heidi (2009a), 'Compounding in Distributed Morphology', in Rochelle Lieber and Pavol Štekauer (eds), *The Oxford Handbook of Compounding*, Oxford: Oxford University Press, pp. 129–144.
Harley, Heidi (2009b), 'The Morphology of Nominalizations and the Syntax of vP', in Anastasia Giannakidou and Monika Rathert (eds), *Quantification, Definiteness, and Nominalization*, Oxford: Oxford University Press, pp. 321–343.
Harley, Heidi (2014), 'On the Identity of Roots', *Theoretical Linguistics* 40: 225–276.
Harris, James W. (1991), 'The Exponence of Gender in Spanish', *Linguistic Inquiry* 22: 27–62.
Harris, Zellig S. (1951), *Methods in Structural Linguistics*, Chicago: University of Chicago Press, repr. as *Structural Linguistics*, 1960.
Hellman, Bo, Arne Wallgren and Claes Hellerström (1962), 'Two Types of Islet A Cells in Different Parts of the Pancreas of the Dog', *Nature* 194: 1201–1202.
Heyvaert, Liesbet (2009), 'Compounding in Cognitive Linguistics', in Rochelle Lieber and Pavol Štekauer (eds), *The Oxford Handbook of Compounding*, Oxford: Oxford University Press, pp. 233–254.
Hilpert, Martin (2020), 'Lexicalization in Morphology', in Rochelle Lieber (ed.), *The Oxford Encyclopedia of Morphology*, New York: Oxford University Press, pp. 1721–1733.
Hippisley, Andrew (2020), 'Network Morphology', in Rochelle Lieber (ed.), *The Oxford Encyclopedia of Morphology*, New York: Oxford University Press, pp. 1082–1098.
Hjelmslev, Louis (1943), *Omkring sprogteoriens grundlæggelse*, Copenhagen: Bianco Lunos.
Hockett, Charles F. (1942), 'A System of Descriptive Phonology', *Language* 18: 3–21.
Hockett, Charles F. (1947), 'Problems of Morphemic Analysis', *Language* 23: 321–343.
Hockett, Charles F. (1954), 'Two Models of Grammatical Description', *Word* 10: 210–231.

Hockett, Charles F. (1958), *A Course in Modern Linguistics*, New York: Macmillan.
Hoeksema, Jack (2020), 'Derivational Networks in Dutch', in Lívia Körtvélyessy, Aleksandra Bagasheva and Pavol Štekauer (eds), *Derivational Networks across Languages*, Berlin: De Gruyter Mouton, pp. 137–146.
Hoffmann, Benedikt (1777), *Lateinische Sprachkunst, zum bessern Gebrauche der Jugend tabellarisch abgefasset*, 6 vols, Bruchsal: Hoffmann (I, VI); Frankenthal: Segel (II); Mannheim: Kurfürstl. Hofdruckerei (III); Karlsruhe: Machlott (IV, V).
Holton, David, Peter Mackridge and Irene Philippaki-Warburton (2004), *Greek: An Essential Grammar of the Modern Language*, Abingdon: Routledge.
Horecký, Ján (1959), *Slovotvorná sústava slovenčiny*, Bratislava: Vydavateľstvo SAV.
Horecký, Ján (1964), *Morfematická štruktúra slovenčiny*, Bratislava: Vydavateľstvo SAV.
Horecký, Ján, Klára Buzássyová and Ján Bosák (eds) (1989), *Dynamika slovnej zásoby súčasnej slovenčiny*, Bratislava: Vydavateľstvo Slovenskej akadémie vied.
Hough, Carole (ed.) (2016), *The Oxford Handbook of Names and Naming*, Oxford: Oxford University Press.
Huck, Geoffrey J. and John A. Goldsmith (1995), *Ideology and Linguistic Theory: Noam Chomsky and the Deep Structure Debates*, London: Routledge.
Hüning, Matthias and Geert Booij (2014), 'From Compounding to Derivation: The Emergence of Derivational Affixes through "Constructionalization"', *Folia Linguistica* 48 (2): 579–604.
Hüning, Matthias (2018), 'Foreign Word-Formation in Construction Morphology: Verbs in -ieren in German', in Geert Booij (ed.), *The Construction of Words: Advances in Construction Morphology*, Cham: Springer, pp. 341–371.
Hymes, Dell (1971), 'Competence and Performance in Linguistic Theory', in Renira Huxley and Elisabeth Ingram (eds), *Language Acquisition: Models and Methods*, London: Academic Press, pp. 3–24.
Ivanová, Martina (2020), 'Derivational Networks in Slovak', in Lívia Körtvélyessy, Aleksandra Bagasheva and Pavol Štekauer (eds), *Derivational Networks across Languages*, Berlin: De Gruyter Mouton, pp. 93–104.
iWeb (2018), *The iWeb Corpus*, Provo, UT: BYU, https://corpus.byu.edu/iweb.
Jackendoff, Ray (1975), 'Morphological and Semantic Regularities in the Lexicon', *Language* 51: 639–671.
Jackendoff, Ray (1983), *Semantics and Cognition*, Cambridge, MA: MIT Press.
Jackendoff, Ray (1990), *Semantic Structures*, Cambridge, MA: MIT Press.
Jackendoff, Ray (1997), 'Twistin' the Night Away', *Language* 73: 534–559.
Jackendoff, Ray (2002), *Foundations of Language: Brain, Meaning, Grammar, Evolution*, Oxford: Oxford University Press.
Jackendoff, Ray (2009), 'Compounding in the Parallel Architecture and Conceptual Semantics', in Rochelle Lieber and Pavol Štekauer (eds), *The Oxford Handbook of Compounding*, Oxford: Oxford University Press, pp. 105–128.
Jackendoff, Ray (2010), *Meaning and the Lexicon: The Parallel Architecture 1975–2010*, Oxford: Oxford University Press.
Jackendoff, Ray (2016), 'English Noun-Noun Compounds in Conceptual Semantics', in Pius ten Hacken (ed.), *The Semantics of Compounding*, Cambridge: Cambridge University Press, pp. 15–37.
Jackendoff, Ray and Jenny Audring (2016), 'Morphological Schemas: Theoretical and Psycholinguistic Issues', *The Mental Lexicon* 11: 467–493.
Jackendoff, Ray and Jenny Audring (2020), *The Texture of the Lexicon: Relational Morphology and the Parallel Architecture*, Oxford: Oxford University Press.

Jackendoff, Ray (2022), 'Alternative Theories of Morphology in the Parallel Architecture: A Reply to Benavides 2022', *Isogloss* 8 (1)/12: 1–10.
Jakobson, Roman (1932), 'Zur Struktur des russischen Verbums', in *Charisteria Guilelmo Mathesio quinquagenario a discipulis et Circuli linguistici Pragensis Sodalibus oblata*, Prague: Cercle Linguistique de Prague, pp. 74–84.
Janssen, Theo M. V. (2012), 'Compositionality: Its Historic Context', in Markus Werning, Wolfram Hinzen and Edouard Machery (eds), *The Oxford Handbook of Compositionality*, Oxford: Oxford University Press, pp. 19–46.
Jarošová, Alexandra (2000a), 'Lexikalizované spojenie v kontexte ustálených spojení', in Juraj Dolník (ed.), *Princípy jazyka a textu: Materiály z medzinárodnej vedeckej konferencie konanej 9.–10. 3. 2000 na Katedre slovenského jazyka Filozofickej fakulty Univerzity Komenského*, Bratislava: Univerzita Komenského, pp. 138–153.
Jarošová, Alexandra (2000b), 'Viacslovný termín a lexikalizované spojenie', in Klára Buzássyová (ed.), *Človek a jeho jazyk 1: Jazyk ako fenomén kultúry*, Bratislava: Veda, pp. 481–493.
Jespersen, Otto (1934), 'Gruppegenitiv på Dansk', in *Studier tilegnede Verner Dahlerup*, Copenhagen: Aarhus University Press, pp. 1–7.
Joseph, John (2002), *From Whitney to Chomsky: Essays in the History of American Linguistics*, Amsterdam: John Benjamins.
Katamba, Francis and John Stonham (2006), *Morphology*, 2nd edn, New York: Palgrave Macmillan.
Kiparsky, Paul (1973), '"Elsewhere" in phonology', in Anderson, Stephen R. & Kiparsky, Paul (eds.), *A Festschrift for Morris Halle*, New York: Holt, Rinehart & Winston, pp. 93–106.
Kiparsky, Paul (1982), 'Lexical Morphology and Phonology', in *Linguistics in the Morning Calm: Selected Papers from SICOL 1981*, vol. 1, Linguistic Society of Korea, Seoul: Hanshin, pp. 3–91.
Kiparsky, Paul (1983), 'Word-Formation and the Lexicon', in Frances J. Ingeman (ed.), *1982 Mid-America Linguistics Conference Papers*, Lawrence, KS: Department of Linguistics, University of Kansas, pp. 3–29.
Kiparsky, Paul (2000), 'Opacity and Cyclicity', *The Linguistic Review* 17 (2/4): 351–366.
Kiparsky, Paul (2005), 'Blocking and Periphrasis in Inflectional Paradigms', in Geert Booij and Jaap van Marle (eds), *Yearbook of Morphology 2004*, Dordrecht: Springer, pp. 113–135.
Koch, Peter (2001), 'Bedeutungswandel und Bezeichnungswandel: Von der kognitiven Semasiologie zur kognitiven Onomasiologie', *Zeitschrift für Literaturwissenschaft und Linguistik* 121: 7–36.
Koch, Peter (2002), 'Lexical Typology from a Cognitive and Linguistic Point of View', in Martin Haspelmath, Ekkehard König, Wulf Oesterreicher and Wolfgang Raible (eds), *Language Typology and Language Universals: An International Handbook*, vol. 2, Berlin: De Gruyter, pp. 1142–1178.
Koliopoulou, Maria (2014), 'How Close to Syntax Are Compounds? Evidence from the Linking Element in German and Modern Greek Compounds', *Rivista di Linguistica* 26 (2): 51–70.
Körtvélyessy, Lívia (2012), *Evaluative Morphology from a Cross-Linguistic Perspective*, Newcastle upon Tyne: Cambridge Scholars Publishing.
Körtvélyessy, Lívia, Aleksandra Bagasheva and Pavol Štekauer (eds) (2020), *Derivational Networks across Languages*, Berlin: De Gruyter Mouton.
Kotyczka, Josef (1976), *Kurze polnische Sprachlehre*, Berlin: Volk und Wissen.

KSSJ (2003), *Krátky slovník slovenského jazyka*, 4th edn, edited by Ján Kačala, Mária Pisárčiková and Matej Považaj, Bratislava: Veda.

Kuryłowicz, Jerzy (1964), *The Inflectional Categories of Indo-European*, Heidelberg: Winter.

Labov, William (1973), 'The Boundaries of Words and Their Meanings', in C.-J. N. Bailey and R. W. Shuy (eds), *New Ways of Analyzing Variation in English*, Washington DC: Georgetown University Press, pp. 340–373, repr. in Bas Aarts, David Denison, Evelien Keizer and Gergana Popova (eds) (2004), *Fuzzy Grammar: A Reader*, Oxford: Oxford University Press, pp. 67–89.

Lane, M. A. (1907), 'The Cytological Characters of the Areas of Langerhans', *American Journal of Anatomy* 7: 409–422

Langacker, Ronald W. (1982), 'Space Grammar, Analysability, and the English Passive', *Language* 58: 22–80.

Langacker, Ronald W. (1987a), *Foundations of Cognitive Grammar, Volume 1: Theoretical Prerequisites*, Stanford, CA: Stanford University Press.

Langacker, Ronald W. (1987b), 'Nouns and Verbs', *Language* 63: 53–94.

Langacker, Ronald W. (1991), *Foundations of Cognitive Grammar, Volume 2: Descriptive Application*, Stanford, CA: Stanford University Press.

Langacker, Ronald W. (1995), 'Possession and Possessive Constructions', in John R. Taylor and Robert E. MacLaury (eds), *Language and the Cognitive Construal of the World*, Berlin and New York: De Gruyter Mouton, pp. 51–80.

Langacker, Ronald W. (1999), *Grammar and Conceptualization*, Berlin: Mouton de Gruyter.

Langacker, Ronald W. (2007), 'Cognitive Grammar', in Dirk Geeraerts and Hubert Cuyckens (eds), *The Oxford Handbook of Cognitive Linguistics*, Oxford: Oxford University Press, pp. 421–462.

Langacker, Ronald W. (2008), *Cognitive Grammar: A Basic Introduction*, Oxford: Oxford University Press.

Langacker, Ronald W. (2019), 'Morphology in Cognitive Grammar', in Jenny Audring and Francesca Masini (eds) *The Oxford Handbook of Morphological Theory*, Oxford: Oxford University Press, pp. 346–364.

van der Lee, Anthony and Oskar Reichmann (1973), 'Einführung in die Geschichte der Feldtheorie', in Jost Trier, *Aufsätze und Vorträge zur Wortfeldtheorie*, edited by Anthony van der Lee and Oskar Reichmann, The Hague: Mouton, pp. 9–39.

Lees, Robert B. (1960), *The Grammar of English Nominalizations*, Bloomington: Indiana University Press and The Hague: Mouton (reissued 1963, 5th printing 1968).

Lehrer, Adrienne (1974), *Semantic Fields and Lexical Structure*, Amsterdam: North Holland.

Levi, Judith N. (1978), *The Syntax and Semantics of Complex Nominals*, New York: Academic Press.

Lewis, Geoffrey L. (1967), *Turkish Grammar*, Oxford: Clarendon.

Libben, Garry (1998), 'Semantic Transparency in the Processing of Compounds: Consequences for Representation, Processing and Impairment', *Brain and Language* 61: 30–44.

Lieber, Rochelle (1980), *On the Organization of the Lexicon*, PhD dissertation, Massachusetts Institute of Technology, distributed by Indiana University Linguistics Club, Bloomington, 1981.

Lieber, Rochelle (1983), 'Argument Linking and Compounds in English', *Linguistic Inquiry* 14: 251–285.

Lieber, Rochelle (1992), *Deconstructing Morphology: Word Formation in Syntactic Theory*, Chicago: University of Chicago Press.

Lieber, Rochelle (2004), *Morphology and Lexical Semantics*, Cambridge: Cambridge University Press.

Lieber, Rochelle (2009), 'A Lexical Semantic Approach to Compounding', in Rochelle Lieber and Pavol Štekauer (eds), *The Oxford Handbook of Compounding*, Oxford: Oxford University Press, pp. 78–104.

Lieber, Rochelle and Pavol Štekauer (eds) (2009), *The Oxford Handbook of Compounding*, Oxford: Oxford University Press.

Lieber, Rochelle (2016a), *English Nouns: The Ecology of Nominalization*, Cambridge: Cambridge University Press.

Lieber, Rochelle (2016b), 'Compounding in the Lexical Semantic Framework', in Pius ten Hacken (ed.), *The Semantics of Compounding*, Cambridge: Cambridge University Press, pp. 38–53.

Lieber, Rochelle (ed.) (2020), *The Oxford Encyclopedia of Morphology*, New York: Oxford University Press.

Lowenstamm, Jean (2014), 'Derivational Affixes as Roots: Phasal Spell-Out Meets English Stress Shift', in Artemis Alexiadou, Hagit Borer and Florian Schäfer (eds), *The Syntax of Roots and the Roots of Syntax*, Oxford: Oxford University Press, pp. 230–258.

McCawley, James D. (1968), 'Lexical Insertion in a Transformational Grammar without Deep Structure', *Papers from the Fourth Regional Meeting, Chicago Linguistic Society*, pp. 71–80, repr. in James D. McCawley (1976), *Grammar and Meaning: Papers on Syntactic and Semantic Topics*, New York: Academic Press, pp. 155–166.

McGinnis-Archibald, Martha (2016), 'Distributed Morphology', in Andrew Hippisley and Gregory Stump (eds), *The Cambridge Handbook of Morphology*, Cambridge: Cambridge University Press, pp. 390–423.

McMahon, April M. S. (1994), *Understanding Language Change*, Cambridge: Cambridge University Press.

Marantz, Alec (1997), 'No Escape from Syntax: Don't Try Morphological Analysis in the Privacy of Your Own Lexicon', *UPenn Working Papers in Linguistics* 4: 201–225.

Marchand, Hans (1969), *The Categories and Types of Present-Day English Word-Formation: A Synchronic-Diachronic Approach*, 2nd edn, Munich: Beck.

Mathesius, Vilém (1936), 'On Some Problems of the Systematic Analysis of Grammar', *Travaux du Cercle Linguistique de Prague* 6: 95–107.

Mathesius, Vilém (1940), 'Příspěvek k strukturálnímu rozboru anglické zásoby slovní', *Časopis pro moderní filologii* 26: 79–84.

Matthews, Peter H. (1972), *Inflectional Morphology*, Cambridge: Cambridge University Press.

Mauger, Gaston (1968), *Grammaire pratique du français d'aujourd'hui: langue parlée, langue écrite*, Paris: Hachette.

Mayerthaler, Willi (1981), *Morphologische Natürlichkeit*, Wiesbaden: Athenaion.

Mohanan, Karvannur Puthanveettil (1982), *Lexical Phonology*, PhD dissertation, Massachusetts Institute of Technology.

Newmeyer, Frederick J. (1986a), *Linguistic Theory in America*, 2nd edn, New York: Academic Press.

Newmeyer, Frederick J. (1986b), 'Has There Been a "Chomskyan Revolution" in Linguistics?', *Language* 62: 1–18.

Newmeyer, Frederick J. (1998), *Language Form and Language Function*, Cambridge, MA: MIT Press.

OED (2000–2023), *Oxford English Dictionary*, 3rd edn, edited by John Simpson and Michael Proffitt, Oxford: Oxford University Press, www.oed.com.

Ološtiak, Martin (2019), 'To the Relations between Morphemic and Word-Formation Structure of a Word in Slovak', *Journal of Linguistics/Jazykovedný časopis* 70 (3): 545–572, https://doi.org/10.2478/jazcas-2020-0004.

Ološtiak, Martin (2021), 'Poznámky k lexikálnej adaptácii prevzatých pomenovaní v slovenčine (na príklade nominačného hniezda blog)', *Jazykovedný časopis* 72 (3): 769–786.

Ološtiak, Martin and Martina Ivanová (2015), 'Teoreticko-metodologické aspekty', in Martin Ološtiak (ed.), *Kvalitatívne a kvantitatívne aspekty tvorenia slov v slovenčine*, Prešov: Filozofická fakulta Prešovskej univerzity v Prešove, pp. 87–138.

Palmer, Frank R. (1995), 'Firth and the London School of Linguistics', in E. F. Konrad Koerner and R. E. Asher (eds), *Concise History of the Language Sciences: From the Sumerians to the Cognitivists*, Oxford: Pergamon/Elsevier Science, pp. 268–272.

Panocová, Renáta (2015), *Categories of Word Formation and Borrowing: An Onomasiological Account of Neoclassical Formations*, Newcastle upon Tyne: Cambridge Scholars Publishing.

Paul, Hermann (1886), *Principien der Sprachgeschichte, zweite auflage*, Halle: Niemeyer.

Payne, John (2011), 'Genitive Coordinations with Personal Pronouns', *English Language and Linguistics* 15: 363–385.

Pesetsky, David (1979), 'Russian Morphology and Lexical Theory', ms., Cambridge, MA: MIT.

Picallo, M. Carme (2005), 'Some Notes on Grammatical Gender and *l*-pronouns', in Klaus von Heusinger, Georg A. Kaiser and Elisabeth Stark (eds), *Proceedings of the Workshop 'Specificity and the Evolution/Emergence of Nominal Determination Systems in Romance'*, Konstanz: Fachbereich Sprachwissenschaft, pp. 107–122.

Piller, Ingrid (2016), *Linguistic Diversity and Social Justice: An Introduction to Applied Sociolinguistics*, New York: Oxford University Press.

Pollock, Jean-Yves (1989), 'Verb Movement, Universal Grammar, and the Structure of IP', *Linguistic Inquiry* 20: 365–424.

Prince, Alan and Paul Smolensky (2004 [1993]), *Optimality Theory: Constraint Interaction in Generative Grammar*, Malden, MA: Blackwell, originally a technical report of the University of Colorado Computer Science Department and of the Rutgers Center for Cognitive Science.

Radden, Günter and René Dirven (2007), *Cognitive English Grammar*, Amsterdam: John Benjamins.

Radford, Andrew (2004), *Minimalist Syntax: Exploring the Structure of English*, Cambridge: Cambridge University Press.

Radimský, Jan and Pavel Štichauer (2021), 'Nomina Actionis in the Diachrony of Italian: A Paradigm-Based Model of Competition', *Lingue e Linguaggio* 20 (1): 33–55.

Rainer, Franz (2020), 'Blocking', in Rochelle Lieber (ed.), *The Oxford Encyclopedia of Morphology*, New York: Oxford University Press, pp. 1172–1184.

Ritchie, L. David (2013), *Metaphor*, Cambridge: Cambridge University Press.

Robins, Robert H. (1979), *A Short History of Linguistics*, 2nd edn, London: Longman.

Robins, Robert H. (1987), 'Polysemy and the Lexicographer', in R. W. Burchfield (ed.), *Studies in Lexicography*, Oxford: Clarendon, pp. 52–75.

Romieu, Maurice and André Bianchi (2005), *Gramatica de l'occitan gascon contemporanèu*, Pessac: Presses Universitaires de Bordeaux.
Rosch, Eleanor H. (1973), 'On the Internal Structure of Perceptual and Semantic Categories', in Timothy E. Moore (ed.), *Cognitive Development and the Acquisition of Language*, New York: Academic Press, pp. 111–144.
Rosenbach, Anette (2002), *Genitive Variation in English: Conceptual Factors in Synchronic and Diachronic Studies*, Berlin: Walter de Gruyter.
Sambor, Jadwiga (1975), *O słownictwie statystycznie rzadkim*, Warsaw: Państwowe Wydawnictwo Naukowe.
van Santen, Ariane (1979), 'Een nieuw voorstel voor een transformationele behandeling van composita en bepaalde adjectief-substantief kombinaties', *Spectator* 9: 240–262.
Saussure, Ferdinand de (1916), *Cours de linguistique générale*, edited by Charles Bally and Albert Sechehaye, Édition critique préparée par Tullio de Mauro, Paris: Payot, 1981.
Scalise, Sergio (1984), *Generative Morphology*, Dordrecht: Foris, 2nd edn 1986.
Schlücker, Barbara (2013), 'Non-classifying Compounds in German', *Folia Linguistica* 47 (2): 449–480.
Schlücker, Barbara (2016), 'Adjective-Noun Compounding in Parallel Architecture', in Pius ten Hacken (ed.), *The Semantics of Compounding*, Cambridge: Cambridge University Press, pp. 178–191.
Schultink, Henk (1961), 'Produktiviteit als morfologisch fenomeen', *Forum der Letteren* 2: 110–125.
Schultink, Henk (1988), 'Some Remarks on the Relations between Morphology and Syntax in Twentieth-Century Linguistics', in Martin Everaert, Arnold Evers, Riny Huybregts and Mieke Trommelen (eds), *Morphology and Modularity*, Dordrecht: Foris, pp. 1–8.
Sechehaye, Albert (1926), *Essai sur la structure logique de la phrase*, Paris: Champion.
Selkirk, Elisabeth O. (1982), *The Syntax of Words*, Cambridge, MA: MIT Press.
Siddiqi, Daniel (2019), 'Distributed Morphology', in Jenny Audring and Francesca Masini (eds), *The Oxford Handbook of Morphological Theory*, Oxford: Oxford University Press, pp. 143–165.
Siegel, Dorothy (1974), *Topics in English Morphology*, PhD dissertation, Massachusetts Institute of Technology, New York: Garland, 1979.
Simpson, John (2000), 'Preface to the Third Edition of the OED', http://www.oed.com/public/oed3preface/preface-to-the-third-edition-of-the-oed (last viewed 28 October 2011).
Skalička, Vladimír (1958), 'O současném stavu typologie', *Slovo a Slovesnost* 19: 224–232.
SNK (2022), *Slovenský národný korpus*, Bratislava: Jazykovedný ústav Ľ. Štúra, bonito. korpus.sk.
Spencer, Andrew (2019), 'Inflection and Derivation', in Bas Aarts, Jill Bowie and Gergana Popova (eds), *The Oxford Handbook of English Grammar*, Oxford: Oxford University Press, pp. 242–261.
SSSJ (2006–2022), *Slovnik súčasného slovenského jazyka*, edited by Klára Buzássyová and Alexandra Jarosová, Bratislava: Veda, https://www.juls.savba.sk/pub_sssj.html.
Stampe, David (1973), 'On Chapter Nine', in Michael Kenstowicz and Charles Kisseberth (eds), *Issues in Phonological Theory*, The Hague: Mouton, pp. 44–52.
Steedman, Mark (1993), 'Categorial Grammar', *Lingua* 90: 221–258.
Štekauer, Pavol (1998), *An Onomasiological Theory of English Word-Formation*, Amsterdam: John Benjamins.

Štekauer, Pavol (2000), *English Word-Formation: A History of Research (1960–1995)*, Tübingen: Narr.
Štekauer, Pavol (2005), 'Onomasiological Approach to Word-Formation', in Pavol Štekauer and Rochelle Lieber (eds), *Handbook of Word-Formation*, Dordrecht: Springer, pp. 207–232.
Štekauer, Pavol, Salvador Valera and Lívia Körtvélyessy (2012), *Word-Formation in the World's Languages: A Typological Survey*, Cambridge: Cambridge University Press.
Štekauer, Pavol (2014), 'Derivational Paradigms', in Rochelle Lieber and Pavol Štekauer (eds), *The Oxford Handbook of Derivational Morphology*, Oxford: Oxford University Press, pp. 354–369.
Štekauer, Pavol (2015), 'The Delimitation of Derivation and Inflection', in Peter O. Müller, Ingeborg Ohnheiser, Susan Olsen and Franz Rainer (eds), *Word-Formation: An International Handbook of the Languages of Europe*, 5 vols, Berlin: Mouton de Gruyter, pp. 218–235.
Štekauer, Pavol (2016), 'Compounding from an Onomasiological Perspective', in Pius ten Hacken (ed.), *The Semantics of Compounding*, Cambridge: Cambridge University Press, pp. 54–68.
Stump, Gregory (1991), 'A Paradigm-Based Theory of Morphosemantic Mismatches', *Language* 67: 675–725.
Stump, Gregory (2019), 'Paradigm Function Morphology', in Jenny Audring and Francesca Masini (eds), *The Oxford Handbook of Morphological Theory*, Oxford: Oxford University Press, pp. 285–304.
Sussex, Roland and Paul Cubberley (2006), *The Slavic Languages*, Cambridge: Cambridge University Press.
Suter, Rudolf (1992), *Baseldeutsch-Grammatik (3. überarbeitete Auflage)*, Basel: Merian.
Taylor, John R. (2000), *Possessives in English: An Exploration in Cognitive Grammar*, Oxford: Oxford University Press.
Taylor, John R. (2002), *Cognitive Grammar*, Oxford: Oxford University Press.
Thèses (1929), 'Thèses présentées au Premier Congrès des philologues slaves', *Travaux du Cercle Linguistique de Prague* 1: 5–29, translated in Josef Vachek and Libuše Dušková (eds) (1983), *Praguiana: Some Basic and Less Known Aspects of the Prague Linguistic School*, Amsterdam: Benjamins, pp. 77–120.
Thomas, Claire (2013a), *Characterizing the Polysemy of French and English Deverbal Nominalization Suffixes*, PhD thesis, Swansea University.
Thomas, Claire (2013b), 'Lexicalization in Generative Morphology and Conceptual Structure', in Pius ten Hacken and Claire Thomas (eds), *The Semantics of Word Formation and Lexicalization*, Edinburgh: Edinburgh University Press, pp. 45–65.
Thorne, James Peter (1965), 'Review of Postal, Paul (1964), *Constituent Structure: A Study of Contemporary Models of Syntactic Description*, The Hague: Mouton', *Journal of Linguistics* 1: 73–76.
Tieken-Boon van Ostade, Ingrid (2011), *The Bishop's Grammar: Robert Lowth and the Rise of Prescriptivism*, Oxford: Oxford University Press.
Timberlake, Alan (2004), *A Reference Grammar of Russian*, Cambridge: Cambridge University Press.
Trier, Jost (1973), *Aufsätze und Vorträge zur Wortfeldtheorie*, edited by Anthony van der Lee and Oskar Reichmann, The Hague: Mouton.

Trubetzkoy, Nikolaj S. (1939), 'Grundzüge der Phonologie', *Travaux du Cercle Linguistique de Prague* 7.
Uriagereka, Juan (1998), *Rhyme and Reason: An Introduction to Minimalist Syntax*, Cambridge, MA: MIT Press.
Vennemann, Theo (1983), 'Theories of Linguistic Preferences as a Basis for Linguistic Explanations', *Folia Linguistica Historica* 4: 5–26.
Voegelin, Charles F. (1958), 'Review of Chomsky, Noam (1957), *Syntactic Structures*, 's-Gravenhage: Mouton', *International Journal of American Linguistics* 24: 229–231.
Whitney, William Dwight (1879), *A Sanskrit Grammar, Including both the Classical Language, and the Older Dialects, of Veda and Brahmana*, Leipzig: Breitkopf & Härtel.
Wiedenhof, Jeroen (2004), *Grammatica van het Mandarijn*, Amsterdam: Bulaaq.
Wray, Alison (2002), *Formulaic Language and the Lexicon*, Cambridge: Cambridge University Press.
Wurzel, Wolfgang Ullrich (1984), *Flexionsmorphologie und Natürlichkeit: Ein Beitrag zur morphologischen Theoriebildung*, Berlin: Akademie-Verlag.
Wurzel, Wolfgang Ullrich (1987), 'System-Dependent Morphological Naturalness in Inflection', in Wolfgang U. Dressler, Willi Mayerthaler, Oswald Panagl and Wolfgang Ullrich Wurzel (eds), *Leitmotifs in Natural Morphology*, Amsterdam: John Benjamins, pp. 59–96.
Wurzel, Wolfgang Ullrich (1989), *Inflectional Morphology and Naturalness*, Dordrecht: Kluwer.
Zubiri Ibarrondo, Ilari (2000), *Gramática didáctica del euskera*, Bilbao: Didaktiker.
Zwicky, Arnold M. (1987), 'Suppressing the Zs', *Journal of Linguistics* 23: 133–148.

Author index

Abney, Steven Paul, 86, 134
Alexiadou, Artemis (et al.), 84
Allen, Margaret Reece, 38, 89, 92
Amacker, René, 23
Anderson, Stephen R., 50, 68–9, 80
Andreou, Marios, 107–8
Archangeli, Diana (and Langendoen), 100
Aronoff, Mark H.
   1976, 37, 89, 93, 132, 247–8
   1994, 227
Audring, Jenny (and Masini), 50, 128–30, 142, 146, 169; *see also* Booij, Geert; Jackendoff, Ray
Aufinger, Sara, 22

Baayen, Harald, 151
Bagasheva, Aleksandra *see* Körtvélyessy, Lívia
Bally, Charles, 63
Bar-Hillel, Yehoshua (et al.), 128
Barz, Irmhild *see* Fleischer, Wolfgang
Bauer, Laurie
   1983, 13
   2003, 220
Beard, Robert, 50, 118
Beekes, Robert S. P., 20
Benavides, Carlos, 171, 240, 257
Benjamin, Carmen *see* Butt, John
Bennis, Hans, 66
Bermúdez-Otero, Ricardo, 100
Bianchi, André *see* Romieu, Maurice

Blank, Andreas, 193
Blevins, James P., 90
Bloch-Trojnar, Maria, 50
Bloomfield, Leonard, 16, 25–8, 90
BNC, 2–3, 33, 63, 123
Bobaljik, Jonathan D., 51, 68–9, 75, 81–2
Bochner, Gregory, 3
Bonet, Eulàlia, 68
Booij, Geert
   1977, 51, 127
   1994, 116
   1995, 58
   1996, 116
   2000, 2004 (et al.), 127
   2002, 76, 138
   2004 (and Lieber), 117
   2009, 169
   2010, 52, 127–35, 140, 142–3, 146–7, 149, 151, 163, 169–70, 248
   2013, 127, 129
   2015 (and Masini), 132, 140
   2016, 127–9, 133, 137, 139, 144, 147–8
   2017, (and Audring), 150
   2018, 127
   2020, 127–8, 130, 134, 141, 147, 191, 256
   see also Hüning, Matthias
Borer, Hagit
   2013, 119
   2014, 83, 88

Author index

Bornemann, Eduard (and Risch), 17, 139
Bosák, Ján (and Buzássyová), 46; see also Horecký, Ján
Brinton, Laurel J. (and Traugott), 12
Brown, Dunstan, 49
Butt, John (and Benjamin), 18
Buzássyová, Klára see Bosák, Ján; Horecký, Ján

Carstairs, Andrew
   1981, 80
   1987, 97
Carstairs-McCarthy, Andrew
   1992, 50, 89
   1994, 80
ten Cate-Silfwerbrand, Ragnhild, 18
Ceranowicz, Piotr (et al.), 155
Cetnarowska, Bożena
   2015, 134
   2018, 134, 136–7, 146
CHN, 248
Chomsky, Noam
   1953, 31
   1957, 29–31, 38, 69, 111
   1965, 8, 30–1, 33–4, 38, 41, 254
   1968 (and Halle), 90–1
   1970, 30, 33–5, 38, 51, 69, 90, 108, 149, 238, 253
   1973, 69
   1977, 69
   1980, 8, 252
   1981, 69, 241, 248
   1986, 8, 253
   1993, 69, 248
   2000, 69
Cieszkowski, Jakub see Ceranowicz, Piotr
Clark, Billy, 247
COBUILD, 65, 85, 104, 122–3, 145, 166, 189, 229, 245
COCA, 2, 39–40, 57, 111, 176, 254
COED, 10
Collins, 17
Corbett, Greville G. (and Fraser), 49, 80
Corbin, Danielle, 151, 218
Coulmas, Florian, 9
Craigie, William A. (and Onions), 4

Creemers, Ava (et al.), 78–9
Croft, William, 128
Cubberley, Paul see Sussex, Roland
Culicover, Peter W. (and Jackendoff), 130, 134, 257

van Dale, 76
Dembiński, Artur see Ceranowicz, Piotr
Depecker, Loïc, 22
DeReKo, 10, 64, 73, 222
Di Sciullo, Anna Maria (and Williams), 2, 85, 163
Dirven, René see Radden, Günter
Dokulil, Miloš
   1962, 43–5, 47, 49, 63, 140, 205, 208–9
   1964, 44
   1968, 45, 47, 63, 220, 228
   1994, 43–7
Don, Jan see Creemers, Ava
Downing, Pamela Ann, 58, 97
Dressler, Wolfgang U.
   1985, 53, 216, 219
   1987 (et al.), 216, 224, 227, 239
   1988, 216, 219
   1990, 221
   1994, 225
   1994 (and Merlini Barbaresi), 225
   1999, 217
   2000 (and Ladányi), 216
   2005a, 216–20, 222, 225, 228, 230–1, 253
   2005b, 221, 223, 229, 231
   2006, 216, 239
   2020, 216
Duden, 64, 121

Eliyahu Shamir see Bar-Hillel, Yehoshua
Everaert, Martin (et al.), 41
Evers, Arnold see Everaert, Martin

Fenger, Paula see Creemers, Ava
Fernández-Domínguez, Jesús, 193
Fleischer, Wolfgang (and Barz), 47, 56, 121, 165
Fraser, Norman M. see Corbett, Greville G.

Fudge, Erik C., 25
Furdík, Juraj
  1978, 48
  2004, 47–9, 140, 201, 256

Gaeta, Livio
  2006 (and Ricca), 227–8
  2019, 226–8, 231
Gaifman, Chaim see Bar-Hillel,
    Yehoshua (et al.)
Garrett, Andrew, 90
Geerts, G. see Haeseryn, W. (et al.)
Gilliver, Peter, 4
Giovanelli, Marcello (et al.), 173
Goldberg, Adele, 52, 127
Goldsmith, John A. see Huck,
    Geoffrey J. (and Goldsmith)
Grandi, Nicola (and Körtvélyessy),
    205
Greenberg, Marc L., 9
Gregová, Renáta, 60, 99
Grimm, Jacob, 20
Grzega, Joachim, 193

de Haas, Wim (and Trommelen), 76
ten Hacken, Pius
  2007, 8, 27, 29, 31, 111
  2009a, 250
  2009b, 32
  2011, 111
  2011 (and Panocová), 13, 23, 212
  2012, 4–5
  2013a, 59, 67, 158–60
  2013b, 13
  2014, 58, 183, 243
  2015, 63
  2019a, 13, 67, 84, 132, 143, 151,
    157, 171, 240, 248, 257
  2019b, 56
  2019c, 30
  2020a, 8, 250
  2020b, 55
  2020c, 30
  2020d, 8
  2022 (and Panocová), 8, 227
Haeseryn, W. (et al.), 17–18, 58–9
Halle, Morris
  1973, 30, 35–8, 41–3
  1985 (and Mohanan), 92
  1993 (and Marantz), 51, 68–9, 71
  see also Chomsky, Noam
Hanks, Patrick, 65
Harley, Heidi
  1998 (and Noyer), 71
  2003 (and Noyer), 71, 75
  2009a, 69, 72, 75
  2009b, 84
  2014, 83
Harris, James W., 183
Harris, Zellig S., 27–8, 31
Harrison, Chloe see Giovanelli,
    Marcello (et al.)
Hellerström, Claes see Hellman, Bo
    (et al.)
Hellman, Bo (et al.), 155
Heyvaert, Liesbet, 172, 178–9
Hilpert, Martin, 65
Hippisley, Andrew, 49
Hjelmslev, Louis, 25
Hockett, Charles F.
  1942, 27–8, 30
  1947, 27
  1954, 28, 31, 50, 108, 251
  1958, 71
Hoeksema, Jack, 62
Hoffmann, Benedikt, 16
Holton, David (et al.), 18
Horecký, Ján
  1959, 44, 46, 252
  1964, 46
  1989 (et al.), 49, 61, 140
Hough, Carole, 3
Huck, Geoffrey J. (and Goldsmith),
    149
Hüning, Matthias
  2014 (and Booij), 130, 145
  2018, 143
Huybregts, Riny see Everaert,
    Martin
Hymes, Dell, 8

Iordăchioaia, Gianina see
    Alexiadou, Artemis (et al.)
Ivanová, Martina, 62; see also
    Ološtiak, Martin
iWeb, 4–6, 10

Jackendoff, Ray

1975, 30, 35–8, 41–3, 128, 135, 149, 151, 169
1983, 3, 52, 150
1990, 12, 141, 150
1997, 150, 154
2002, 52, 127–8, 150, 159, 239, 244, 254, 257
2009, 52, 150, 155, 167, 169
2010, 149–51, 155
2016, 155, 167, 171
2016 (and Audring), 149, 151
2020 (and Audring), 52, 149–54, 157–8, 160–5, 169–70, 244
2022, 171
see also Culicover, Peter W.
Jakobson, Roman, 24
Janssen, Theo M. V., 178, 245
Jarošová, Alexandra, 201
Jespersen, Otto, 97
Joseph, John, 25

Katamba, Francis (and Stonham), 89–90, 92, 99–101
Kiparsky, Paul
1973, 93
1982, 51, 89–93, 95–8, 100, 103, 105–6
1983, 89, 92–4, 103–4, 106
2000, 89, 100
2005, 89, 101–3, 106
Koch, Peter
2001, 193
2002, 193
Koliopoulou, Maria, 157
Körtvélyessy, Lívia
2012, 205
2020 (et al.), 62, 207–8
see also Grandi, Nicola (and Körtvélyessy); Štekauer, Pavol
Kotyczka, Josef, 18
KSSJ, 11, 65, 246
Kuryłowicz, Jerzy, 116
Kuśnierz-Cabala, Beata see Ceranowicz, Piotr

Labov, William, 3
Ladányi, Maria see Dressler, Wolfgang U.

Lane, M. A., 155
Langacker, Ronald W.
1982, 172
1987a, 52, 128, 172–3, 178–9, 186, 189, 192
1987b, 181, 183, 187–9, 191
1991, 52, 172, 183
1995, 181
1999, 178
2007, 172–3, 190, 231, 253
2008, 172–3, 175–8, 181–3, 186, 190–1
2019, 172, 175–7, 179–80, 184–6, 190–1
Langendoen, D. Terence see Archangeli, Diana
van der Lee, Anthony (and Reichmann), 117
Lees, Robert B., 30–3, 40–3
Lehmann, Christian see Booij, Geert
Lehrer, Adrienne, 117
Levi, Judith N., 30, 40–3, 213
Lewis, Geoffrey L., 102–3
Libben, Garry, 230
Lieber, Rochelle
1980, 91–2
1983, 51, 107
1992, 51, 68–9, 107
2004, 51, 107–8, 110, 112, 114–18, 120, 122–3, 126
2009, 107–9, 112, 120, 122
2009 (and Štekauer), 169
2016a, 51, 107–12, 115–17, 119–21, 123, 191, 249
2016b, 107
2020, 50, 62, 243
see also Booij, Geert
Lowenstamm, Jean, 75, 78–9

McCawley, James D., 39
McGinnis-Archibald, Martha, 51, 68, 79–80
Mackridge, Peter see Holton, David
Marantz, Alec, 75; see also Halle, Morris
McMahon, April M. S., 226
Marchand, Hans, 121
Masini, Francesca see Booij, Geert; Audring, Jenny

Mathesius, Vilém
  1936, 23, 252
  1940, 24
Matthews, Peter H., 90
Mauger, Gaston, 139
Mayerthaler, Willi, 53, 216; *see also* Dressler, Wolfgang U.
Merlini Barbaresi, Lavinia *see* Dressler, Wolfgang U.
Mohanan, Karvannur Puthanveettil, 89, 93; *see also* Halle, Morris
Mugdan, Joachim *see* Booij, Geert

Newmeyer, Frederick J.
  1986a, 38–9, 52, 149, 172
  1986b, 29
  1998, 1
Noyer, Rolf *see* Harley, Heidi
Nuttall, Louise *see* Giovanelli, Marcello

OED, 4–6, 10, 22, 37, 84, 246
Ološtiak, Martin
  2015 (and Ivanová), 48
  2019, 47
  2021, 62, 82
Onions, C. T. *see* Craigie, William A. (and Onions)

Palmer, Frank R., 25
Panagl, Oswald *see* Dressler, Wolfgang U.
Panocová, Renáta, 209; *see also* ten Hacken, Pius
Paul, Hermann, 20–2, 228, 231
Payne, John, 202
Pesetsky, David, 93
Philippaki-Warburton, Irene *see* Holton, David
Picallo, M. Carme, 84
Piller, Ingrid, 9
Pollock, Jean-Yves, 241
Prince, Alan (and Smolensky), 89, 94, 100

Radden, Günter (and Dirven), 173
Radford, Andrew, 257
Radimský, Jan (and Štichauer), 227
Rainer, Franz, 248

Reichmann, Oskar *see* van der Lee, Anthony (and Reichmann)
Ricca, Davide *see* Gaeta, Livio
Risch, Ernst *see* Bornemann, Eduard
Ritchie, L. David, 235
Robins, Robert H.
  1979, 15, 19
  1987, 19
Romieu, Maurice (and Bianchi), 18
Romijn, K. *see* Haeseryn, W. (et al.)
de Rooy, J. *see* Haeseryn, W. (et al.)
Rosch, Eleanor H., 3
Rosenbach, Anette, 96

Sambor, Jadwiga, 48
van Santen, Ariane, 41
Saussure, Ferdinand de, 15, 22, 66, 108, 212
Scalise, Sergio, 35
Schlücker, Barbara
  2013, 58, 157
  2016, 155–6, 170
Schultink, Henk
  1961, 151, 169
  1988, 251
Sechehaye, Albert, 63
Selkirk, Elisabeth O., 97
Siddiqi, Daniel, 51, 68–9, 71, 79–80
Siegel, Dorothy, 89–90
Simpson, John, 4
Skalička, Vladimír, 219
Smolensky, Paul *see* Prince, Alan (and Smolensky)
SNK, 10, 60, 206
Soare, Elena *see* Alexiadou, Artemis (et al.)
Spencer, Andrew, 202
SSSJ, 81
Stampe, David, 53
Steedman, Mark, 128
Štekauer, Pavol
  1998, 52, 193–6, 198–200, 202, 204, 206, 209
  2000, 89
  2005, 53, 193, 198–200
  2012 (et al.), 53
  2014, 61–2, 140, 206–8
  2015, 243

2016, 53, 193, 198–200
   see also Körtvélyessy, Lívia;
     Lieber, Rochelle
Štichauer, Pavel *see* Radimský, Jan
Stonham, John *see* Katamba, Francis
Stump, Gregory, 49–50
Sussex, Roland (and Cubberley), 16
Suter, Rudolf, 16

Taylor, John R., 173
Thèses, 23, 43
Thomas, Claire
   2013a, 84, 248
   2013b, 12
Thorne, James Peter, 29
Tieken-Boon van Ostade, Ingrid, 16
Timberlake, Alan, 18
van den Toorn, M. C. *see* Haeseryn,
   W. (et al.)
Traugott, Elizabeth C. *see* Brinton,
   Laurel J. (and Traugott)
Trier, Jost, 117
Trommelen, Mieke *see* Everaert,
   Martin (et al.); de Haas, Wim
   (and Trommelen)

Trubetzkoy, Nikolaj S., 24

Uriagereka, Juan, 8

Valera, Salvador *see* Štekauer, Pavol
Vennemann, Theo, 217
Voegelin, Charles F., 29

Wallgren, Arne *see* Hellman, Bo
   (et al.)
Warzecha, Zygmunt *see* Ceranowicz,
   Piotr (et al.)
Whitney, William Dwight, 17, 90
Wiedenhof, Jeroen, 18
Williams, Edwin *see* Di Sciullo,
   Anna Maria (and Williams)
Wray, Alison, 236, 254
Wurzel, Wolfgang Ullrich
   1984, 53, 216, 219
   1987, 225–7, 231
   1989, 225
   see also Dressler, Wolfgang U.

Zubiri Ibarrondo, Ilari, 18
Zwicky, Arnold M., 202

Example index

Czech
hravost, 208
nástěnné, 208
pád, 208
sladkost, 208–9

Dutch
Amsterdammer, 142
apotheker, 142
biertje, 115
boompje, 77
broer, 76
dagje, 115
donkere kamer, 136
gebergte, 219
goed, 78
harinkje, 77
huisje, 58
  in DM, 77
  in RM, 158–9
  in NM, 224
huizen, 59
  in DM, 76
  in LMP, 98
  in CxM, 137–8
  in RM, 158–9
  in CG, 184
  in NM, 224
kaartje, 60
  in DM, 79
  in the onomasiological theory, 205
  in NM, 225
kast van een huis, 130
klopper, 142
kommetje, 77
onverwoestbaar, 131, 248
prachtvrouw, 130
propeller, 184
scholier, 76
schrijver, 142
stokje, 60
  in DM, 79
  in LMP, 98–9
  in CG, 185, 192
  in the onomasiological theory, 205, 214–15
suikers, 159
suikertje, 159
uitsmijter, 66, 246
  in DM, 85
  in LMP, 104
  in LSF, 124
  in RM, 167–8
  in the onomasiological theory, 210–11
  in NM, 230
vogels, 59–60, 240–1, 253
  in DM, 75–6
  in LMP, 98, 106
  in LSF, 115
  in CxM, 137–8, 147
  in RM, 158
  in CG, 184
  in the onomasiological theory, 204
  in NM, 224

Example index

vogeltje, 59–60, 241
   in DM, 75, 77, 79, 87
   in LMP, 98, 106
   in LSF, 115
   in CxM, 137, 147
   in RM, 158–9
   in CG, 184
   in the onomasiological theory, 205
   in NM, 224
vrije trap, 136, 147
weekendje, 77–9, 87, 192
wijntje, 78
winkelier, 76
woordenboek, 13–14

English
abolitionism, 132
acceptable, 45
aggression, 37
airman, 24, 47
almsgiving, 96–7
altruism, 132
altruist, 132
ambitious, 152
anonymizer, 199
apple juice seat, 97
applicant, 93
arrival, 35
assassin, 152
assembly plant, 32, 42
baker, 153
behaviourism, 163
beta cell, 155
bird's nest, 57, 237
   in DM, 74, 86
   in LMP, 96–7, 105
   in LSF, 113, 125
   in CxM, 136
   in RM, 157
   in CG, 181
   in the onomasiological theory, 202–3, 214
   in NM, 223
blackbird, 36–7, 178
blackboard, 179
blogger, 218
blood donor, 40
body scan, 209
brush, 104

categorization, 83
cell division, 40
Chicago postman, 58
Chicago suburb, 57, 237
   in DM, 74
   in LMP, 97, 105
   in LSF, 114, 125
   in CxM, 136, 147
   in RM, 157
   in CG, 182, 191
   in the onomasiological theory, 203–4, 213
   in NM, 223
circumstances, 254
collapser, 4–5
comfort eater, 197–8
communism, 132
commuter suburb, 57, 237
   in DM, 74
   in LMP, 97, 105
   in LSF, 114, 125
   in CxM, 136
   in RM, 157
   in CG, 182, 191
   in the onomasiological theory, 203, 213
   in NM, 223
computer, 189–90
constitutional amendment, 40
construction, 164, 249
contain, 195
container, 196
conventioneer, 115
cooker, 91
cranberry, 195, 221
dancer, 129, 131
decision, 36–7, 219
dishwasher, 219
Do you know what time it is?, 247
dogbed, 122
dollarless, 175, 192
doorman, 65–7, 245–6, 249, 256
   in DM, 85, 87
   in LMP, 104, 106
   in LSF, 122–3
   in CxM, 144–5
   in RM, 166–8, 171

doorman (*cont.*)
   in CG, 189, 192
   in the onomasiological theory,
      210, 212, 214
   in NM, 229–30
driver's licence, 96
eagerness, 33–4
ear witness, 235
easiness, 33–4
excess profits tax, 96–7, 202
exploration, 63, 65
   in DM, 82–3
   in LMP, 103
   in LSF, 118
   in CG, 187
explosion, 187–9, 191
feet, 93
flirtatious, 152
flutist, 225
foodist, 199
high-school, 222
hipster, 115
honeymoon, 42
industrial equipment, 40
influencer, 91
inforamtion, 111
innocuous, 100–1
installation, 63–5
   in DM, 83–5
   in LMP, 104, 106
   in LSF, 119, 122
   in CG, 188
   in the onomasiological theory,
      209–10
   in NM, 228, 231
journalist, 207
kill, 39–40
kritharaki, 4–5
langauge, 6, 111
Leyden jar, 155
lice-infested, 96
love song, 40
Mendelianism, 93
methode, 76
moonless night, 178
neck (of a violin), 235
nose job, 42
on a moonless night, 177
opaqueness, 220

pacifism, 163
paddle, 104
pala, 9–10
parks commissioner, 97
peel, 9–10
pilot, 24, 47
pizza shovel, 9
polycystid, 4–5
possible, 195
presidentialness, 142
printer, 50, 189–90
propeller, 189
quillet, 22
readable, 34
redden, 39
refusal, 253
representation, 209, 214
ring, 176
sloppiness, 141, 191, 256
song bird, 40
spaceship, 235
speared, 6
stander, 129
sugar cube, 40
sunny day, 175
teacher, 207
teapot, 2
textile mill, 32
thigh bone, 179
transformational, 37
underwhelmed, 235
unknown, 100–2
unvaccinated, 199
violinist, 167
walker, 129–30
water, 115
whitefish, 95
worse, 102
writer, 110

French
recevoir, 139–40

German
Abgabe, 121
Anrufbeantworter, 255
Bildung, 121
Computer, 10, 235
Fälschung, 143

Example index

Hartkäse, 55–6, 237
  in DM, 72–3, 87
  in LMP, 95, 105
  in LSF, 112–13, 125
  in CxM, 133, 146
  in RM, 154, 156
  in CG, 179–80
  in the onomasiological theory, 201
  in NM, 222
Hohepriester, 221
installieren, 143
Installierung, 64–5, 241–3, 247–8, 255–6
  in DM, 84, 87
  in LSF, 120–2
  in CxM, 142–4, 148
  in RM, 164–6, 171
  in CG, 188, 192
  in the onomasiological theory, 210, 215
  in NM, 229, 231
Normalform, 73
Rechner, 10–1, 235
Sammlung, 166, 171, 215, 248
Türsteher, 66, 246
  in DM, 85
  in LMP, 104
  in LSF, 124
  in RM, 167–8, 171
  in the onomasiological theory, 210–11
  in NM, 230

Italian
cambiamento, 227
trasformazione, 227

Polish
dział finansowy, 134, 146

Slovak
atašé, 80
blog, 62, 236
  in DM, 81
  in LMP, 106
  in LSF, 117
  in CxM, 140
  in RM, 162–3, 170–1
  in CG, 186

bloger, 62
  in DM, 81–2
  in LSF, 117
  in RM, 162–3
  in the onomasiological theory, 206–7
blogerka, 81–2, 162–3
blogovať, 81, 117, 162–3, 170–1
blogový príspevok, 236
čajový, 86
čajová lyžička, 56, 237
  in DM, 73–4
  in LMP, 96, 105
  in LSF, 113, 125
  in CxM, 134
  in RM, 156, 169
  in CG, 181
  in the onomasiological theory, 201, 213
  in NM, 222
computer, 11
dobré ráno, 237
domov, 207
dopravná informácia, 86
drevorubač, 46
gitara, 61, 240–1, 253
  in DM, 79–80
  in LMP, 102–3, 106
  in LSF, 116
  in CxM, 139–40
  in RM, 161–2
  in CG, 185–6
  in NM, 225–6
inštalácia, 64–5
  in DM, 84
  in LSF, 120–2
  in CG, 188, 192
interview, 13–14, 246
jazykoveda, 45
lavička, 60
lyžička, 86
nadstavba, 81
nočný stolík, 135
počítač, 11
potrebná informácia, 86
rýchlosť, 46
školská lavica, 135
stromček, 60, 225
učiť, 48–9

učiteľka, 47–8, 81
ulica, 186
vankúšik, 60
vyhadzovač, 66, 246
  in DM, 85
  in LMP, 104
  in LSF, 124
  in RM, 167–8
  in the onomasiological theory, 210–11
  in NM, 230

zamestnávateľ, 45
zamestnávateľka, 46
zoo, 80

Turkish
el, 102–3, 106

Subject index

A-Morphous Morphology, 50–1, 68
A+N compound, 95, 146, 155
　in RM, 156
A+N names, 136
ablaut, 162
action modality, 167–8
adjectival inflection (in CG), 180
affix
　in LMP, 91, 105
　in LSF, 110
affixoid, 130
agreement, 56, 134–5, 138, 241
allomorph, 76–8, 159
allomorphy, 159
American linguistics, 25
American structuralism, 16, 252
analogy, 235–6
analysability, 179
Ancient Greek, 17, 139
arbitraire du signe, 23, 66
argument structure (in LSF), 243
association, 175, 190
ATK nominalization, 119, 121
Audring, Jenny, 150
augmentative, 59
authority, 5, 6–7, 10
automatization, 175, 190, 192
autonomy of morphology, 251

Bally, Charles (1865–1947), 21, 23
Basel German, 16
basic functions for compounding (in RM), 155, 167

Basque, 18
behaviourism, 26
bilateral sign, 195
biuniqueness, 219
blocking, 247–8, 255
　in LMP, 93, 95, 101
　in LSF, 121
　in the onomasiological theory, 215
　in NM, 231
Bloomfield, Leonard (1887–1949), 25
body (in LSF), 109
Booij, Geert, 51, 127, 149–50
Bopp, Franz (1791–1867), 19
borrowing, 5, 10–11, 13, 19, 62, 235–6, 246, 254–5
　in DM, 80, 82
　in RM, 163
　in the onomasiological theory, 193, 195
bound morpheme, 145
bound stem, 132
boundary
　type of, 243
　see also fuzziness of boundaries
Bounded (feature in LSF), 115
Bracketing Erasure Convention, 93–4

Categorial Grammar, 128
categorization, 175–6, 190
Cercle linguistique de Prague, 23, 43–9; see also Prague School
Chinese see Mandarin

Chomsky, Noam, 149–50
Chomskyan revolution, 29
circularity, 27, 30
circumfixation, 219
clitic, 55, 97, 113
coercion (in CxM), 144; see also contextual coercion; onomasiological coercion
cognitive function of language, 216–7, 253
Cognitive Grammar (CG), 52, 172–92, 230–1, 239–40, 244–5, 249, 251, 254
cognitive manifestation of words, 7
coindexation, 238, 240, 243, 256
   in LSF, 110, 113–14, 119, 122–6
   in RM, 169
collocation, 24–5
communication, 7
communicative/interactive function of language, 173, 190, 216–7, 234, 252–4
comparative, 81, 102, 144
competence, 8, 31, 111
competition, 10–11
completeness, 101–3, 106
complex affixation schema, 131
component (in CG), 178
Composed of Individuals (feature in LSF), 115
composite structure, 178
compositionality, 12, 178–9, 218, 222, 245, 247, 254
compound schema, 155, 167
compounding, 21, 31, 40, 54–5, 237, 239
   in LMP, 92
   in LSF, 110
   in NM, 221
   see also basic functions for compounding (in RM); synthetic compounding
concept, 1–3, 10, 12
   definition, 3, 14
conceptual level, 197
conceptual overlap, 181
conceptual recategorization, 200
conceptual semantics, 52
conceptual structure, 141, 150, 153

conceptualization, 45, 194, 231
conceptualizing function of language, 253–4
constructicon, 129, 133
construction (Bloomfield), 26
Construction Grammar, 127–8
Construction Morphology (CxM), 52, 127–49, 152, 168–9, 171, 239–40, 243, 249, 251, 256
constructionalization, 130, 145
contextual coercion, 119–20, 123, 249–50
contextual inflection, 116
conversion, 107, 110, 200, 218
corpus, 4–6, 10, 27–8, 31, 110–11
corpus linguistics, 16, 25
countability, 84
cumulative exponence, 161
cyclicity, 90, 94
Czech, 16

declension, 80
decomposition, 2
deep structure, 30, 32–3, 35, 38
deictic compound, 58, 97, 125, 147, 191
deictic strategy, 182
delimitation of inflection, 58
derivation
   definition, 62–3
   in LSF, 110
derivation and inflection, distinction between, 240, 243
   in LMP, 98, 100, 105
   in LSF, 115–16, 125
   in CxM, 137
   in RM, 158, 161
   in the onomasiological theory, 204, 208
derivational chain, 49
derivational ecosystem, 117, 126
derivational nest, 49
derivational network, 62
derivational paradigm, 49, 61–2, 236
   in CG, 186, 191
   in CxM, 140, 147
   in DM, 81
   in LMP, 103, 106

in LSF, 117–18, 126
in NM, 227
in RM, 162–3, 170–1
in the onomasiological theory, 206–7
derivology, 43
description, 9, 13
descriptive expression, 234, 251
descriptive grammar, 16
descriptive strategy, 182
diachronic, 28
diagrammaticity, 218
dictionary, 4–7, 10
dictionary of words, 35–6
diminutive, 56, 58–60, 241
in CG, 184
in CxM, 137–8, 147
in DM, 75, 77–9, 87
in LMP, 98–9, 106
in LSF, 114–16
in NM, 224
in RM, 158–61, 170
in the onomasiological theory, 204–5
Distributed Morphology (DM), 51, 68–88, 124, 126, 146, 238, 244, 249, 251, 253
Dokulil, Miloš (1928–2002), 43, 193
DP-analysis, 86
Dressler, Wolfgang, 53
Dutch, 16, 20
dynamic (feature in LSF), 109, 120
dynamic morphology, 220, 228

E-language, 8
economy, 106
in SOT, 101–2
Elsewhere Condition, 93, 97
empty category, 38
Encyclopedia (in DM), 70–1, 73–4, 79, 82, 84–8, 146, 239, 244, 249
English, 20
entrenchment, 175, 186, 254
error, 6, 8
euphemism, 254
European linguistics, 25
European structuralism, 16, 252

European structuralist linguistics, 238
expressiveness (in SOT), 101–2, 106
Extended Ordering Hypothesis, 92
f-morpheme, 71, 75–9, 87, 244
faithfulness constraint, 100–1
feature (in LSF), 109
field linguistics, 26
figure-ground preference, 219
filter, 35–6, 42
Finnish, 48
Firth, J. R., (1890–1960), 25
formulaic language, 236, 254
foundation (Prague School), 47–9
frame (in CG), 185
Frege, Gottlob, 178
French, 22, 48, 139
frequency, 152
Fula, 59
full entry theory, 36, 42, 128, 149, 169
function word, 2
functional category, 72–3, 79
functional onomatology, 252–3
functional–structural aspect of word formation (Prague School), 45
functional syntax, 252–3
functionalism, 43–9, 52
fuzziness of boundaries, 190–1

gemination, 100–1
gender, 161–2
  Dutch, 59
gender assignment, 152
gender marker, 183
generative linguistics, 16, 29–43
generative morphology, 51, 68
generative semantics, 38–41, 52, 172
genetic aspect of word formation (Prague School), 45
Geneva School, 23, 63
German, 22
Germanic languages, 20
Glossematics, 25
government, 241

grammar
  definition (Prague School), 44
  see also Categorial Grammar;
    Cognitive Grammar;
    Construction Grammar;
    descriptive grammar;
    normative grammar; space
    grammar; traditional grammar
grammaticalization, 130
Grimm, Jacob (1785–1863), 19
Grimm's Law, 19–20
grounding strategy (in CM), 182

Harris, Zellig (1909–1992), 25–6
head
  in CxM, 130
  in NM, 219
headedness, 131
historical–comparative linguistics, 15, 19–21, 25
Hjelmslev, Louis (1899–1965), 25
Hockett, Charles (1916–2000), 25–6
Horecký, Ján (1920–2006), 43, 193
Hungarian, 48

I-language, 8
iconicity, 218, 229–30
idiom, 71, 95, 128, 130, 150, 239; see also lexical idiom
implicational paradigm structure condition, 225; see also morpheme
incidental naming, 235
incorporation, 72, 87
INDEF (in PA), 153
index (in RM), 164–6
indexicality, 218
Indo-European languages, 19–20
inflection, 44, 235
  in LSF, 114
  in the onomasiological theory, 214
  see also adjectival inflection;
    contextual inflection;
    delimitation of inflection;
    derivation and inflection,
    distinction between; inherent inflection
inflection class, 139, 141, 225
inflectional category, 225

inflectional paradigm, 61, 236
  in DM, 80
  in LSF, 116–17
  in CxM, 139, 147
  in the onomasiological theory, 206
  in NM, 225–6
information structure, 253
inherent inflection, 116
inheritance, 130–2, 141, 143, 145, 169
inheritance hierarchy, 152
initial specialization, 41–3
institutionalization, 13
intended performance, 11, 234–6, 244, 253–4
interface link, 153
interfix, 223; see also linking element
interlevel, 24
interpretation, 13
intuition (linguistic), 111
irony, 241
irregular form, 186
isolation, 21
Item-and-Arrangement (IA), 108, 251–2
Item-and-Process (IP), 50, 251

Jackendoff, Ray, 52, 149
Jakobson, Roman (1896–1982), 23

Karcevskij, Sergej (1884–1955), 23

l-morpheme, 71, 75, 77–9, 87, 244
Langacker, Ronald, 52, 172
language academy, 9
language change, 228
langue and parole, 22, 212
last resort, 248
late insertion, 85
Latin, 17, 20, 80, 139
level-based morphology, 78–9
level-ordering, 89–90, 92, 98
levels of adequacy, 111
levels of analysis (Post-Bloomfieldians), 27
levels of representation (Prague School), 24, 201

lexeme, 58, 236
  in DM, 79–80
  in LMP, 90
  in LSF, 112, 116
  in RM, 163
Lexeme-Morpheme Base Morphology (LMBM), 50
lexical component (in the onomasiological theory), 194–6, 204
lexical entry (in RM), 151
lexical idiom, 134
lexical insertion, 33, 35, 69–70, 75
lexical morphology, 43, 89–107
Lexical Morphology and Phonology (LMP), 51, 124, 126, 145, 238, 243, 249, 251
lexical rule, 91, 94–6
Lexical Semantic Framework (LSF), 51, 107–27, 145, 148, 171, 238, 240, 243, 249, 251, 256
lexical word, 2–3
lexicalist hypothesis, 34–8, 51, 69, 90, 108, 149, 238
lexicalist model, 41–3
lexicalization, 11–13, 41–2, 65–6, 99, 104, 124, 145, 189, 229, 236–7, 255
lexicographic manifestation of words, 6–7
lexicography, 28
lexicology (Prague School), 45
lexicon, 31, 33–5, 41
  in DM, 70–2, 86
  in CxM, 129
  in CG, 175–6
  see also mental lexicon
Lieber, Rochelle, 51
linguistic phenomenon (definition), 54
linguistic wars, 38, 52, 149, 172
linking element
  in LSF, 113
  in RM, 157
  see also interfix
list of morphemes, 35–6
listeme, 85
loan translation, 11, 235; *see also* borrowing

Logical Form (LF), 69, 72
logical spectrum, 197
Lowth, Robert (1710–1787), 16

Mandarin, 18
markedness, 24–5, 46, 53, 138, 216, 228, 231
markedness constraint, 100–1
mass noun, 78
material (feature in LSF), 109, 118, 120
Mathesius, Vilém (1882–1945), 23, 44, 47
Mayerthaler, Willi, 53
meaning extension, 195
mental lexicon, 10–11, 37, 234–7, 242, 254
mentalism, 26–7
merge, 70
metaphor, 235
Minimalist Program (MP), 69
Modern Greek, 18
modificational onomasiological category, 45–6, 205
morphematic structure, 47
morpheme, 30–1, 238
  in CxM, 129
  in LSF, 108, 124
  in SOT, 101
  in the onomasiological theory, 195
morpheme-based morphology, 251–2
Morpheme-to-Meaning-Assignment Principle, 198
morphological paradigm, 185
Morphological Structure (MS) (in DM), 69
morphome, 162
morphophonology, 24
morphosemantic transparency, 218, 230
morphotactic transparency, 219
motivation, 11, 66–7, 235
  Prague School, 47–9
  see also onomasiological motivation
move α, 248

multi-word unit, 56
  in the onomasiological theory, 202
multiple-affix problem, 108, 115
mutational onomasiological
  category, 45–6

named language, 8–9, 250
naming, 1–14
  in Bloomfield (1933), 26
  definition, 11
  in Paul (1886), 21
  Post-Bloomfieldians, 27
  Prague School, 24
  in Saussure (1916), 22–3
naming and deep structure, 32–3
naming and description
  in CxM, 135
naming expression, 233–45, 251
naming need, 255
naming unit (in CxM), 146
native speaker, 9
Natural Morphology (NM), 53,
  216–32, 239–40, 245, 251, 253
Network Morphology, 49, 80
noeme, 197
nominal compound, 131, 134
nominalization, 34, 40–1; *see also*
  ATK nominalization
non-inflectional word formation,
  114
norm, 10, 15–16
normative grammar, 16
noun incorporation, 74
numeration, 70, 72

Occitan, 18
onomasiological approach, 257
onomasiological base (OB), 46,
  198–9, 201, 205
onomasiological category (OC), 45
onomasiological coercion, 13, 65–7,
  245–7, 249–50, 255–6
  definition, 67
  in DM, 85, 87
  in LMP, 104–6
  in LSF, 120, 122–4, 126
  in CxM, 144, 148
  in RM, 166–8, 171
  in CG, 179, 189–90
  in the onomasiological theory,
    210–12, 214–15
  in NM, 229–30
onomasiological connective, 198
onomasiological level, 196–8
onomasiological mark (OM), 46,
  198–201, 205
onomasiological motivation, 248–9,
  255–6
onomasiological theory of word
  formation, 52, 193–215, 231,
  238, 240, 243, 250–2, 256
onomasiological types (OTs), 198–9,
  203, 211–13
onomastics, 3
onomatological level, 196, 198
opacity, 100
Optimality Theory (OT), 89, 94, 100
order of derivation (in the
  onomasiological theory), 207
ordering principle, 92
orthography, 2
overgeneration, 32, 41–3, 248
Oxford English Dictionary (OED), 4

Pāṇini, 90
paradigm, 35, 60, , 87, 242–4
  in DM, 79–82
  in RM, 161–3, 170
  in the onomasiological theory,
    195, 204
  see also inflectional paradigm;
    derivational paradigm,
    morphological paradigm; word
    formation paradigm
Paradigm Function Morphology, 49
paradigm structure condition, 231
paradigmatic relations, 25
paradigmaticity, 101–3, 106
Parallel Architecture (PA), 52, 127–8,
  149–50, 168, 239–40, 244, 257
parole, 212; *see also* langue and
  parole
passive, 35
Paul, Hermann (1846–1921), 20–2,
  129
performance, 8, 31, 111; *see also*
  intended performance
Phase Theory, 69–70

Subject index

Phonological Form (PF), 69–70
phonological level (in the onomasiological theory), 196–8
plural, 58–60, 241, 244
  in DM, 75–7, 79, 87
  in LMP, 97, 99, 106
  in LSF, 114–16
  in CxM, 137–8, 147
  in RM, 158–61, 170
  in CG, 184, 191
  in the onomasiological theory, 204
  in NM, 224
pluralia tantum, 97
Polish, 18
polysemy, 115
polysemy of affixes, 108
pomenúvacia funkcia jazyka, 44, 252
Post-Bloomfieldian linguistics, 16, 25–8, 30, 111
post-lexical rule, 91, 94–6, 105
potentiality, 208
pragmatic predisposition, 123
pragmatics, 250
Prague School of linguistics, 16, 23, 52–3, 63, 193–6, 212
predicate-argument structure, 124
primary affix, 91
priming, 236
principle of coindexation, 110, 112, 120
privative feature, 158
process reading, 64, 248, 255–6
  in DM, 84
  in LSF, 119, 121–2
  in CxM, 142–4, 148
  in RM, 165, 171
  in CG, 188, 192
  in the onomasiological theory, 215
  in NM, 229
productivity, 34, 56, 62, 67, 151–2, 161, 169, 171, 220, 227–8, 244
projection, 134, 137, 146
projection level, 239
proper function, 168
proper name, 3
prototype, 3, 7
  in NM, 221

quantity feature, 115

Rask, Rasmus (1787–1832), 19
readjustment rule, 77
reanalysis, 129
Recoverably Deletable Predicates (RDPs), 40, 42
redundancy rule, 36–7, 135, 149, 151–2, 160
reference-point relationship, 181
referential argument, 122
relational adjective (RA), 40, 56, 60, 236, 239, 256
  in CG, 181
  in CxM, 134–5, 146
  in DM, 73–4, 86
  in LMP, 96
  in LSF, 113, 125
  in NM, 223
  in RM, 156, 169–70
  in the onomasiological theory, 213–14
relational hypothesis, 151, 169
relational link, 152–3, 169
relational morphology (RM), 52, 149–71, 239, 244, 249, 251
research programme, 29
result reading, 65, 248, 255
  in CG, 188, 192
  in CxM, 142–4, 148
  in DM, 84
  in LSF, 119, 121–2
  in NM, 229
  in RM, 165, 171
  in the onomasiological theory, 215
resyllabification, 219
root (in DM), 72
root incorporation, 239
Russian, 18, 48

S-Structure, 69
Sanskrit, 16, 19, 90
de Saussure, Ferdinand (1857–1913), 21
Saxon genitive, 57, 96–7, 156, 202
scalar (feature in LSF), 109
schema, 135, 145–6, 151–3
  in CG, 177
  in CxM, 129

schema (*cont.*)
  see also complex affixation schema; compound schema; second-order schema
schema unification, 131–2
schematic assembly, 178
schematization, 175–6, 190
Sechehaye, André (1870–1946), 21, 23
second-language acquisition, 11
second-language learning, 18
second-order schema, 132, 138–41, 144, 147, 163, 170, 243
secondary affix, 92
SEM (in CxM), 239, 240, 244, 256
semantic field theory, 117
semantic interpretation, 32, 38
semantic level (in the onomasiological theory), 196–8
semantic representation, 39
semantic specialization, 192, 249–50
  see also specialization of meaning
seme, 198
semi-productivity, 151
semiological function of language, 173
sense extension, 10–11, 193
Separation Hypothesis, 50
sign Σ (CG), 173, 245
sign language, 253
signe (Saussure), 23–4, 108
  see also bilateral sign
Sir William Jones (1746–1794), 19
sister schema, 163, 170, 244
skeleton (in LSF), 109, 115
Slovak, 16, 48
space grammar, 172
Spanish, 18, 183, 185–6
specialization of meaning, 12
  see also initial specialization; semantic specialization
speech community, 12–3, 22–3, 175, 191, 193–8, 200, 212, 255
Spell-Out, 70, 72, 83, 244
split morphology, 80
standard, 12, 16, 18
static morphology, 220, 228
Štekauer, Pavol, 52

stimulus-response model, 25–6
storage, 237, 254
Stratal Optimality Theory (SOT), 89, 94, 100
structure-preserving rule, 94
subcategorization, 36–7, 91
subtraction, 218
superlative, 81–2
suppletion, 219
surface structure, 30, 32–3, 35, 38
Swedish, 18
symbolic assembly, 174
symbolic complexity, 174, 177, 186
symbolic function of language, 173, 190, 253
symbolic structure, 173–5, 177
symbolic unit, 172
synchronic and diachronic perspectives, 22, 28
syntactic category (in LSF), 109–10
syntactic component (in the onomasiological theory), 194, 196, 200, 204
syntagmatic relations, 25
syntax and the lexicon (distinction between), 237
synthetic compounding, 66, 167, 255
system adequacy (in NM), 216
system-dependent naturalness (in NM), 217, 219–20, 225

tableau (OT), 100–1
traditional grammar, 15–19, 43, 80
transformation, 30, 32, 34
transformational model, 41–3
transposition, 62–5, 235–6, 241–3, 253, 256
  definition, 63
  in CG, 187–9, 191
  in CxM, 141–4, 147
  in DM, 82, 87
  in LMP, 103–4, 106
  in LSF, 118–25
  in NM, 227–9
  in RM, 164–6, 171
  in the onomasiological theory, 208–10, 214
transpositional onomasiological category, 45

Subject index

truncation rule, 132
Turkish, 102
typological adequacy (in NM), 216–17, 219–20

unintentionality, 152, 169
universal markedness theory, 217
universal naturalness, 220
universal preferences (in NM), 216–17
unlabelled trees, 51
usage-based manifestation of words, 6–7
usage event, 173, 190
usúvzťažňovacia funkcia jazyka, 44, 252

variable (in RM), 153–4
virtual paradigm space, 79
Vocabulary (in DM), 70–2, 74–5, 86
vowel harmony, 102

word, 2, 237
 definition, 55
 see also function word; lexical word

Word-and-Paradigm morphology, 90
word-based morphology, 251–2
word formation
 in Saussure (1916), 23
 in Bloomfield (1933), 26
 Prague School, 24
 Post–Bloomfieldians, 27
word formation and inflection, distinction between, 44, 170, 224
 see also derivation and inflection, distinction between
word formation chain, 48
word-formation component, 194–6, 198, 200, 213, 238, 256
word formation nest, 48–9
word formation paradigm, 48, 61
word formation pattern, 128
word formation rule, 13, 35–6
 in CxM, 129
Wortgebildetheit, 47, 220, 228
Wurzel, Wolfgang, 53

združené pomenovania, 56, 201, 213
zero-derivation, 108

EU representative:
Easy Access System Europe
Mustamäe tee 50, 10621 Tallinn, Estonia
Gpsr.requests@easproject.com

www.ingramcontent.com/pod-product-compliance
Lightning Source LLC
Chambersburg PA
CBHW050208240426
43671CB00013B/2251